BETTER *in the* *Poconos*

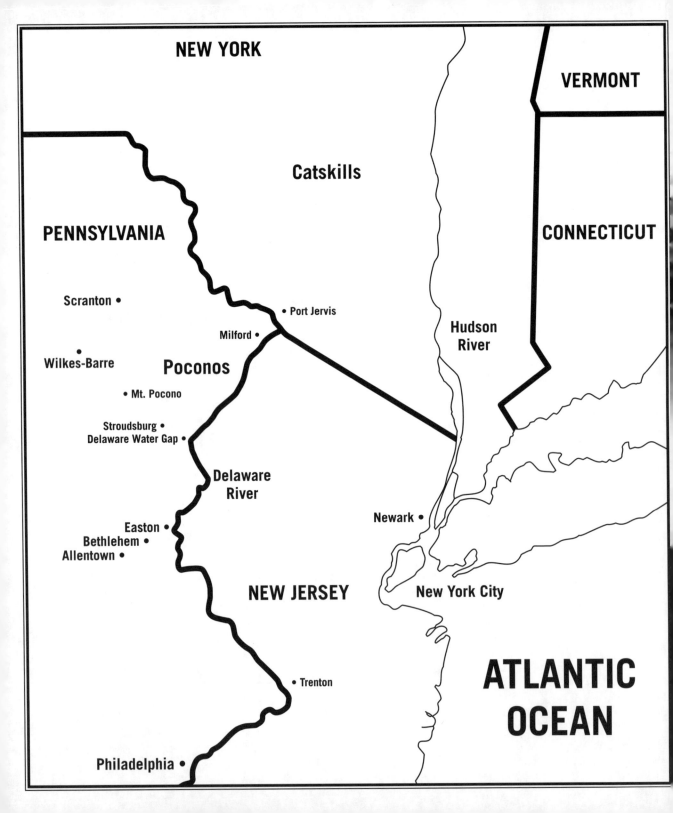

BETTER *in the* Poconos

The Story of Pennsylvania's *Vacationland*

Lawrence Squeri

The Pennsylvania State University Press | University Park, Pennsylvania

A Keystone Book is so designated to distinguish it from the typical scholarly monograph that a university press publishes. It is a book intended to serve the citizens of Pennsylvania by educating them and others, in an entertaining way, about aspects of the history, culture, society, and environment of the state as part of the Middle Atlantic region.

Library of Congress Cataloging-in-Publication Data

Squeri, Lawrence Louis, 1942–
Better in the Poconos : the story of Pennsylvania's vacationland / Lawrence Squeri.
p.   cm.
Includes bibliographical references and index.
ISBN 0-271-02157-8 (cloth : alk. paper)
1. Pocono Mountains (Pa.)—History. 2. Pocono Mountains (Pa.)—Social life and customs. 3. Vacations—Pennsylvania—Pocono Mountains—History. 4. Resorts—Pennsylvania—Pocono Mountains—History. I. Title.

F157.M6 S68 2002
974.8'2—dc21
2001035925

It is the policy of The Pennsylvania State University Press to use acid-free paper for the first printing of all clothbound books. Publications on uncoated stock satisfy the minimum requirements of American National Standard for Information Sciences— Permanence of Paper for Printed Library Materials, ANSI Z39.48–1992.

To *Rosemarie* and *Nick*

CONTENTS

List of Illustrations   ix

Acknowledgments   xiii

Preface   xv

(1) A Niche Resort: The Antebellum Years   1

(2) Here Come the Vacationers: The Poconos After the Civil War   15

(3) Never Sit Still: Surviving the 1890s   37

(4) The Glory Days, 1900 to 1914   55

(5) City Meets Country   79

(6) An Archipelago of Fun, 1914 to 1929   99

(7) Guess Who's Coming to the Poconos?
The Rise of Ethnic Resorts   123

(8) Laurel Blossom Time: Surviving the Great Depression   143

(9) The Poconos at Midcentury: The Last of the Good Old Days   169

(10) Prelude to Reinvention   191

(11) Welcoming a New Millennium   207

Epilogue   229

Notes   233

Bibliography   257

Index   271

ILLUSTRATIONS

1   Mount Tammany and Mount Minsi

2   Tom Quick memorial

3   The "Palace Car"

4   Dingmans Falls

5   Swimming at the Bluff House

6   The Kittatinny Hotel and the Water Gap House

7   Brodhead Cottage

8   Boating in Delaware Water Gap

9   Joseph Jefferson's cottage

10   Main Street, Delaware Water Gap

11   A lone kayak on the Delaware River

12   One hour's catch

13   The Spruce Cabin Inn

14   Delaware House, Delaware Water Gap

15   Mount Pleasant House, 1911

16   Pocono Hay-Ven

17   A tour group, Delaware House, 1902

18   Cyclists in front of the Delaware House

19   Phoebe Snow

20   The Delaware River, the Delaware Water Gap station of the Lackawanna Railroad, and the Delaware House

21   A bridge is born

22   The Delaware Valley Railroad

23   Outdoor recreation at the Water Gap House

24   The Churleigh Inn

25   The easy life after 1900

26   Theodore Roosevelt at the Water Gap House

27   Pocono Manor after the turn of the century

28   Playing Croquet at the Inn at Buck Hill Falls

29   The original Barrett Friendly Library

30   Barrett Township Fair, August 1914

31   Echo Lake House and trees

32   Grey Towers

33   Bears on display

34   Stroudsburg fairgrounds

35   Lice Clarke and friend

36   A W.C.T.U. memorial

37   The Barrett Township Fair, August 1918

38   The Fulmer House

39   The Penn Stroud

40   Monroe County Courthouse

41   A scenic route

42   Autos conquer the trolley

43   Island Park beach, Delaware Water Gap

44   Swimming at the Buckwood Inn

45   First night in the country

46   Independence Day, 1915

47   Dogsled at Buck Hill

48   Play Club, Buck Hill, 1929

49   Unknown resort musicians

50   Forest Park

51   "Appreciation of Art" lecture, Unity House, 1925

52   Folk dancing at Unity House

53   Sandyville

54   An indoor race at Camp Tamiment

55   Eleanor Roosevelt at Buck Hill

56   On vacation in the mid-1930s

57   Laurel Blossom Time

58   The queen of laurel blossoms

59 Violet Clark and her masks

60 Women on the links

61 The annual sports trophy exhibit at Skytop Lodge

62 Frolicking at Skytop in the 1930s

63 Equine etiquette

64 A successful catch

65 Russian dancers at Camp Tamiment

66 Buck Hill lifeguards during World War II

67 Boulder field, Hickory Run State Park

68 "Switzerland of America"

69 Stone Row, Race Street

70 Tobogganing at Skytop

71 Charlie Walker

72 Fred Waring and the Pennsylvanians

73 Swimsuit contest at Kamp Karamac

74 Where the girls are: Kamp Karamac

75 The honeymoon business

76 Remains of the Interboro bridge

77 Tocks Island

78 Ben Josephson and Willi Brandt

79 Traditional transportation

80 Walt Disney—and other lawn bowlers

81 The magnificent Oak Grove hotel

82 Ice skaters at Buck Hill

83 Up, up, and away at Camelback

84 Snow tubing aficionados wait their turn

85 A winter wonderland

86 John Kiesendahl and Debbie Martin, Woodloch Pines

87 Champagne glass whirlpool bath

88 Entrance to the "Land of Love"

89 The Pocono Garlic Festival

90 The Annual Scottish and Irish Games and Music Festival, Shawnee Mountain

ACKNOWLEDGMENTS

This book is largely based on archival sources—and as a result, my debts are legion. I have spent countless hours at the Monroe County Historical Association in Stroudsburg. Special thanks are due to Vertie Knapp, Janet Mishkin, Candace McGreevy, and Amy Leiser. They have been particularly patient with my questions and requests for information.

I also wish to thank Bill Kiger, Bob Longcore, and the staff of the Pike County Historical Society. The Barrett Friendly Library in Mountainhome, Pa., was very cooperative. Rae Donnelly kindly loaned many photographs from that library's Buck Hill Collection. Jean K. Wolf shared information on Pocono Manor that she had collected for the National Register of Historic Places. Susan Kopczynski, historian of the Delaware Water Gap National Recreation Area, has been very helpful. Nancy Van Solkema of Skytop Lodge has graciously loaned photographs from the Skytop Collection. Cheryl A. Trecoske, of Caesars Pocono Resorts, updated my material and granted permission to use a photograph from a Caesars publicity brochure. In addition, John Kiesendahl and Debbie Martin of Woodloch Pines took hours from their busy schedules in order to show me the resort.

The librarians at the Kemp Library of East Stroudsburg University were pleasant and efficient, as always. They are Angella Angelini, Leslie Berger, Paul Graham, Ramona Hylton, Pat Jersey, John Lalley, Kay Lavelle, Michelle Star, and Susan Ziegenfus. Judith Feller, recently retired from the Kemp Library, provided documents from her father's resort. And Alan Semon of the University Computing Center shared his knowledge of computer images with this technologically challenged author.

Some of the research was done outside of the Poconos. Faculty Development Grants from East Stroudsburg University paid for travel expenses. Thanks to Peter Hawkes and Jack Truschel. The State Archives in Harrisburg contain useful information on the origins of Pennsylvania's state parks and forests. The Department of Special Collections of the Syracuse University Library houses the corporate records of the Lackawanna Railroad. The UNITE Archives at the Kheel Center for Labor-Management Documentation and Archives, Cornell University, contain the Unity House papers. The Camp Tamiment materials are housed at the Tamiment Institute Library, New York University. The author appreciates the kind assistance of Paulette Manos and Barbara Morley of the UNITE Archives,

Diane Cooter of the Syracuse University Library, and Erika Gottfried of the Tamiment Institute Library. I would also add that the New York Public Library is a wonder of the modern world.

I wish to thank the numerous people who shared their impressions of the Poconos. Those who were formally interviewed are listed in the bibliography. Two of my graduate students, Ian Geffers and Christopher Brooks, did some of the research. Peter Potter at the Penn State Press has always given excellent advice. I am also indebted to my colleagues at East Stroudsburg University, Pat Crotty and Joseph Jarvis, who read this manuscript and offered their guidance. The same thanks is given to Richard Earley. Of course, I assume all responsibility for any errors in the work—although unlike a Roman of old, I will not fall on my sword when the inevitable mistakes that authors never catch are brought to my attention.

My dear wife, Rosemarie, deserves my gratitude for a multitude of reasons. She read the manuscript, made wise suggestions, and shot the photographs that are otherwise not attributed in the text. Most important, she listened with great patience to my expositions on the Poconos.

Finally, a few words about my four cats. While sitting in front of my Macintosh Performa, I sometimes would notice the felines staring at me, entranced. They were present when this book was written. And in their own mysterious way, they were part of the process.

PREFACE

This book could begin with a memoir of my very first visits to the Pocono Mountains in Pennsylvania. I could lyrically describe pleasant memories of idyllic vacations with my parents. This might be charming indeed—but my family never went to the Poconos. People in my New York City neighborhood, Astoria, went to the Catskill Mountains in upstate New York; my parents were no different. During the summer, they would take us to the Catskills, where we'd spend a week in a small boardinghouse that catered to New Yorkers from northern Italy.

I first learned of the Poconos when I went to Philadelphia to attend the University of Pennsylvania. Hearing about the Poconos on KYW radio, I became interested in this alternative to the Catskills, located in northeastern Pennsylvania. Even then, though, I did not visit the area. I was busy with academic pursuits, and I did not have the money for a vacation. Still, my curiosity had been piqued. It was reinforced every time I listened to the Philadelphia news. More than once I wondered about the Poconos, these fabulous mountains of honeymoon havens, ski lodges, children's camps, summer homes, and resorts.

When I finally saw the Poconos, I have to admit that I was somewhat surprised by their popularity. I have seen higher mountains. I could understand why Philadelphians found them exciting: they are the closest mountains to the city of brotherly love. Why New Yorkers went there when they had the Catskills was still a mystery. But gradually, the truth dawned on me. The Poconos are an acquired taste. They have to be sampled, experienced over again, like a good wine. The winding roads, the gentle hills, the idyllic waterfalls, the placid Delaware River that separates the Poconos from New Jersey—all have a charm that grows on a person.

The story of Pocono vacationing really begins in the nineteenth century. The factories that created the big cities also created a middle class with disposable income and a taste for annual trips. All over America, mountains, seashores, and lakes that were near urban centers and railroads became likely spots for resorts.

The Poconos had a great location. Stroudsburg, which is the largest town in the region, is located roughly one hundred miles west of New York City and one hundred miles north of Philadelphia. The

New Jersey suburbs of New York City and the northern suburbs of Philadelphia are closer. Even nearer are the small cities of Wilkes-Barre, Scranton, Trenton, Easton, Bethlehem, and Allentown. (Only thirty miles separate Easton from Stroudsburg.)

Despite their location, though, the Poconos were not necessarily destined to give rise to resorts. If the region had been blessed with good soil, the local residents might have become happy farmers in the years after the Civil War. Instead, the poverty of the mountain soil forced them to supplement their incomes by housing summer boarders. Successful boardinghouse keepers gave up farming altogether, while ambitious city people moved to the Poconos and opened their own resorts. Eventually, the large number of boardinghouses and hotels redefined the Pocono economy—and farming and lumbering evolved into a service economy of leisure. All this happened long before deindustrialization made service economies fashionable.

At the beginning of the twentieth century, resort keepers banded together to create a trade association to promote the Poconos. The resort keepers believed that they needed such promotion. Although the area had its natural attractions, it also had serious competition from Niagara Falls and the New Jersey shore. Visitors from New York could not be taken for granted, because they could easily travel to the Catskills or the Berkshire Mountains of Massachusetts. The trade association wanted to stimulate an already existing flow of tourists, and Pocono innkeepers were not shy in letting the public know of the area's many assets, such as the Delaware Water Gap and the scenic waterfalls.

In the long run, though, the natural beauties of the Poconos were less important to the success of the vacation industry than that industry's ability to renew itself. The Poconos originally appealed to sportsmen (fishermen and hunters) and to tourists who, in the years before the Civil War, preferred the scenic to the fashionable. After the Civil War, the Poconos developed a mass market. Along with their picturesque attractions, they offered the refinements of the Victorian vacation, including carriage rides, lectures, and card parties.

In the twentieth century, the public became more demanding. Resort keepers responded with golf courses and swimming pools, and by the 1920s, they were providing social directors to keep guests busy. In the 1940s, clever entrepreneurs realized that newlyweds had money for honeymoons. They transformed the Poconos into the "land of love" by opening honeymoon hotels, which evolved into couples resorts—the institutions whose garish heart-shaped bathtubs have become Pocono icons. In the 1950s, alert resort keepers saw that young singles had money and the freedom to enjoy it. This was the golden age of the singles resorts, where twentysomethings could meet and connect. In today's market, people look for nightclub entertainment and family fun, and again, the large resorts oblige.

The greatest act of reinvention after World War II, however, was the introduction of skiing. Although snowfall in the region tends to be uncertain, the Pocono ski runs can offer artificial snow. Neither Colorado nor Vermont feel threatened, but Pocono skiing does fill a niche for nearby skiers on tight budgets. It is no accident that the Pocono Mountains Vacation Bureau called the area "the near country."

Aside from their capacity for reinvention, the Poconos stand out for their close relationship with Philadelphia. Although the Poconos drew tourists from New York City and Philadelphia—perhaps even more from New York, which is larger and had a direct rail connection to the Poconos—the region has been a peculiarly Pennsylvanian resort. It is almost an extension of Philadelphia. To begin, there is the proprietary attitude Philadelphians have toward "their" Poconos. For Philadelphians, the Poconos are the only accessible mountains within a reasonable travel time. It is telling that the New York City media never mention the Pocono weather, leaving the curious to settle for the forecast in "western New Jersey." By contrast, Philadelphia radio and television always mention Pocono weather, as if the Poconos were as close as the backyard.

The Poconos have also shown their Philadelphia connection by sharing the same ethnic culture. Philadelphia was unique among the old East Coast cities in that its "ethnic" citizens accepted Protestant dominance. As late as the 1940s, Philadelphia elected Protestant Republican mayors. Likewise, ethnic diversity was never a dominant feature of the Poconos. Although the Poconos had Jewish resorts and Italian resorts, the great majority of resort owners had northern European names, giving Pocono vacationing a WASP image. The Poconos, then, were quite unlike the Catskills, which were defined in the twentieth century by a heavy Jewish presence from New York City.

Another trait of Philadelphia is its relaxed, understated tone. Philadelphia was founded by Quakers, modest people who frowned upon ostentation and braggadocio. Long after the Quakers lost political control of Philadelphia, their ethos continued to influence the city's culture. Philadelphia has not cared to compete with other cities, never becoming a metropolis boasting skyscrapers and spectacles. Its famous Mummers Parade aside, Philadelphia is not a city of popular display. Its New Year's Eve celebration cannot compare to New York's. Philadelphia has no Rockefeller Center or Times Square. The Philadelphia tourist bureau tacitly admits that visitors may not be fully satisfied: aside from recommending the city's colonial buildings and museums, the tourist bureau urges side trips outside of Philadelphia to Atlantic City, Valley Forge, and Longwood Gardens in the distant suburbs.

The Poconos, too, have been quiet and unobtrusive. The region has never been known for monumental hotels, neon, glitter, or world-class hanky-panky. When the very famous visited the Poconos, they did not call attention to themselves. Even the couples resorts have plain exteriors. An uninformed traveler would never guess that the walls hide "love nests" that, according to one's point of view, are either tacky or colorful.

The Poconos have survived, though, in the very competitive vacation business. The region attracted vacationers prior to the Civil War, thrived in the late Victorian era, remained a major resort center during the twentieth century, and enjoyed great business at the end of the 1990s. The future looks bright in the new millennium. This book is the history of this successful vacation region, of its renewal and reinvention, and of its status as a particularly Pennsylvanian resort. The book pays attention to children's camps, bungalow colonies, hunting clubs, and day-tripper attractions, but it concentrates on the resorts. Without them, the Poconos would lack vacation glamour.

Finally, the task remains of defining and locating the Pocono region. The eastern boundary of the region is the upper Delaware River, which separates the states of New York and New Jersey from Pennsylvania. The much smaller Lehigh River is sometimes considered a southwestern boundary. The Blue (Kittatinny) Mountains separate the Pocono region from the Lehigh Valley to the south. The opening through these mountains is the famous Delaware Water Gap, through which flows the Delaware River. Even today, because of Interstate 80, Delaware Water Gap remains a gateway into the Pocono region from New Jersey.

The Pocono region contains two distinct mountain chains: the Blue (Kittatinny) Mountains and the Pocono Mountains proper. The Pocono Mountains are located inland from the Delaware River. They are, in fact, a hilly plateau, an eroded remnant of mountains formed in the Cambrian Period, before the dinosaurs. This plateau has definite boundaries. It covers the north and west of Monroe County and adjacent chunks of Pike, Wayne, Carbon, Luzerne, and Lackawanna Counties.

In the nineteenth century and in the first decades of the twentieth century, residents used precise language when referring to local geography. The term "Pocono" referred only to the plateau. The thirty-five miles along the Delaware River from Milford to Delaware Water Gap was called the Upper Delaware Valley or the Minisink, its Indian name. The mountains around Stroudsburg and Delaware Water Gap were called by their correct names of the Blue or Kittatinny Mountains. But in ads that appeared in the New York City press, the entire region was occasionally called "Pennsylvania Mountains."

These assorted names can pose problems. Outsiders might confuse a name that contains "Delaware" with the state of Delaware. Milford, too, is common. Stroudsburg might be confused with Strasburg, a village in Lancaster County's Amish Country. And much of Pennsylvania is mountainous, as travelers know. As a result, around World War I or so, the area adjacent to the plateau—even the Blue Mountains—began to be known as "the Poconos." Local purists resisted the change, but the term "Pocono," with its Indian origin, is unique. Referring to the region as "the Poconos" has been a stroke of genius.

This larger region, occupying the plateau and beyond, is the vacationland of northeastern Pennsylvania. It is what the modern public calls the Pocono Mountains. And in this work, I use the term "Pocono" to refer to this larger area.

The Pocono region, though, still has uncertain boundaries. It may be easiest to define the vacation hub by ignoring geographic features and concentrating instead on political divisions. During the nineteenth century and much of the twentieth, the Pocono vacationland consisted of Monroe and Pike Counties. (This book focuses on these two counties.) When the modern-day Pocono Mountains Vacation Bureau was founded in 1948, however, it added Carbon County (which lies southwest of Monroe County) and Wayne County (which lies north of Monroe County and west of Pike County) to the original two. The Poconos thus officially became a four-county region.

Since the word "Poconos" conjures vacation glamour, the Pocono region will continue to expand. Ambitious real estate developers are already stretching the boundaries at the fringes. Lately, the

Scranton and Wilkes-Barre area to the northeast has been occasionally included in the Poconos. In the new millennium, the Pocono region may eventually include *all* of northeastern Pennsylvania. The only certainty is that the Delaware River will continue to define the eastern boundary of the region. There are no indications whatsoever that the Pocono region, like George Washington, will cross the Delaware and conquer the New Jersey side.

A Niche Resort
The Antebellum Years

In October 1846, the poet William Cullen Bryant visited the Delaware Water Gap, the spot where the Delaware River cuts through the Kittatinny (or Blue) Mountains. When Bryant saw Mount Minsi and Mount Tammany, the "lofty peaks" that flanked the Gap, he was impressed. But when his poet's ear heard the river running "noisily over the shallows," he was inspired. He wrote that the river was "boasting" of the victory it had won "in breaking its way through," and he described the area around the Gap as a hunter's paradise abundant with deer.

Bryant, who was based in New York City, often depicted exotic locales for its press. In his *Letters of a Traveller,* he told the story of a little boy who had been playing near the Delaware River when a copperhead bit him on the leg. The boy cried violently and attracted the attention of a nearby innkeeper, who cut the wound, allowing the blood to flow. The boy was given milk mixed with a mountain herb. Despite these ministrations, the leg swelled terribly, causing ten days of agony. But the boy survived.

Having painted the Poconos in primitive colors, Bryant then assured his readers that he had not strayed beyond the pale of civilization. As if he were contrasting darkness with light, he mentioned the "excellent hotel" near the northern entrance of the Gap. This "resort of summer visitors," as he called it, stood on a cliff and rose "more than a hundred feet almost perpendicular from the river." While dining at the hotel, Bryant gazed at the Gap and again was inspired, sketching a scene in which the "mountains shut in one behind another, like the teeth of a saw."[1]

In his few pages on the Delaware Water Gap, Bryant summed up the appeal of the Poconos for American vacationers of the 1840s. The imposing Gap and poisonous snakes called up the "sublime," the dominant aesthetic or theory of beauty in the literature and arts of the day. According to this theory, nature was a locus of danger and spectacle, one that aroused both fear and awe. Edgar Allan Poe's moody pieces (such as his short story, *The Maelstrom*) and Samuel Taylor Coleridge's *Rime of the Ancient Mariner* gave literary expression to the sublime. Educated people—the only tourists of the day—would have been familiar with the idea of the sublime, and their cultural upbringing conditioned them to enjoy scenery that evoked it.[2] The Gap was such a spectacle. If hikers reached the heights of

Mount Minsi (on the Pennsylvania side) and looked downward, the view could make them dizzy. If hikers looked upward from the river before beginning their ascent, they would face the shadows cast by the twin peaks that stood, sentinel-like, over the Gap. The Delaware Water Gap offered all this—along with its poisonous snakes.

Bryant's reference to deer hunting pointed to the appeal of the Poconos for sportsmen. In the 1840s, the Poconos had been barely settled. Although mountain lions and elk were extinct, their passing had been so recent that hunters might still expect to find them. Bear and deer were plentiful; rattlesnakes, ubiquitous. Fishing was an attraction that has not yet faded. The eastern Poconos are still noted for their many streams, full of mountain trout that invariably find their way to the Delaware River. The sportsmen of this era stayed in travelers' hotels or in fishing lodges such as the Henryville House, which began its 150-year existence in the 1830s.[3]

The Kittatinny Hotel

The "excellent hotel" that Bryant mentioned was the Kittatinny, founded in 1829 to take advantage of the emerging vacation business in America. The Kittatinny was the first tourist hotel in the Poconos (and remained a leading resort until fire destroyed it in 1931). The hotel became widely regarded as the best Pocono hotel of the nineteenth century, marked by elegance and refinement. However, in its early years, it was as insignificant as its location—a rustic village that itself had only just appeared on the scene.

The founder of the village of Delaware Water Gap—as well as the Kittatinny Hotel—was Antoine Dutot. Dutot had ambition, but he was an extraordinarily unlucky man. His travails started early. He had the misfortune of being a planter in Haiti when the slaves rebelled and expelled the French. Dutot went to Philadelphia before settling in the wilds of the Delaware Water Gap in 1793 and reinventing himself. Formerly a slaveholder and planter, he became a frontiersman, hoping to find fame and fortune. Instead, he found failure. When he opened a toll road at the Gap, travelers often pretended that they did not understand his accented English and left without paying. A poor road master, Dutot also failed at prospecting, wasting a good deal of money in fruitless searches for precious metals. He wasted even more money in lawsuits against Ulrich Hauser, a neighbor from Germany whose English was as broken as his. It was said that neither man could understand the other's insults. If nothing else, the frivolous litigation showed that Dutot, the immigrant, had become a real American.

Another debacle for Dutot was the Kittatinny Hotel, which he started in 1829 and sold, unfinished, three years later, when he ran out of money. A sad description of Dutot is found in the diary of a German nobleman, Prince Alexander Philip Maximilian of Weid, who visited the Gap on August 23–25, 1832. The Prince wrote that all of Dutot's speculations had failed, forcing him to sell his property and reducing him to great poverty, an object of pity for passing travelers.

Dutot's bad fortune continued even after he died in 1841. He had named the village that he had founded "Dutotsburg," but in 1856, it was renamed "Delaware Water Gap" to reflect its famous natural asset. The twelve buildings that Dutot had erected as a nucleus of a metropolis were gone by the 1860s. Other plans had gone awry as well. For instance, Dutot had bought a cannon and a bell for the town, and he requested that the cannon be fired over his grave and the bell rung when a railroad went through his village and a steamboat appeared on the Delaware River. When the tracks of the Lackawanna Railroad were laid down in 1856, the cannon had already exploded during a patriotic holiday; the bell had been moved to Stroudsburg. His grave on Sunset Hill was neglected and its location is today unknown. Dutot is remembered mainly as the founder of the Kittatinny Hotel.[4]

Isaac Bickley bought the hotel. A wealthy Philadelphia bachelor, Bickley made it his fishing lodge in the spring and his hunting house in the fall. In the summer, the Kittatinny catered to vacationers, housing twenty-five in 1833. In these early days, the Gap Hotel, as it was then called, also relied on the patronage of rafters, who floated logs downriver every spring and would spend the night at the hotel. Since Bickley was based in Philadelphia, he leased the hotel to Samuel Snyder, who was the superintendent of the slate quarries below the Water Gap. The real manager of the hotel was Snyder's wife. So began the Pocono tradition of wives running hotels while husbands worked elsewhere.[5]

The First Vacationers

In 1820, Delaware Water Gap had seen its first vacationers, Quakers from Philadelphia, who had been attracted by coreligionists who had settled in the area. Staying in private houses and at an inn, the Quaker visitors were not seeking comfort. They had chosen a summer locale with abundant wildlife, off the beaten track, and with a touch of the primeval. The journey from Philadelphia was similarly primitive: a two-day stagecoach ride of bumps and groans over unpaved roads that would keep many other potential travelers at home.[6]

In the 1840s and 1850s, the few vacationers attracted to the Poconos defined themselves by their lodgings. If they did not stay at the Kittatinny or at fishing lodges, they stayed at the handful of hotels in Stroudsburg and Milford, which ordinarily catered to travelers and farmers visiting the county seat. Although little is known of these antebellum vacationers, a few remarks can be made. According to the ledger of the Stroudsburg House, most guests in the summer of 1859 were men traveling alone. Presumably, they were on business, because men were not likely to bring their wives and children along on commercial trips. Conversely, the Philadelphia families seen on the register most likely were vacationers. These families had names such as Buzby and Longstreth, which today are considered old Philadelphia names.[7]

These scarce data give the impression that Pocono vacationers of this era were not status seekers, people who wanted to be noticed. This does not necessarily mean that they were urban laborers and clerks, men of modest incomes who would not have been able to afford a traveler's vacation, and in any case would not have received vacation time from their employers. Only the wealthy self-employed—such as merchants, professionals, and southern plantation owners—had both the leisure time and income to take a holiday. Visitors to the Poconos, then, had money, but they were looking for a different vacation experience. It was no accident that Bryant had referred only to the "excellent hotel," as if few of his readers would recognize the Kittatinny by name. Bryant was admitting that the Gap was rather out of the way, even though it did have great scenery.[8]

By the 1840s, America had its own Grand Tour of important places that anyone with social pretensions had to see. The American Grand Tour mimicked the European version; rich Britons customarily made the rounds of the Continent's highlights, which (as a minimum) consisted of Paris, Florence, and Rome. The rich and educated of America visited the Hudson River Valley, the White Mountains of New Hampshire, Niagara Falls, or went to fashionable shore resorts. But by and large they avoided the Gap. The guidebooks of the era usually ignored it. The Poconos were a niche region, visited by hunters, fishermen, and those tourists who did not care for status and fashion—those for whom a vacation was country living instead of display.[9]

Some Philadelphians found the niche character of the Poconos appealing. They were usually Quakers whose seventeenth-century ancestors had founded Philadelphia as a haven where they could practice their radical version of Christianity. The early Quakers were rebels, neither removing their hats in the presence of their betters nor deferring to their social superiors. They were also outsiders, because as pacifists, they refused to defend their community—thus automatically disqualifying themselves from public office. By the nineteenth century, Quakers had long lost political control of Philadelphia, but they had overachieved in other areas. Their aversion to vices (both major and minor), their plain living and work ethic, and even their clannishness had made them very successful merchants. Success created a unique dilemma: Quakers had money to spend, but also had scruples about spending it. Quakers of the nineteenth century often solved the dilemma by leaving the fold and becoming respectable Episcopalians. If Quakers kept the faith, wanting to remain a plain people who frowned upon ostentation, they would have to master the art of spending without being arrogant, of living well and being humble. Not surprisingly, people of this persuasion would not like the Grand Tour, which would attract all sorts of name droppers and businessmen who believed that humanity was eager to hear of their success. The Poconos aptly suited the Quaker ethos.[10]

Resort Competition

The Poconos were a niche resort partially because of poor accessibility. Prior to the building of railroads, Americans avoided land travel as much as possible, preferring river or sea travel to stagecoach rides over unpaved roads. For this reason, the rich often chose to vacation at Atlantic Ocean resorts, which they could easily reach by sailing up and down the coast. Prior to the Civil War, Cape May and Long Branch in New Jersey, Bar Harbor in Maine, and Newport in Rhode Island emerged as leading seaside resort communities and social centers for high society.[11]

A comparison of the Poconos with the Catskill Mountains of the Hudson River Valley underscores the importance of good transportation. Before the railroad era, steamboats carried New York

City's tourists up the Hudson River to the Catskill region. By contrast, the upper Delaware River was unfriendly to traffic. The rapids and low waters below Delaware Water Gap prevented Philadelphians from reaching the Poconos by steamboat. In the Pocono stretch of the river, from Delaware Water Gap to Port Jervis, navigation was nearly impossible, except for rafts. Later in the nineteenth century, small steamers occasionally attempted to reach Port Jervis. If they succeeded and managed to return to Delaware Water Gap, they rarely repeated the adventure. Not surprisingly, the Catskills developed a brisk vacation trade earlier than the Poconos.[12]

Aside from access, the Catskills had the good luck of favorable publicity. Many noted painters and writers based their works on the Hudson River Valley, and the Hudson River's storms and fogs were painted by the first major landscape school of American artists. Thomas Cole, perhaps the most famous member of the Hudson River School, went a step further. He argued that water at rest could stir the soul. Nature at peace was not the original sublime, but it was reassuring. It made the sublime more accessible to the timid.[13]

The Poconos also attracted artists. Landscape painters Thomas Birch, Karl Bodmer, George Inness, and lesser-known figures painted the famous Delaware Water Gap. From the river, depending on the time of day, Mount Minsi (on the Pennsylvania side of the river) and Mount Tammany (on the New Jersey side) would cast ominous shadows. Artists loved to paint rowboats on the still waters with the twin peaks looming in the background. The overall effect is not the sublime of thunderous, misty Niagara Falls, but a gentler sublime, one that invites contemplation. It is the sublime of Thomas Cole, who heard sound in silence and saw fury in peace. According to Cole's schema, the Gap should have been considered as worthy a subject as the Hudson River Valley, but the art world did not agree. Pocono artists never received the acclaim of their counterparts in the Hudson River School.[14]

The Hudson River School also had the adjunct advantage of a literary tradition. The emerging literature of the young American Republic was inspired by the Catskill Mountains that overlooked the Hudson River Valley. Washington Irving placed *The Legend of Sleepy Hollow* and *Rip Van Winkle* in this setting. Rip Van Winkle seized America's imagination, and Irving helped the legend along by calling the Catskill Mountains the fairy region of the Hudson. Likewise, James Fenimore Cooper, another early American writer who reached a national audience, used the Catskills as the setting for two of his novels: *The Spy* (1821) celebrated the Revolution, and *The Last of the Mohicans* (1826) took up the French and Indian War. Along with the landscape artists, Irving and Cooper established an atmosphere of adventure and mystery for the Hudson River Valley that permeated the national consciousness throughout the century. As early as the 1850s, this free publicity helped create a Catskill resort culture that was far better known than its Pocono counterpart.[15]

Aside from the family trade, the Poconos also attracted city anglers whose favorite pastime was spending hours at a mountain stream, trying to snare the elusive trout. Fly-fishing was an art in itself with a lore and a rich literature. Here again, the Catskills won the publicity war. According to fly-fishing historian Ernest Schwiebert, American popular culture places the cradle of fly-fishing innovation in certain streams of the Catskills. Schwiebert begs to differ. He writes:

FIG. 1
Mount Tammany and Mount Minsi. Mount Tammany, in New Jersey, and Pennsylvania's Mount Minsi face each other at the Delaware Water Gap. Artists and poets in the nineteenth century found the view inspiring, but hikers found it challenging. If they reached the top, they could look directly down to the Delaware River. After 1900, vacationers had the option of riding burros to the top of Mount Minsi. Buck Hill Collection, Barrett Friendly Library.

[I]n recent years, considerable evidence has emerged that the lesser-known Brodheads [creeks] in the Poconos of Pennsylvania is probably the true wellspring of American trout-fishing tradition.

There is also considerable evidence that Henryville House on its laurel-sheltered upper reaches is the oldest trout-fishing hotel in America, and its rambling clapboard structure sheltered every major American angler from its establishment in 1835 until the Great Depression of the nineteen thirties.

Indeed, the Poconos deserve attention if only for the famous people who fly-fished in the mountain streams. Among the famous fishermen of later years were Presidents Benjamin Harrison, Grover Cleveland, Theodore Roosevelt, and Calvin Coolidge. Harrison and Cleveland, in fact, were guests during the same week prior to their 1888 election campaigns—the campaigns in which they ran against each other.[16]

Pocono History and Its Neglect

If the Poconos had inspired a great literature, the region would have attracted greater numbers of visitors and much more attention. The problem with the Poconos was not an absence of literary material, for the Poconos did have the stuff of historical fiction. In the eighteenth century, the Lenape Indians were driven off their lands, but got their revenge during the French and Indian War of 1754–63—and again during the Revolution, when they killed isolated farmers. Nonetheless, they were defeated, and they eventually left. As for the colonists, they produced a great villain in Tom Quick, who allegedly murdered nearly a hundred Indians during and after the Indian wars. In explaining why he had killed an Indian baby, he replied that "nits make lice." On his deathbed in 1796, instead of thinking of sweet things and Jesus, he asked for one more Indian to kill.[17]

Quick was an Indian killer, not a patriot. He sat out the American Revolution, unlike many Pocono residents who volunteered to serve in Washington's army. The patriots who stayed home lost several minor engagements. The worst was the Wyoming Massacre, which took place in the Wyoming Valley (at the edge of the Poconos) when a mixed Indian-Tory force routed American militiamen. The Indians ran amok and took 227 scalps. The survivors, mostly women and children, fled through wilderness and swamps, reaching Dansbury (East Stroudsburg) only after a long trek and near starvation. Here were martyrs for the new Republic whose sad and inspiring story was the stuff of mythology. These American heroes were begging for an immortality that would make them standard fare in textbooks. All they needed was a bard, a latter-day Homer. None came forth.[18]

If bizarre encounters were desired, Judge Daniel Dingman, a Pocono original, could have inspired a tale or two. The associate judge of the Pike County court, Dingman served on the bench for twenty-six years, beginning three years before the creation of the county in 1814. Although his office proclaimed dignity, Dingman was uneducated and boorish. He addressed a fellow judge as "Bub" and occasionally held court barefoot and in shirtsleeves. One time, Dingman was passing sentence on a vagabond accused of theft. According to Alfred Mathews's *History,* the judge looked severely at the culprit and said: "You ought to be hung, but the sentence of this court is that you be banished from the face of the earth. Go get off the face of the earth." The thief asked how he could get off the face of the earth. Dingman answered: "You can go to Jersey." It was said that the thief immediately swam across the Delaware River to New Jersey.[19]

Authors could have found literary material among the rafters, too. Rafters were often farmers who saw more money in cutting trees and floating them to market than in tilling the stony soil. All along the upper Delaware Valley, on the New Jersey and New York banks as well as on the Pocono side of the Delaware River, trees were cut, lashed into rafts, and floated during the spring, when flooding raised the low water level of the river and allowed rafts to clear the rocks. Some rafters rode the current as far as Philadelphia. After arriving, the rafters broke the rafts, sold the wood, and took the stagecoach back—or saved money by walking.

The first rafter in the area, a man named Daniel Skinner, dates back to colonial times. In his early days, Skinner sailed in the Caribbean Sea and saw ships with pine masts. He realized that a market existed for the tall white pine trees back home in Wayne County. After his first rafting attempt failed, he succeeded with a second; he reached Philadelphia in 1764 and sold his wood for great profit. His exploits on the river earned him the unofficial title of "Lord High Admiral of the Delaware."[20]

Over the decades, rafting involved much hard work, some danger, and a unique form of life that is long gone. Rafters lived in shanties on their rafts, but they would stop at night, unwilling to navigate the river in darkness. A favorite destination was Milford. As many as two hundred rafters would stay overnight, drinking and carousing, giving Milford the flavor of a frontier town. The hard work created great appetites. A legend has it that one rafter ordered two dozen eggs, a dozen fried and a dozen boiled, at a restaurant in Belvidere, New Jersey. A rafters' hotel in Dingmans Ferry served pancakes by the barrel along with gallons of molasses. The bony Delaware shad was a popular dish. It was said that eating fish was akin to eating corn. The fish entered in the east corner of the mouth and emerged from the west corner, a perfect skeleton.[21]

Little was written about these colorful characters, and ignorance is no excuse. During the nineteenth century, rafting was a well-known activity. It peaked in the 1850s, but some 3,190 rafts passed through Lackawaxen in Pike County as late as 1875. The last rafters floated down the Delaware River in the early twentieth century.[22] Although vacationers came to the Poconos after the spring rafting season, they surely must have heard of the rafters. People living downstream likewise must have known of them. The Delaware River rafters were the equivalent of the boatmen of the Mississippi River, needing only an eastern Mark Twain to make them part of American lore. No such writer appeared, and no great novel was written. The Delaware River rafters were fated to end up as footnotes to history, omitted from the main narrative.

All of Pocono history has suffered the same neglect. The region had eccentrics, soldiers, and Indians. There were battles and, ultimately, genocide, for the Indian population disappeared after the wars of the eighteenth century. The Pocono mountains held much literary raw material—yet, incredibly, inspired little literature.

FIG. 2
A monument to Tom Quick was erected in 1889 and stood in the middle of a Milford street until 1999, when Native American activists vandalized it. The monument now sits in storage. It resembled a cemetery stone, and the message at its base was equally somber, stating that after the "Savages" killed his father, Tom Quick "never abated his hostility to them to the day of his death."

Quaker Modesty—and Its Consequences

Why eastern Pennsylvania produced a meager literature on the Poconos is difficult to explain. Philadelphia had its share of literate persons who were aware of the Poconos. An explanation for the absence of a Pocono literature may have been given by E. Digby Baltzell, a sociology professor at the University of Pennsylvania, who wrote *Puritan Boston and Quaker Philadelphia.* The book is a remarkable analysis of how Philadelphians think—and, by extension, how their neighbors in eastern Pennsylvania think as well. (Much of eastern Pennsylvania was settled by sects that valued Quaker pacifism and modesty.) Baltzell claims that Bostonians are chauvinistic about their town, while Philadelphians are negative about theirs. Anyone who has heard Philadelphia sports fans jeer the home team—the unforgiving storm of catcalls for the slightest mistake—will understand what Baltzell means.

Baltzell explains the difference between the two cities by pointing to their respective religious heritages. He argues that Boston's Puritans saw themselves as God's chosen people; Boston was God's town as well as their own. A residue of Puritanism survived in Boston's civic pride, which explains why nineteenth-century Boston dubbed itself "the hub of the universe." By contrast, Quakers were modest people, suspicious of authority. During the French and Indian War, their pacifism drove them out of Philadelphia politics. They retreated into their private worlds, doomed to be perennial outsiders who denied greatness in themselves and in others. Baltzell accuses Quakers of being smug and contented, but having little ambition for Philadelphia.

Baltzell adds that Quakers and Episcopalians of Quaker descent had the drive to make money but refused the civic obligations of wealth. An economic elite that refused to lead, Quakers had an enormous impact on nineteenth-century Philadelphia. According to Baltzell, their civic absenteeism explains why local pride was weak, why Philadelphia lost economic leadership to New York City, and why the city did not care if its museums and schools were inferior to those of New York and Boston. Philadelphia's writers, often mediocre to begin with, showed little interest in Pennsylvania's past.[23]

The Baltzell thesis can explain the literary neglect of the Poconos. No literature on the Indian wars and the Revolution would come from a pacifist environment, nor would a region obsessed with modesty celebrate its scenery and lore. But if residents of eastern Pennsylvania would not call attention to themselves, neither would anyone else. As a result, the Poconos never penetrated the American mind as deeply as the Catskills. This was true in the nineteenth century—and it remains true today.

Railroads Create Vacationland

The Poconos stopped being a niche region and entered the mass age of Victorian vacationing when the railroads came. The reinvention of the Poconos was somewhat fortuitous. There was no master plan in the Poconos, no clever entrepreneur who decided to kick-start a vacation economy by bringing in the railroad. The Poconos were quite different from Atlantic City, where savvy businessmen of the 1850s laid out a railroad to Philadelphia, realizing that a seashore resort would attract city folk who needed something to do on a Sunday afternoon.[24]

The needs of New York City explain rail service in the Poconos. Completed in 1851, the Erie Railroad carried freight to and from the city; it also connected the city to the Poconos, although it was in the paradoxical situation of never stopping there. The nearest station the Erie had to the Poconos was at Port Jervis, across the Delaware River in New York State. The distance between Milford and Port Jervis was eight miles and required a river crossing, but, as matters turned out, this was close enough.

Vacationers who wanted to stay in the northern Pike County resorts stopped at the Erie's Port Jervis station and took the stagecoach to Milford.

The Delaware, Lackawanna and Western Railroad, commonly called the "Lackawanna," was similarly serendipitous for the future resort industry. Completed five years after the Erie Railroad, the Lackawanna Railroad was also a freight carrier: it supplied New York City with Pennsylvania coal. Although the Lackawanna Railroad regarded passenger service as secondary, it allowed Monroe County and southern Pike County to tap the prospective vacation markets of northern New Jersey and New York City. The orientation of the vacation business in Monroe County changed forever as its hotels and boardinghouses began to cater to New Yorkers as well as Philadelphians.

Unlike the Erie Railroad, which skirted Pike County, the Lackawanna Railroad had eight stations in Monroe County. Four of these stations would be magnets for numerous hotels and boardinghouses. In these early days, the Delaware Water Gap station had the most vacation traffic. Its location—across the Delaware River from New Jersey—made it the closest Pocono rail station to New York City. Without this station, the village would have remained a backwater. Three miles to the northwest was the East Stroudsburg station, which was responsible for making the Stroudsburgs another vacation center. Twenty miles inland lay the mountain stations of Cresco and Mount Pocono. Their importance would come later in the century.

Another way in which the Lackawanna Railroad boosted vacation travel in these years was by improving service. In 1864, the Lackawanna shortened travel time between Philadelphia and the Poconos by arranging a connection between its trains and the Pennsylvania Railroad at Manunka Chunk in New Jersey. Passengers from Philadelphia left the Pennsylvania Railroad train at the Manunka Chunk station, crossed the platform, and boarded the Lackawanna from New York. New York City also benefited from the Lackawanna's improved service. Prior to the Civil War, a rail trip from New York to Delaware Water Gap took more than five hours. In 1868, though, the Lackawanna shortened this travel time, moving its "New York City" passenger terminal from Elizabeth, New Jersey, to Hoboken (also in New Jersey, but closer to Manhattan). New Yorkers saved an hour of travel time. By 1881, five trains left New York City every day for the Poconos. The trip to Delaware Water Gap took fewer than three and one-half hours from both New York City and Philadelphia. Of course, the entire trip from New York City took far more time, for a horse and buggy were needed to reach a railroad station. Moreover, river tunnels did not yet exist. New Yorkers needed to ferry across the Hudson River to reach the Lackawanna station in Hoboken. The Poconos were not close, but still, they were not very far. Excessive travel time would not ruin a short vacation.[25]

Accommodating the City People

A stay at a nineteenth-century resort was a social ritual that was identified with refinement. Middle-class vacationers would not have stayed where the social climate was boorish. When straying from

FIG. 3
The age of railroads was also the age of the stagecoach, since travelers needed a ride to and from the train station. Passengers on this coach—the "Palace Car"—were probably vacationers from New York City who had taken the Erie Railroad to the Port Jervis station. Pike County Historical Society.

the resort, they might have been willing to countenance a few country bumpkins, but they would not want regular contact with the crass and the vulgar. In the first half of the nineteenth century, the Poconos were not yet ready to become a resort area. The isolated region was home to farmers, lumberjacks, and tanners whose hardscrabble lives would not suit a resort culture. There was a lady lumberjack, for instance, who smoked a pipe and drove a team with masculine abandon. She was not exactly the sort that refined city women who discussed the latest English novels cared to meet. Milford had the flavor of a frontier town. It was said that elections were won by the candidate who supplied the most free liquor.[26]

Milford also lacked churches, which were the taming, civilizing influence of the nineteenth century. Before the 1820s, not a single church member lived in Milford, but this was to change. By the

1840s, both Methodists and Presbyterians were active. Their impact is seen in Mathews's *History* (1883), which reported that Milford had fewer licensed establishments than formerly. In other words, the Milford that featured resorts had fewer bars than the Milford that featured lumberjacks and rafters. In Stroudsburg, roughly thirty-five miles downstream from Milford, a population of seven hundred supported five churches during the 1840s. By 1860, Monroe County had thirty-three churches and all that churchgoing implied: a culture that frowned upon swearing and drinking.[27] Although the Poconos would always have their share of crude people, the rules of proper behavior were now known. Gentility was necessary for a resort climate, since many guests were women. The spinster teachers, librarians, and housewives whose husbands worked in the city would frown upon bad habits.

Along with a resort atmosphere, the residents of the Poconos had to be willing to accommodate vacationers. At the very minimum, entrepreneurs were needed to start resorts; cooks, chambermaids, and laborers, to work in them. The world beyond the grounds of a resort was also important. An enjoyable vacation required guides to lead hunters, liveries to rent horses, and tradesmen to provide services and souvenirs.

A workforce emerged because the urban demand for vacations came at a time when the Pocono economy needed renewal. Its primary industries were declining. Farming had become less profitable because the stony mountain soil of the Poconos could not compete with the fertile farms of the Midwest. And lumberjacks were putting themselves out of work: by the end of the century, the virgin forest was nearly extinct.[28] The other great forest industry was tanning, which required tannic acid from the bark of hemlock trees. Most Pocono tanneries started in the thirty years before the Civil War and lasted as long as the bark did. Since tanning a single hide required ten pounds of bark, the hemlocks eventually disappeared. By 1890, nearly all the tanneries had shut down, and one can see the same pattern in the shoe peg and clothespin factories that used local wood. They flourished as long as the wood lasted. Bluestone and flagstone quarries supplied city streets for a time, but they too ceased operating when the stone was exhausted.[29]

Aside from natural resource depletion, the Poconos had to cope with the national economy. The Panic of 1873 ruined many tanneries, preventing Pocono farmers from exchanging hemlock bark for food and dry goods at the general store. Farmers needed this source of income to supplement the meager returns from the soil. In addition, the late nineteenth century was not the best of times for agriculture. Around the nation, low commodity prices ruined many farmers, even where the soil was rich and fertile. The *Jeffersonian* reported sheriff's sales in the countryside and empty houses in Stroudsburg. The 1890 census registered population declines in both Monroe and Pike Counties.[30]

The residents of the Poconos, then, had few choices. They could give up and move elsewhere, or they could turn to new occupations. More than one farmer realized that city boarders would offer an income supplement, just as lumbering and tanning had done in the old days. Others sought work in the new economy. Farmers' daughters became waitresses and chambermaids; farm laborers became cooks and porters; teenagers carried dishes and did odd jobs. These were the more visible of a vast army of workers, ranging from plumbers to stableboys, who would make up the infrastructure of the resort industry. The emergence of this labor pool meant that a major resort economy was possible.

The birth of the resort economy can be seen in the expansion of the Kittatinny Hotel. William Brodhead bought the hotel from Isaac Bickley in 1851, and increased its capacity to 65 guests. Two years later, the hotel held 75 guests. Another renovation in 1860 increased the hotel's capacity to 150 guests. Business was so good that his brother, Luke Brodhead (who joined William in 1857), planned another large hotel. Stopped by the Panic of 1857, he had to wait until the Civil War had ended before returning to this project—the future Water Gap House.[31]

By the eve of the Civil War, the Kittatinny Hotel had outgrown its original incarnation as a dual-purpose inn for vacationers and rafters. With the exception of the fishing lodges, the Kittatinny was the only resort hotel in the Poconos, although vacationers could stay at the traditional travelers' hotels. The success of the Kittatinny—along with the new rail service—demonstrated the potential for a Pocono vacation trade. In the decades after the Civil War, the emerging labor and entrepreneurial pools, as well as a proper resort climate, allowed Pocono vacationing to reinvent itself.[32]

2

Here Come the Vacationers
The Poconos After the Civil War

More than anything else, what drew vacationers to the Poconos was their fatter wallets. After the Civil War, the United States became industrialized, urbanized, and wealthy, with income per capita nearly doubling by 1900. The American middle class could eat well, dress up, drop a few coins in the Sunday collection plate, and still have cash for baubles and frivolities. Vacationing became a national habit. Wherever suitable locations existed—by lakes, rivers, mountains, or the ocean—new resort hotels and boardinghouses opened their doors. The American resort industry had arrived.[1]

For once, the Poconos had an advantage over the Catskills. Whereas the Catskills catered mostly to the New York City metropolitan area, the Poconos had a wider orbit. Within a mere hundred miles from Stroudsburg lay the supercities of Philadelphia and New York City. Even closer were the smaller cities of Allentown, Bethlehem, and Easton in Pennsylvania's Lehigh Valley, which was roughly midway between the Poconos and Philadelphia. Also close were Scranton and Wilkes-Barre, which lay about forty miles northwest of Stroudsburg. The small cities of northern New Jersey were likewise closer to the Poconos than the Catskills. The population of all these cities doubled or tripled between 1860 and 1900. Here was a host of potential vacationers—only several hours by train from the Poconos.[2]

Health and Nature in the Poconos

America's new vacationers were, on average, less educated and less fussy than the elites of the antebellum years. Their ostensible reason for a vacation was to enjoy nature, which they regarded as healthy as well as scenic. There was a widespread belief that the mineral water in spas could restore health and that the invigorating breezes of the ocean were similarly therapeutic. Although the Poconos lay far from the ocean and had no spas, the region still attracted the health-conscious by offering an alternative recipe for well-being: pure mountain air, sweet clean water, and a quiet country lifestyle that overstressed city people found relaxing.[3]

The Poconos had a great asset in its "pure air," because the people of the nineteenth century worried over just that, having a false belief in miasmas, the allegedly poisonous gases given off by decaying organic matter such as urban garbage. If nothing else, this quackery encouraged people of means to leave the stinky, crowded cities of the day and spend time in the country, where their lungs could breathe uncontaminated air.[4] References to "clean mountain breezes" were common in Pocono advertising. A railroad promotional booklet once claimed that Mount Pocono had "the breath of the primeval forests."[5]

Pure water was another urban need. The cities of the nineteenth century were plagued by the common waterborne diseases of dysentery, typhus, and cholera. By contrast, mountain streams in the Poconos had never been contaminated, and their water was safe to drink. The potable water of the Poconos was very much a drawing card for tourists. The *Jeffersonian* summed up the therapeutic case for the region: "[C]ity folks are enjoying the hygienic benefits of our pure mountain air and water. A few weeks spent with us will soon supplant the chalkish, sickly pallor of their countenances with the ruddy red of full health, and enable them to return to the city with a new lease upon life."[6]

A subtle rejection of the Puritan work ethic found expression in the growing belief in the psychological *need* for a vacation. This new idea appeared in the Bachelder travel guide of 1874, in which a "typical" family asked: "Where shall we spend the hot months of summer? A change is required: we must go somewhere. The father has become overtaxed by the cares of business; the mother is wearied by household duties; the children need a respite; the health of all demands this change."[7]

Where could this family relieve stress? In the Poconos, the *Jeffersonian* answered proudly. It claimed that city visitors returned home "with system thoroughly braced and strengthened for the labors, trials and tribulations of the coming year."[8] The Pocono formula for stress relief was the simple life. In contrast to the noisy crowds of the cities and of rival vacation points such as Niagara Falls and the seashore, the Poconos offered quiet villages with authentic farmers who milked real cows. A vacationer could walk on a country road and be alone, with only the birds for company. He could sit on a rock by a brook, contemplate the great questions, and wait for the fish to bite. For many city people, this was happiness.

Aside from the pursuit of health, a vacation also offered city dwellers a chance to get close to nature. Vacationers of the nineteenth century (and those of today) looked for different degrees of exposure to the alien environment of nature. Although the very vigorous would want a rough camping vacation of several weeks, they were the exception. Most city folk preferred rest and relaxation, wanting no more exertion than a hardy hike in the woods.[9]

In the immediate postwar years, travelers occasionally wrote that the Poconos had an appealing "wilderness." They really meant that enough of the wilderness had survived to give the illusion of danger, but enough had been erased to make the Poconos safe. No one worried over the once-abundant mountain lions and wolves, extinct in the postbellum Poconos. On the other hand, deer, the smaller wildlife, and an occasional black bear all reminded visitors of the real wilderness that had once existed. The best reminders of primeval nature were probably rattlesnakes. Although common in the backwoods, they were less frequently seen along the Delaware River, where most postwar resorts were located. In Delaware Water Gap, the local druggist preserved and displayed a long serpent in alcohol—a sign of man's dominance over nature.[10]

A good example of this safe wilderness was the Cold Air Cave. Located two miles from the Delaware Water Gap train station, the cave was a natural refrigerator. The cold inside was so intense that the wood-chopper who first discovered it retreated after fifty feet. His dog ran farther in and never returned. The mouth of the cave had a draft of air so strong that trees thirty yards distant constantly moved. The unexplained, mysterious nature of the cave was an obvious attraction in the age of the sublime.[11]

The Poconos appealed, then, mostly to vacationers who wanted a modified version of the wilderness. In Delaware Water Gap, they would find a sanitized nature, renovated for their comfort. The Gap was as wild as a modern national park: its mountain trails were marked in colors for hikers, and it was dangerous only if a vacationer became lost or was drowned in the Delaware River. It was no accident that in the decades immediately after the Civil War, Delaware Water Gap was the leading resort town in Monroe County.

The Poconos also pulled in visitors by catering to the urban demand for the picturesque. The aesthetic of the picturesque emerged from the same body of theory as the sublime. It held that natural scenes, such as trees, rivers, and lakes, had beauty if they followed the rules of painting.[12] The Poconos had the good fortune of an abundance of water, the substance of countless trout streams, lakes, and endless cascades of idyllic beauty. Caldeno Falls in Delaware Water Gap stood conveniently near many resorts. Several miles farther along the same stream lay the equally scenic Marshalls Falls and Buttermilk Falls.

Pike County alone had some five hundred waterfalls. The most scenic—and still a major attraction—was Bushkill Falls near the Monroe County line. According to the *New York Times,* the rocks at the bottom of the Falls were three hundred feet high, and the visitor would "find himself in the realm of perpetual shadow," only to turn away "with a shudder." Whether the visitor had this reaction is beside the point. The *Times* was using the accepted language of the sublime. Nearer to Milford were Dingmans Falls and Raymondskill Falls. The latter consisted of a series of cataracts that started their descent two miles from the Delaware River on Raymondskill Creek. The top cataract poured water into a pool, which fed a new waterfall to its side, which in turn begat a new waterfall. The overall sight was of an angular terrace whose lack of symmetry gave it a touch of the baroque.[13] Whereas Niagara Falls was huge and overpowering, the Pocono waterfalls were small and pretty. Their effect may have been cumulative, built up after many visits. Or they may have had the appeal of bonsai plants, dwarfed versions of larger ones. Just as some connoisseurs might prefer the elegance of the small oak grown in a flowerpot and eschew its larger outdoor version, some nature lovers might prefer a miniature Pocono waterfall to the vast, noisy falls of Niagara.

The Resort Business and the Right Stuff

What God had wrought was not enough. The Poconos became a summer attraction because of man. Resort proprietors, promoters, souvenir sellers, laborers, and service workers performed the minor miracle of popularizing a region that few vacationers had noticed before the Civil War. Residents of the Middle Atlantic states realized that there was an alternative to the Catskills and New England. In

FIG. 4
Dingmans Falls. Located near the River Road (today's Route 209) some ten miles from Milford, Dingmans Falls was a favorite tourist site in the nineteenth century and remains one today.

the Poconos, city visitors could spend their hard-earned money, do little of importance, and enjoy themselves.

Resort proprietors stand out. Lured by the American dream of making money and running their own business, these bold men tried their luck in a new industry, confident enough to believe that they could earn money to pay the bills and have enough left over to live well. One resort keeper in Milford was able to visit his native Switzerland every winter. Although resort keepers in the Poconos never did become super-rich, they achieved the goal of being self-employed, having more control over their lives than salaried employees in cities. The resort business was especially enticing because it did not require specialized skills. The job needed generalists who could handle money, had common sense, and were sensitive to urban wants. Good managers instinctively realized that city people expected good food, clean rooms, and a wholesome environment and that they would recoil from a foul-smelling latrine that ruined the effect of healthy air.[14]

A resort had the added attraction of employing the entire family, making the business a celebration of family values—nineteenth-century style. Children were unpaid servants. Wives were indispensable; they cooked, cleaned rooms, greeted guests, and supervised the help. Victorians would not object to a woman playing a key role, since a resort was seen as an extension of the home, the natural domain of women. When husbands died, widows often continued the business. In some cases, women started a resort from scratch. Women were especially noticeable in boardinghouses, the private residences that took in summer guests. If the boardinghouse were a farm, the husband worked the farm and the wife dealt with the guests. Although advertisements for farm boardinghouses usually listed the husband's name, the wife was usually the real manager.

A boardinghouse offered the personal touch. The personalities of the owner and his wife were all-important. They were the hosts who led the singing and chose the games; like parents, they visibly set the tone of the house. This required a small operation. Proprietors of boardinghouses (and even of hotels) were pygmies in comparison to the great captains of industry, the Rockefellers and Carnegies of the nineteenth century. Resort proprietors were much like the clergy of their communities, mentioned in the local press, but rarely known beyond the county line.[15]

The first resorts were often recycled mountain and river inns that needed new customers to replace the shrinking pool of tanners and lumberjacks, victims of the disappearing virgin forest. These remote inns did not have a travelers' trade, unlike their counterparts in Milford and Stroudsburg. They had to find new customers, and luckily for the rafters' inns, they already had the advantage of location. The same Delaware River that had been used for rafting could also be used for water sports. Many old rafters' inns along the Delaware River evolved into hotels for vacationers. In Dingman Township, along the Delaware River, the Dingman House was renovated in the 1860s for summer guests. In Lehman Township, the Cove Hotel—which had opened in 1838 for rafters—became the Riverside Hotel. These resorts along the Delaware River served as models for the old mountain inns that had formerly housed tanners and lumberjacks. Laurel Grove, Pine Knob, and Hotel Canadensis, all of which had once served tanners, transformed themselves into hunting and fishing lodges.[16]

Everywhere, entrepreneurs could sense where the money was. Although inns in Milford could always count on a backwoods clientele that would be visiting the county seat, they nevertheless welcomed the vacation business. One example was the Crissman House, which dated from the 1820s and had been known as the Pike County House before Cyrus Crissman bought it in 1853 and renamed it. By the eve of the Civil War, the hotel was hosting city vacationers during the summer, but staying open in the winter for its old clientele. When the Crissman House advertised fine liquors and cigars in 1876, it was obviously not thinking of city spinsters and librarians. After the summer crowd was gone, the Crissman House was very much a typical, small-town American hotel. Unlike European inns of the nineteenth century, which limited themselves to meals and bedding, American inns were community centers. Crissman's hotel was a meeting house for Milford's politicians. Democrats met there for party business.[17]

Another old Milford inn, the Dimmick House, followed a similar path. However, the great claim to fame of its founder, Samuel Dimmick, was not so much his work than his encounter with the famed Horace Greeley, editor of the *New York Tribune* and national leader of the Whig Party. Dimmick had the distinction of failing to recognize Greeley when rain and mud had caused the great man's stage-coach to break down near Milford in the 1840s. Greeley entered Dimmick's place to have his dirty boots cleaned, but Dimmick did not recognize him and sent him instead to the public pump down the road. Like a common yokel, the nationally famous Greeley had to clean his own boots. The humiliation ended when the local head of the Whig Party recognized Greeley. Taken back to Dimmick's, Greeley was given a pair of slippers and a place to sit while his boots were cleaned. Greeley never forgot, later claiming that Pike County was the home of "rattlesnakes, Democrats, and bad whiskey."[18]

Samuel Dimmick's daughter, Frances, was by far the most colorful innkeeper in Milford. Having inherited the hotel, Aunt Fan, as she was called in later years, was an eccentric woman who fiddled at parties, but who also liked to hunt and fish. Although handy with gun and rod, she held her own among the cultured, serving as president of the genteel Village Improvement Society. Her neighbors were amazed that at the age of sixty she rode a double-decker bicycle through Milford. She had the *Milford Dispatch* captivated: in 1891, the newspaper called her an amazing person who would never grow old. Of course, she did. Frances Dimmick died in 1910 at the age of seventy-nine. In its obituary, the *Milford Dispatch* noted her "marked masculine exterior" and her "peculiarities in dress," but added that she had been "feminine and a lady in all her tastes."[19]

A conventional hotel owner of these early days was Henry Fulmer, a petty capitalist. He was president of the First National Bank of Easton as well as the owner of slate quarries and other properties. In 1874, he bought the Stroudsburg House, a forty-year-old travelers' hotel on Main Street, which he expanded for the vacation trade. He tripled its size, put water and gas in every room, and installed new furniture and bedding. A busy man, Fulmer rented the hotel to lessees, renaming it the Burnett House (1875). (Over the years, the hotel has also been called the Fulmer House [1907] and the Penn Stroud. Today it is the Best Western.[20])

The chief rival to Fulmer's Stroudsburg House was another former travelers' inn, the nearby Indian Queen, which had a name common to the tavern business. Many towns had an "Indian Queen" tavern with an Indian maid on the sign above the door. In 1867, Jacob Shafer bought the Indian Queen in Stroudsburg, which entered a new phase as both a resort and travelers' hotel. Shafer enlarged it in 1873 to serve a growing patronage. He kept the name "Indian Queen," although Indians had killed his great-uncle. The needs of business trumped sentiment.[21]

Starting from Scratch

Instead of recycled travelers' inns, the typical Pocono resorts in the years after the Civil War were more likely to be original creations for vacationers. In some cases, the founders were outsiders who came to the Poconos with money in hand. More often, they were natives with deep roots in the Poconos, people who could enter the resort business because their families had slowly enriched themselves over the generations. Besides, capital requirements were minimal for opening a boardinghouse, since it was the owner's residence. Building or buying a hotel required more money, but not an impossible sum. By century's end, many proprietors were not even owners, but lessees, often from the cities.

Samuel Peters of the Gonzales House in Bushkill traced his maternal lineage to a Spanish ancestor of the 1750s. His father was a shopkeeper, farmer, lumberman, and the owner of a gristmill. In 1874, Samuel Peters built on his father's work when he made the great career move of his life, erecting the Gonzales House on his family's 130-acre farm. Its twenty-five rooms accommodated forty guests. Samuel's brother Peter had already moved up: in 1861, he had opened a ten-bedroom hotel, the Peters House. Like many resort owners, Peters reinvested his profits. Only a few decades later, his hotel had seventy-five bedrooms.[22]

The Hausers of Delaware Water Gap also traced their lineage to the eighteenth century. Theodore Hauser was a carpenter who joined his brother to build the Mountain House, which opened in 1870. With their own hands, the Hauser brothers expanded the facilities—a little every year—until, by the end of the century, the Mountain House accommodated seventy-five guests. Doing their own work allowed the Hausers to advertise that they had the lowest rates in Delaware Water Gap.[23]

In some instances, resorts were launched with profits from "old money," which in the Poconos meant income derived from tanning and logging. Lumberman Isaac Stauffer was a short, ruthless man with a Van Dyck beard. He called himself the "king of the Poconos" because he had cut so many trees. Stauffer invested his money in a resort, and in the 1880s, his Laurel Inn could accommodate over one hundred guests. The *Stroudsburg Times* gave the Laurel Inn a favorable write-up and mentioned its beautiful bathtubs.[24]

In Canadensis, the father of the Price brothers, Milton and Wesley, had erected a sawmill on the family homestead. The lumber money financed Wesley's education, after which Wesley worked in New York City for a drug wholesaler before returning home. In 1887, together with Milton, Wesley erected the Spruce Cabin Inn on the family farm. The brothers catered to wealthy sportsmen.[25]

Still another scion of Pocono "old money" was Philip Fulmer. His father had been a shopkeeper, tanner, and banker. The family money sent Philip to Lafayette College in Easton and to the University of Pennsylvania Medical School. When Philip returned home, he practiced medicine and ran the family tannery. Sensing changing times, Philip sold the tannery in 1865 and bought Judge Dingman's old inn, enlarging it to accommodate two hundred guests. He changed the name to High Falls Hotel. For a while, it was the largest Pocono resort outside of Delaware Water Gap.[26]

Paradoxically, a Civil War death explains the birth of Delaware Water Gap's oldest surviving hotel, the Glenwood. It had been a boys' boarding school opened in 1855 by Reverend Horatio Howell. While serving as a chaplain and nurse, Howell was killed at the Battle of Gettysburg. Samuel Alsop took over the school, saw more money in innkeeping, and the Glenwood Hotel was born.[27]

Of the outsiders who opened Pocono resorts, F. Wilson Hurd stands out. Born in Connecticut in 1830, Hurd spent his early years as a sailor. In 1857, seeking better health, he took the so-called water cure; he found not only relief, but also his life's mission. He would promote the water cure (or hydropathy), a school of medicine that shunned drugs and stressed the curative powers of water, hygiene, exercise, and positive thinking. The following year, with two partners, Hurd opened the Dansville Water Cure in New York State. He sold out his interest in 1868. After searching for a suitable location, he settled in North Delaware Water Gap (today's Minisink Hills), deeming the region both scenic and healthful.

In 1871, Hurd opened a sanitarium, the "Wesley Water Cure." Many patients came with their families, thereby giving the sanitarium the air of a resort. Contemporaries would not have been surprised, since the state of one's health often justified a Victorian vacation. The distinction between Hurd's sanitarium and a resort was in fact so loose that Hurd advertised in resort publications and provided amusements, such as fireworks on the Fourth of July. After 1900, he joined the newly formed resort owners association.[28]

Hurd was rather eccentric. He believed that chickens had to be two years old before they were fit for human consumption. His hatred of salt was so intense that his stablehands had to sneak it to the animals. Hurd also hated ice cream, but in this case, he could not meet his own high standards. Like the celibate who succumbs to the charms of the painted woman, he fell from grace: his staff once saw him at a Stroudsburg drug store, eating ice cream with evident enjoyment.[29]

A touch of class—quite unexpected in rural Pennsylvania—was provided by the cluster of French hotels in Milford. The owners of these hotels may have been attracted to Milford by the French colony that had its origins in Napoleon's defeat at Waterloo. After 1815, some of Napoleon's die-hard supporters left France for America, and a handful ended up in Milford.[30] Although Emile Schanno arrived in later years, he also was a refugee. In 1870, his native Alsace was annexed to the newly created German Empire after France lost a war with Prussia. Schanno fled in 1876 so that his sons would not serve in the German army. He started a hotel in Milford and, after he died in 1883, his children ran it. Another Francophone innkeeper was Louis Fauchere, who left Switzerland in 1851. He first worked as a chef at the famed Delmonico's restaurant in New York City and then ran a French hotel before coming to Milford in 1867. His Hotel Fauchere established Milford's reputation for French cuisine.[31] Another French hotel, LeClerc's, was the summer home of many French celebrities of the New York stage.[32]

The resorts saved Milford. Bypassed by the Erie Railroad, Milford seemed doomed to obscurity, of interest only to the declining rafter population in need of overnight rest and to the backwoods people who attended its courts. Instead, by the mid-1870s, Milford contained twelve hotels and many boardinghouses. The largest hotel was the two-hundred-room Bluff House, opened in 1873. Its name came from its location on a steep bank overlooking the Delaware River.[33]

The popularity of the Poconos was noticed by the *New York Times.* In 1877, it estimated that the thirty-five-mile stretch along the Delaware River from Milford to Delaware Water Gap expanded by five thousand souls during the summer, while twice as many vacationers made transient visits. Three years later, the *Times* said that the upper Delaware Valley was "almost a continuous summer resort." The main attraction was the Delaware River, with resorts clustering on its Pennsylvania bank. Only later in the century did the inland areas, especially the Pocono plateau, draw vacationers.[34]

The Brodhead Clan of Delaware Water Gap

If any name stands out in these early years of Pocono vacationing, it is "Brodhead." The Brodheads were an old Pocono family with a hand in every aspect of the vacation business. Aside from promoting the Delaware Water Gap area, the Brodheads provided bed and board in their excellent hotels—and if the city folk wanted to leave the resort grounds for amusement, the Brodheads provided services that ranged from golf to river cruises. If Pocono vacationing were a republic, the Brodheads would have been its first citizens.

Although the founder of the Brodhead clan did not come over on the *Mayflower,* his background would have allowed him to do so. Daniel Brodhead was born in Yorkshire, England, in 1631, and he arrived at Esopus (Kingston), New York, in 1667. Daniel was a very fertile progenitor who had thousands of descendants. A grandson with the same name moved to Pennsylvania in 1737 and bought one thousand acres in the area of the future Stroudsburgs. He died in 1755. His house stood roughly where the Pocono Medical Center stands today.

Daniel's grandson was Luke Brodhead. He ran the inn in Delaware Water Gap where the first tourists stayed in the 1820s. He died in 1845, leaving nine children, the sixth generation of Brodheads in America—four of whom (Benjamin Franklin, William, Thomas, and Luke) would figure prominently in the Gap's resort industry.[35]

The sixth-generation Luke was born in 1821. Innkeeper, archaeologist, and promoter of Delaware Water Gap, he contributed to the *Philadelphia Public Ledger,* the *New York Times,* and travel publications. In 1867, Luke Brodhead published the first edition of his most enduring work, *The Delaware Water Gap: Its Scenery, Its Legends and Early History.* Although the book was ostensibly a guide to the Gap's scenery, it had the far wider effect of enhancing the Gap's resorts, especially the Kittatinny Hotel.

To succeed, Brodhead had to work on his readers—expand their imaginations and change their perceptions. Vacationers would visit the Gap only if they would see in a hill more than a mound of trees, and in a brook, more than a rapid current. Natural sites needed new frames of reference that pointed to European counterparts or to literary and historic symbols. Luke followed conventions already laid down for New England and New York tourism. He used history, romance, and the

Bluff House and Bathing Beach   Milford, Pa.

FIG. 5

The Bluff House, near Milford, overlooked the Delaware River. As this postcard shows, its patrons could bathe in the river—a common practice for vacationers until swimming pools were introduced in the twentieth century. Fire destroyed the Bluff House in 1948. Pike County Historical Society.

sublime to transform geologic features into tourist scenery. He gave literary associations and cultural resonance to ordinary streams, waterfalls, and trails. To some degree, Brodhead was shamelessly imitative. Fanciful place names in the Gap, such as "Diana's Bath" and "Lover's Leap," would have been familiar to tour veterans of Niagara Falls and New England.

Calling a pool of water "Diana's Bath" had all sorts of implications. It was a coded name that separated the cultured folk from the common. In Roman mythology, Diana (to the Greeks, Artemis) was the goddess of the hunt, yet chaste as a Victorian maiden. One time, she was bathing when a mortal hunter, Actaeon, meandered into her presence. The outraged Diana turned the hunter into a stag, who was pursued and devoured by his own dogs. This tale would be known to the educated, because anyone who went to school in the nineteenth century studied Latin and Greek culture. Aside from its obvious snob appeal, the name "Diana's Bath" also implied nudity and voyeurism. Female guests might have also enjoyed Diana's complete power over Actaeon, a man.

Brodhead used his interest in archaeology and his collection of Indian artifacts to good advantage. By describing his excavations of Indian graves, he implied that the Kittatinny's guests could join him on a dig, and at the very least, they could peruse his artifacts. The Indian collection may have served to engender a sense of mystery as well. The Indians were vaguely similar to the unknown makers of Stonehenge and to the Druid priests of prehistoric England. They were a mixture of physical remains, legend, and whatever the modern imagination wished to add: the stuff of poetry and legend.

Brodhead's bones and arrowheads told little about the personal lives of the Indians. Such remains are silent: they do not reveal whether their owner had had one spouse or several, or whether the person had been good or evil. Brodhead's Indian artifacts needed a life. He obliged, endowing them with drama by retelling the legend of Winona, the Indian princess, who jumped off a cliff after her lover left. The fact that other parts of the Poconos also claimed Winona was irrelevant. Like other tourist sites around the nation, Delaware Water Gap needed a romantic Indian legend, and Brodhead provided one.

Luke Brodhead was hoping to reach as many readers as possible. He often referred to young lovers. No one would have guessed from reading the book that resort hotels catered heavily to spinsters and families. Luke Brodhead's success is difficult to assess. Though his book was second-rate literature, it would have been first-rate promotion, if his development of scenery attracted vacationers to the Gap.

In August 1871, a visitor noted that the Kittatinny Hotel was very crowded with guests sleeping on cots. The good business may have encouraged Luke to start his own hotel. Besides, his brother, William, owned the Kittatinny, and William's sons, Edward Livingston (b. 1840) and John Davis (b. 1844), wanted to take it over. On June 20, 1872, Luke Brodhead's Water Gap House accepted its first guests.[36]

The Water Gap House captured attention. Erected on Sunset Hill, the Water Gap House stood four hundred feet above the Delaware River—twice the height of the Kittatinny Hotel, its main rival. It represented the cutting edge in hotel design with its gaslights, mansard roof, and secluded setting. The hotel was surrounded by thick old trees and outer walls that hid it from the nearby train station. Several guests (perhaps articulating the old view that a building should stand free of the "wilderness") suggested that Luke should cut the trees. But Luke refused. His position reflected the new trend of surrounding urban and suburban houses with greenery—in a sense, bringing nature to civilization. In fact, four hotels in the Gap were not visible to each other, although they were only minutes apart. The local correspondent for the *New York Times* boasted of the Gap's "primitive character." He knew that city people liked the illusion of being in the wilds.[37]

As always, Luke was a success. Although the Water Gap House did not sell liquor, the hotel made money. The accepted wisdom held that a large hotel needed profits from liquor. Luke proved his critics wrong. He may have anticipated the growing temperance movement, and he realized that a dry hotel would serve as an alternative to the wet Kittatinny. Besides, Luke was a teetotaler.[38]

After Luke died in 1902, his wife Margaret ran the hotel for three years before selling it to Atlantic City businessmen. Luke's older brother, Thomas, died in the same year. He ran the Brainard House in Delaware Water Gap. It was smaller than the grand places that his brothers operated. The youngest of the brothers was Benjamin Franklin Brodhead. He owned a large general store in Delaware Water Gap, and in the summer he ran the Brodhead Cottage.[39]

The family trade of catering to vacationers was followed by the seventh generation of Brodheads. William's sons, John Davis and Edward Livingston, took over the Kittatinny Hotel when their father died in 1880. Edward Livingston Brodhead died in 1900, and his brother retired. In 1901, the Kittatinny was sold.[40]

As for the other Brodheads of the seventh generation, Horatio and Harry (along with John Davis of the Kittatinny Hotel) went into the boat tour business. In 1879, John Davis and Horatio bought a narrow, sixty-foot steamboat with side-wheels. They named it the *Kittatinny,* and soon after it arrived, they showed it off in a clever publicity stunt by sailing upriver from Delaware Water Gap to Milford. The following year, a more ambitious trip was taken past Milford to Port Jervis, a distance of over forty miles in all from Delaware Water Gap. The Brodheads did not tempt fate again. The upper Delaware River has shallow waters and is not suited for navigation. The steamer stayed in the Gap area and carried vacationers on moonlit cruises. When a storm destroyed it in 1898, another steamer, the *Kittatinny II,* replaced it.[41]

Jesse Graves: Public Relations, Souvenirs, and Photos

The greatest promoter of Delaware Water Gap in the nineteenth century was a transplanted New Yorker, Jesse Graves. Unlike the Brodheads, who had deep Pocono roots, Graves was born in Brooklyn and moved to Delaware Water Gap in 1867 at the age of thirty-two. He became the best-known person in the Gap, serving as the local photographer and also as postmaster for a number of years, the result of his staunch Republican politics—and the Republican control of the White House after the Civil War.[42]

Graves lived at the Gap when the resort trade was having its great expansion: the number of boardinghouses and hotels jumped from six in 1867 to twenty in the 1890s. Graves himself never ran a resort; instead, he promoted the vacation business and provided services. His photo shop was so busy during the summer that he had to employ two assistants. His souvenir store sold photos of the local scenery as well as "shell work . . . Indian work baskets . . . Swiss goods"—the usual junk vacationers buy and ignore when they return home. In 1879, Graves published a guidebook that listed the Gap's carriage rides, hiking trails, and scenic sights. A year prior to his death in May 1895, he was using an incubator to hatch pheasant eggs. Local game birds were in short supply, and hunters had to be attracted. Graves was the perpetual promoter.[43]

The leading service Graves performed for the Gap was literary. The local correspondent for out-of-town newspapers, Graves began publishing his own journal in 1879—the *Mountain Echo,* a vacation newspaper that he distributed locally, at the seashore, and at urban vacation bureaus. Although the *Mountain Echo* concentrated on the Gap, it also covered the other resorts along the Delaware

FIG. 6
The Kittatinny and the Water Gap House were the leading hotels in Delaware Water Gap. In this postcard, the two hotels are seen from the Delaware River. The Kittatinny was closer to the river, but its rival was on higher ground. Today, the site of the Kittatinny is a National Park Service lookout post over the Delaware River. The site of the Water Gap House is in the woods of Sunset Hill and nearly forgotten. This undated postcard features the renovated Kittatinny of the 1890s, and it clearly predates the 1915 fire that destroyed the Water Gap House. Monroe County Historical Association.

River. It occasionally printed ads from resorts as far away as Milford. After Graves died, the *Mountain Echo* appeared intermittently until the early 1920s.

The *Mountain Echo* entertained and informed. It regaled the summer crowd with social events, local history, and resort gossip. By printing the names of resort guests, it satisfied readers' curiosity about who was visiting the Gap. And by printing news on railway schedules, mail deliveries, and local merchants, it provided useful information. Graves and his *Mountain Echo* told the outside world that Delaware Water Gap was no isolated backwater. Only a transplanted New Yorker like Graves would recognize the need to announce to the folks back in Brooklyn that the Gap was worth visiting.

Graves was smart enough to admit that the Gap had serious competition. On July 9, 1881, the *Mountain Echo* conceded that Niagara Falls was bigger than Delaware Water Gap's Caldeno Waterfall,

FIG. 7
The Brodhead Cottage, owned by Benjamin Franklin Brodhead. Subsequent owners kept changing its name. It was St. Elmo, then Courtney Lodge, and in the 1930s, it was reborn as a dude ranch. Monroe County Historical Association.

that Mount Washington in New Hampshire was higher than Mount Minsi, and that bathing in the Delaware River did not match the experience of the New Jersey shore. Having admitted all this, Graves defended the Gap, claiming that its rivals suffered from "excess"—in effect, suggesting that less was more. Graves insisted that Delaware Water Gap was "enjoyable." As evidence of boom times, Graves naively added that arson was unknown in the Gap. Resort owners made money and had not been forced to collect on their insurance policies.

Graves worked alone. No chamber of commerce or resort association existed in his day. If not motivated by civic pride, Graves was, at least, motivated by self-interest: more vacationers coming to Delaware Water Gap meant more business for his photo and souvenir shops. His sons also catered to vacationers. Albert rented rowboats in the Delaware River, and Joseph managed hotels after the turn of the century.

Railroad Promotion

The Poconos were served by three railroads. The Lackawanna and the Erie Railroads were based in New York City; the Pennsylvania Railroad had its headquarters in Philadelphia. The Pennsylvania Railroad typified the Philadelphia ethos, with its long tradition of modesty toward local achievement. The railroad never promoted the Pocono resorts, although many Philadelphians rode it halfway to the Poconos before switching to the Lackawanna in New Jersey.

There was no such modesty from the Erie and the Lackawanna Railroads. In the 1870s, the Lackawanna decided to boost the inland mountain town of Mount Pocono. It sponsored a resort hotel, the Mount Pocono House, which accommodated three hundred guests—a huge number by Pocono standards. To some degree, the Lackawanna was responsible for the transformation of Mount Pocono, "a wild, rugged looking spot" in the 1870s that became, only two decades later, a cute resort town of five hotels and boardinghouses, as well as a church, three stores, and thirty dwellings. Located twenty miles from Delaware Water Gap, Mount Pocono had emerged as a rival for the vacation trade.[44]

The Erie Railroad brought attention to Pike County by publicizing its waterfalls. An 1883 public relations pamphlet would not be accused of modesty. It claimed that Pike County's waterfalls were worth "going a thousand miles to see," because none could be "surpassed for beauty," and several outdid the others by being "grand and awe-inspiring." The same pamphlet noted that many "labor-surfeited mortals" were allowed "only a week for their year's vacation." It had a solution: a rigorous itinerary of sightseeing that only a restless city person could appreciate. The traveler would leave New York City on Monday, take a side trip from the Port Jervis station, stay overnight at Milford, and visit the nearby Sawkill Falls and Raymondskill Falls or other cataracts farther south. Resuming his journey, the traveler would arrive at Niagara Falls on Wednesday, leave on Friday, and on the return trip make side excursions to see a coal mine in Scranton and, in Honesdale and Hawley in Wayne County, to ride on gravity railroads—precursors to roller coasters. The traveler would be back in New York on Saturday, either exhilarated or exhausted.[45]

The Vacationers

Why did vacationers choose the Poconos? Whatever the reason, it was not because they lacked alternatives. Philadelphians could read ads in their city press about resorts in the suburban counties and at the New Jersey shore. New Yorkers had nearby resorts in the suburbs, the Long Island beaches, and the Catskills. Like the Poconos, small New England towns were reversing their fortunes with tourism. Old whaling ports and the colonial architecture of New England were assets that the Poconos could never match. In addition, vacationers could choose more distant destinations around the nation and in Europe.[46]

FIG. 8
Horatio Hauser and Albert Graves rented rowboats to vacationers in Delaware Water Gap. The *Kittatinny* steamer is in the background. Monroe County Historical Association.

The full story of how the Poconos penetrated the urban mind will never be known. The impact of the public relations campaigns of Brodhead, Graves, and the railroads is impossible to judge. One certainty is that the Poconos gained popularity after the Civil War. Another is that resorts advertised in New York and Philadelphia newspapers. On July 7, 1866, the *New York Times* printed an ad from the Kittatinny Hotel, which noted that the trip from New York City took fewer than five hours. The Highland Dell advertised in both the *New York Times* and the *Philadelphia Inquirer* on July 1, 1872. The ads alluded to the major themes of the immediate postwar era: health, scenery, and location. Likewise, when Philip Fulmer's High Falls Hotel advertised in the *New York Times,* the ad noted the scenery and the cool mountain air as well as the hotel's main asset, its location near the Delaware River, which meant boating and bathing.

A common promotional theme was nature's bounty. A Rev. Theo Cuyler, who had summered at the Kittatinny Hotel, wrote to the *New York Independent* and noted the grandeur of the Gap area, calling it "a wilderness of beauty." When a New York newspaper lauded Milford, it highlighted the absence of steamboats, gas, phones, theaters, and beer gardens. The attractions were pure mountain air and water as well as delightful walks and picturesque scenery. In the same vein, a Wilkes-Barre reporter wrote that he loved Stroudsburg because he had nothing to do but enjoy nature and walk around.[47]

The peculiar appeal of the Poconos helps define the summer guests. Vacationers who were satisfied with a jaunt in the woods or a rowboat ride on the Delaware River were not conspicuous consumers. Nor would they be the social climbers who flocked to Newport and other society watering holes. When the local press named businessmen who were staying at Pocono resorts, it never added that they were in the Social Register. In the two decades after the Civil War, the Pocono resorts drew people who could not compete in a peacock parade with the very rich or who simply liked the region's simplicity and lack of artifice. In short, the Poconos were demonstrating a kind of continuity. Their appeal, largely unchanged since the Civil War, was drawing from a larger pool of people.

On those occasions when the local press mentioned the occupations of individual vacationers who were not businessmen, it named clergymen, reporters, teachers, professors, politicians, and actors. A few examples will suffice. The High Falls Hotel and Dr. Fulmer, its refined owner, appealed to physicians and clergymen—among them Rev. Dr. McCosh, the president of Princeton University.[48] In 1871, the ambassador to Sardinia (Italy) stayed at the Kittatinny. In September 1877, the former Secretary of the Navy stayed at the Water Gap House. Two years later, the famous guest was George McClellan, the Civil War general. Meanwhile, the Burnett House in Stroudsburg housed the head of the Modern Language Department at the United States Naval Academy, a Philadelphia newspaper writer, and a Philadelphia clergyman. Many New York stage actors stayed at Delaware Water Gap.[49]

Actors with less money went inland. Barton Hill, the actor, stayed in Paradise Valley (about twelve miles from the Gap) for three months in 1864.[50] Joseph Jefferson had stayed there in 1859. While reading Washington Irving, he was inspired to create the Rip Van Winkle stage character that made him famous. Referring to the cultural inferiority that nineteenth-century Americans felt toward Europe, Jefferson wrote in his memoirs that the prospect of an American actor in an American story by an American writer so excited him that he made his Rip Van Winkle costume even before he wrote a line of the play.[51]

Most of the Gap's guests came in equal numbers from New York and Philadelphia. On the other hand, Milford attracted more New Yorkers, many of them artists and literary figures. The artist Winslow Homer stayed at Dimmick's. Many New York newspapermen preferred the Wells House. The village of Dingmans Ferry downriver attracted a literary crowd. The family of Lincoln's Secretary of War, Edwin Stanton, spent several seasons at Behre's, one of the French hotels.[52]

Two notable literary figures went so far as to buy houses and become residents of Pike County. The philosopher Charles Sanders Peirce was so impressed by the "picturesque" Delaware Valley that he settled near Milford, where he lived until his death in 1914. He once wrote that the vistas from his window always gave him "refreshment."[53] Western novelist Zane Grey came later. He arrived in Pike County in 1904 and met his future wife, who was also vacationing. While living in the village of Lackawaxen, in Pike County, Grey started writing his famous Western novels. Grey stayed in Pike County until 1917, when he moved to California because his books were being made into movies. Although Grey spent his last years on the West Coast, he always regarded Pike County as his home, where he hunted and fished with neighbors whom he knew well. He and his wife are buried in Lackawaxen.[54]

Delaware Water Gap hosted a substantial number of day-trippers, who came to swim, fish, hike, or row in the Delaware River. In August 1871, some 3,500 persons attended a religious camp meeting at the Delaware Water Gap's campgrounds. The following year, over 4,000 arrived for a camp meeting. The press reported a huge demand on the local liveries, suggesting that many had not spent the entire day in prayer. Some excursions had no religious connections. In July 1879, the Eagle Hose Company organized a special train from Pittston, in Luzerne County, so that 300 excursionists (along with a cornet band) could spend the day picnicking and sightseeing. The Scranton Home for the Friendless sent nine train cars in June 1880.[55]

These excursions must be considered when assessing Delaware Water Gap's social standing. The Scranton Home for the Friendless and the employees of the Eagle Hose Company would not have been seen at Newport or other high-society resort areas. These working-class vacationers were not even typical for the Poconos. They probably would have gone to Atlantic City, with its lowbrow attractions, if it had been closer.

If Pocono vacationers of these years project any picture, it is that of people congregating with their own kind, whether the group is defined by class, religion, education, occupation, or interests. Of course, homogeneity *would* typify a vacation area; birds of a feather flock together. What distinguished the Poconos may have been the lack of extremes—neither great wealth nor, with a few exceptions, poverty. The natural attractions of the Poconos themselves defined the Pocono vacationer. Their subdued quality suggested a vacationer who did not seek the pretentious and the showy. The Poconos were quiet and relaxed. In their own way, they were about lifestyle.

Vacation Pastimes

As with all human activity, more is known of licit pleasures than illicit. A fishing club in Monroe County had a caretaker with a compliant daughter, who presumably was not listed in the day's catch. No written documentation exists of this club's special services, which are a memory handed down by word of mouth, flowing into the vacation underground of whispers and gossip (gossip that the press ignored). The best source of the vacation underground of the nineteenth century would be eyewitnesses, but they have long since died. Then, as now, some vacationers must have been breaking taboos: unmarried couples who sought anonymity and "kinky" individuals who sought the freedom absent in their communities.

The so-called Swiftwater Monks, who were guests at the Swiftwater Inn, were one such group of free spirits. They liked to drink—but they lived in an age when the respectable, especially women, equated booze with bestiality. These disciples of John Barleycorn solved their problem by meeting in a cellar, denying entrance to their wives, and calling themselves "monks." They furthered the charade by dressing in monkish robes and cowls. In this private world of parody and irony, the monks, who were businessmen in real life, thumbed their noses at Victorian virtue and indulged themselves with adult beverages. Like monks of old, they achieved a certain measure of immortality.[56]

The local press ignored the monks, preferring to focus on respectable vacationers. These were either "consumers" who participated in resort and community life without leaving tangible traces, or they were "developers" who changed the physical environment. The possibility of vacationers leaving their mark on the landscape may have been, in fact, why visitors described the Poconos as "wild." There were sites still without a permanent name. Three visitors from Philadelphia named Caldeno Falls in 1851, using parts of their surnames: Pascal, Ogden, McDoud.[57]

Other early "developers" were the "Sappers and Miners," Kittatinny guests who labored to "beautify" the scenery before the Civil War. In 1875, the "Minsi Pioneers" came into being. Buying uniforms and axes, the Pioneers cut trees, erected bridges, blasted boulders, removed stones, and filled cavities, a labor that made Mount Minsi accessible from all directions. At their annual banquet in 1879, the Pioneers reported spending $1,400. Why they worked so hard is an interesting question. Assuming that altruism was not their only motive, they may have been fighting boredom or seeking excuses to exercise. Or they may have been on a mission, taming the "wilderness" by emulating their forefathers and the Western settlers of their own day. After all, they did call themselves "pioneers."[58]

George W. Childs was a Minsi Pioneer and one of its financial backers. A wealthy philanthropist and publisher of the *Philadelphia Public Ledger,* he was a "developer" in his own right. In Delaware Water Gap, he created "Childs Arbor," which consisted of a Japanese-style pagoda along with stairs, railings, and other woodwork. In later years, Childs turned his attention to Pike County, where he purchased fifty-three acres near Dingmans Ferry. The property, which included the scenic Factory Falls, came to be known as Childs Park.[59]

By making scenic spots accessible, George Childs added to his philanthropic reputation. In 1912, his widow donated Childs Park to the State of Pennsylvania. It carries his name today, giving Childs a limited immortality. By contrast, Antoine Dutot, who desperately sought to be remembered, suffered the posthumous insult of having his name removed from the village he had founded. "Dutotsburg" became Delaware Water Gap because Dutot had been self-centered, concocting schemes that never bettered his neighbors. He never realized that philanthropy is the best self-promotion.

Although conspicuous, developers like the Minsi Pioneers or George Childs were anomalous. Most vacationers did not have an active relationship with the physical environment. They were consumers who took what was offered, but left the region unchanged—and so needed to find ways to pass the time. They got little help from resorts. Americans of the nineteenth century were expected to be rugged individualists who ran their own lives and created their own vacation. Resorts of the 1870s and 1880s did not plan activities from sunrise to sunset nor provide social directors to prevent boredom. Too much play was considered hedonistic. Besides, few games existed: golf, tennis, and winter sports were European, and they had not yet arrived in the United States.[60]

The Cottage where Jos. Jefferson lived 40 years ago,
and old barn where he dramatized the play
"Rip Van Winkle."

FIG. 9

Joe Jefferson slept here. Jefferson was the stage actor who achieved lasting fame for his portrayal of Rip Van Win-kle. He received the inspiration for the play while staying at this cottage. The cottage itself still stands in Paradise Falls, some ten miles from Stroudsburg. Monroe County Historical Association.

All this does not mean that resorts had *no* social life—only that it was meager by later standards. In the 1870s, bowling, croquet, and billiards were among the few pastimes. In 1878, the *Jeffersonian* reported that guests at the Burnett House were playing charades. The article's tone implied that the game was a novelty. Guests occasionally amused themselves by giving lectures. Minnie Swayze spoke on women rulers in history. Although she claimed that women were capable of wise leadership, she assured her audience at the Kittatinny that women belonged at home. Ms. Swayze herself was a pro-fessor of elocution at Vassar—a careerist who was mouthing Victorian pieties that she did not practice.[61]

At night, hops were popular. According to the *Mountain Echo*, pretty girls and infectious music swept shy middle-aged men onto the dance floor. In 1884, the Water Gap House held a hop in which guests dressed as Mother Goose characters. By then, the Glenwood had hops every Saturday night. The Bur-nett House in Stroudsburg once held a hop with 150 Chinese lanterns decorating the walls. The Poconos were reflecting national trends. In the 1880s, modern resort entertainment required a ballroom dance.[62]

FIG. 10

Main Street, Delaware Water Gap. This old postcard shows a bucolic view that in fact did not exist. The real Delaware Water Gap would have been teeming with vacationers during July and August. Monroe County Historical Association.

Resort life could not fill a day. Guests often left the resorts on carriage rides. Aside from their intrinsic enjoyment, the rides were necessary if visitors wanted to see scenic places. Laughing, singing vacationers occasionally passed through Stroudsburg on hay rides. Picnics were popular. One farmer near Delaware Water Gap catered to what he believed were urban fantasies. He advertised that city people could drive his cows to pasture, milk them, and churn his butter. He would provide "shepherds" with both flocks and crooks. If requested, he would provide Watteau costumes or appropriate ceremonies adapted from the novels of Thomas Hardy. Whether many city people were this willing to play at farming and make fools of themselves is not known.[63]

The Delaware River offered much. It had salmon-stocked waters and a beach on the New Jersey bank across from Delaware Water Gap. Picnickers and bathers could reach this beach by taking the tiny Brodhead steamer, the *Kittatinny.* A Mrs. Barry of New York did not need it. She got her proverbial

FIG. 11

A lone kayak on the Delaware River near Delaware Water Gap. Today's river is far less crowded than it would have been in the late nineteenth century, when it was the main attraction of the Pocono vacation industry.

fifteen minutes of fame by swimming the river where it was eight hundred feet wide and returning without taking a rest.[64]

Mrs. Barry was atypical in that she was not forgotten. Her name and the memory of her feat, if nothing else, survive. Her presence in the Poconos, along with that of countless other vacationers, indicated that the region had finally created a viable economy. Though farming was not very profitable and the forest industries not renewable in the short term, vacationing would have a long future. As the 1890s approached, the Poconos were no longer a backwater of stony hills and poor soil.

3

Never Sit Still
Surviving the 1890s

"He who stops is lost," a politician once said. This aphorism is very true for the resort business. A smart resort keeper can never rest easy. Entering the trade does not require a lot of talent or money, and as long as the resort business appears profitable, someone else will try his (or her) luck, hoping to steal customers away from established resorts. A resort keeper who believes that he has achieved perfection, that he no longer needs to improve his facilities, cook better food, offer new creature comforts, and provide novelties to titillate the public—in short, the resort keeper who believes that he can rest on his laurels—is a resort keeper who should start preparing for bankruptcy.

In the 1890s, resort keepers were facing new competition. Their services were no longer essential for vacationers, who had other options. Vacationers could join a private club and stay at the attached hotel or at a cottage on the club grounds. If vacationers liked being alone, they could buy or rent a summerhouse. Still another option appealed to vacationers with little money: instead of staying at a budget boardinghouse, they could enjoy a day-tripper outing.

The Importance of Being Different

Resort alternatives were still in their infancy in the 1890s. Resorts reserved their greatest suspicion for each other. Monroe and Pike Counties had a minimum of one hundred hotels and boardinghouses, all of which would compete not only against each other, but also with rivals in other parts of the country. Throughout the East Coast, like wildflowers after a spring rain, many resorts had arisen—each of which would try to push its competitors aside.

To survive, a resort had to insist that it was better than the rest. But the chief attraction of these country resorts was nature, and in each place, nature looked essentially the same. Smart resort keepers knew this. They knew that the Pocono sun shone for them exactly as it did for the competition's place down the road. Even more disconcerting was the fact that the sun looked just as warm and bright over the rival Catskills or at the New Jersey shore. Area trees did not offer much help to resort keepers, either. A spruce was a spruce, whether in Milford, Mount Pocono, or the Catskills. Clearly, the resort keepers had to convince the public that nature was not the only attraction—and that they offered superior service. If a resort keeper could go a step further and actually convince the public that the charms of nature were, in fact, richer at his location, so much the better. In a sense, resort keepers had a trace of Barnum. They sold hokum and snake oil because they aimed to create the illusion of being unique. Each wanted the public to believe that a particular service, attraction, amenity, or experience was only available at his resort—just as the Eiffel Tower could only be seen in Paris and the Statue of Liberty in New York.

Once resorts had developed a unique product, or at least something that could pass for it, they took the next step: telling the public. Aside from free publicity in the press, Pocono resorts had the options of advertising in newspapers, sending brochures to prospective clients, and placing ads in the passenger directories of the Erie and the Lackawanna Railroads. As a rule, these strategies followed the conventions of the nineteenth century, making frequent references to health and nature—the mantra that would justify a vacation over work. References to creature comforts and amusements were fewer. They might raise unsettling fears of hedonism, still considered a moral failing in the 1890s.

Nature Is Better in the Poconos

While resorts fought each other for the vacationers already coming to the Poconos, the Erie and the Lackawanna Railroads sought to entice more visitors to the area. Their vacation directories aimed to steal business from the Catskills, the New Jersey shore, and wherever else a potential Pocono vacationer might be lured.

The railroad directories insisted that nature excelled in the Poconos. Fishing was better, and scenery was more eye-catching and picturesque. Consider the following effusion about Monroe County: "We have stood on the top of Pike's Peak, . . . beheld with wonder and admiration the snow-capped peaks of Mount Tacoma . . . , Mt. Shasta, Mt. Baker and Mt. Hood; . . . fished in the streams of the Cascades, beheld a sunset through the Golden Gate, but no where do we have so many of the above features so neatly combined in miniature form than here."[1] The words "miniature form" were typical of Pocono publicity—making a virtue of what some vacationers may have seen as a shortcoming.

Pike County was not to be outdone. The 1896 Erie directory described Milford as "exceptionally charming," standing "on a broad plateau . . . above the river." It added that "a lofty peak one thousand feet above the village" allowed a view "for a distance of forty miles." The 1898 Erie directory noted that the railroad's twenty-six-mile stretch in Pike County had been blasted out of a mountainside, creating "some of the most magnificent scenery on the continent." For good measure, it asserted that the blasted rock had created a solid foundation and that the double track guaranteed absolute safety. Presumably, readers with long memories who recalled accidents along the Erie would be reassured.

Guests who preferred the strenuous life could enjoy nature by hunting and fishing. Numerous advertisements in the railway directories assured sportsmen that fishing was better in the Poconos. In

1896, the Erie Railroad's passenger directory claimed that a deep spot in the Delaware River had "wily bass" and lurking pickerel, an astounding fish story; the railway directory implied that Pocono fish were smarter and more of a challenge. Fish, it seems, were *not* the same everywhere.

The Poconos also accommodated weekend warriors who liked the hunt, but did not care for its stress. Although these city people wanted to play macho games, they were soft, having neither the stamina nor the patience to stalk wild animals. Nor would they be able to cope with the wounded

FIG. 12
One hour's catch. The truth about
Pocono fishing, or a real fish story?
Monroe County Historical
Association.

bears and stags that, objecting to being killed, had been known to turn against their pursuers. These hunters would worry about safety. The solution was simple: to bring these sportsmen to the Pocono woods, hunting lodges would drain the danger and work from the joy of the kill—much like the way in which a modern amusement park ride provides speed and thrills, but eliminates the risk.

A lodge could accommodate fearful "hunters" by allowing them to capture hunting trophies, risk-free. The president of the Philadelphia Stock Exchange once caught a bear in a trap and killed the defenseless beast. The bear was skinned and made into a smoking room rug—an emblem of the hunter's courage. Other Philadelphians trapped a bear near the Spruce Cabin Inn. Instead of quickly killing the beast, they freed it near the woods, giving it a chance to escape. Before reaching safety, the bear was gunned down.[2]

Bird hunting was safer, but tedious. The hunters had to tramp through the woods, wait in ambush, and endure hours of sweat and boredom for a few seconds of shooting. The solution to their discomfort was a pigeon shoot. One hundred and fifty birds were the targets at a shoot organized at

A CORNER OF THE EXCHANGE, SPRUCE CABIN INN, CANADENSIS, PA.

FIG. 13

The Spruce Cabin Inn. The hunting and fishing lodge was run by Milton and Wesley Price in the mountain village of Canadensis. Note the deer heads on the walls. Another sign of masculinity: the well-stocked bar (not shown here). Monroe County Historical Association.

Tannersville in 1895. Two years later, the owners of the Spruce Cabin Inn held a bird shooting contest in which the winner killed thirteen of his fifteen target birds. The kill had become so easy that nature *was* truly better in the Poconos.[3]

Healthier in the Poconos

While staying in the Poconos, city people had the assurance that they were less likely to get sick. The Erie 1898 directory claimed that Milford had "ideal conditions for rest and relaxation." A letter in the *Milford Dispatch* claimed that the Delaware River Valley from Milford to Delaware Water Gap was free of malaria and mosquitoes—a healthful Eden, in contrast to the Hudson River, whose malaria belt extended as far as sixty miles from New York City. As if this slap at the Catskills were not enough, the letter added that the New Jersey shore as well as Long Island and Staten Island were infested with mosquitoes.[4] The assertion that the Poconos were healthier was a staple in advertisements, as resorts bragged of a mountain purity unknown to the New Jersey shore.

Mount Pocono made much of its high location, where the "overworked seeker of health and happiness" and "persons afflicted with hay fever and asthma" would find strong and bracing air. New Yorkers who had sweated through summer nights would find "cool nights and great sleeping." The Clairmont House outdid its Mount Pocono rivals, claiming that its summer air came "from the North and Northwest through dense pine forests," making it "healthy and unusual" and "high, dry and piney."[5] A careful reader might have perceived a critique of Delaware Water Gap and Milford, which were lower-lying and river bound. Clear mountain water also had its appeal. The Mount Pocono House bragged of drinking water that was "perfect" and "invaluable in kidney troubles."[6]

Aside from nature's bounty, a healthy environment depended on human concern. The Erie Railroad noted that breathing was easier for its passengers because its locomotives had clean smoke, the result of burning hard or anthracite coal instead of the more common and dirtier soft coal.[7] The Lackawanna Railroad likewise showed its concern for passengers: it installed electricity and steam heat at its East Stroudsburg station so that city people would not catch an October chill when they came to see the autumn foliage. The recently renovated Kittatinny Hotel declared the same awareness of the public's needs when it announced its steam heat.[8]

By the 1890s, health-conscious Victorians understood the need for cleanliness. Knowing this, many resorts advertised hot and cold baths. The Burnett House in Stroudsburg went a step further by having bathtubs on every floor. Several resorts also realized the selling power of sanitation. The Delaware House in Delaware Water Gap advertised "complete sanitary arrangements," presumably meaning city-style water closets. The best appointed of the Mount Pocono resorts was probably the Mount Pocono House. It advertised in the 1899 Lackawanna directory that it had the most recent sanitary arrangements: sewer pipes separate from laundry pipes and ventilated at the roof, along with state-of-the-art plumbing that would keep the building free of deadly "sewer gas" (the methane gas

from sanitary facilities that worried many Victorians). If things went wrong, there was the reassurance that "competent physicians" were nearby.[9]

For some reason, less attention was paid to the other end of the alimentary canal. Resorts tended
to ignore food, neither publicizing menus nor trumpeting the virtues of a healthy diet. The cliché
about "being what you eat" was evidently unknown. The village of Henryville, however, constituted
an exception to this neglect of diet: it reassured the few food faddists of the day by claiming that its
resorts served "clean and fresh food."[10]

The great fear, in all resorts, was tuberculosis. This contagious disease of the lungs seized the imagination of the nineteenth century much as cancer frightens us today. The standard treatment, which
was country rest, created the suspicion that the resort guest with a persistent cough was not a smoker
but a consumptive. A fair number of resorts protected themselves by refusing to accept victims of
tuberculosis, and they proclaimed this exclusion in their ads, thereby pacifying the health-conscious.
Consumptives were expected to stay at special rural sanitaria, which were not plentiful in the
Poconos, although a few did exist in Tobyhanna. An old lumber town tucked away in the northwest
corner of Monroe County, some twenty-five railroad miles from Stroudsburg, Tobyhanna needed a
new mission after its trees were cut. Tuberculosis was this mission. Tobyhanna bragged of being
"famous as a resort for people affected with pulmonary diseases."[11]

Meanwhile, F. Wilson Hurd's Water Gap Sanitarium in Delaware Water Gap was still going strong,
but Hurd's ads give the impression that he did not treat consumptives. Hurd catered to patients with
"tired and debilitated nerves and wasted energies." He was obviously treating "neurasthenia," which
physicians of the late nineteenth century had identified as a mental disease of worry and depression.
Although Hurd was keeping abreast of the times by treating faddish ailments, his treatments were his
usual "baths" and "rubbings" and whatever else was "suitable."[12]

Greater Comfort in the Poconos

Masochists enjoy misery; the rest of mankind prefers comfort. Even so, Americans of the 1890s had a
problem with the easy life. Though naturally drawn to it, they nonetheless needed to justify it, to convince themselves that a particular service or creature comfort was not hedonistic. Once convinced that
it was necessary, they would enjoy it. Pocono resorts would claim to supply these justifiable luxuries.

Travel and communications were practical concerns for Victorians. If they worried about reaching
the hotel after getting off the train, they would find reassurance from the Pocono resorts that advertised
a waiting stagecoach at the train station. If vacationers arrived unexpectedly, they would have liked the
Peters House. Boasting one of the first telephones in the Poconos, the Peters House reduced anxiety
by allowing vacationers to phone from the East Stroudsburg train station. Once ensconced at a resort,
vacationers needed transportation to reach the scenic sights. Many resorts satisfied this need as well.
They advertised that vacationers could rent horses and carriages at nearby livery stables. Workaholic
businessmen may not have cared for country jaunts, but if they wanted instant communication with

their offices, they could stay at the Kittatinny Hotel and use its long-distance phone. The Conashaugh Spring House outdid the Kittatinny by offering not only a telephone but also telegraph service and a second mail delivery each day.[13]

An icon of the late nineteenth century was the home and its domesticity. Vacationers who appreciated small resorts, with their implied cordiality, would have liked Milford. In 1898, the Erie directory listed the sizes of nineteen Milford resorts. Their average capacity was 46.6 guests; only two of the nineteen could hold more than 100 guests. Other vacationers sought domesticity through familiar faces. The Mount Pocono House advertised the same management for twenty-one years. The Locust Grove House in East Stroudsburg boasted forty-one years of continuity. Neither resort could match the Kittatinny Hotel's claim of having pioneered the resort trade in Pennsylvania and of being the best-known and largest hotel along the Delaware River.[14]

In an age when a pretty sight, either natural or man-made, was an acceptable pleasure, the Kittatinny Hotel offered its architecture. In the early 1890s, extensive renovations had removed its original appearance, giving the Kittatinny a very up-to-date exterior, with mansard roof, dormer windows, gables, and porches. These features allowed the Kittatinny to stand in sharp contrast to many resort buildings in the Poconos, especially the dull-looking and functional boardinghouses, which had originated as farmhouses or residences and had added extra rooms as business expanded.

Such modern architectural choices implied that the vacation experience would be up-to-date as well. Not surprisingly, newer resort buildings had a late Victorian appearance. The newly built Central House in Mount Pocono had a double veranda and two conical roofs. For sheer ostentation, however, the Delaware House stood alone. Directly across from the Delaware Water Gap railroad station, the Delaware House caught the tourist eye with a double veranda graced with gingerbread railings; it hinted at domestic sentimentality with its six dormer windows. Its conical turrets in the corners and flagpole tower in the middle of the building were nearly overwhelming, but the stylish mansard roof managed to assert itself. The overall effect was of excess that was nonetheless pleasing.

A modern resort of the 1890s did not necessarily need all the typical features of Victorian architecture. More than one resort building lacked bay windows, towers, and turrets—features that were ornamental—but at the very least, a resort needed a veranda or porch, an accessory that was functional. Guests needed a porch for exercise, for conversation, and for sitting down to observe the passing world. A porch represented modern comfort, making a resort that lacked this key item of 1890s modernity seem hopelessly old-fashioned.

Some resort architects believed in redundancy. They designed buildings with two verandas. The Mount Pleasant House in Mount Pocono stood out with three floors of verandas. The Mount Pocono House bragged that it had "over 17,000 feet" of verandas that stood "on three sides at every story, measuring fully a quarter of a mile on a straight line." By contrast, Milford's Hotel Bellevue was modest. In 1893, it was content to widen its porches and to add a few more ornaments.[15]

Reflecting the slowly changing cultural standards at the end of the nineteenth century, several resorts offered creature comforts that had a whiff of indulgence. In this regard, a leader among Pocono resorts was the Conashaugh Spring House, whose ads proclaimed it a "headquarters for amateur photographers." Its darkroom permitted vacationers who had bought the new handheld Eastman camera to have instant gratification. Another kind of gratification was the Conashaugh's beds, "all furnished with wire woven springs and the best of hair mattresses." By advertising comfortable beds and a concern for hobbies, the Conashaugh clearly previewed the hedonism of the twentieth century.[16]

Prime Pocono Pastimes

In the 1890s, fun and gaiety were being redefined. Although the Victorian work ethic was still powerful, Americans were increasing their interest in recreation. The conformist, respectable norms of the

FIG. 14
Two hotels near the Delaware River were known as the "Delaware House." The one in Delaware Water Gap was directly across from the train station. Unlike the rather plain-looking farmers' boardinghouses, the Delaware House was probably designed to attract travelers getting off the train. Owned by James Yarrick of Philadelphia, it was operated by his widow after his death. Although Victorians believed that women should eschew business, they did not object to female innkeepers. Monroe County Historical Association.

FIG. 15

Mount Pleasant House, 1911. Over the years, the Mount Pleasant House in Mount Pocono changed its appearance. In 1911, it was very much an example of Victorian excess: gabled roofs, polygonal pointed towers, and three-tiered veranda. Monroe County Historical Association.

post–Civil War period were weakening. An urge to be "young, masculine, and adventurous" expressed itself in new styles of popular music, in the sports revolution at colleges, and in the emergence of the "new woman." Newspapers published sports pages and new magazines focused on fun.[17]

In the reorientation of American popular culture, the Poconos did not lead. But the area still had to project a modern image. The local press, always a booster of the vacation economy, was quick to report the details if the Poconos seemed to be following national trends. One example was the "new woman." Although created elsewhere, she was seen in the Poconos. The press would have it no other way.

The "new woman" was "new" in that she boldly sought the outdoors. Unlike her sisters of previous generations, she was not a delicate creature whose face betrayed the pallor of an indoor, sedentary lifestyle. The "new woman" proudly sported a suntan. Called the "summer girl" by the *Stroudsburg Times,* she threw herself into the latest crazes. She bicycled, rowed, golfed, and danced, and men admired her. In Milford, the "new woman" played softball—so much, in fact, that a local politician was scandalized. He introduced a bill in the state legislature to ban women from the game. His colleagues laughed, but he insisted that softball had "ruined" innocent young women. Whatever was going on in Milford, the little resort village was achieving notoriety. If a unique vacation atmosphere was the goal, Milford had gone a long way toward achieving it.[18]

Less dramatic—but also gaining attention in the Poconos—was the trend of going hatless. In 1899, the *Stroudsburg Daily Times* announced that summer people no longer feared sunburnt faces, preferring a healthy color to "fairy whiteness." The newspaper added that the hatless fad was spreading from the ultra-fashionables at the Mount Pocono and Delaware Water Gap resorts to Stroudsburg. It feared that the venerable custom of men tipping their hats to ladies would end.[19]

The hatless fad and the "summer girl" pointed to the emergence of a distinctive resort culture. Resort life was no longer city living placed in a country setting, no longer the pursuit of health, education, or aesthetic development. Rather, resort life was becoming self-conscious, a unique way of life,

FIG. 16
Pocono Hay-Ven. In 1932, Dr. William Howard Hay turned the old Mount Pleasant House into a health resort. (The producer of this postcard chose to use the plainer name of "Pocono Haven.") Monroe County Historical Association.

the antithesis of the mundane, run-of-the-mill routine in the cities. This in itself would make vacationing different and more appealing.

The new self-conscious resort culture should not receive too much emphasis. Although new and expanding, it was not yet the norm. The "summer girl" received attention; she was chic and eye-catching, but she was not the typical resort woman. Librarians, schoolteachers, and married women with children stayed for the season and continued to dominate resort life. Even men—the supposed lords of the manor in the Victorian era—counted for less. Married men worked in the city and came on weekends, strangers to the gossip of resort cliques and outsiders on the veranda or porch, where spinsters and housewives sat and talked. The porch institutionalized a sedentary, conversational culture. It empowered women, albeit the ones of a traditional bent.[20]

On the other hand, men did not have to play the ladies' game of sitting on the porch and sharing polite chitchat. Among the selling points of the Pocohasset in Mount Pocono and the Central House in Delaware Water Gap were their smoking and reading rooms for men. In an era when good Christian men were not expected to smoke, a smoking room hinted at masculine naughtiness.[21]

But Pocono pastimes were rarely naughty. Only the most puritanical could take offense at the presentation of tableaux: performers donned costumes that reminded audiences of familiar scenes or people, and the participants then froze onstage for a few moments. Local newspapers would mention imaginative tableaux. Two New York girls at Stroudsburg's Burnett House staged eighteen scenes in 1890. Several years later, Mother Goose inspired a tableaux series in Milford's Brown Hall.[22]

Some bluenoses would object to dancing and card playing, but the resort industry did not care. By mid-decade, Milford resorts were taking turns hosting biweekly hops. The Burnett House once held a "phantom party," in which masked men dressed in white walked in with candles. After the unmasking, couples danced until midnight. When the Brookside Inn in Canadensis held a progressive euchre party, it glamorized this card game by having a very exotic setting. The lawn was illuminated with Japanese lanterns and the parlor decorated with flowers. First prize was a silver-plated pair of scissors for ladies and a pearl-handled pocket knife for men. A few weeks later, the Brookside Inn held a "donkey party" and, amid much laughter, awarded a booby prize.[23]

At times, villages sought to create particularly memorable events. In 1890, Milford celebrated the Fourth of July with firecrackers and bunting. Stores closed and hotels printed fancy menus. The Crissman House printed its menu in Spanish, French, and German.[24] In 1897, Delaware Water Gap took advantage of its riverside location and held a river carnival. The carnival took place at night with three outdoor bands and lights on the bathing beach. Hotels competed to present the best parties and illuminated boats. Although the carnival was showy, it probably was unsuccessful, since it did not become an annual affair.[25]

The main draw of the Poconos was, of course, the outdoors. Although sunshine and fresh air were shared by the Pocono vacation spots, resort guests were by no means alike. The timid might prefer to enjoy their fresh air without leaving the grounds. Many resorts accordingly advertised swings, lawn tennis, and croquet. More adventuresome vacationers might prefer sunshine in an open field.

Their game would be golf (recently arrived from Scotland), and by the turn of the century, they could play nine holes in Delaware Water Gap. Golf was also available in Milford.[26]

Carl Tilennius provided the ultimate in managed nature. In 1880, he had bought one thousand acres of Mount Pocono land, part of which he turned into an elk park, a private zoo of sorts. Tilennius catered to urbanites who wanted to see wild animals in a controlled environment and have the illusion of being close to nature. Tilennius converted the rest of the grounds into a riding school. He owned a New York City restaurant, and he had a shrewd eye for urban needs. Although gentlemen were expected to be horsemen, they would have little need to ride a horse in the cities, where omnibuses, carriages, and the new electric trolleys had turned them into passengers. Tilennius solved their problem—killing the proverbial two birds with one stone—by providing a European riding instructor to teach equestrian skills, thereby allowing city folk to learn a valuable social skill while vacationing.[27]

Day-Tripping in the Poconos

Around the nation, one-day outings were becoming increasingly popular. Although never threatening the expensive resorts, they did represent an alternative to the budget boardinghouses—especially by the 1890s, when the nation's rail network had nearly reached its full expansion, making the countryside more accessible than ever. The harried city worker who could not budget time to stop overnight would welcome the brevity of the day trip, as would the penny-pincher who could not afford the expense of an overnight stay.

Not all day trips were equal. Social class and breeding created an informal ranking. At the bottom of the social totem pole stood the "trashy" day-tripper places. These catered to elements in the working class that wanted excitement, that ignored the culture of their "betters," and that would frequent the dance halls, saloons, and other questionable haunts of the city.[28]

The Poconos never did offer the mechanical rides that were the main attraction of Coney Island, nor the raucous bars, brothels, and ballyhoo of Atlantic City. Shohola Glen came the closest, although it never sank to Atlantic City lows. Located in Pike County, Shohola Glen was a tree-lined cleft in the rocks. John Kilgour bought it in the early 1880s with money made by selling Pocono bluestones to the cities. Kilgour constructed booths, walks, picnic tables, refreshment stands, shooting galleries, a merry-go-round, and a dancing platform. A gravity railroad gave thrill rides. At its height, Shohola attracted annual crowds of one hundred thousand visitors. Hordes of holiday revelers required seven special trains; groups of travelers took the Erie from New York City and the coal regions of Pennsylvania. Drinking and gambling were common, although in 1894 the press reported that new owners were cracking down on gambling. A Brooklyn man was arrested for setting up a "three card monte game" to fleece the "greenhorns." Released on bail, he forfeited the money when he did not appear for his trial. Shohola Glen closed in 1907, when the Erie Railroad canceled its excursion fares.[29]

By contrast, other day-tripper spots in the Poconos were respectable. Island Park was in the Delaware River, just off staid Delaware Water Gap. In 1890, it offered a merry-go-round as well as dancing and refreshments. Picnic parties came from Wilkes-Barre, Trenton, and Philadelphia. Nonetheless, serpents had crept into Eden. Island Park could not escape urban malaise. The press reported that a party of "city toughs" had amused themselves by getting drunk and firing pistols, leaving before they could be apprehended.[30]

Located about ten miles from Stroudsburg, Lake Poponoming (Saylors Lake) was very respectable. Instead of artificial, man-made amusements, its main attractions were fishing and boating in a very scenic lake surrounded by trees. As early as the 1870s, Lake Poponoming was attracting picnic parties. The atmosphere was so wholesome that churches held camp meetings on the grounds.[31] The 1888 extension of the Lehigh and Lackawanna Railroad to Saylorsburg, about a half-mile from the lake, was a significant event. No longer would proper residents of Monroe County have Lake Poponoming to themselves. They would have to share it with the people of the Lehigh Valley cities of Allentown, Easton, and Bethlehem. Despite the crowds, decorum was maintained, by and large. In 1892, a reporter for the *Stroudsburg Times* visited Lake Poponoming on a crowded Sunday and reported having seen "few intoxicated persons." Six years later, the *Stroudsburg Times* assured its readers that tales of Sunday law violations were untrue. Although the lake grounds were crowded and bicyclists had "overrun the place," things seemed innocent enough. Youngsters were enjoying the swings. Farmers' daughters were flirting with city chaps, trying "to imitate the ways of girls from town in the lowering of the eyes and the small smile of encouragement."[32]

If press inattention meant anything, the least popular day-tripper spot in the Poconos of the 1890s was Hygiene Park. Hygiene Park suffered from its location near Marshall Falls: it was several miles from Delaware Water Gap and required an extended trip by horse and buggy from the train station. In June 1889, when seventy-two persons came by rail from New Jersey, they brought along teamsters to drive carriages from Delaware Water Gap to the Park. Hygiene Park charged an admission of fifteen cents, which permitted guests to walk on the paths, fish in the lake, sit by the fountains, or play tennis and croquet. Since these pleasures were found elsewhere, Hygiene Park needed a gimmick. As the park's name suggests, health *was* that gimmick. According to advertisements, Hygiene Park was "a complete out-of-door and in-door sanitarium" with gymnastic and swimming facilities and other forms of "healthful recreation."[33]

The health formula evidently did not work; though it seemed to anticipate the evolution of the modern health spa, Hygiene Park was too far ahead of its time in the 1890s. After the turn of the century, Hygiene Park stopped hawking health and became a regular resort named "Titania." The name was painted in huge letters across the front of the building, making the Titania easy to find. But the name of the resort marked it in another unusual way: while other resorts often had names that reflected natural themes, such as "Maple Grove," Titania House broke the mold by referring to Shakespeare. In *Midsummer Night's Dream,* Titania was the queen of the fairies, a character that

FIG. 17
A tour group posing outside the Delaware House in Delaware Water Gap, 1902. Their sober faces were typical of Victorians who took their vacations seriously. Monroe County Historical Association.

stretched the imagination. If planning and thinking of a vacation was part of the fun, a resort named Titania would associate the countryside with enchantment and help create the right mood.[34]

Private Club Resorts: Keeping Out Undesirables

The manager or proprietor of a resort was the gatekeeper. He decided which applications to accept and which to reject. If the gatekeeper admitted an obnoxious guest, the other guests had to endure his unpleasant company. If the gatekeeper admitted a guest with different interests, the other guests would be bored. Here was a situation that cried out for an alternative to the resort and its gatekeeper. The result was a resort hybrid, one that combined a private club with a hotel and a cottage colony. The private club screened membership, thus creating a proper social environment. Members had the choice of staying at the club hotel or at a nearby cottage, which they could buy or rent. The cottage option allowed both privacy and conviviality, since cottagers had the services of the hotel at their disposal.

The first Pocono example of this hybrid arrangement—the private club resort—was the Blooming Grove Park Association, an exclusive hunting and fishing club for rich city men who shared a common interest in field sports. The Association exemplified a new interest for the upper classes. In the eighteenth century, American gentlemen had been bored with the outdoors and had relegated hunting and fishing to the poor and the hungry. In the nineteenth century, gentlemen redefined themselves: they believed that they had to re-create pioneer values and to approach nature through wildlife. This new code for the urban upper class required a nearby supply of fish and game, but such a supply was nearly nonexistent, due to the spread of civilization. Private fishing and hunting clubs to breed and stock wildlife provided a solution. By 1878, about twenty-five thousand Americans belonged to six hundred of these clubs. Among the leaders was the Blooming Grove Park Association.[35]

Promoted by two New Yorkers—Fayette Giles, a gentleman jeweler, and Charles Hallock, the future founder of *Field and Stream* magazine—the Blooming Grove Park Association received a charter from the Commonwealth of Pennsylvania in 1871. Within a year, over one hundred sportsmen from twelve states had joined, and by the 1890s, membership had doubled.[36] That the Association members were well-off is obvious, but in addition, they were on the technological cutting edge. Like their e-mailing, faxing, cellular-phoning descendants of the new millennium, they were wired. They had strung telephone wire over fourteen miles of forest so that they could enjoy the latest news from the New York Stock Exchange.[37]

The Blooming Grove Park Association was a product of the Gilded Age and testified to the wealth and arrogance of the period. It was inspired by the European game parks at Baden and Fontainebleau, which were private preserves for the nobility. The promoters had grandiose plans from the start, buying a huge tract of 12,000 acres in Blooming Grove, Porter, and Greene Townships in Pike County, and leasing another 2,000 acres. In all, the tract was twenty times larger than New York City's Central Park. After the purchase, money poured in. Within two years, a clubhouse and a gamekeeper's lodge were built, a kennel of dogs collected, and a deer-breeding park of 620 acres enclosed with an eight-foot-high wire fence. The promoters wanted to introduce exotic game, such as German wild boars, buffalo, moose, and elk. In this, they evidently failed, for by the 1890s, none of these animals lived in the park. The power of money had its limits.[38]

The Blooming Grove Park Association had the Commonwealth's permission to make its own game laws. It punished poachers with severe penalties that ranged from a two-dollar fine for a fish to a three-hundred-dollar fine for an elk.[39] The club's neighbors were not amused. Poor farmers and woodsmen had previously roamed the territory at will. Wildlife that once had been theirs now belonged to rich city people. They hated the club and they initially refused to work for it. By the 1890s, they had learned to tolerate the club—but under duress.[40]

The Blooming Grove Park Association exemplified the paradox that selfishness can serve the public interest. Although the Association members were snobbish, they performed an environmental service. To create their private playground, they had bought nearly worthless land ravaged by lumberjacks and had restored it, allowing trees to grow back and protecting the wildlife. By practicing integrated natural resource planning, the Association was years ahead of the public sector.[41]

The Association exuded nineteenth-century masculinity, but it was not a male preserve. Its charter stated that the "better class of gentlemen" preferred the presence of women. If wives and daughters did not care to fish and shoot, they had the options of playing croquet, swimming in the club's lake, or canoeing. Private cottages on the grounds made the Blooming Grove Park Association a family resort from the beginning.[42]

Another private club resort devoted to hunting and fishing was the Forest Lake Club, which was founded in 1882 in Pike County. Within a decade, the Forest Lake Club boasted an elegant Victorian clubhouse and five cottages amid three thousand acres. Forest Lake was very respectable. An 1896 visitor noted religious services and the absence of gunning and fishing on the Sabbath.[43]

The Blooming Grove and Forest Lake clubs were assets to the Pocono economy. They paid taxes, hired local labor, and bought local services and goods. But for the established resorts, especially the hunting and fishing lodges, they were a threat. Private club resorts had the advantage of allowing members to decide the guest list and to control field sports. Consider the following event at the Spruce Cabin Inn. In 1895, guests, a guide, and Wesley Price, the owner, went hunting. Price and the guide killed a bear and two deer; the city people had to settle for several pheasants. By shooting the best game, Price and his guide clearly did not defer to the guests. Instead, they acted as their equals. This rural effrontery would not have taken place at the Blooming Grove and Forest Lake clubs. The guests owned the clubs, hired the staff, and they would have shot the bears and deer. The hired help would have watched and applauded.[44]

The Solitary Vacation

Regular resorts, private club resorts, and day-tripper attractions all provided a communal experience. Mingling with other vacationers was the norm for day-trippers. Likewise, house rules set the tone for cottagers and hotel guests at private clubs such as Blooming Grove. Resorts offered the least privacy: guests could not escape each other. They ate in a common dining room, bumped into each other in hallways, shared the bathroom at the end of the corridor, and congregated on the porch—the center of gossip. Someone who did not care for the conversation was isolated. Moreover, guests had to look their best, since they were always under scrutiny, risking humiliation for wearing clothes that were not fashionable or were just plain wrong. Resorts were not for nonconformists, the shy, or those who believed that a vacation meant solitude. These outcasts could find relief, though: they could vacation alone.

FIG. 18

Cyclists in front of the Delaware House. This Delaware House was the one in Dingmans Ferry. It stood on the River Road—today's Route 209. (The gentleman in the middle was Randall Van Gorden, the owner.) During the cycling craze of the 1890s, city folk often stopped at the inns along the River Road, coming south from Milford on their way to East Stroudsburg or Delaware Water Gap to catch the Lackawanna train back to New York City. Pike County Historical Society.

The easiest way to avoid people and have a solitary vacation was to rent or buy a summer cottage. In 1893, *Harper's Weekly* noted a growing national trend in this direction. A few years later, Mount Pocono had enough cottage owners for a Taxpayers Protective Association.[45] In the next century, the cottage alternative would cut into resort business. In the 1890s, however, vacation cottages were still atypical of the Poconos. Their day would come only with the widespread use of the automobile.

The cheapest solitary vacation was a bicycle jaunt in the country. Cycling was the great fad of the 1890s. Throughout the nation, the bicycle seemed necessary—and became ubiquitous. In the city, cyclists could pedal directly to their destination and avoid the hassles of public transportation. In the country, cyclists could spend a day or two traversing country roads at will and avoiding the intermediary of carriage and driver. Cyclists were the horseback riders of the railroad age.[46]

The Poconos were a popular attraction for New York City cyclists, who had several options. For a one-day outing, cyclists brought their bicycles to the country, stayed near the railroad station, and used the station as a base for riding around. Cyclists with more time rode the Erie Railroad to the Port Jervis station and crossed the Delaware River to Pike County. Then they cycled down the River Road (today's Route 209), the same scenic route by the Delaware River that vacationers took to the waterfalls. Since the road was mostly downhill, the trip was not fatiguing. After stopping overnight at an inn, cyclists returned to New York City via the Lackawanna Railroad at the East Stroudsburg station or farther down at Delaware Water Gap.[47]

The reasons given for the bicycle's popularity would later apply to the automobile. The bicycle meant freedom from the crankiness of the horse and the inefficiencies of public transportation. The bicycle fad of the 1890s clearly shows that the public was ready for personal, mechanical transportation; in its own way, the bicycle presaged the automobile and the end of the nineteenth century's reliance on the railroad and the horse. When the automobile finally came, it would accelerate the competitive stress that emerged in the 1890s—providing even more mobility to the consumer. The railroad created the Pocono vacation, but the automobile would profoundly change it.

4

The Glory Days, 1900 to 1914

In the first years of the twentieth century, Americans had reason to feel satisfied. Their country had become an economic giant that was flexing its muscle in readiness for world leadership. At home, the economic doldrums of the 1890s had come to an end. Americans were again enjoying prosperity.

The future looked even better. The new president was the dynamic Theodore Roosevelt, a man of many parts—a reformer who fought corruption and political abuses, a hero of the Spanish-American War, a man who seemed all the more heroic because of his love of the outdoors. Roosevelt was a former Western rancher and very much still a big-game hunter. When Roosevelt preached the virtues of forests and wide-open spaces, he spoke from experience.

All in all, the new century offered a great opportunity for Americans to leave the cities and see their "outback." Like Walt Whitman, that most American of poets, some felt a bit untamed, wanting to sound their "barbaric yawp." After shedding a few inhibitions, they would roam and play around the nation, if not the world.

Unfortunately, most people in the Middle Atlantic states had neither time nor money to travel afar. Europe and beyond were out of the question. Much of the United States was equally remote. Typical residents of Pennsylvania, New York, and New Jersey would not spend the summer hunting in the Far West, seeing Old Faithful at Yellowstone Park, gazing at the stately redwoods of California, or marveling at the beauties of Yosemite Park. Exotic vacations could beckon, but they would remain in the realm of dreams. Most vacationers had to settle for the near and familiar. As always, they could visit the Poconos—and they did so in record numbers. The first decade and a half of the new century would be the best of times for the Pocono resorts along the Delaware River.

Feeling Good About Fun

Americans were enjoying themselves as they had never done before. Once diffident about fun, Americans had learned how to play—a great change noted by a national publication in 1911, when it pointed out that rich Americans of the 1870s played in old clothes (because they rarely played), but in the new century, they were spending a fortune on casual clothes. Aside from playing, Americans increasingly did the formerly unthinkable. After the turn of the century, women drank cocktails in public and men smoked at dinner. Traditional norms were eroding.[1]

Mores and manners had changed because many Americans had moved to the cities. When they left the countryside and small towns behind, they also left old ways behind. In return, the new city dwellers acquired free time, the great advantage of urban jobs. Unlike farmers, they did not have to fret at night over the sudden birth of a calf nor stay near barnyards to keep foxes at bay. When not at work, they could play, leave home, or do anything they wished without having to think of their jobs—a freedom that the great majority of people through history had never enjoyed. The result was the emergence of new games and pastimes, which city people considered natural and guiltless.[2]

The growing acceptance of leisure could be seen in resort life. In the 1870s, a vacation was a serious affair. If vacationers did not have the motive of improving their health or relieving stress, they were at least expected to appreciate nature or to expand their minds through an educational trip. With each passing decade, resort life gradually loosened up. Not only did resorts offer new pastimes, but their traditional parlor games and dances also showed more imagination and variety. Individual resorts needed to gain an advantage over rivals, and this hastened the change. By the eve of World War I, the full amusement resort had been born. Unlike the old days, when a resort was a home base from which guests would leave, the full amusement resort had the goal of keeping guests occupied during their entire vacation.[3]

It was no accident that the promotional literature of the new century referred to the Poconos as a "playground." The vacation industry was frankly admitting that city folk were enjoying themselves when they visited the Poconos. Resort ads in the Lackawanna directories were longer and more explicit. Resorts bragged of amusements and comforts that gave new excitement to the traditional bed and board.

A Better Lackawanna Railroad

The Lackawanna Railroad exemplified the changing attitudes toward fun. Its new promotional campaign centered on a pretty young woman, the fictional Phoebe Snow, the star of the railroad's ads and posters. Phoebe was seen golfing, swimming, bicycling, horseback riding, and playing tennis. Traveling alone, she was the independent woman of the early 1900s. Phoebe exuded sex—not by exposing her flesh, but by implying her sensuality. Her beauty and flair stimulated men into using their imaginations; Phoebe received fan mail and offers of marriage.

Phoebe Snow was also the butt of vaudevillian humor, perhaps because she spoke in jingles (an advertising strategy much in vogue in the period). The Calkins and Holden ad agency devised about seventy jingles from 1900 to 1917. The first of the series captured what was to follow:

FIG. 19

Phoebe Snow, the Lackawanna Railroad's lady in white. The model in this photograph may have been Marion F. Murray, who posed as Phoebe until 1907. Delaware, Lackawanna and Western Railroad Records, Syracuse University Library, Department of Special Collections.

> Says Phoebe Snow
> About to go
> Upon a trip
> To Buffalo
> "My gown stays white
> From morn till night
> Upon the road of Anthracite."

And another poster placed her at Delaware Water Gap.

> It's time to go
> Where records show
> It's cooler ten degrees or so
> By Fahrenheit
> Each summer night
> Along the road of Anthracite.

Phoebe wore white to show that she did not fear soot and cinders because the Lackawanna's loco-motives burned clean anthracite coal. Other railroads used dirty soft coal. The real reason why the Lackawanna used anthracite coal was less a concern for passenger cleanliness than the simple fact that the Lackawanna owned anthracite coal mines. Small pieces of coal, called "culm," had no market value; they would burn in locomotive furnaces, however.[4]

Although Phoebe Snow did not exist, she had a real message: service was better than ever on the Lackawanna Railroad. The improved service was due to William Truesdale, who had become the rail-road's new president in 1899. He believed that the railroad had become overly reliant on the coal business and that it had to boost passenger traffic. Aside from the Phoebe Snow advertising campaign, Truesdale sought to attract passengers by promoting the Pocono resorts and by modernizing the rail-road's facilities.[5]

In the years before World War I, Truesdale spent forty million dollars of the railroad's profits on improvements. He had stations adorned with flower beds and painted. If aging, they were replaced, along with aging track and rolling stock. Truesdale paid special attention to the Poconos. In 1903–4, he replaced the old wooden station at Delaware Water Gap with a new brick structure. In 1908, he com-menced a project to shorten the New York City-Pocono route. The cutoff from Slateford (on the Penn-sylvania side of the Delaware River) to Port Morris, New Jersey, was the greatest improvement in the history of the Lackawanna Railroad. Completed in 1912, the cutoff eliminated a number of steep grades and difficult curves, shortening the distance to New York by eleven miles. Railroad ads boasted that New Yorkers could reach Delaware Water Gap in a little over two hours. Riders on the Mountain Spe-cial could visit their vacationing families on weekends without neglecting business in the city.[6]

FIG. 20

The Delaware River, the Delaware Water Gap station of the Lackawanna Railroad, and the Delaware House. Today's view differs. The Delaware House is gone, and the trees have returned; the area between the river and the train station is thick with vegetation. The once proud train station stands empty and is deteriorating. Monroe County Historical Association.

The cutoff was symptomatic of the new leisure ethic. Passenger comfort had become a top priority, unlike the old days, when passengers were expected to endure a rough ride. Truesdale knew what he was doing. He justified the expense of the cutoff by noting that coal did not mind being jostled, but passengers would complain.[7]

The Lackawanna's Passenger Directories

During the summer, when the coal business lagged, equipment and crews were idle. The railroad needed passengers in order to stay busy. Truesdale drummed up new business by promoting the resorts. He looked at the resort directories issued by his predecessor and saw an ugly collection of ads and train schedules. His solution was a new series of resort directories, printed on glossy paper, with color drawings and an eye-catching format. The cover of the 1909 directory had a charming color print of a train coming through the Water Gap. The pleasures of vacationing were proclaimed.

The new directories sought to be modern without being offensive. They reassured traditionalists by continuing to refer to health and nature. At the same time, they were modern: they embraced the recreation ethic. They called the Poconos "a summer pleasure ground." Their drawings and photos

FIG. 21

A bridge is born. In 1908, the Lackawanna Railroad started work on a cutoff in New Jersey that shortened the route to New York City. The cutoff required a new bridge over the Delaware River. Monroe County Historical Association.

focused on vacationers at play. The directories both satisfied readers' curiosity and excited their imaginations. Fantasizing about a vacation is half the fun.

The greatest change in the directories was the hint of sex. The 1903 directory broke new ground with a love story. The love story in the 1906 edition took place in the Poconos and in New York City. It ended with the following effusion: "He caught her close in his arms and kissed her; kissed her full on the soft, appealing curve of her throat. Then he fled shamelessly into the night—just a common thief, after all." Aside from the love story, the 1906 edition featured Phoebe Snow on the cover, as well as a drawing of Phoebe and her beau facing the title page. Phoebe was looking toward the reader, but the young man was obviously love-struck. His eyes could only see Phoebe. Single women could dream of similar conquests: even romance was better in the Poconos.[8]

In accordance with Pennsylvania tradition, though, the directories downplayed certain elements of Pocono history. The Truesdale directories paid little attention to the early pioneers, the Indian wars, and the Revolution. Nor did the directories imitate the nostalgia motif of many New England resort communities and romanticize area farmers. Rural New England may have been sold to city folk as the repository of national virtue, but for the Poconos there was no such nonsense. After all, the Civil War (which many could still recall) produced more than its share of draft-dodgers who hid in the Pocono Mountains. In short, the Lackawanna Railroad implied that the attractions of the Poconos were neither the people nor the history, but the amenities of the resorts, the gifts of nature, and—for the young at heart—a chance at romance.[9]

One defect of the Lackawanna directories is understandable. They ignored much of the Poconos because their focus was on the villages and resorts near the Lackawanna's stations. In effect, they stressed Monroe County and the southern fringe of Pike County, and they ignored the northerly Milford area, which was located in the Erie Railroad's orbit. The Erie did not address this omission: it ceased publishing directories in the twentieth century. This may be one reason why Monroe County increasingly became the center of the Pocono vacation business.

Promoting the Resorts

The masterstroke of the Lackawanna Railroad was the sponsorship of a badly needed resort association. The loss of business resulting from the 1901 Pan American Exposition in Buffalo had alarmed the resort proprietors. The possibility that more sanitaria for consumptives would locate in the Poconos also had them worried. When they met at Mount Pocono in January 1902 to discuss the formation of a trade association, they spoke mostly about tuberculosis, perhaps concerned about the movement to establish summer camps for its victims on state land near Bushkill. Speakers warned about the sad fate of Liberty, New York, which had been a thriving resort center, but had drastically declined after sanitaria for consumptives opened. With several sanitaria already existing in Monroe County, the fate of Liberty was ominous. The future of the Pocono resorts was at stake—or so it was feared.[10]

In April 1902, the Monroe County Mountain Resort Association was formally established. Its major promoter was the Lackawanna Railroad, which guided the Resort Association until the First World War. It says much about the ethos of eastern Pennsylvania that the impetus and direction for the resort association came from New York City. The Pennsylvania Railroad, by contrast, never promoted the resorts, reflecting the individualism and atomization in Philadelphia that E. Digby Baltzell regarded as a pernicious Quaker legacy. The need for direction from New York shows how much the Pocono resorts were part of the culture of eastern Pennsylvania, in which hardworking entrepreneurs knew how to make money, but were less likely to unite for the common good or a grand vision.

At the initial meeting in April 1902, Wendell Colton, the advertising manager of the Lackawanna Railroad, was in charge. He promised to place large seven-by-six-inch block ads in New York City and Philadelphia newspapers. The ads had the double purpose of publicizing Monroe County and of listing its individual resorts by name, proprietor, and size. By May, the Resort Association had collected a $2,200 advertising budget. The Lackawanna had contributed $500 to this budget, four local banks another $100, and resorts had chipped in the rest. The railroad also sponsored a Pocono outing for newspaper reporters and set up a resort information bureau in New York City. The results were spectacular. So many vacationers came to Monroe County in 1902 that resorts turned 20,000 away. August was so busy that resorts placed cots in halls, parlors, and cellars.[11]

During the course of 1903, resort proprietors contributed $5,500 to the common advertising budget. The Lackawanna contributed an additional one-third. According to Colton, the railroad placed 61,000 lines of advertising in New York and Philadelphia newspapers, far surpassing the previous year's 14,000 lines. The Lackawanna also printed 50,000 copies of the resort directory. The success of the Lackawanna's promotion of the resorts can be seen in passenger receipts. During June, July, and August 1899, the Pocono route had collected about $10,000. In 1902, revenues increased to $68,492, and in 1903, they reached $130,412![12]

The Lackawanna also encouraged business from Philadelphia by bringing the Pennsylvania Railroad to Stroudsburg. Prior to 1903, both lines met at Manunka Chunk in New Jersey, about eleven miles from Delaware Water Gap, where passengers switched trains. The Lackawanna persuaded the Pennsylvania Railroad to send its trains to the East Stroudsburg station. Pocono-bound passengers from Philadelphia would no longer have to brave the elements at Manunka Chunk. The Pennsylvania Railroad was less accommodating with its money, however. In the best tradition of Philadelphia individualism, it refused to contribute to the 1903 resort advertising fund.[13]

A small addition to the rail network was the Delaware Valley Railroad. Launched in 1901, it ran on a single track from East Stroudsburg to Bushkill, a distance of eleven miles. At the height of the tourist season, five trains made the thirty-five-minute daily run. The tiny railroad arranged its schedules to meet the Lackawanna trains at the East Stroudsburg station. Although the Lackawanna was not responsible for the creation of the Delaware Valley Railroad, it regarded the smaller line as a branch. The Delaware Valley's Marshalls Creek, Coolbaugh, and Bushkill stations served many resorts.[14]

Aside from better rail service and more vacationers, the Resort Association achieved its original goal of keeping new tuberculosis sanitaria out of the Poconos. Protecting the resort industry was so important that when a young man with advanced tuberculosis arrived in the village of Mount Pocono, he was hurried off by a local physician, despite the fear that he would die. The young man managed to reach the train station, only to die at home two days later. Constant vigilance was necessary: in March 1903, the Resort Association successfully lobbied in Harrisburg against a proposed sanitarium in the Poconos. Later in the year, news came that a Camden group wanted to locate a sanitarium in the Mount Pocono area. In 1904, Pittsburgh promoters were also considering a sanitarium. A. Mitchell Palmer, a Stroudsburg attorney and future Attorney General of the United States, took up the cause, representing a citizens' group that fought to keep the Poconos free of carriers of contagious diseases.[15]

The Automobile Boosts Business

The successful battle against sanitaria cleared the way for continued growth in the vacation business. To accommodate the growing hordes of vacationers, new resorts opened, and many old resorts modernized and added new wings. In this first decade of the century, the automobile contributed to the boom in a surprising way: locked into old habits, new car owners drove to the familiar hotels and boardinghouses of the railroad age.

At first, resorts reacted to the automobile by believing that the new contraption would be an additional attraction for vacationers. In 1905, Delaware Water Gap had a "touring car" that sat forty and made daily trips around the county. In the following year, according to the *New York Times,* more than one Pocono resort had touring cars for its guests. Resort ads noted "automobiling" as a diversion along with the traditional hiking, riding, and river bathing. The auto tour had replaced the carriage ride.[16]

Another quasi-novelty was the "auto carnival," an event vaguely similar to a horse race. The carnival of 1908 consisted of a series of car races and hill climbs, nine in Delaware Water Gap and nine in Canadensis. Most races were limited to cars within specific price ranges. The Monroe County Mountain Resort Association gave the auto carnival its full endorsement. Unlike the auto carnival, however, the "auto run" was a use of the automobile that resorts could not control. City people would organize a train of cars—sometimes as many as a hundred—and take long treks into the countryside. They might stop at a resort for meals, or they could bypass the resorts and picnic by the side of the road. In 1911, the Lehigh Valley Motor Club sponsored a large Pocono auto run. Eighty-one cars left Allentown at nine in the morning and rode forty miles to the Buckwood Inn in Shawnee, where the 319 motorists visited the Worthington aviary and its "wonderful collection of birds."[17]

The fun of an "auto run" consisted of riding over unpaved, dusty roads, knowing that mechanics were far apart and that a breakdown was stressful, but not dangerous. An "auto run" was controlled

"Bushkill Flyer", D. V. R. R., Bushkill, Pa.

FIG. 22

The Delaware Valley Railroad. It was no colossus: it had one track, and once the train reached Bushkill, it made the return trip backward. But it got the job done. Farmers, schoolchildren, and lumbermen—as well as vacationers—used it for the seventeen-mile journey from the Lackawanna station in East Stroudsburg to Bushkill. Monroe County Historical Association.

adventure for the modern age. It was also conspicuous consumption, for poor people did not own cars. The well-to-do had the thrill of speeding past common yokels who rode horses or whose poverty forced them to walk. On the unpaved roads of the day, pedestrians literally ate dust, clouds of earth churned into the air by high-speed cars.[18]

Resort owners had to get used to the new technology. Unlike railroads, automobiles had no schedules. Auto parties arrived at all hours without warning. On Memorial Day in 1910, the Kittatinny Hotel was flooded with 350 unexpected visitors. On July 4, an observer counted over 500 cars in Delaware Water Gap. On a Sunday in August, autos overran Stroudsburg and filled local garages. The Sunday traffic jam in the Bushkill area—which today's vacationers and residents know well—already existed in 1911.[19]

FIG. 23
Outdoor recreation at the Water Gap House. Note the automobile in the center of this postcard. Motor driving had joined horseback riding and canoeing as a leisure activity. Monroe County Historical Association.

Expansion of the Resort Industry

During the new century's first decade, the traditional resort communities along the Delaware River were flourishing. According to the Lackawanna resort directories, Monroe County contained 152 hotels and boardinghouses in 1905. Four years later, Monroe County had 204 (this figure does not include the smaller resorts that did not advertise in the Lackawanna directory). In August 1910, the *Monroe Democrat* noted that Delaware Water Gap's resorts were overflowing, having their best August on record and diverting the overflow to Stroudsburg and Mount Pocono.

In this golden age—the best of times for the Pocono resorts—life was to be enjoyed, slowly and with grace, as on a luxury liner. Several resorts deserve mention because of their size, their opulence, their creature comforts, and (in some cases) their builders. Not only were these builders bold businessmen, but they were also inexorably tied to their resorts, which were temples of pleasure and monuments honoring their founders.

In 1909, Dimmick Drake completed the Castle Inn, destined to be the last great hotel in Delaware Water Gap. An energetic businessman, Drake had settled in Delaware Water Gap a few years before, and he counted commercial entertainment among his projects. He erected a casino, or music hall, next to the Castle Inn so that the Gap could keep up with the latest trends—having a building devoted to recreation. The casino had five thousand square feet of uninterrupted space, which could be used for conventions, dancing, plays, or dining in what was the area's largest banquet hall. Dancing and vaudeville were the usual fare.[20] On Labor Day in 1910, soft-shoe dancers, a comedian, and a quick sketch artist performed. In August 1913, the John Philip Sousa band played to a huge audience. According to a 1913 ad, the casino was open to all vacationers in Delaware Water Gap.[21] The casino was detached from the hotel, as was the fashion of the day, so that the Castle Inn's patrons could have the illusion of going somewhere special, or could sleep undisturbed.[22]

Another Pocono entrepreneur was Charles C. Worthington, a New York millionaire whose factories manufactured pumps around the world. Worthington liked to vacation in the Poconos and stayed at the Water Gap House before finally deciding to erect his own resort, which he completed in 1911 and called the Buckwood Inn. It was located at Shawnee-on-Delaware, several miles north of Delaware Water Gap. With accommodations for one hundred guests and fifty private baths, the Buckwood Inn won the unofficial lavatory competition in the Poconos. A golf enthusiast, Worthington had his own private nine-hole course on an island in the Delaware River, conveniently near the Buckwood.[23]

Most men would be content with a personal golf course. But Worthington was not an ordinary man; he was rich. A nature lover who did not wish to be bored, Worthington had no intention of spending hours in a forest waiting for a favorite bird or animal to wander by. Instead, he created his own aviary for bird-watching. Likewise, he created a private deer park on the New Jersey side of the Delaware River. He surrounded thirteen hundred acres with a nine-foot-high fence of closely knit barbed wire, trapping skunks and foxes inside, and had his men kill them. After this victory, Worthington stocked the park with deer imported from Wisconsin, giving life to his own vision of nature: an Eden with no predators. He was a throwback to the nineteenth-century "developers" who had created accessible scenery by carving out trails and roads.[24]

The Montanesca in Mount Pocono had a brief but glorious life of ten years. When completed in 1901, it boasted more private baths than any other Pocono hotel. Its verandas were imposing—among the largest in the Poconos. In 1902, the Montanesca had the honor of hosting Admiral George Dewey, the hero of the Spanish-American War. When Dewey arrived, a large crowd greeted him at the train station, and this was only the beginning. During the course of his vacation at the Montanesca, the admiral could not escape the local press; he could not even walk in the woods without making the front page. This was great publicity for the Montanesca. Unfortunately, its glory was short-lived. A fire destroyed it in 1911.[25]

The Churleigh Hotel was built one year after the Montanesca, and in comparison, it was smaller and less plushy. It had no private bathrooms in its forty-five bedrooms, thus forcing guests to line up in the corridor the old-fashioned way. The Churleigh's claim to fame was its location and appearance. It stood some eight hundred feet above Stroudsburg on a spur of the Blue Mountain, giving a view that stretched for twenty miles on a clear day. The Churleigh's exterior was always worth a second look, if not a third. The architecture was a version of the Queen Anne style, a promiscuous mix of parts that did not match, a collage of broken lines and differently sized turrets. It did not offer the symmetry of nature, in which trees seem to glide into each other. The Churleigh, in its Queen Anne glory, radiated a lack of balance and boldly stood out from its surroundings.[26]

The Kittatinny, the oldest resort hotel in the Poconos, was by no means resting on its laurels. In the ten years after 1903, it increased its capacity from three hundred to five hundred guests and added another story that supplied seventy more rooms. A new power plant provided the gifts of the electric age—not only indoor lights but also a fountain that treated spectators to a different light display every minute. Erected in 1905, the fountain's only equal in Pennsylvania was found in Willow Grove Park in suburban Philadelphia. The Kittatinny's greatest asset may have been its grounds, though. Its private mountain park of over 150 acres doubled in size within a decade, and according to the 1913 Lackawanna directory, it contained "beautiful walks, lakes, lawns, waterfalls, cascades, electric fountains." The grounds were so well manicured that there was no pretense of the nineteenth-century fantasy of being in the wilderness. The closest that guests got to nature was seeing the Kittatinny's pet deer and collection of stuffed animals. One observer regarded the Kittatinny as probably the only first-class hotel in the entire Poconos with the whole apparatus: electric bells, elevators, private baths, bedrooms with hot and cold running water, and most important of all, liveried servants and bellboys. By 1913, guests could amuse themselves by bowling at the bowling alley, shooting billiards, and playing shuffleboard. A private riding academy allowed them to practice horsemanship.[27]

In 1915, the Kittatinny was bought by John Purdy Cope, who was perhaps the best-known resortman of the century's early decades. He was the brother of G. Frank Cope, who had bought the Kittatinny Hotel in 1907. Both Copes came from Atlantic City, but John Purdy, unlike his brother, stayed in the Poconos. First, he ran the Water Gap House, which he bought in 1907, and—after fire destroyed it in 1915—he bought the Kittatinny. During his Water Gap House days, Cope doubled the hotel's capacity to five hundred, spent sixty thousand dollars on renovations, and added a new electric power plant. A hotel always needs to persuade the public to choose it over its rivals, and in the Water Gap House's case, that rival was the Kittatinny. The Water Gap House stood higher than the Kittatinny, and Cope built a rooftop observatory that maximized the already magnificent view of the Gap. For the more sensuously inclined, the Water Gap House offered gourmet food prepared by French chefs. It also advertised an "entire white service," perhaps in an effort to distinguish itself from the Kittatinny, which had long employed black waiters.[28]

John Purdy Cope was a community leader as well as an innkeeper. He ran for the State Senate in 1916 as a "Wilsonian Democrat," but lost. He was more successful when he ran for the Delaware

Water Gap borough council. On a less exalted note, Cope became a local celebrity of sorts in 1911, when he and his second wife became the first couple to file for divorce in Monroe County. According to the local press, the wife insisted that she had been beaten, but Cope replied that he was the victim, accusing his once beloved of having temper tantrums and striking him.[29]

How Low Can You Go?

To say that the Poconos were becoming more comfortable with fun does not mean that they were hosting Roman orgies. It simply means that compared to the immediate years after the Civil War,

FIG. 24
The Churleigh Inn perched on a spur of the Blue Mountain above Stroudsburg. While some resorts advertised "all white service," the Churleigh employed black waitresses. In 1920, they organized a jazz ball that was a social event for African Americans, attracting guests from out of town. In the same year, the management announced plans to add fifty additional rooms. Fire destroyed the Churleigh in the 1920s. Monroe County Historical Association.

there was a greater acceptance of pleasure. Whether the Poconos would completely abandon traditional standards still remained an issue, however. For contemporary observers, the extremes of virtue and vice were embodied at the New Jersey shore. On the one hand, Atlantic City was noted for its vulgarity and vice. On the other, Ocean City and Asbury Park were Methodist resort towns noted for their very wholesome atmosphere. So where did the Poconos fall between these extremes?[30]

By most standards, some of the Pocono pastimes were inoffensive—such as the burro rides at Delaware Water Gap. According to the *Morning Press,* the burros made jaunts to the woodlands and mountains "less tiresome." Vacationers could easily reach the lookout points on the top of Mount Minsi and enjoy a great view of the Delaware River. Donkey rides may have been morally neutral, but they were a concession to ease and indicative of the new times. Vacationers of an earlier era would have been expected to walk.[31] Another innocent pastime was golf, which was rapidly gaining popularity around the nation. Several Pocono resorts had their own courses. The best one was attached to the Buckwood Inn, whose owner, Charles C. Worthington, hosted the first Professional Golfers Association tournament in 1912. Pocono golfing had achieved national status.[32]

The emerging singles scene could give offense, though. The Kittatinny Hotel had a program of Sunday college dances. Waltzing, two-stepping, and square dancing were popular with students from Moravian College, Lehigh, and other institutions of higher learning. East Stroudsburg Normal School was only several miles from the Gap, and its students, including Mary Owens Ballard, attended these dances. In a 1989 interview, Ballard recalled the gentility and innocence of these events, the fine clothes and the chaperons. Despite Ballard's sweet memories, some of the religious people of her day, especially Methodists—who strongly disapproved of dancing—would be critical. Other aspects of the singles scene would raise more eyebrows. Young adults stayed overnight at the Glenwood and at the Bellevue, resorts in Delaware Water Gap. The Bellevue had opened in 1906, and it was so successful that its owners opened a second hotel at the Gap.[33]

Moralists who disapproved of the stage would also censure the vaudeville that had become a staple in Delaware Water Gap. In 1902, a vaudeville troupe arrived with John L. Sullivan, the retired heavyweight boxing champion, who played Simon Legree in a presentation of *Uncle Tom's Cabin.* More vaudeville came after the mayor of Atlantic City, G. Frank Cope, bought the Kittatinny Hotel in 1907. Cope announced that the Kittatinny would stay open during the winter: its main attraction would be entertainment, similar to Atlantic City's. Open-air motion pictures, a circus, and a dog and pony show were among one year's attractions. In 1917, the Kittatinny waiters (who were black) put on a minstrel show. Two years later, they were replaced by professionals, described in a local newspaper as "some of the best-known colored actors and actresses." After the show, they performed a cakewalk. Although Cope talked of importing a bit of Atlantic City to the Poconos, Delaware Water Gap never sank to the level of New Jersey's "Babylon" at the shore, which complemented the sand and surf with seedy bars, brothels, and gambling dens. Cope obviously meant to import the best of Atlantic City.[34]

Milford's driving park for horses was the lowest of the new amusements. Good Christians were not supposed to gamble, and during this period, nearly all Americans paid lip service to Christian

Mt. Minsi or bust--Delaware Water Gap.

FIG. 25

The easy life after 1900! Vacationers at Delaware Water Gap could rent a burro at a stand located at the site of today's post office and could ride to the top of Mount Minsi—assuming that the burro was willing to move. As this postcard shows, burros can be contrary, providing unanticipated adventure for visitors. Monroe County Historical Association.

ideals. But Pike County was always considered backward, with hinterlands that rarely saw a clergyman. The *Milford Dispatch* was not upset by the track, perhaps because the gamblers were city vacationers. Although the driving park attracted a crowd of nearly one thousand on July 4, 1903, a smaller turnout was the norm. Revenues barely met expenses and could not satisfy the mortgage. The driving park survived for only four years and was sold at a sheriff's sale in 1905.[35]

Liquor sales annoyed Pocono moralists. They reacted by trying to outlaw alcohol, and they always failed. The Poconos preferred choice in this matter, and they never became another Ocean City. Opponents of liquor could take comfort in knowing that most Pocono resorts were dry, the most famous being the Water Gap House. There was enough virtue to allow a Monroe County newspaper to boast of the morally clean atmosphere and to claim that resort proprietors, as a rule, were "God-fearing people" who led "clean Christian lives."[36]

Despite claims of Christian virtue, the Pocono press was far more likely to notice the rich and famous than the saintly. What counted was the size of a guest's wallet or reputation, not piety. Guests who were ministers received far less attention in 1910 than in 1870. At times, the Pocono press gave the impression that the importance of the vacation industry lay in the number of rich people it attracted. When six millionaires stayed at the Kittatinny in 1902, the *Mountain Echo* was quick to notice. On another occasion, the newspaper proclaimed a particularly good season: the guests had been of "a better class." Former president Grover Cleveland's fishing trip to Pike County was big news in 1907. The trip was billed as the biggest event in the county since the visit of Horace Greeley prior to the Civil War. In August 1910, Theodore Roosevelt was driving through the Poconos and he stayed overnight at the Water Gap House. The always ebullient ex-president attended a reception in his honor and posed for photographs, providing more fodder for the Pocono publicity mill.[37]

The Pocono region, then, was torn between extremes. Its heart was closer to the wholesome seaside communities of Asbury Park and Ocean City, but the money came from being closer to Atlantic City. The Poconos wanted to seem virtuous, but would overlook sin, provided that it was discreet. The region had mastered the art of compromise. Mammon may have been condemned as a false god, but the worship of Mammon paid the bills.

The Quaker Resorts

The eternal tug-of-war between Zion and Sodom can be seen in two Quaker resorts. The Inn at Buck Hill Falls opened in 1901, and Pocono Manor opened the following year. Part of the old Philadelphia elite, Quakers tended to feel uncomfortable about their wealth. Yet they kept their riches, and, perhaps by way of compensation, they adhered to a strict code of morality that made them wary of the latest fads.

The very origin of the Inn at Buck Hill Falls had its roots in virtue. A Quaker, Samuel Griscom, owned the site of the future Inn at Buck Hill Falls in Barrett Township. At the turn of the century, Griscom, getting on in years, wanted to sell his property, which he believed would make an excellent resort. A New York hotelman made a good offer, but he intended to sell liquor. Griscom refused, as a good Quaker would. Realizing that he had to sell to his own people if he wanted to maintain his standards, Griscom badgered Howard Jenkins, editor of the *Friends Intelligencer* of Philadelphia. In August 1900, Jenkins consented to inspect the property. Along with his three sons and a friend, Jenkins visited the Griscom estate and was impressed. The site of the prospective resort stood one thousand feet higher than Delaware Water Gap, twenty miles inland on the Pocono plateau, and—with the Cresco station of the Lackawanna Railroad nearby—had the advantage of being accessible. That autumn, a corporation was formed and stock sold.[38]

On Saturday, June 22, 1901, the still-unfinished Inn at Buck Hill Falls opened. Some of its staff members had to sleep on cots. The Inn exuded Quaker modesty: its twenty rooms had no private baths, and the hotel used kerosene lamps, not the electric lights that were becoming the standard in new resorts. Nonetheless, Quakers came to the resort. During the summer of 1903, the Inn was filled, despite bad weather. As was the case with some of the hunting and fishing clubs, guests had the option of buying lots and erecting cottages on the grounds. In less than two years, the Buck Hill estate contained seventeen cottages. The venture was profitable for its 89 stockholders, who enjoyed a 6 percent return on their capital.[39]

Meanwhile, Quakers were giving birth to a second resort. In 1902, the Pocono Manor Association and its 145 Quaker shareholders purchased 750 acres of Little Pocono Mountain, a site not ten miles from Buck Hill and close to the Mount Pocono station of the Lackawanna Railroad. Pocono Manor

FIG. 26
Theodore Roosevelt, the former president, spent the night at the Water Gap House on August 2, 1910. He was driving through the eastern United States. Monroe County Historical Association.

stood about 1,800 feet above tidewater. A publicity brochure noted the healthy location and the "refreshing coolness and dryness." Pocono Manor opened in August 1902, an immediate success that sparked expansion. In October 1908, a winter building opened, making Pocono Manor a year-round resort, one of the first in the Poconos. Like its Buck Hill rival, Pocono Manor sold lots for private cottages.[40]

Pocono Manor's opening on August 15, 1902—just a year after Buck Hill's—was not accidental. Pocono Manor was the work of a rival branch of the Philadelphia Quaker community, the Orthodox Friends, who belonged to the Arch Street Yearly Meeting. The Buck Hill Quakers were Hicksites, whose ancestors had followed the radical egalitarianism of Elias Hicks and had left the Orthodox fold. This schism, or "separation," occurred in 1827. Afterward, the Hicksite and Orthodox Friends ignored each other, but also competed—as much as pacifists could. They lived in different neighborhoods of metropolitan Philadelphia, sent their children to different private schools, and erected rival colleges. The Orthodox Friends educated their children at Haverford and Bryn Mawr Colleges. The Hicksites sent theirs to Swarthmore. This friendly rivalry explains why the Orthodox Friends erected a resort in Monroe County once the Hicksites did.[41]

As was the rule with outsiders who came to the Poconos, Quakers brought their worldview—a perspective manifested, for instance, by the roads at the Inn at Buck Hill Falls. Instead of being named after people, the roads had names such as Rock Oak Road, Rabbit Run, Laurel Lane, and Pines Road. The explanation for this emerges from deep within the Quaker psyche. It refers to the iconoclastic streak that made the early Quakers refuse to defer to their "betters"—the contrariness that explains, in part, why William Penn named the streets of Philadelphia after trees (Walnut Street, Spruce Street, and so on) instead of famous people. Whether the Buck Hill Quakers consciously knew of their cultural baggage when they laid out and named the roads is beside the point. People often act with little awareness of the tradition that guides them.[42]

By World War I, the Inn at Buck Hill Falls was surrounded by 125 cottages and was becoming a leading Pocono resort. Along the way, the lean simplicity of its origins was discarded in favor of electric lights, an elevator, and long-distance telephones. Steam heat allowed a winter trade. Recreational facilities kept pace with creature comforts: an outdoor pool, built in 1908, was placed under the supervision of an experienced instructor. Tennis courts were equipped with night lights and attracted famous athletes, such as the future tennis legend, Bill Tilden, who played at Buck Hill in 1913. In 1920, Tilden achieved tennis immortality by winning at Wimbledon. Far more important, though, was golf. A 259-acre farm was bought in 1907 and a nine-hole course quickly laid out. A golf pro was hired in 1909, and the course itself was extended to sixteen holes in 1916 and to twenty-seven holes by 1920. The course was so popular that in 1912, golfers had to wait ninety minutes for a tee time. It was said that more than anything else, the golf course kept the men from leaving their wives at Buck Hill and returning to their city jobs. In 1915, twenty-five Boy Scouts from Lansdale (a Philadelphia suburb) were imported as caddies.[43]

Buck Hill reflected the age-old Quaker dilemma. Quakers were expected to live simple lives, yet their frugal lifestyle and work ethic made them rich. Quakers had a constant problem of reconciling their principles with Mammon, the simple life with wealth. In the course of the nineteenth century, Philadel-phia's Quakers often resolved the dilemma by leaving the fold. They became respectable Episcopalians.[44]

At Buck Hill, Quakers followed the simple lifestyle, as they defined it. The 1912 promotional brochure warned that Buck Hill was an "early to bed settlement" and that "common sentiment" frowned upon a commotion after 10 P.M. It bragged that the Inn had withstood "the inroads of fash-ion." Only two cottages were built with plaster; the others had wood-lined walls. Card playing, danc-ing, alcohol, dogs, and professional entertainers were forbidden. For a long time, Buck Hill held out against automobiles, since they frightened the horses. Not until 1916 were cars allowed on the grounds—and only between the public road and individual cottages. Auto travel between cottages remained forbidden. Despite these gestures, the truth was that the Buck Hill Quakers had chosen Mammon, running the Inn as a business and selling lots to non-Quakers, who as early as 1907 owned 30 percent of the cottages. Moreover, Buck Hill's 1912 brochure warned that admittance was denied to consumptives and guests to whom "a reasonable moral, social, racial or physical objection" could be raised. In the following year, the guest newsletter lamented that women were dressing up for the afternoon teas and that the simplicity of 1902 was gone. Somehow, the idea that simple folk do not have afternoon teas in the first place did not occur to the newsletter editor.[45]

Quakers seeking the simple life avoided Buck Hill and Pocono Manor. They stayed at a third Quaker enterprise. Pocono Lake Preserve had its origins in 1904, when a band of Quakers asked the Pocono Mountain Ice Company for permission to camp near Pocono Lake. In 1908, along with new recruits, they bought 3,300 acres by the lake. For legal reasons, they organized as a hunting club, and by 1913 the eighty-five members had ninety-nine-year leases on lots. The Preserve had no hotel building, only modest houses called "camps." When a member brought in the first bathtub, his neigh-bors objected: "We don't think thee is the sort of person we want at Preserve." As late as the 1940s, some of the camps had outhouses in lieu of indoor plumbing. Pocono Lake Preserve was both a poor man's Buck Hill and a lifestyle choice. Isaac Sharpless, president of Haverford College and a promi-nent Quaker, summered there, although he could have afforded to vacation elsewhere.[46]

Leisure and Camping for Children

Children can ruin a vacation. They are cranky, they cry, and they fight. When parents want to enjoy themselves, they wish that they did not have to referee and lecture the kids. Although Victorians had made a virtue—in fact, a near religion—of domestic life, some of them eventually discovered the joys of being without the children. Conveniently for them, the growing interest in leisure and amusement ended up embracing children and relieved vacationing parents of their burden. After the turn of the century, high-priced resorts offered children's recreation that gave adults a respite from parenting. The Water Gap House had a children's room; Pocono Manor, a special playground and equipment. The Kittatinny offered a daily play hour that physical education professionals from the city supervised.

FIG. 27

Pocono Manor after the turn of the century. Note the absence of automobiles. Quakers frowned upon conspicuous consumption. Monroe County Historical Association.

Buck Hill affirmed its love of the outdoors with a nature club that had children hiking in the woods and working on projects.[47]

In the late nineteenth century, children's camps were born. They reflected the late Victorians' interest in the outdoors: unlike their ancestors, those living at the turn of the century had lost their fear of nature. They no longer saw it as the wilderness, a place of dread where hunters would be lost, attacked by animals, or beset by the vagaries of the weather. By the twentieth century, the wilderness had been tamed and understood. And once it no longer terrified, it became nature—appealing, even suggesting maternal connotations. Not coincidentally, this was the era of the silly Tarzan novels, whose hero is a superior person because he lives outdoors and knows nature. In a more serious vein, the first decade of the twentieth century saw the emergence of the Boy Scout movement and its glorification of nature. Children's camps were a logical outgrowth of the back-to-nature movement.[48]

Although New England was the home of most early children's camps, some did open in the Poconos. Oneka was the first girls' camp south of New York. Ernest Siple and his wife opened it in

FIG. 28
Playing croquet at the Inn at Buck
Hill Falls. Buck Hill Collection, Bar-
rett Friendly Library.

1907. Dan Beard, a founder of the Boy Scouts in America, ran a Pocono camp that was very exclusive. Two of Theodore Roosevelt's sons stayed there. By World War I, the Pocono press often mentioned local camps. The Pine Tree Camp for girls was established in 1914 by a Philadelphia school
principal. Forty girls from this camp once hiked from Cresco to East Stroudsburg, staying overnight
at the Normal School (the future East Stroudsburg University).[49]

Rabbi David Davidson ran a unique boys' camp that met the recreational needs of both parents and children. The parents of many of its boys stayed at the nearby Forest Park resort, where they enjoyed the best of both worlds—vacationing without the children, yet having them nearby. As part of Forest Park's Fourth of July celebration in 1900, the boys entertained at dinner. Aside from learning how to play and sing, the boys also studied at a summer school attached to the camp.[50] All this seemed innocent enough, yet Rabbi Davidson was a subversive. By allowing parents to get rid of the children in order to vacation with other adults, he supported the rejection of Victorian domesticity. Of all the indications of relaxed standards, whether they were play clothes, golf, or other amusements, summer camps may have best symbolized the new world of the twentieth century, in which the highest goal of living was pleasure.

City Meets Country

Hot days, sweat, and a wistful desire for cool breezes are traditional signs of summer in the cities of the Northeast. In the Poconos, another sure mark of the season was the arrival of vacationers who crowded the roads, shops, and churches. Many natives of the Poconos were peeved. They tried to ignore the city folk as much as possible, treating them to the same indifference that they reserved for hoboes and other migrating creatures. Others were hostile, feeling that city people were odd and snooty—good only for their money and little else.

The Pocono press was less narrow in its view of the relationship between city and country. Speaking for the resort industry, as it always did, it hailed city vacationers, knowing well the positive effects they had on the local economy. But the press rarely saw the big picture. City people had an effect on the Poconos that went far beyond money. Vacationers were emissaries of sorts, the means by which urban customs—even urban plans for changing the countryside—arrived in the Poconos.

City "Strangers"

The vacation impact must be placed in context. During the nineteenth century, country people lived far from the centers of civilization and were isolated. They did not have radio to feed their imaginations nor television and cinema to provide images of distant peoples and places. Unless country people traveled, they had to rely on the printed word to satisfy their curiosity. Pocono newspapers tried to meet this need. They were full of stories of strange people who lived in strange corners of the nation and the world. They had a special fondness for features that portrayed nearby New York City as exotic, full of colorful criminals and bizarre businessmen—people who might, for instance, stage a duel between sewer rats and a bull terrier.[1]

City vacationers gave country folk the chance to see the outside world in the flesh. The *Jeffersonian* once noted "the beauty of the lady equestrians" at the Kittatinny Hotel, adding that a horsewoman "attracted a large share of attention" when she rode into Stroudsburg. Pocono residents witnessed big-city sophistication firsthand. They were affected in ways known only to their private selves, even though they did not speak to the frosty horsewomen.[2]

At times, resort guests and the local population did mix—far more, in fact, than they would today. The nineteenth century was a world without automobiles, which forced vacationers to stay near their resorts and sometimes meet their neighbors. Information is sparse, for the press was usually silent on this subject, but there are hints. An occasional contact ground was baseball, the new game that was sweeping the nation. Resort guests formed baseball teams and played against local teams. In 1874, guests at the Water Gap House challenged Stroudsburg's baseball team and won. The rematch drew a large crowd, including many young ladies. This time, the hotel team lost.[3]

Although city and country folks sometimes became friends, often attending the same parties and outings, resort guests and locals usually did not mix. Instead of the links between town and country, the Pocono press of the 1870s preferred to see the distances. It bluntly called the city folk "strangers." Even those vacationers who spent the entire summer at the resorts were not members of the tribe, but considered transient, like migrating birds that would stop, feed, and never be seen again.

In reporting on vacationers and local residents, the *Jeffersonian* used different yardsticks. The newspaper was not above lecturing natives on civic behavior, once displaying great shock when several girls in Stroudsburg smoked cigarettes in public. It was even more scandalized when "a young miss of this borough" walked down a street smoking a pipe. The *Jeffersonian* promised that if the young lady smoked in public again, an exposé would make her "hang her head in shame." By contrast, it did not criticize vacationers. When it referred to "the pranks of the exuberant city visitors," it did so in good humor. "Let them gush," it wrote. Since resorts enriched the local economy, tolerating the summer crowd was good business. The *Jeffersonian* preferred to believe that the local folk would not be contaminated.[4]

A Helping Hand

Compared to their descendants, Americans of the mid-nineteenth century were religious. The first vacationers occasionally contributed to local churches, a benevolent act that was also a form of missionary work; prior to the Civil War, settlers arrived in the Poconos before organized religion did. It was not unknown for a Pocono couple to begin housekeeping and wait for a preacher to visit the backcountry to legalize matters. The rural folk needed to be uplifted and churchgoing encouraged. Guests at the Locust Grove resort in East Stroudsburg once collected money for the local African Methodist Church. In most cases, however, hotel guests donated to white churches. Some of the Kittatinny guests went further. Feeling deeply about Delaware Water Gap's spiritual needs, they built the "Church of the Mountain" in 1854, deeded it to the Presbyterians, and continued to support it afterward.[5]

Urban largess could also be secular. While on vacation, Joseph Jefferson, the actor who played Rip Van Winkle, introduced new potato seeds to local farmers. After the turn of the century, when the Milford dramatic society staged a benefit for the Milford Lyceum, vacationers dominated the audience. Likewise, vacationers donated books in response to the Lyceum's appeal on behalf of the local library.[6]

Books, however, only helped the literate. A systemic improvement in the lives of rural folk required far more effort. The wife of Charles C. Worthington conceived of a project to combat rural unemployment. She had the women of Shawnee-on-Delaware make baskets for sale in the cities. She was inspired by the English Arts and Crafts movement that came to the United States in the 1890s. The movement was a revolt against machine-made goods, which were perceived as dehumanizing, as opposed to handmade goods, seen as both natural and uplifting. As many as thirty women worked for Mrs. Worthington. They made forty varieties of baskets, which included waste paper baskets and hanging baskets as well as sewing, yarn, and sandwich baskets. The venture began in 1909 and ended in 1915, when World War I made raw materials scarce. Besides, the Arts and Crafts movement was dying, bedeviled by the expense of its goods and by the machinery that easily copied them. Mrs. Worthington's good intentions went for naught.[7]

The Buck Hill Quakers also believed that their neighbors needed uplifting. Mrs. Charles Thompson, the manager's wife, was the prime mover in opening the Barrett Friendly Library, which served Barrett Township. Buck Hill vacationers donated money for books and for a permanent building. In 1910, the need for library money led to the first Barrett Township Fair. Proceeds of future fairs were used for library maintenance and, during World War I, were donated to the Red Cross and the American Friends Service Committee. Charity aside, the city folk did seem to enjoy themselves. They became involved not only in organizing the fairs, but also in the entertainment, especially the minstrel shows.[8]

The Barrett Fair aimed to improve relations between the Buck Hill vacation colony and local farmers, who needed reassurance that they would not be pushed off their land. The Fair allowed farmers to exhibit and sell handmade goods, fruits, vegetables, poultry, and livestock. Another Buck Hill goal was to raise local incomes by allowing farmers to sell to resorts and by disseminating scientific farming information. Charles Jenkins, the son of the Buck Hill founder, was the editor of an agricultural journal and superbly qualified for this task. He introduced Ayrshire cattle to local farmers.[9]

How the recipients of this urban concern felt is a mystery. Newspapers only printed stories of the giving, not the taking. The need for the Pocono press to remind its readers of the importance of the vacation economy does suggest a certain popular indifference. There are indications that the people of the Poconos had a quiet resentment against city folks, who offended by being alien and better off. A prominent Buck Hill Quaker later recalled the community's mistrust, which he blamed on resentment of Buck Hill's wealth and social standing.[10] If the Buck Hill experience is typical, the relationship (where it existed) between giving vacationers and taking natives may have been that of unrequited love.

FIG. 29
The original Barrett Friendly Library, donated by the Buck Hill vacationers to the local community. Note the logs that were part of the wall. The city Quakers knew little of country living, and they did not treat the wood—providing a feast for the insects. Eventually a new library had to be built. Buck Hill Collection, Barrett Friendly Library.

Resorts and the Economy

Although the resort industry created jobs, no one knows how many. Good statistics do not exist, not even in the census returns. The census was taken in the spring and did not count city workers who had not yet arrived for resort work. Nor did it include local teenagers who would regard resort work as a temporary pastime before they moved on to greater things. Farmers' wives and daughters may also have been undercounted, since they may have seen resort work as marginal to their household duties. Likewise, the census may have omitted men who worked in resorts but regarded their winter jobs as more important. In sum, the census listed only those Pocono residents who saw resort work as their vocation.[11]

FIG. 30
Barrett Township Fair, August 1914. This Buck Hill vacationer in Scottish dress was participating in a minstrel show. Buck Hill Collection, Barrett Friendly Library.

The press rarely noticed resort workers. Many came from the cities, to which they returned in the fall. Whether they were natives or city imports, resort workers appeared in the newspapers only when they were victims of tragedy or accused of crime. An exception to the press's near silence occurred when the Spruce Cabin Inn burned in 1920 and closed. According to the *East Stroudsburg Press,* the village of Canadensis suffered a "death blow." "Employed were 27 waitresses, 2 head waiters, 2 pastry cooks, one chef, 2 bellhops, and several chambermaids, largely recruited from the neighborhood."[12] If these statistics were typical for the industry, most resort workers were women who were supplementing the family's income.

The economic impact of the resort industry was far-ranging. Aside from their obvious contribution—the money that vacationers paid for lodgings, meals, souvenirs, liveries, and, after the turn of the century, for rented cars—resorts affected the regional economy indirectly as well. Local farmers sold produce to the resorts, which in turn could boast of serving farm-fresh vegetables. Craftsmen and construction workers erected resort buildings. Electricians and plumbers modernized them. In addition, the very presence of resorts gave a glamour to the Poconos that attracted vacation homes and day camps. Realtors were needed to buy, sell, or lease land; lawyers, to write contracts; banks, to handle the money. Not surprisingly, the small twin towns of Stroudsburg and East Stroudsburg had five banks by 1914.[13]

Barrett Township contained the resort villages of Cresco, Mountainhome, and Canadensis, which revealed in microcosm the dramatic effect of the vacation industry. In the 1900 census, under the heading of "occupation," only three of Barrett's residents listed "resort keeper." In the 1910 census, fourteen did so. The key reason for the increase was the new Quaker colony at Buck Hill, which made Barrett Township very fashionable. The 1900 and 1910 censuses also reported an increase in carpenters—from five to thirty-three. These were the men who erected the Buck Hill cottages as well as forty other wooden houses. In addition, old houses were refurbished and an electrical power plant was installed. Barrett Township was changing. Compared to ten years earlier, the 1910 census reported fewer farmers and farm laborers, but an increase in merchants, tradesmen, and craftsmen. By 1914, Barrett Township had the standard accessories of a resort community: a photographer, souvenir stands, and soda fountains. A local newspaper proudly noted them as well as the new public school and Methodist church.[14]

Saving the Forest

In the Poconos—or, for that matter, almost anywhere in Pennsylvania—country folk saw forest fires as self-correcting phenomena that would burn until they died of their own accord. In the meantime, people hoped for the best. Quakers were not so resigned. Their urban love of nature gave them a deep concern for forest fires. In 1902, resort Quakers and hotelmen representing 80,000 acres of Pocono land met at the Stroudsburg law office of A. Mitchell Palmer (who himself was a Quaker), and they created the Pocono Protective Fire Association, or PPFA. The PPFA assessed its members one cent per acre to have eight fire wardens patrol the forest and to pay fifty-dollar rewards if arsonists were arrested and convicted. The PPFA was the first private association of its kind in the United States.[15]

The Pocono Protective Fire Association had to deal with both nature and man. Forest fires periodically waxed and waned, according to the weather. In 1908, a bad year for fires, over 11,000 acres in Monroe and Pike Counties were lost. According to the *Monroe Democrat*, volunteer firemen barely stopped flames from destroying the Tilennius elk park—a rare admission from the press that forest fires could affect the vacation industry. Fires were not always acts of God, either. Huckleberry pickers often lit fires to provide a fresh growth of berry trees. At times, the pickers were Slavic coal miners who hoped to earn extra money during the summer slow season. The miners brought their families, lived in tents, and enjoyed the poor man's vacation. Fires were also lit by the needy farmers of the scrub oak barrens, where trees grew no higher than a tall person. The farmers wanted to clear the underbrush to create fresh pasturage for their cattle. Unfortunately, a "controlled burn" can be an oxymoron, and at times, the huckleberry pickers and the poor farmers could not control what they had started.[16]

As a rule, residents of the Poconos had little aesthetic interest in trees. The rural poor regarded trees as the raw material of railroad ties and hoop poles, which they could exchange for flour and tobacco. They could not see any other purpose for trees. The experiences of Rev. Charles Van Allen, a resort keeper in Echo Lake (near Bushkill), are revealing. In the 1870s, when he planted trees along the side of a road, his neighbors resented his "folly," fearing that the trees would shade the road and keep it muddy and damp. A few of his neighbors went beyond disapproval and tried to destroy his trees.[17]

Fire prevention soon became subordinate to the larger issue of conservation. During the nineteenth century, Pennsylvania had been a leading lumber state. When lumberjacks had clear-cut the forests, they had caused erosion and the depletion of the water table, which, in turn, led to many fires. The Poconos were no exception. In 1902, the *Stroudsburg Times* pointed out that the Pocono plateau had been stripped nearly bare of trees, adding that during a rail ride from Paradise Valley in Monroe County to Elmhurst (near Scranton), a distance of over thirty miles, only blackened stumps could be seen. By the twentieth century, the virgin forest was long gone. The forest of today is a second (and in some places, a third) growth.[18]

The rebirth of Pennsylvania's forests was due to urban pressures. In 1886, the Pennsylvania Forestry Association was launched in Philadelphia, and it issued a periodical, *Forest Leaves*, that warned about disappearing woodlands. The Association's first president was Joseph Rothrock of Mifflin County, a physician and botanist who lobbied intensely for the creation of a State Forestry Commission. When the State Department of Agriculture opened in 1895, Rothrock was the logical person to serve as Forestry Commissioner.[19]

Rothrock believed that Pennsylvania should protect forest land by buying it. In 1897, the state government authorized the purchase of unseated (abandoned) lands. This marked the beginning of the Pennsylvania State Forest Reservation system. The following year, the first purchase of lands on which taxes were in arrears took place—some 39,277 acres in five counties, of which 7,407 acres were in Pike County and 1,244 in Monroe County. Right from the start, much of the history of conservation in Pennsylvania would occur in the Poconos.[20]

The creation of the State Forest Reservation had wide support. Conservationists were excited, but so were landowners and lumber companies, who had no further use for their land after cutting the trees. The state thus created a true rarity: a government program that nearly everyone liked. The exception to this near-universal applause came from Pike County, where residents of the backwoods saw that they would lose the free land that they had used for game and firewood. Rothrock was aware of the hostility. He tried to convince the rural folk that in return, they would gain jobs in the forest service. He also made it clear that he would enforce poaching laws.[21]

According to official statistics, by January 1, 1910, the Commonwealth of Pennsylvania had purchased 916,440 acres of woodlands, including 6,246 acres in Monroe County and 53,249 in Pike

State Highway and Echo Lake House, near Bushkill, Pa.   13628   1931

FIG. 31

Echo Lake House and trees. Could these have been the trees that Rev. Charles Van Allen planted in the nineteenth century, precipitating a mini-crisis with his tree-hating neighbors? Not only did he offend by planting trees (whose shade would keep the road muddy), but Van Allen was also a prominent advocate of temperance. An obituary in 1919 focused on this latter trait, not his love of nature. Monroe County Historical Association.

County. The land was bought in order to restore trees. The first step took place in Pike County, where 1,000 Carolina poplar seedlings were planted in the fall of 1899. Due to poor soil, fire, and competition from scrub oak, the trees died. In 1908, the state resumed the reforestation of the Poconos, and within eight years, over 240,000 trees had been planted in Pike and Monroe Counties. Along the way, the state enlisted the aid of the public. In 1909, Public Law 115 authorized the Commonwealth to distribute surplus seedlings. In 1912, J. Sequine of the Pocono Protective Fire Association requested 2,200 seedlings. Soon the PPFA was distributing seedlings to Monroe County schools. Meanwhile, the Quaker resorts joined the crusade. Pocono Manor was responsible for planting 10,000 trees in 1915. Not to be outdone, the people at Buck Hill planted 60,000 trees in 1918, helping to make Monroe County second in Pennsylvania in terms of trees planted that year.[22]

In the long run, the state forests served the public by providing recreation. One of the first state properties used for this purpose was Promised Land State Forest. Its peculiar name dates back to the original settlers, the Shaker religious sect of the nineteenth century, who had been "promised" good land in Pike County. When the Shakers saw that the land was an isolated wilderness, they left. Eventually, lumberjacks came, and by the time the state bought the land, much of it was burnt and barren. In 1905, the Promised Land State Forest was opened for camping. A decade later, 466 campers stayed overnight and 276 campers held three-week permits. In addition, Boy Scout parties, Sunday school picnickers, and high school botany classes were using the site. According to a "fish story" in an official report, fishing in the 232-acre lake was so good that everyone caught at least a few.[23]

FIG. 32
Grey Towers, the Milford home of Gifford Pinchot, pioneer conservationist. It is ironic that Pinchot hailed from an area that did not appreciate his protective view of nature. Built in 1886, Grey Towers is maintained by the Forest Service of the U.S. Department of Agriculture.

Hunting and Fishing

Aside from recreation, the state forest system allowed common people, both from the cities and the Poconos, a chance to hunt and fish. They needed this public land. By the 1890s, rich people had bought much of the Poconos, causing the local press to sound the alarm. The *Stroudsburg Times* rhetorically asked where "the formerly free people of Pike" would fish and hunt. When Jacob Otten-heimer purchased the huge tract for the future Forest Park resort, the *Stroudsburg Times* noted that city people already owned six hunting and fishing preserves in Pike County. In 1898, the *Milford Dispatch* reported that sporting associations owned or controlled most lakes in Pike County. Monroe County was suffering a similar fate. The *Stroudsburg Times* feared that many of its popular waters were being set aside for the "pleasure of the few."[24]

Two residents of the Poconos struck back. In 1899, a fish warden arrested two members of the Pohoqualine Club and fined them one hundred dollars. The alleged offense was using a hand net in fishing. The warden misinterpreted the law against fishing nets in order to harass the fishermen. Meanwhile, the Blooming Grove Park Association and its neighbors were still at odds. In 1891, a poacher on Blooming Grove property was arrested and fined. He refused to pay, and he was jailed.[25]

As it turned out, the Blooming Grove Park Association members overplayed their hand. They would not obey the Lacey Law, the federal legislation that forbade the transport of dead game birds across state lines. In October 1901, the Blooming Grove president and six others were carrying one hundred dead pheasants in unmarked satchels when they were caught at a train station in Pike County by State Game Commissioner Jacob Kalbfus. Tried in a local court, they were surprisingly acquitted. The judge ruled that they had not yet crossed the state line when arrested. A Pocono newspaper angrily claimed that the defendants had entertained the judge before the trial. Kalbfus kept on punching. Late the following year, he accused fifty club members of violating game laws. He laid down the rules. Out-of-state hunters had to eat their catch in Pennsylvania, since federal law did not allow them to cross state lines with dead birds.[26]

In October 1903, the high-flying Blooming Grove Park Association had its wings clipped when the Pennsylvania Supreme Court found its charter unconstitutional. The Association lost the sovereign power to enforce game laws on its property, and it decided to dissolve. Its members reorganized as the Blooming Grove Hunting and Fishing Club, a new entity that avoided controversy. Although problems still existed, they were caused not by people, but by nature. Game birds that the Club bred had the nerve to leave the grounds, and they were shot by local hunters. One Mongolian pheasant crossed two rivers before being caught in Poughkeepsie, New York. In addition, snakes (a perennial nuisance in Pike County) threatened the game birds. In 1912, wildcats emerged as a menace. The Club declared war and killed twenty-eight cats in thirty days, to the great joy of cat haters.[27]

The anti-feline crusade typified the thinking of many urban hunters who wanted fish and game to be tightly managed. They claimed that quail and pheasants were scarce because of foxes, wildcats, and other "noxious" animals. In 1904, they demanded a bounty law. In 1905, a bill in the Pennsylvania legislature proposed bounties on alleged pests such as hawks, owls, foxes, and skunks. The *Milford Dispatch* was furious. It noted that so-called noxious animals destroyed rodents, the bane of farmers—and that farmers would suffer losses if game birds were protected for city people.[28]

City and country also clashed over bears, although their roles were reversed in this case: city folks wanted to protect the cuddly beasties. Farmers hated bears, and they had allies. According to the Pocono press, bears were a dangerous nuisance. They frightened children on their way to school, invaded barns and houses, and killed livestock. In one bad year, bears killed fifty-seven sheep on a single Pocono farm. Bear stories in the press rivaled the best tall tales of fishermen. One man insisted that bears were "too dinged smart." He claimed that he had seen a bear put fence rails in the middle of the road in order to stop an automobile. The bear then revealed herself, frightening the driver and the passengers, who fled, leaving their picnic basket behind. When the bear finished her feast, she left. The frightened picnickers returned and drove immediately to the state line. Regardless of whether this story was true, there was no doubt that residents of the Poconos considered bears to be pests and city people to be fools for liking them.[29]

Fantasies about bears were not limited to country people. When two Philadelphia brewers, Christian Hess and George Weissbrod, helped create the 5,000-acre Porter Lake Club, their original notion was to stock the grounds with European wild boars and hunt them from horseback—European style. This grandiose scheme allegedly ended when a lightning bolt killed five of the breeding boars. If there were no boars to kill, bears would do. In 1905, a Philadelphia newspaper printed a fantastic tale. Weissbrod and Hess were deer hunting when bears surrounded them. By the time the "battle" ended, they had killed twenty-six bears. Weissbrod claimed that he killed a 600-pounder with his bowie knife. A local newspaper quoted an old woodsman in response: "What infernal liars these city fellows be."[30]

The exclusive hunting and fishing clubs of rich city people set an example for moneyed local r esidents, who opened their own clubs after the turn of the century. Compared with the Blooming Grove Club, or even the Porter Lake and Forest Lake Clubs, the local clubs were small and more likely to specialize in fishing than hunting. The Pocahontas Rod and Gun Association in Lehman Township had only 450 acres, a limit of fifty members, and a long waiting list. The Manzanedo Rod and Gun Club in Price Township was smaller, owning a mere 100 acres and a lake. It was organized in the office of Cicero Gearhart, a Stroudsburg attorney. The president of the Maskenozha Club was E. L. Kemp, the principal of the East Stroudsburg Normal School. The local clubs had gobbled up the remains left by the rich city clubs. If it were not for the state forests, the common people would have had nothing.[31]

Pollution, Eyesores, and the Resorts

In the 1890s, the realization had not yet taken hold that the Pocono economy was best suited for recreation. Since the dying tanning and wood industries needed to be replaced, Monroe County hoped that the presence of the railroad and of nearby cities would attract new industry. A Board of Trade was launched in 1888. The opening of the International Boiler Works, with 125 employees, was a major achievement. Nonetheless, the Poconos could not escape their destiny. Industries based in the Poconos tended to exploit the local environment—as evidenced in the cases of the furniture firm that used the remaining lumber trees, the short-lived glass companies that fed on local deposits of sand, and the transitory brick firms that took advantage of nearby clay deposits.[32]

Civic boosters could not see that industry and resorts were incompatible. Factory smoke contaminated the clear air that city people sought in the country. Factory emissions in creeks around Stroudsburg reduced the trout population. A nasty accident at the Stroudsburg brewery once caused fifty to one hundred pounds of ammonia to pour into Brodhead Creek, killing thousands of fish. Nonetheless,

78D:-CAN'T BEAR TO LEAVE THE DELAWARE WATER GAP, PA.

FIG. 33

Bears on display. Rural folk who once regarded bears as pests had to readjust their thinking. By the 1930s, bears were featured at Arthur Cox's road stand near Delaware Water Gap. Motorists stopped to watch the caged bears drink bottled milk chocolate, which Cox sold for ten cents a bottle. One bear drank so much milk chocolate that he was noted in Robert Ripley's "Believe It Or Not." Cox claimed that the bears kept him going during the Depression. Monroe County Historical Association.

in a supreme act of denial, the press gave the impression that overfishing was a greater problem for the local streams than industrial pollution.[33]

Industrialists were not alone in being callous toward the vacation industry. Residents of the Poconos cared little if their low standard of cleanliness gave city vacationers a bad impression. As far back as the early 1870s, the *Jeffersonian* decried odors and garbage in the alleys of Stroudsburg. In 1890, the *Stroudsburg Daily Times* hailed the monetary value of neatness, noting that pretty houses and farms attracted city people. Nevertheless, progress seems to have been slow. It was not until 1895 that the Stroudsburg borough council forbade throwing rubbish into streets. A year later, the *Daily Times* warned that decaying animals in back streets endangered public health. Referring to the miasma theory, it warned that the stink would cause disease.[34]

Milford was not any better. During 1903–4, the *Milford Dispatch* kept on insisting that the town was ugly. Rubbish was everywhere; weeds covered yards and lawns; old dilapidated sheds and outbuildings had become "eyesores." Worst of all, parts of Milford were impassable, because buildings, yards, and bushes were intruding on sidewalks. The borough council must act, insisted the newspaper, or else it would be pointless for the resorts to advertise the "beauties" of Milford. On another occasion, the *Milford Dispatch* pointed out that heavy rainfall had washed out the Catherine Street approach to the Delaware River, causing summer visitors to complain.[35]

This nagging had some effect. With an eye toward the sensitivities of city folk, the Milford borough council banned the keeping of pigs. Milford's one hundred swine had an estimated worth of five hundred dollars, far less than what vacationers spent on a good day. In 1909, the borough council appropriated one hundred dollars to oil streets. The Village Improvement Society contributed another one hundred dollars and took charge of civic betterment.[36]

Although the Village Improvement Society did good work, it was a private organization; its very existence testified to popular indifference. It relied on contributions from resort proprietors and vacationers. Area voters would not tax themselves to beautify Milford. Indifference was also the rule elsewhere. Resort owners in Delaware Water Gap, for example, had to dig into their pockets to oil streets and repair mountain paths. In Barrett Township, the wives of leading resortmen set up the Civic Club, which studied public health, tried to prevent speeding, and erected public signs and streetlights.[37]

Nonetheless, popular indifference could not be blamed for the biggest eyesore, the stone crusher that the Lackawanna Railroad placed on the side of Mount Minsi in Delaware Water Gap. The crusher scarred the mountain and ruined the scenery. Although concerned for the vacation business, the Lackawanna Railroad obviously believed in the greater importance of the crusher, since it provided stone for track beds. The railroad refused to remove the crusher despite the pleas of the Gap's borough council. Resort interests and nature lovers were furious, writing nasty editorials and scheming to have the area declared a state park in order to remove the crusher. Finally, the borough council did the American thing. It went to court and obtained an injunction. In 1907, the Lackawanna agreed to remove the crusher and to plant shrubbery in the scarred areas.[38]

The Mystique of the Common Folk

The ugly, filthy eyesores confirmed that two societies coexisted in the Poconos: the genteel world of vacationers and the crude world of the lower classes that respectable folk, both local and urban, wanted to ignore. At times, however, this crude world could not be ignored. In 1894, a lynching took place—the only one in Monroe County's history—when a black railway worker accused of murdering a local citizen was hanged. After the hanging, many spectators carried away bits of the tree and bought pieces of the rope. This gruesome lust for souvenirs hinted that the real Monroe County differed from the genteel world of the vacationer, although the vacation industry preferred to project an image of gaiety in which the crudeness of the lower classes did not exist.[39]

For the people at the bottom of society, life was hard and, by the standards of the twenty-first century, a little primitive. Old women smoked so much that their teeth were as black as stoves. Beer drinking at the 1902 Stroudsburg Fair led to "a free-for-all" fight. In the following year, at the hanging of a murderer, over three hundred spectators squeezed into the Stroudsburg county jail, while fifteen hundred waited outside. After the execution, the crowd was admitted inside to file past the corpse, and many women became hysterical when they saw the dead man's face. By contrast, another woman remained cool when a policeman served her a warrant. Not only did she assault the cop, but she also bragged that she was the only woman in Monroe County who had the reputation of "doing up an officer." Compared to Monroe County, Pike County was less populated and even more wild. Its colorful residents received much attention from the Pocono press. People in the Pike County backwoods ignored hunting and fishing laws, hunted on the Sabbath, and refused to pay debts. Vacationers were scandalized at the sight of young men and women bathing nude in the Delaware River.[40]

The great social event of the 1890s in Pike County may have been an execution. It was said that cash-poor authorities in Pike County ignored murders to avoid prosecution costs. The murderer Herman Paul Schultz was the exception, perhaps because he was a New Yorker. He had come from the city to kill his wife, who had left him. He was hanged in the Milford jail on December 7, 1897, with a gallows borrowed from New Jersey. In the history of Pike County, Schultz was the first person (and the last) to be executed. His fate drew the curious from the backcountry who packed the local hotels.[41]

Bizarre behavior in Pike County did not necessarily harm the vacation business. A case could be made, in fact, that it was an asset. It created the distinctiveness that every vacation region needed, reinforcing the quaint image of Pike County that had been sold to the urban press, beginning in 1879 with Edward Mott. A Milford journalist and publicist for the Erie Railroad, Mott wrote dialect stories of Pike County life that first appeared in the *New York Sunday Sun.* A book eventually followed. Mott created vivid portraits of Pike County originals: the Old Settler, the Sheriff, and the Judge lived in an almost foreign preindustrial world that city people with rural roots may have found familiar. Mott was packaging Pike County as nostalgia. Whereas Luke Brodhead wrote of the very refined, Mott used a formula that was not uncommon in the promotion of rural vacation areas. He painted a picture of a backward countryside that stood in sharp contrast to the modernity of the cities.[42]

By the 1890s, city reporters were echoing Mott. They were spinning their own fantasies about Pike County and its primeval backwoods. According to the *Philadelphia Times,* Porter Township was a hunter's paradise of forty-five thousand acres, where deer and bears were abundant and pheasants too numerous to count. Even the people were amazing, insisted the reporter. Because of the bracing air, they seemed to live forever in their rough, unspoiled Eden. Another Philadelphia reporter wrote about the Pike County woman who saw a bear lurking in the back of her cabin and ran to a hunting lodge for a gun. Meanwhile, the bear escaped. Returning disappointed, she threw a dead rattlesnake on the ground. "You can have the skin," she said to the reporter, who wrote: "That is a Pike County woman!"[43]

Still, the *Stroudsburg Times* was somewhat skeptical, and once hinted that neighboring Pike County deliberately created tall tales for urban consumption. There was the story of the bear with a taste for beef that allegedly prowled the area for heifers. More believable was the tale of a wounded buck that turned on two Philadelphia hunters and nearly killed them. A Methodist church official in Paterson, New Jersey, once said that Pike County was in need of missionary work as much as "the heart of Africa." He claimed that Pike's people "lived and died without having any religious instruction."[44]

No one denied that Pike County was infested with rattlesnakes. According to one estimate, Pike County averaged 150 rattlesnakes per acre. The reptiles were so numerous that they gave rise to a unique lore. Elsewhere, people told fish stories, but in Pike County they bragged of huge serpents they had allegedly killed or they told fantastic snake stories. In 1897, the *Milford Dispatch* printed one such story: the tale of the mouse who had killed a rattlesnake. A guest at the Hotel Fauchere was keeping the snake in a box for study. A mouse was placed in the box as food, but the mouse eluded the rattler, "to the great amusement of the guests at the hotel." The next morning, the snake was found dead. It was surmised that the mouse had bitten and broken the snake's head. Another newspaper story carried the headline "Big Snake Yarn." A quarry worker insisted that rock blasting threw snakes into the air, causing him to dodge falling snakes. Especially frightening was the big critter that fell on his head. More seriously, a Jersey City man accepted a wager to put his hand in a barrel full of snakes. He ended up in the hospital.[45]

Some backwoodsmen were quite comfortable with snakes. One of the first snake handlers to achieve notoriety was Lije Pelton. When he went off to fight in the Civil War, he took along a box of serpents—probably his way of avoiding homesickness. His protégé was Jack McConnell, who toured the big cities with his snake act. City folk paid good money to see McConnell stroke and fondle his snakes. Although bitten seven times, McConnell survived, and he retired in Pike County, still an avid snake man.[46]

How did backwoodsmen fit into the vacation world? The answer is complex. The backwoodsmen were mostly invisible, but not irrelevant. In the horse-and-buggy age, it is unlikely that many city vacationers ventured far from the resorts along the Delaware River. Only hunters went inland and saw the exotic Pike County depicted in the press. Nevertheless, the backwoodsmen, by their very existence, created the mystique that sold Pike County. They did not necessarily have to be spoken to

FIG. 34
Stroudsburg fairgrounds. Before the widespread use of the automobile, a county fair gave people an excuse (then rare) to travel and congregate. The Stroudsburg Fair was noted for its tippling revelers; in 1902, a drunken brawl spoiled the fun. Since the 1920s, Stroudsburg High School has stood on the site of the old fairgrounds. Monroe County Historical Association.

or even seen in order to be appreciated. As we know from today's international travel, tourists are content to gaze from afar at exotic people. No deeper contact is necessary to enjoy a vacation.[47]

Prohibition and the Resorts

Respectable people in the Poconos felt that they had an explanation for the cursing and uncouthness of the lower orders. That explanation was alcohol. The solution was prohibition, the crusade against

FIG. 35
Lice Clarke and friend. A book in the Pike County Historical Society offers a note on this photograph: "Snake charmer, Lice Clarke, who worked in the blacksmith shop, entertained villagers by his handling of rattlers. He was also a prankster. One day when John Snyder was a boy, he drove his father's mule team and wagon to the village. Lice Clarke sneaked a rattler beside him. John has never forgotten the frightful experience. It was July 4th, 1905." Pike County Historical Society.

"demon rum" that was intensifying around the nation. In the Poconos, the genteel ladies of the Women's Christian Temperance Union, or W.C.T.U., were very active. Like prohibitionists everywhere, they had a double goal: first, they would outlaw alcohol in their communities, and then they would fight for a national ban.

Prohibition threatened the Pocono vacation industry. Although most resorts were too small to have a bar, the larger ones usually served alcohol. A local prohibition would have reduced the Poconos to a country version of Ocean Grove in New Jersey or Rehoboth Beach in Delaware, both Methodist beach communities that specialized in ultra-clean fun, in which spittoons were not seen nor "damns" heard.[48] Whether an alcohol-free Poconos could have competed against these well-entrenched, semireligious resorts is open to question. The Pocono advocates of prohibition saw matters differently. They were Methodists and Presbyterians on a mission from God. Their scale of values ranked the economic effects of a localized prohibition far below the social wreckage of alcohol—drunken men who cursed, smoked, and in general acted badly, losing their jobs and beating their wives and children. Prohibition was identified with family values.[49]

Beginning in 1909, the dry forces in the Poconos followed the strategy of the statewide dry movement: they waged remonstrance or no-license campaigns. They tried to pressure judges of the quarter sessions court, who had the sole authority to grant retail liquor licenses, to revoke existing liquor licenses, and to refuse new ones. The judges were locally elected and were caught between the dry forces and the wet forces. Their solution was a compromise of sorts that probably displeased both camps. Judges offended prohibitionists by renewing existing liquor licenses. In other words, they did not close bars without good cause. Yet a concession was made to the dry lobby as well. Judges promised to be tough when liquor laws were violated. In 1911, Judge C. B. Staples warned hotel keepers about serving liquor to minors and to the inebriated. The judge was serious. In March, after many witnesses testified that the Maple Grove House in Bushkill allowed Sunday sales, underage drinking, and gambling, he revoked its license, although it had a large summer clientele.[50]

In the decade prior to World War I, judges gave the dry forces a second concession. They refused to approve new liquor licenses. As could be expected, the W.C.T.U. and local clergymen opposed new wet resorts in the Poconos, but opposition also came from owners of dry resorts. In 1911, when the Buckwood Inn applied for a license, I. R. Transue and H. A. Croasdale, who both came from old families and ran dry resorts, testified on behalf of the W.C.T.U. Although the Buckwood's owner was Charles C. Worthington, who was well known in the Poconos and an international businessman, the court was not impressed. John Purdy Cope of the Water Gap House also applied for a license. But Luke Brodhead, the former owner of the Water Gap House, had been a teetotaler, who left instructions in his will to keep the hotel dry. Cope argued that times had changed, but the court did not agree. Cope did not get a liquor license. But despite these small victories, the dry forces failed to get judges to legislate prohibition on a piecemeal basis in the Poconos. From 1909 to 1919, the no-license strategy caused seventeen counties in Pennsylvania to go dry. None was in the Poconos.[51]

FIG. 36
This cement flowerpot stands in front of the Monroe County courthouse. Erected by the Women's Christian Temperance Union in 1907, it originally served as a horse trough. The W.C.T.U. seemed invincible a century ago, but it eventually lost its version of the culture war. Indeed, several taverns are found within several hundred feet of this monument.

Prohibition agitation in the Poconos served several ends. In part, it was what it claimed to be—an attempt to rid society of drunkenness. In part, however, it was also an expression of class arrogance, because it originated with refined people and was directed at the unrefined. Prohibition may have also been an episode in the gender wars. Its driving force, the W.C.T.U., was female, but men did most of the drinking. When a prohibition amendment to the Pennsylvania Constitution had appeared on the election ballot, most men in Monroe County voted against it.[52] Since women could not vote, that settled the issue. The ladies could only complain or nag. From an economic point of view, however, the prohibition movement in the Poconos was a short-sighted attack on the resort business. Its existence showed that many in the middle class were as indifferent to the resort economy as the people at the bottom of the social ladder. If they gave any thought to the resorts, they were complacent, believing that the present was permanent and that vacationers would always come in great numbers.

6

An Archipelago of Fun, 1914 to 1929

The beginning of the 1900s coincided with the appearance of the automobile, easily the most popular invention of the century. It freed Americans from train schedules and enabled them to drive where they pleased. The automobile was obviously a boon for travelers, but at the same time it was a challenge for the Poconos. Vacationers would no longer visit the Pennsylvania mountains simply because railroads would take them there.

As early as 1909, the *New York Times* was claiming that the automobile had changed the American vacation. Families were replacing a short stay at a resort with weekend jaunts in an automobile.[1] In later years, other observers noted that fewer vacationers were spending the entire summer at a resort. Even more disconcerting to traditional resorts, their main asset—a nearby railroad station— had become irrelevant to automobile owners.

Bad News in the Poconos

How well were the Pocono resorts doing? Old newspapers, usually the best source of information for resorts, are ambiguous. Seeing themselves as cheerleaders for the local economy, they invariably celebrated the sunny side of life. Newspapers would never report that resorts were having a bad season, although if record business was not mentioned, the season had been disappointing. There are signs that after 1910 the Pocono resort economy was stagnating. Resorts were not rebuilt if destroyed by fire. The Montanesca, the Conashaugh, the Water Gap House, and the Spruce Cabin Inn were prominent examples, suggesting that business could have been better. In addition, beginning in 1913, the Lackawanna Railroad directories contained fewer resort notices, a dark hint that some smaller, marginal resorts had folded.

George A. Cullen, passenger agent of the Lackawanna Railroad, provides the best evidence of a sluggish resort economy. In addressing the Monroe County Mountain Resort Association in 1916, Cullen bluntly stated that the resort business was changing. He blamed the automobile, which allowed guests to drive away and stay for shorter periods. As a result, large resorts were no longer full during the summer. Cullen added that resorts had to stay open during the winter and offer winter sports in order to make a profit.[2]

Cullen meant well, but winter sports were not an immediate solution. Although skating was popular, few Americans, aside from those of Scandinavian descent, were skiers. The market for winter sports needed more development. Besides, many Pocono resorts had a particularly vexing problem: the weather. Delaware Water Gap and the other communities by the Delaware River did not receive enough snow. The future belonged to the higher, colder locations farther inland on the Pocono plateau. Pocono Manor and the Inn at Buck Hill Falls had stayed open during the previous winter, testing the ice, as it were. And at the 1917 Hotelmen Show in Philadelphia, Monroe County had two scenes in its display: a summer scene with a golf course and a winter scene with a woman on skates.[3]

Resorts Fight the Great War

Meanwhile, the world was busy with death. World War I broke out in August 1914, when the Allies—consisting of Great Britain, France, Russia, and later, Italy—went to war against Germany and Austria-Hungary. The United States was neutral until April 1917, when Congress declared war on Germany.[4]

For the Pocono resorts, the war was a nasty little interlude of declining business. The Lackawanna Railroad had fewer passengers and canceled the extra trains it ran at the peak of the season. In the summer of 1918, McMichael's Resort had an excess of women. Young men were in the army or working in war industries. The Kittatinny Hotel suffered badly. At war's end, creditors were hounding its owner, John Purdy Cope. According to the *Times Democrat,* Cope had neglected the hotel because he had been chairman of the Monroe County National Defense and Public Safety Committee. In addition, the Kittatinny had suffered from the "general war conditions" of 1918 and from the "gasless Sundays" that had affected other hotels of its "standing and character." Presumably, the Kittatinny was already heavily dependent on a weekend auto trade.[5]

If nothing else, World War I allowed the resorts to show off their patriotism. This was especially necessary for the Quaker resorts, which were full of pacifists who refused conscription. At a time when German Americans were under suspicion, with sauerkraut renamed "liberty cabbage" and many high schools dropping German as a foreign language, Quakers at the very least needed to show their loyalty. Pocono Manor and the Inn at Buck Hill Falls honored "gasless Sunday" by refusing to serve meals to Sunday motoring parties. Among the booths at the 1918 Barrett Fair were "Nail the Kaiser" and "Bomb Hindenburg." (Hindenburg was a top German general for whom the famous dirigible of the 1930s was later named.) Fair profits were donated to the Red Cross and to the American Friends Service Committee. Like other leading resorts, Buck Hill supported the Liberty Bond drive. By October 1917, Charles Thompson, the manager of Buck Hill, had sold $4,500 worth of war bonds to his employees.[6]

FIG. 37
The Barrett Township Fair, August
1918. The fair concentrated on the
First World War. This young lady was
billed as "a Maiden of the Reconstruction." Like most Americans,
vacationers at the Inn at Buck Hill
Falls hoped that a better world would
result from the War's bloodshed.
Buck Hill Collection, Barrett Friendly
Library.

The federal government also financed the war by selling war savings stamps, which some Pocono
resorts sold to their guests. By July 1918, the Buckwood Inn alone had sold $500 worth of stamps. Sev-
eral Pocono resorts combined stamp sales with recreation, holding dances that charged a gentleman a
war stamp every time he took a lady to the floor. The Glenwood in Delaware Water Gap held a dance
contest in which the winner won war stamps paid by an assessment of fifteen cents on each guest.[7]

According to a wartime slogan, food would win the war. To feed themselves as well as their foreign
allies, Americans had to sacrifice by enduring rationing and possible food shortages. Citizens were
encouraged to have "Wheatless Mondays" and "Meatless Tuesdays." Like the rest of the nation, the
Poconos and the resorts had to cope with this food situation. Because sugar was scarce, resort kitchens
used substitute ingredients in cakes and breads. C. H. Palmer, Food Administrator for Monroe

County and himself a resortman, admitted that substitute ingredients cost more, but insisted that guests at his hotel were willing to pay the extra price.[8]

In the last months of the conflict, the so-called Spanish influenza swept the world and claimed twenty million lives. In the United States, 2 percent of the population died. In October 1918, the local press reported that the influenza had arrived in the Poconos, bringing sickness and death. The press gave no statistics, but evidently, Monroe County suffered severely, for the recently built county hospital was inadequate. Temporary hospitals were established at two resorts: the Prospect House in East Stroudsburg and the Fulmer House in Stroudsburg. Helen Dietz recalls being told by her mother that residents in the mountains beyond the Stroudsburgs did not wish to see city vacationers, fearing that they would bring the dreaded influenza along with their money.[9]

FIG. 38

The Fulmer House. Aging Pocono hotels needed to project a fresh appearance. Today's Best Western—located on Main Street in Stroudsburg—started life in 1834 as the Stroudsburg House. Over the years, the hotel went through many owners, names, and renovations. During World War I, it became the Fulmer House, and it was used as a temporary hospital during the influenza epidemic of 1918. Monroe County Historical Association.

Perhaps the War's greatest effect on the resort industry was severing the link between the Monroe County Mountain Resort Association and the Lackawanna Railroad. Beginning with the founding of the Resort Association in 1901, the railroad's publicity staff had written resort advertisements and placed them in city newspapers. During the First World War, this benign paternalism ended, as the federal government nationalized American railroads. To increase efficiency and maximize the war effort, the government ended all competition among railroads, forbidding them to advertise.[10]

The Resort Association was on its own. It stopped receiving an advertising subsidy from the Lackawanna Railroad as well as a directory to advertise the resorts. The separation was inevitable. Sooner or later, the Resort Association would have had to grow up and take charge of its public relations. The growing popularity of the automobile would leave it no choice, because the Lackawanna could not be expected to incorporate motor vehicles in its advertising campaigns nor give directions for

THE PENN-STROUD HOTEL, STROUDSBURG, PA.   113620

FIG. 39

The Penn Stroud. In the 1920s, new owners changed the name of the Fulmer House to the Penn Stroud, and they gave it a new exterior look. Boxer Gene Tunney stayed here in 1926 when he trained for his championship fight with Jack Dempsey. Monroe County Historical Association.

FIG. 40
The Monroe County Courthouse was built in 1890. Here, the statue of the World War I soldier in the foreground makes up for the lack of a Civil War monument—a standard ornament of small Pennsylvania towns. "Lincoln's War" was unpopular in the Poconos, where draft evaders hid in the mountains. Monroe County Historical Association.

highway traffic. In any case, during the war, the Resort Association hired its own advertising agency to handle publicity.[11]

What potentially might have been the resort industry's biggest sacrifice for the war effort never came to pass. The federal government planned to convert Delaware Water Gap hotels into one huge convalescent camp for soldiers. By December 1917, the War Department had rented the Hillcrest for the duration of the conflict, with the option of purchase. The same arrangement was planned for other winter-heated hotels: the Castle Inn, the Delaware House, the Forest House, and the Riverview.

These resorts were to house one thousand convalescents from the Lehigh and Delaware Valleys. The press was careful to note that none of the convalescents would be sick with disease. As it turned out, the press never again mentioned the proposed convalescent camp. For some reason, the federal government sent the war's maimed elsewhere.[12]

Driving in the 1920s

On November 11, 1918, Germany signed an armistice and the war ended. The United States was the big winner, because it had sold billions of dollars of munitions to its allies but had escaped the war's destruction. The end of the war left Americans prosperous, with jobs and money—and ready to buy what they would always buy in the twentieth century with discretionary income. They bought automobiles. In 1914, there was one auto in Pennsylvania for every seventy persons. In 1919, one in twenty Pennsylvanians owned a car. Four years later, one million Pennsylvanians owned automobiles. Americans truly had had a good war.[13]

In 1920, Monroe County voters approved a bond proposition for better roads. Many existing roads were paved with concrete or macadam. The crown jewel of the road system was the so-called Lackawanna Trail (today's Route 611), which ran from Scranton southward through Monroe County to Easton. In 1921, the paving of the Trail was mostly finished, giving rise to pageants, speeches, and parades. However, the final portion from Stroudsburg to the Northampton County line was not completed until 1930, giving rise to a second round of festivities.[14]

Roads encouraged driving. The more people drove, the less they used other forms of transportation, causing interurban trolley lines and railroads to lose business. Prior to World War I, trolleys had connected Delaware Water Gap with Philadelphia, but in the 1920s they ceased operating. Another casualty was the little Delaware Valley Railroad that ran from East Stroudsburg to Bushkill. Automobiles, buses, cabs, and the paving of the River Road between Stroudsburg and Milford (today's Route 209) all contributed to its decline. In the summer of 1924, the railroad tried to attract passengers by offering four weekday trips and three Sunday trips. Increasing service at a time of declining revenue was a bold move, but it failed. The last passenger train ran in 1927. The freight service lingered until 1937, when the Delaware Valley Railroad finally collapsed and died. Its tracks were removed and sold as scrap.[15]

The automobile encouraged new kinds of vacations. In the 1920s, more than ever, city people rented or bought summer homes, stayed overnight in state forests, and sent children to camps. In addition, day-trippers increasingly drove to the Poconos, creating a need for gas stations, souvenir stands, and tearooms. Hotel and resort restaurants saw an extra source of income by opening their dining rooms to these casual tourists.[16]

To take advantage of the auto trade, clever businessmen packaged Pocono scenery. Charles Peters was a minor genius who understood that the automobile had created the one-day vacation. Peters owned Bushkill Falls and enhanced it by adding footpaths, bridges, and observation platforms. Even

FIG. 41
The completion of the Lackawanna Trail (or Route 611) through Delaware Water Gap occasioned a celebration in front of the Kittatinny Hotel. Monroe County Historical Association.

during World War I, when business flagged, he added improvements such as a gazebo. Peters also understood the importance of public relations; he advertised heavily in New York and Philadelphia newspapers. His masterstroke was avoiding the appearance of greed by restricting shops to the entrance of the Falls, thereby allowing him to feign indifference to money while making it. In the summer of 1916, Bushkill Falls attracted more than thirty thousand visitors.[17]

Beautiful View of Delaware Water Gap from Trolley.

FIG. 42
Not even their picturesque views could save the trolleys from competition by automobiles. By the 1930s, the trolley lines were gone from the Poconos. Monroe County Historical Association.

The Resort Business in the 1920s

In 1919, people drove out of the cities to forget the war, the rationing, and all the other petty sacrifices and privations. The Memorial Day business that year in the Poconos was the best yet. The Fourth of July crowd was probably one-third to one-half larger than in the preceding year. The Lackawanna Railroad reported its busiest Independence Day (although most tourists came by car, as they had been doing in recent years). Delaware Water Gap "was gay with varicolored dresses and parasols and automobiles. The river was alive with boats and canoes. The mountain paths were thronged." The Labor Day crowd exceeded the average of previous years by about three thousand. Since the Poconos could always expect large holiday crowds, more telling was the regular weekday trade. In June 1919, many resorts in Monroe and Pike Counties reported that they were sold out for the summer.[18]

In the following year, 1920, huge Memorial Day crowds filled the boardinghouses and hotels. The overflow slept on cots in hotel lobbies and railroad stations. The Indian Queen in Stroudsburg had enough applicants to fill twice over. Huge crowds again arrived for the Fourth of July holiday. Private homes took in guests. And still, rooms were lacking: vacationers slept in cars, barns, porches, and in the woods. Impromptu auto camps were set up in Mountainhome, Buck Hill Falls, Tannersville, and Bushkill.[19]

Even John D. Rockefeller, the richest man of his day and a retired octogenarian, visited the Poconos in 1920. Rockefeller did not sleep in the woods. Coming with a large staff of bodyguards and chauffeurs, he drove around to see the scenery and he stopped at the Buckwood Inn to play golf.[20]

Rockefeller never returned, nor did the huge crowds of 1919 and 1920. Although the Pocono press always remained upbeat, printing the handouts of the vacation industry, newspapers never reported in the later years of the 1920s that resorts and private residences were filled beyond capacity and that auto parties were sleeping outdoors. Cots were no longer seen in hotel lobbies. The super-boom of 1919–20 had been temporary.

To complicate matters, some resorts were less favored than others in the automobile age. Resorts near the Delaware River were among the losers, sharing a nearness that had been an advantage in the railroad age but made vacationers feel crowded in the 1920s. The vacation industry in Delaware Water Gap and Milford did not expand, a sure sign that existing resorts were not packed and turning away visitors. The press also hinted at stagnation. It never reported that all the Delaware Valley hotels were full for the season. Business moved from along the Delaware River to the plateau, where greater distances separated resorts. Vacationers had the advantage of being isolated and still being in auto contact with the outside world. Pocono Manor and the Inn at Buck Hill Falls both shared this advantage, and they emerged as the leading resorts of the 1920s.

A bad sign for Delaware Water Gap was the disappearance of its horse show, which had started after World War I. In the early 1930s, the horse show was revived in Mount Pocono—another indication that the higher elevations on the Pocono plateau had overtaken the Gap. A further blow to the Gap was the increasing use of swimming pools and lakes for recreation, which made the Delaware River no longer needed for water sports. A resort could be deep in the mountains and still offer water recreation. Especially damaging to the Gap was the creation of Lake Wallenpaupack, the largest lake in Pennsylvania, on the shared border of Pike and Wayne Counties. Lake Wallenpaupack was created to produce electricity, but it was also used for recreation. Speedboat races on the Delaware River were eventually moved to this lake.[21]

A problem shared by the entire region was the lack of public support. Both the Commonwealth of Pennsylvania and municipalities in the Poconos refused to publicize their vacation industry, forcing the Monroe County Publicity Bureau, which was launched in 1925, to rely on private financing. Businessmen, resort proprietors, and public-spirited citizens had to dig into their own pockets to keep the Monroe County Publicity Bureau afloat. By contrast, in many other vacation regions, local governments were promoting tourism by using tax revenues. In the mid-1920s, the Miami Chamber of Commerce was receiving one hundred thousand dollars of public money for publicity.[22]

A full-time professional ran the Monroe County Publicity Bureau. He was W. L. Caley, who also served as general secretary of the Monroe County Automobile Club and of the Mountain Resort

Association. As could be expected of a publicity man, Caley was very energetic. In 1929, aside from doing his regular job of mailing out literature, recommending hotels to tourists, and placing advertisements in newspapers (especially the ones in the traditional New York, New Jersey, and Pennsylvania markets), Caley also erected displays at the Broad Street railway station in Philadelphia and in the windows of urban newspapers. As in the past, newsmen from metropolitan New York were entertained at the leading hotels. Caley was so busy that he had to hire a full-time assistant in the summer of 1929.[23]

Vacation Fun in the Roaring Twenties

Although part of the Pocono resort industry was showing signs of maturity, it was not dying. A mature industry can still have a long life. Whether Milford and Delaware Water Gap were less crowded than in the old days was irrelevant to vacationers who came to enjoy themselves. They could have an old-fashioned vacation or they could delight in some of the new fun.

In the America of the 1920s, the press usually ignored traditional diversions, preferring to focus on rebellion. Nonconformity had been redefined. It was listening to the jazz of black musicians, dancing the Charleston—and for women, it was wearing short dresses and claiming fuller sex lives than their mothers. Likewise, attention was paid to men who showed their trendiness by carrying a flask of illegal whiskey and to mobsters who murdered to supply that whiskey. This violence defined the "Jazz Age." Many Americans were mesmerized by the mobsters who sold alcohol and by the knowledge that allegedly law-abiding citizens bought it.

What of the Poconos? Here, too, rules were broken, but the overall impression is of an accelerated evolution of earlier trends. There was no sudden, sharp break. Many people in the Poconos drank before Prohibition and continued to drink during Prohibition. Farmers had always used the produce of their orchards to make applejack, saw no reason to stop, and continued to share with neighbors. Like the rest of the nation, speakeasies were present in the Poconos. When the state police raided a Pike County speakeasy in 1924, the *Morning Press* reported that they had found "pretty women, each with a silken foot on the bar rail." The hussies were holding "a glass on one hand, while the fingers of the other delicately held between aromatic puffs, a cigarette." Here was a portrait of modern sin in the heart of Pike County. But even before Prohibition, some bars flouted liquor laws. Besides, Pike County had a long tradition of thumbing its nose at authority.[24]

The press did not report liquor raids on the resorts, which suggests that they obeyed the law. After all, most resorts had been dry before Prohibition. A large resort had much to lose by selling liquor, although employees could privately supply it. This happened at the Bluff House in Milford, where state police, pretending to be vacationers, asked the bellboy for liquor. When the bellboy used a phony prescription to buy alcohol from a local pharmacy, he was arrested. But his understanding employer paid the bail. Although the bellboy broke the law, he was no mobster.[25] By the standards of the big cities, the Poconos come across as relatively clean. Dead gangsters riddled with bullet holes

BATHING BEACH AT DELAWARE WATER GAP, PA.   2

FIG. 43
Island Park beach at Delaware Water Gap. The growing popularity of swimming pools made the Delaware River beaches less desirable. Monroe County Historical Association.

were not found on streets. No one accused Stroudsburg or Milford of being wide-open. Lawbreaking was done discreetly.

As for the alleged immorality of the 1920s, vacationers in the Poconos had to respect the proprieties. The tale of a Broadway actress illustrates this point. In 1922, she and her boyfriend stayed at the Renleigh Hotel in Delaware Water Gap, where they slept in separate bedrooms. At night, however, the staff heard the pitter-patter of feet in the corridor. The boyfriend was sneaking into her room. Whatever the actress and her beau may have done in the City, they did not openly break the rules in the Poconos. It should never be forgotten that whatever the desires of city people, they had to behave in public when they went to the Poconos. In 1930, two women were arrested for wearing shorts in the streets of East Stroudsburg.[26]

Sex aside, the decade was the age of the outrageous. Americans had prided themselves on being a serious people, yet publicity seekers of the "roaring twenties" danced for hours, sat on flagpoles, and swallowed goldfish. The silliness of the roaring twenties mesmerized contemporaries and still has a certain fascination today. But the great change of the 1920s Poconos was not this new silliness; rather, it was the death of the old belief that a vacation had to be justified in terms of personal improvement. The evolution toward open hedonism that had started in the late nineteenth century had reached fruition. Vacationers occasionally were silly in the old days: the Swiftwater Monks, for example, with their clerical dress and drinking bouts, were both silly *and* subversive. But the Monks carried out their antics behind closed doors.[27]

In the 1920s, by contrast, people acted silly in public without justifying themselves. At the Hotel Edgewood in Delaware Water Gap, when both sexes played baseball after dinner, a woman slid into home plate after a rain shower—and she was wearing a seventy-five-dollar dress. The Mountain Lake House—a new resort founded after the First World War—advertised "Egyptian dances," mind reading, guessing contests, and jokes. Although located in Marshalls Creek, a declining resort area near the Delaware River, the Mountain Lake House was successful because it catered to modern trends. It also survived the Great Depression.[28]

At Cleo's Pavilion, a mock marriage united Miss Crab to Mister Worm. The Rev. Nut presided and intoned: "Miss Crab, are you willing to take this worm until he wiggles away with another fish? . . . Mr. Worm, do you take this crab until she is caught in another net? . . . If so, you're hooked." The guests howled with delight.[29]

Now that fun was fully out of the closet, the expensive resorts hired social directors to plan and lead amusements so that vacationers would be occupied for the entire day. Long gone was the expectation that vacationers would fend for themselves and perhaps suffer moments of boredom. In a sense, social directors were the high priests of hedonism. Their presence proclaimed the new religion of enjoyment.

Water sports came into their own. The *Mountain Echo* of 1922 printed a photo of Saylors Lake and its happy bathers. Although vacationers had long used Saylors Lake, the novelty here was showing real people having fun. At Milford, recreation in the Delaware River took on a new dimension. "Professor" Norman Coykendall organized water sports and performed stunts in the river. The "human fish," as he was billed, spent his winters in Florida, where he managed a similar beach. Coykendall exemplified the foolishness of the 1920s.[30]

The growing popularity of swimming pools ended the fiction that water sports brought one closer to nature. The chlorinated water of swimming pools reeked of artificiality, yet vacationers preferred it to the real thing. Although the Buckwood Inn was adjacent to the Delaware River, only a few steps from the water, its management realized that guests preferred a swimming pool to river bathing. Aside from divorcing vacationers from nature, swimming pools were lazy recreation—in a sense, a modern replacement for the porch. Pools, though, had a hint of the naughty, putting guests in situations of controlled voyeurism and exhibitionism.

Another novelty of the 1920s was public sponsorship of recreation. The borough of Stroudsburg led the way after the war by organizing block dances. In 1920, the Ladies Auxiliary of the Pocono

Hospital sponsored a horse show in Delaware Water Gap. In the 1921 show, horsemen showed off their talents in a polo game, riding exhibitions, and steeplechase races. A British flying ace and a representative of the Curtis Aeroplane Company entertained the two thousand spectators with barrel rolls and tailspins.[31]

In 1925, the Milford Chamber of Commerce decided to exploit the growing American interest in winter sports. A skating pond was laid out on the old racetrack that had closed in 1905, and a 250-foot toboggan slide was constructed on the side of a hill. To finance advertising in city newspapers, the Chamber launched a campaign to raise $1,200. Among the contributors was Governor Gifford Pinchot, a native of Pike County. A press account from January 1926 noted that 150 people were seen enjoying themselves in the snow and ice. Whether the crowd consisted of local residents or vacationers was not mentioned.[32]

In 1928, the three-year-old Monroe County Publicity Bureau announced a new amusement policy of continuous gratification for both vacationers and residents. The Publicity Bureau was not speaking idly. In the following year, it sponsored a variety of events, including its second amateur golf tournament (consisting of forty-two matches at seven courses in the county), a tennis tournament that attracted thirty-five players, and contests in the lakes as well as speedboat races on the Delaware River. These events attracted resort guests and local residents from throughout the Poconos, creating spectacles that would have been difficult to arrange in the horse-and-buggy age. The Publicity Bureau was making creative use of the automobile, linking resorts and creating an archipelago of fun. According to the *Morning Press,* the "gayest of regions in the gayest of months" had taken on even more life and color. It added that Europe had long understood the psychology of public amusements, but that America had far to go.[33]

1920s Modernism Versus an Old-Fashioned Vacation

Along with sports and zany amusements, city sophisticates expected city comforts. They wanted indoor toilets instead of outhouses, electric lights instead of gaslights, and antiseptic water from faucets instead of the unsafe stuff from wells and brooks. Another source of delight was the refrigerator that protected the freshness of milk and meat. The old-fashioned ice house in the backyard was strictly for country rubes. City people even *looked* modern in their stylish clothes. Small-town folk knew it. There were people in Stroudsburg who went to the train station to check out city tourists and see the latest fashions.[34]

Resorts had to cater to big-city modernity. The Buckwood Inn of the 1920s advertised "all the comforts of city living." No details were given, but the nature of these comforts may be seen by comparing the ads in the *Mountain Echo* of 1922 with the 1917 edition. The ads reveal a greater attention to private baths and electric lights, precisely the conveniences whose absence made a rural area backward. Telephones also defined city life in the 1920s. The Pennlyn resort in Stroudsburg assured the public that it had private phones in every room.

Even better if an entire town were modern! In 1922, the Milford Chamber of Commerce published a publicity brochure that took pains to note that Milford was no hick town. The brochure boasted of electric lights that kept Milford bright at night, of main streets paved in concrete, and of side streets that were oiled. Resorts advertised in the brochure that they welcomed auto parties and served meals to passing motorists. The brochure seemed to protest too much. Many motorists probably did regard Milford as a "hick town," good only for passing through. But motorists who chose to stay were assured that hotels had nightly dancing. Single ladies were further guaranteed that they would not be lonely. Many young men lived in Milford, and, the brochure added, there were "some handsome ones."[35]

Although booze, zaniness, and creature comforts captured the imagination of contemporaries, 1920s modernity would not appeal to all vacationers. Older adults had been raised in less sophisticated times. Some would prefer an old-fashioned vacation of well water, outhouses, and timeless simplicity. Walking in a forest and feeling twigs crunching beneath the feet, smelling the fragrance of the

FIG. 44

Swimming at the Buckwood Inn. The Buckwood was adjacent to the Delaware River. To remain a leading resort, though, the Buckwood needed a swimming pool and chlorinated water. Vacationers no longer wanted to swim in the river. Monroe County Historical Association.

morning dew, that rush of discovery when a wild critter runs by—those experiences would be just as rich in 1925 as in 1900. In a world that was changing—and, in the opinion of many, not necessarily changing for the better—a simple vacation offered solace.

In 1963, an Easton banker recalled joining the Maskenozha Club in 1923. The only heating facilities in the clubhouse were the fireplaces in the rest rooms and the kitchen stove. A windmill pumped water from a spring to a water tank. When winter came, the tank and all the pipes had to be drained, making the bathroom facilities unusable. Living like this in the 1920s was nostalgic. It was also slumming: the rural poor lived like this not by choice but by necessity. Only the well-to-do had electric generators for water pumps.[36]

Ken Bates remembers the Meadowbrook House, a farmer's boardinghouse in Canadensis run by his parents, Robert and Harriet. The Meadowbrook House offered much of the lifestyle of a previous generation. It had no electric line to supply unlimited energy for appliances. In fact, the Poconos gained access to a power grid only in the late 1920s, when the Pennsylvania Power and Light Company dammed Wallenpaupack Creek in Wayne County and created cheap hydroelectric energy. Like many other innkeepers, Bates's parents used an electric generator to light the guest rooms. But the generator was too weak to run pumps. Bates's father installed a waterwheel in a nearby stream to pump water into a reservoir above the farm, and gravity pressure supplied running water to each room. A freezer was out of the question. An old-fashioned ice house made of stone and filled with blocks of winter ice provided limited refrigeration for foods. The elder Bates fed guests with his own vegetables and with meat from cows, pigs, sheep, and chickens that he raised and slaughtered. Since the ice house preserved meat poorly, extra meat was given to nearby boardinghouses that in turn shared their surplus. Here was the neighborliness for which city people yearned. The elder Bates had about one hundred sheep that he sent to a nearby mountain to fend for themselves during the summer. The sheep provided meat and wool. The younger Bates recalls the kitchen stove, which was an army surplus wood burner. Gas and electric stoves were for city people. As with the Maskenozha Club members, Meadowbrook House patrons gave up city comforts to enjoy the simple life.[37]

A cheaper and more rustic vacation was possible with a cabin on state land. A 1913 state law authorized the leasing of suitable campsites to build cabins of approved design. By the 1920s, the State Department of Forests and Waters was leasing tracts of land, 75 by 100 feet in extent, for ten dollars a year. Leases ran for ten years with the privilege of renewal and with the requirement that leaseholders erect a cabin within two years. By 1926, the state had issued 366 cabin permits in Pike and Monroe Counties. Nearly 150 of these cabins were at Peck's Pond in Pike County, where vacationers had set up a colony that had its own grocery store.[38]

Vacationers who wanted a bare-bones vacation in the woods could, as always, go camping. The State Department of Forests and Waters was very accommodating, creating "Class A" camps that were accessible to motorists. Class A sites had fireplaces, tables, benches, comfort stations, garbage bins, and cleared spaces for tents. In Pike County, they were located at George Childs State Park and at Promised Land State Park.[39]

1:—FIRST NIGHT IN THE COUNTRY.

FIG. 45
First night in the country. This postcard expressed the urban view of country living. Monroe County Historical Association.

Quakers Rising

Between the extremes of the bare-bones vacation on the one hand and noisy zaniness on the other, there was room for a third way, neither frenetic nor spartan, and having just enough culture to attract vacationers with money but dubious about the latest fads. The Quaker resorts had come into their own. During the 1920s, both Pocono Manor and the Inn at Buck Hill Falls grew enormously. In 1923, Pocono Manor completed that absolute necessity for a modern vacation, an eighteen-hole golf course. Three years later, it added a brick wing, a nine-story addition with 113 rooms. By 1928, a 300-seat auditorium had been added. Likewise, Buck Hill also opened an addition in 1925, the fireproof central section, that gave the Inn 214 bedrooms. Good business begat additional expansion. By 1930, Buck Hill had 309 bedrooms; 105 of these had a lavatory and 26 had both a lavatory and toilet.[40]

The many rooms at Buck Hill without running water suggested that the Inn did not offer the best and latest facilities. The Quakers would not have cared. Pocono Manor and Buck Hill were great resorts not because of their creature comforts but because of their refinement, culture, and the Quaker ethos that eschewed conspicuous consumption and created an alternative definition of the good life. Although neither resort strove to be fashionable, both were exclusive and selective. Both places had rules—but as with the British Constitution, the rules were unwritten ones. Many things simply were not done. Guests did not flaunt money, nor did men wear evening clothes. Guests were expected to observe and learn that the guiding principle was understatement. Guests who understood were included in the "family." Those who did not pick up on hints, body language, and example were not allowed to return.[41]

Culture was important at the Quaker inns. In the early days, reading aloud in the evenings and discussing books had been a favorite pastime. At Buck Hill, a first concern had been the Greenleaf Library, which originally consisted of a few shelves of donated books. By 1922, the library was receiving two hundred donated books every season. A new library building completed in 1923 contained thirty-seven hundred volumes.

The well-educated Quakers had a keen interest in the outside world. The Pocono Manor Association often invited speakers on human rights and social issues. On August 11, 1911, African American leader Booker T. Washington spoke to guests and cottagers. Pocono Manor periodically held peace conferences; a popular theme, in 1917, was reconstruction after the First World War. By 1928, many of these lectures were being held in the new auditorium. At Buck Hill, the Foxhowe Association started its series of current events lectures in 1924. In the following year, Buck Hill established the International House, which invited a distinguished foreign guest for a week's residency. The guest served as a focal point for discussion groups and lectures. In 1927, thirty-seven guests—representing fourteen nationalities—spoke at Buck Hill. Most were European, either in nationality or origin. By the standards of the 1920s, when Africa and most of Asia were ignored, non-American whites (unless they were British) were exotic: the International House was, then, a very multicultural place, a miniature League of Nations in the mountains of Pennsylvania.

Although "music has charms to soothe the savage breast," the laid-back Quakers did not need the tranquilizing effects of music. They listened to chamber music because they enjoyed it and also because it was a traditional sign of breeding. A trio of distinguished musicians from Philadelphia played at Buck Hill for twenty years, starting in 1922. The trio was led by the assistant violoncellist of the Philadelphia Orchestra.

Quakers were not opposed to fun, as long as it was clean fun that even Methodists would approve. In 1907, the Quaker inns began their annual Labor Day contests, held in even years at Buck Hill and in odd years at Pocono Manor. Buck Hill won most of the tennis tournaments; Pocono Manor was superior at bowling. Golf was about even. One Buck Hill cheer borrowed the tune of "When Johnny Comes Marching Home."

> Oh, Buck Hill teams have come again,
>> Hurrah! Hurrah!
> Oh, Buck Hill teams have come again,
>> Hurrah! Hurrah!
> We'll beat you at bowling and tennis, too,
> Oh, Pocono teams we are ready for you!
> Oh, we'll beat you, sure, with racket and ball to-day!
> Oh, we'll beat you, sure, with racket and ball to-day!

By the late 1920s, the rivalry was attracting so many spectators that box lunches were served. In 1932, at the height of the Great Depression, the games were discontinued. They were no longer fun.

Both sides chanted the following:

> We're two Quaker inns, Rah, Rah,
> We're two Quaker inns, Rah, Rah,
> However it ends,
> We'll always be friends,
> We're two Quaker inns, Rah, Rah.

With a cheer like this, the Hicksites and the Orthodox Friends were destined to end their schism. (The two Quaker branches officially kissed and made up in 1955.)

Although the ancestors of the pacifist Quakers did not fight in the American Revolution, a major event at Buck Hill was Independence Day. Guests usually dressed up in colonial costumes, but on July 4, 1923—the summer following the discovery of King Tut's tomb—the annual pageant took on a note of whimsy. To the sound of martial music, a sarcophagus was borne onto the stage. The mummy was unwound, and from the bandages emerged Charles N. Thompson, the general manager of the Inn at Buck Hill Falls. According to the narration, Tut had died because ancient Egypt was dull without an Inn at Buck Hill Falls.[42]

Another annual event was the Barrett Fair. It did not survive, although it had been heavily attended, attracting over seven thousand people after the War. It had been so successful that the *Morning Press* opined that the Fair had surpassed its origins as a township event and had become a county event. Such popularity raises the question: why did the Fair close?[43] The official explanation in the Buck Hill Annual Report of 1926 was less "enthusiasm." The Annual Report for the previous year noted that the township had drastically raised the tax assessments on the hotel property and cottages, causing the Buck Hill community to be annoyed. Maybe a connection existed between the higher assessments and Buck Hill's cancellation of the Fair, or maybe not. Coincidences do occur.

The ideal at both Pocono Manor and the Inn at Buck Hill Falls was progressive recreation within a framework of social conservatism. Nothing bore this out so well as the winter sports program, which was avant-garde even in the 1920s. The Quaker inns started to offer sledding, skating, and tobogganing before World War I, and they added skiing in the 1920s. Hockey also emerged. Guests from Pocono Manor and Buck Hill formed teams that played each other. The one restriction on the winter sports program was something beyond Quaker control—the weather. Although the plateau received more snow than Delaware Water Gap and the Stroudsburgs, the snowfall was irregular. Buck Hill tried holding an annual winter carnival, but it had to be discontinued when the Inn could not guarantee a blanket of snow.[44]

Although Pocono Manor and the Inn at Buck Hill Falls could not coax snow from the heavens, they could change the public's perceptions. The Quaker inns created a wintry image for the Poconos by having Alaskan-style dogsleds. Asie Seppala, a Canadian musher complete with reindeer parka and dogs, became a winter feature at Pocono Manor. The local press noted the birth of five pups to Togo, the head Alaskan husky on Seppala's sled. Seppala and his dogs earned their keep by taking guests for rides.[45]

The friendly rivalry between the Quaker inns even extended to dogsleds. If Pocono Manor had a dogsled team, so would Buck Hill. According to Harry Drennan, the Winter Sports Director, dogsledding came to Buck Hill accidentally. A guest left five husky pups at the Inn and never returned. Drennan raised and trained the orphaned pups, the nucleus of a kennel that would contain as many as forty dogs.[46]

The winter sports program at the Quaker inns presented a modern touch that was not faddish. Pocono Manor and the Inn at Buck Hill Falls had none of the inanities that marked the 1920s. Quakers were too proper to sponsor beauty contests, flagpole sitting, and marathon dancing. Their parties did not revolve around exotic themes. Japanese lanterns were not needed to suggest the Far East. Buck Hill had the real thing—speakers from Japan as well as from China and India.

Also absent were social directors. When the Quaker inns were not sponsoring cultural activities, they expected guests to entertain themselves in the old-fashioned way—by using their wits and imagination. Here was a reflection of the Quaker religion, which valued spontaneity and which differed from other Christian faiths by having neither ministers nor rituals. Services consisted of members of the congregation speaking whenever the "inner light" moved them. The only guideline was having a sense of the meeting, which meant avoiding foolish talk. As a result, the Quaker service embodied a paradox of spontaneity within a framework of custom. Likewise with recreation; guests acted freely within the boundaries set by the resort. Using a social director to lead games was akin to having a minister conduct services. Quakers would have neither.[47]

The Inn at Buck Hill Falls of the 1920s was noted for its taboos. Prohibition was honored both in spirit and in letter. Guests could not bring their own alcohol. Charles Thompson, the general manager, would not allow a guest to return if he had been drinking. Speeding cars were another taboo. Roads at Buck Hill had depressions to prevent motorists from driving fast. Sundays had to be observed. Guests at Buck Hill could neither buy a newspaper nor play golf until the end of Quaker services, which, incidentally, attracted many non-Quakers. Buck Hill was quiet, and many liked it that way. A cottage owner wrote to management: "The day you open dancing, jazz and other lipstick amusements, do me a favor—put my cottage on the market." Despite these restrictions, the Inn at Buck Hill Falls was considered more lively than Pocono Manor. Although card playing was traditionally frowned upon, bridge had crept into the Inn. The pleasurable and social aspects of the game were irresistible. Likewise, Buck Hill compromised with dancing. Although forbidden at the main building, dances were held at the Tennis Tea House, where a college orchestra played.[48]

Skytop Lodge Is Born

Minor concessions to modernity were insufficient for some of the Buck Hill guests, who found the atmosphere a bit stuffy, although they liked the exclusive nature of the Inn. Since Buck Hill would not change, the solution was to create another inn that would also be private, remote, and on a high elevation. The result was Skytop Lodge, destined to be the most exclusive of the Pocono resorts.[49]

FIG. 46
Independence Day, 1915. Independence Day was always celebrated at Buck Hill. In this photograph, guests showed off fancy colonial clothes. The Quakers of the eighteenth century would have been appalled. They preferred plain living—and they dressed down. Buck Hill Collection, Barrett Friendly Library.

FIG. 47
Dogsled at the Inn at Buck Hill Falls.
What did the dogs do when there was
no snow? Buck Hill Collection, Barrett Friendly Library.

The chain of events that led to Skytop was launched by John S. Stubbs, a New York securities dealer and a Buck Hill patron. He was assured by Charles Thompson that the area could support another fancy hotel and that Sam Packer, his nephew and assistant, would make an excellent manager. On July 23, 1925, "Sky Top Lodges, Inc." was incorporated in Pennsylvania, and stock in the new venture was sold. Among the directors were Thompson, Packer, a member of the New York Stock Exchange, and corporation executives.

A mountain plateau about three miles north of Canadensis had long been viewed as the ideal location for another great hotel. The site had it all: elevation, streams, waterfalls, impressive distant views, and the key asset of the automobile age, isolation. Tucked away in a remote part of Monroe County, Skytop would have no resorts nearby. Like medieval nobles who built castles on hilltops, its patrons were safe from the prying eyes of inferiors. They would not be on display—a privilege that the well-to-do usually did not enjoy in the days prior to the automobile. If the rich of the railroad age wished to be near civilization, they had to frequent resort towns like Delaware Water Gap and risk bumping into the less affluent when walking the streets. Best of all, the site of the proposed Skytop resort was available for purchase. The topsoil was generally shallow and unsuited for agriculture, causing many of the farms to be abandoned by the early 1920s. A bushy second growth of small trees had reclaimed the land. Through a series of independent purchases, the Skytop corporation acquired eight contiguous tracts, some twenty-five hundred acres in all.[50]

By Pocono standards, Skytop had history. It overlapped the grounds of the former Janney House hotel, recalled as "a shabby, unattractive brown boarding house where fishermen were entertained." Before 1920, it had been the Mountain Lake House, which had also catered to fishermen. Its owner had been Lafayette Price, the son of Charles Price, a Pocono pioneer who had run a tavern and inn. Among Charles's customers in this remote location had been drovers—a familiar sight prior to railroads and refrigeration. Drovers "drove" or walked livestock and fowl to towns and cities, where

FIG. 48

Play Club, Buck Hill, 1929. Although the children are posing for this photograph, the ideal of the play club was spontaneity. Quaker religious services ran on the same principle. Members of the congregation spoke up whenever the "inner light" moved them. Buck Hill Collection, Barrett Friendly Library.

butchers would slaughter the animals and sell meat that was beyond fresh; the meat had a gamy taste. The humble folk of the nineteenth century could never have imagined that their mountain backwater would become the summer home of moneyed city people. The mountaineers could not foresee that the automobile would reduce distances and make the far seem close.

Although Skytop would compete with Buck Hill, Charles Thompson invested in Skytop, and he served as an adviser during its construction. Along with Sam Packer, he supervised the furnishing of Skytop and the hiring of its personnel. In a sense, Skytop was an offspring of Buck Hill, though it was not formally acknowledged as such. Although proper—after all, in the 1920s, the rich were decorous—Skytop was far more playful than the Quaker resorts and had its priorities straight. When it opened in June 1928, the eighteen-hole golf course was already completed. From the start, card playing was allowed, discreet drinking permitted, and guests danced every Saturday night in the lobby. To make sure that the right people mingled at Skytop, a club was created so that only members and their recommended friends could stay at the hotel. The relaxation of standards had limits.[51]

7

Guess Who's Coming to the Poconos?
The Rise of Ethnic Resorts

Who is an American? On November 1, 1938, the International Ladies' Garment Workers' Union (the I.L.G.W.U.), the owner of a Pocono resort, inadvertently gave its own reply. Its Death Benefit Report broke down 125 deaths by ethnic group. Eighty percent of the deceased members were listed as either "Hebrew" or "Italian." The rest were "Colored," "Polish," and other ethnics from around the world. Six were "American." Presumably, by "American," the I.L.G.W.U. meant an old-stock American, that is, a Protestant of British descent.[1]

The I.L.G.W.U. was mostly Jewish. Its definition of an American was obviously a reaction of its first- and second-generation members to old-stock white Protestants who regarded themselves as "real" Americans. Still, ethnic defensiveness was not entirely due to rejection. To non-British immigrants, "real" Americans were also strange. American boiled meat was insipid, compared with old-country foods, and the English language sounded as foreign to immigrants as Yiddish or Italian did to Americans. Ethnic clannishness resulted from choice as well as from rejection.

Foreigners in the Poconos

These dynamics could certainly be seen in the Poconos, where nativism was strong. In the years after the Civil War, when an occasional "foreigner" wandered into Stroudsburg, he was regarded with curiosity, like a freak in a carnival sideshow. As more immigrants from eastern and southern Europe were encountered, the Stroudsburg press grew less amused and more alarmed. By the turn of the century, it showed its contempt by adopting a double standard for strangers: "Americans" were identified by name, but "ethnics" only by their nationality. For example, in the case of a near drowning, it reported that "a Jew" had been fished out of the river. The press treated Polish and Italian laborers with hostility and condescension. They had "funny" names, ate strange foods, and spoke bad English. (One article quoted an Italian workman who was criticizing "a badda man.") Unlike the local yahoos who gaped at hangings and showed their tobacco-stained teeth, the ethnics offended tribal sensibilities. They really *were* different. But they were needed for heavy labor. In their own way, they were part of the vacation economy.[2]

In the case of the Poles, the local press made the best of their unwelcome presence by regarding them with humor. Polish names were considered hilarious. When a Pole named "Wojciechowski" applied for a wedding license, the *Stroudsburg Times* sarcastically noted that the local prothonotary had "a narrow escape from fracturing his jaw and losing a mouthful of teeth." When Polish railway workers ended their Christmas celebrations with a brawl in which both sexes joined freely, a newspaper claimed that it had no full report because Polish names were "unpronounceable." These Poles and their families lived on "Shanty Hill," which comprised six houses on a bluff in East Stroudsburg overlooking the railway tracks. According to the press, Shanty Hill insulted both the eyes and the nose because of the pigs. When the railroad laid off the Poles in 1899, they left town, and Shanty Hill disappeared. The departure benefited the resorts. Stink and squalor did not appeal to city vacationers.[3]

The next minority to arouse the locals were Italians—or "dagoes," as a local newspaper called them. They had come to work as temporary laborers. They provided the muscle for the infrastructure of the resort economy, building houses, working for the railroads, and digging ditches and sewers around the Poconos. As was the case with many Italian immigrants, the men came alone in order to work hard and send money back to Italy. The Italian workmen lived as bachelors, with all this implied. More than once, the *Daily Record* complained that the railroad "dagoes" were fighting, gambling, drinking, and making passes at local women. At a time when the very respectable neither drank nor gambled, the "dagoes" did so noisily and with strange accents. They obviously were not Methodist men. In 1909, a house full of Italian railway workers provoked a Rev. Francis Craft. He complained to A. Mitchell Palmer, the Lackawanna's attorney in Stroudsburg, who in turn wrote to William Truesdale, president of the railroad. Truesdale, in turn, promised to look into the matter.[4]

One group of foreigners did not raise controversy, partially because they were Protestants of northern European origin and partially because they remained aloof. These were the Norwegians from Brooklyn who hoped to create a utopian cooperative that would let them escape the mean streets of the city, its greedy employers, and the dog-eat-dog routine of capitalism. In 1902, some twenty families created the Norwegian Colony Association, contributed thirty-six thousand dollars, and purchased one thousand acres in Rowland, Pike County. They intended to clear the land, quarry stone, cut timber, lay out farms, and sell produce in Brooklyn. They also planned a resort for workers who had the option of paying cash for their lodgings or working in the fields. This manual labor would support a superior society of literary and physical culture. To some degree, the Norwegians were a throwback to Horace Greeley's Sylvania, a socialist experiment in the Pike County of the 1840s. Just as with Greeley's Sylvania experience, nature was unforgiving. The soil was poor, and once the timber was cut, there was little source of ready cash. The local people could have told the Norwegians the awful truth: good intentions cannot coax a living from the barren soil of Pike County. Most of the colonists soon saw the light and left, but unlike Greeley's Sylvania, the Norwegian venture did not completely disappear. Descendants of the original settlers own summerhouses in Rowland, and Norwegian names grace their mailboxes. Other mementos are the remains of outhouses that once greeted visitors at the edge of the grounds. After the long trip from Brooklyn, people needed relief. The four-seater and six-seater outhouses redefined family values.[5]

Vacationing for the Others

Before 1914, "real" American vacationers could rest assured that they would be safe in the Poconos. They would be among their own. With the exception of Catholics of Irish or British descent, other ethnic elements in the American population were mostly missing in the Pocono resorts. Published names of guests reveal no Slavic names among resort proprietors and guests. The few Jews were safely tucked away in two Jewish resorts. Italians who went to the Poconos stayed at the Brentini and Caprioli resorts in the village of Canadensis. These two boardinghouses advertised Italian food, which, at the time, was a code word for an Italian clientele. "Real" Americans would get the message.

In the years before the First World War, the largest group of ethnic vacationers consisted of native-born Catholics of Irish or British descent. Although not particularly diverse in appearance or speech—and, in many cases, possessed of a long American lineage—these Catholics did not fit the old-stock mold. All this was very clear in Milford, where both Catholics and Protestants vacationed, apparently in the same hotels, for there is no indication of religious segregation. If anti-Catholic prejudice existed, the press and resort literature were silent on the subject.

In 1902, both Protestant and Catholic vacationers staged benefits for their respective churches in Milford. Although northern European Catholics were more Americanized than eastern and southern Europeans, they behaved differently from "real" American Protestants. At Milford, Catholics raised money for St. Patrick's Church by playing euchre (awarding prizes to winners), and when they finished with cards, they danced. After all, in the course of the twentieth century, Catholic parishes would be noted for raising money through parties, bingo games, and lotteries. On the other hand, Protestants neither gambled nor danced at their church benefits. The traditions of their churches frowned on these amusements. The Presbyterian benefit featured a colonial room, "a fancy table," and refreshments. The Episcopalians featured food and drink, as well as a Turkish Room, a Fortune Teller, and a Laundry at which a guest was "attired as a Chinaman and his sister impersonated a negress." Catholics had no need for such exotica. Their Latin Mass, papal loyalties, and rich ritual were exotic enough in the America of 1902.[6]

Beyond the pale were African Americans. They were only mentioned at the resorts as servants who, at times, were treated as curiosities. Guests at the Burnett House once offered fifteen dollars to the hotel's black waiters if they would take part in an hour's "go-as-you-please" race or walking marathon at the Stroudsburg fairgrounds. In 1889, a guest at the Kittatinny Hotel arranged a baseball match between Delaware Water Gap's black waiters and white Stroudsburg players. In 1895, the Cuddleback Farm House offered its guests a demonstration of the high-stepping cakewalk, a dance that originated with African Americans and was crossing over into white society. The three black couples present at the Cuddleback to perform the dance most likely were not guests at the Cuddleback. The search for novelty would have its limits in racial integration.[7]

More threatening than African Americans, though, were Jews. They were white, and some had money, especially German Jews who started to come to America before the Civil War. Several Pocono resorts openly stated that they did not permit Jewish guests. One resort at Delaware Water Gap advertised in the 1905 Trenton phone book that it was free of "Hebrews and tuberculosis patients," thereby incensing Trenton's Jewish community, which threatened the phone company with a boycott. Mostly unwelcome, Jews had the option of patronizing their own hotels, such as Forest Park Hotel in Bushkill. Around the time of World War I, the Highland Dell had a Jewish clientele as well

FIG. 49
Unknown resort musicians. Since this photograph is found in the Jesse Graves Photography Book, these African Americans probably played at the Delaware Water Gap resorts. Regardless of race, the "help" was meant to be largely invisible to guests. Monroe County Historical Association.

as a new proprietor with a Jewish-sounding name. These two resorts were the extent of the Jewish presence. The Poconos definitely were not the Catskills, already known for attracting Jewish vacationers from New York City.[8]

Forest Park

Before 1900, the only ethnic resort in the Poconos was Forest Park, the creation of German-Jewish Jacob Ottenheimer. The immigration agent of the Canadian Pacific Railroad, Ottenheimer came to Pike County to start a colony of German-speaking immigrants. After seeing the land, he opted for a hunting and fishing club. Realizing the work involved, he again changed his mind and decided on a hotel. Ottenheimer bought twelve thousand acres of land in Porter and Lehman Townships—land that included four lakes and fifteen miles of trout streams. By 1892, workmen were cutting trees and laying out roads for a resort near Bushkill, about seventeen miles from the East Stroudsburg railway station. All the construction materials and equipment had to be carted, which put ten teams on the road much of the time and had the side effect of producing work for area farmers.

Local newspapers were impressed. The *Milford Dispatch* wrote that the hotel "must have cost a big sum of money . . . with every imaginable convenience known to modern hotel management, even in the cities." The *Stroudsburg Times* called Forest Park "a perfect paradise" in which guests could amuse themselves with billiards, archery, or cricket; when hungry, they could order filet mignon and spring duck from the so-called random menu. After Ottenheimer died in 1895, his son-in-law, Arthur Lederer, took over and continued the lavish tradition.[9]

To describe Forest Park as Jewish is somewhat misleading. It catered to German Jews whose ancestors came to America around midcentury and who had become middle-class and theologically liberal. These Jews believed themselves to be different from the more recently arrived eastern European Jews, working-class and orthodox, who ate kosher food and honored the Sabbath. By advertising a Vienna Cafe and other Germanic features, Forest Park may have been hinting that eastern European Jews were unwelcome. In short, Forest Park was a unique specialty resort that catered to a minority within a minority.

In 1914, the Forest Park resort was running strong. The new Delaware Valley Railroad from East Stroudsburg eliminated a bumpy horse-and-buggy ride from the train station. But like so many other institutions of the Western world, it would be a casualty of World War I. What exactly happened to Forest Park after America declared war on Germany is unclear. According to a newspaper account written a half-century later, the U.S. government considered Lederer suspicious, because he was closely associated with German steamship lines and because his resort had a German flavor. As a result, according to this scenario, the government forced Lederer to sell his Pocono holdings. In 1918–19, however, Pocono newspapers did not mention these alleged troubles. They simply gave the impression that Lederer had decided to leave the resort business.[10]

FIG. 50
Forest Park was built in the early 1890s, and its owner, Jacob Ottenheimer, spread the news. A publicity brochure contains this drawing of the clubhouse. The brochure boasted of tents for use in warm weather. Fresh food was promised, including frogs' legs from a pond on the property. Monroe County Historical Association.

Lederer found two buyers. In 1919, Locals 22 and 25 of the Dress and Waistmakers' Union of the International Ladies' Garment Workers' Union paid eighty-five thousand dollars for Forest Park's buildings, 750 acres, and a lake. Lederer still had 2,196 acres and Lake Tamiment to sell. In 1920, Lederer sold this remaining property to the Rand School of Social Science in New York City. The Rand School met Lederer's price of twenty-two thousand dollars by selling bonds to sympathizers and by borrowing from banks, one of which was the Stroudsburg Trust Company. Camp Tamiment was created from this second purchase.[11]

Unity House

Locals 22 and 25 of the I.L.G.W.U. built Unity House, a vacation resort for workers and their families. Like most locals in the New York City garment industry, these two consisted mostly of Jewish women imbued with the class consciousness of the period. They believed that humanity was divided into two warring groups: workers and bosses. This made it necessary for workers to stick together, even on days off. As a result, unions acted as social clubs—and at times even as chaperons who protected class virtue. Unions sponsored excursions, hikes, dances, and visits to museums and theaters. By combining social betterment with summer recreation, "unity houses" became the latest expression of this nurturing side of unions. From 1918 to 1920, four garment workers' locals ran unity houses, but only the Pocono Unity House survived.[12]

The purchase of the Forest Park buildings was a coup, allowing the Dress and Waistmakers' Union to brag that workers could vacation in the summer home of millionaires. (Such concern for aping the rich suggests a note of envy, but that is another story.) From the start, a concerted effort was made to publicize the new resort in union circles. Although Unity House was a resort, the Dress and Waistmakers' local never lost sight of the mission to raise the political and intellectual consciousness of working people. Among the guest lecturers in 1923 were Will Durant, the philosopher, and Scott Nearing, the former professor whose radicalism led to his losing two teaching jobs and to his arrest during World War I.[13]

The activists of the Dress and Waistmakers' Union soon realized that they could not run a resort, having neither the expertise nor the money for essential repairs and expansion. In 1924, they sold Unity House to the "International," as the I.L.G.W.U. was often called. The I.L.G.W.U. quickly realized that Unity House needed refurbishing, opened its coffers, and hired an outsider as a full-time manager. To keep Unity House attendance in the family, the I.L.G.W.U. established a three-tier rate structure: its members paid eighteen dollars a week to stay at Unity House; members of other unions paid twenty-three dollars; outsiders paid twenty-six dollars a week. Although income usually did not cover operating expenses and depreciation, the International did not mind. As much as anything, Unity House was a union showcase. In a 1928 report, the General Executive Board of the International boasted that Unity House paid higher wages because its main purpose was not profit but showing "labor in its proper light."[14]

In some ways, Unity House was defined by its promotion. In the 1920s, it was well publicized in the Yiddish press. Unity House also sought to gain the attention of intellectuals by inviting Columbia University faculty. It sent complimentary tickets for its winter reunion at a Manhattan hotel to Harry Laidler of the League for Industrial Democracy and to Norman Thomas, Socialist candidate for President in 1928. Although these names were impressive, the leadership of the International knew that associating Unity House with prominent radicals would not, in itself, attract the rank and file. Union members wanted fun during their week's vacation. Even those Jewish workers who thrived on politics and the life of the intellect would seek simpler pleasures while vacationing. By the end of the decade, Unity House was offering sports, bowling, Ping-Pong, dramatics, and nightly dancing with a jazz orchestra: the usual pastimes of a modern vacation resort.[15]

Camp Tamiment

Camp Tamiment, it should be recalled, was built on the part of Forest Park that was not sold to the Dress and Waistmakers' Union. It had much the same mix—a Jewish clientele, political awareness, and intellectual stimulation—but it also hosted younger guests who, as time went on, became increasingly middle-class. Another difference from Unity House was the absence of children. Tamiment was an adult camp, a popular fad of the 1920s, when twentysomethings discovered the joys of playing in mixed-sex situations. Adult camps were especially liberating for women, since mothers stayed home. In this unchaperoned environment, young women were free to frolic, although they had to live in

FIG. 51

"Appreciation of Art" lecture, Unity House, 1925. Were the kitchen workers at the top right also interested in art, or did they merely want to be included in the picture? UNITE Archives, Kheel Center, Cornell University.

separate quarters from the men and abide by the prevailing rules of decorum. Nonetheless, by the standards of the times, adult camps were progressive. They hinted at forbidden pleasures.[16]

The origins of Camp Tamiment lay in the Rand School of Social Science, a socialist school for workers on New York City's Fifteenth Street. Since the school did not offer summer courses, some of its administrators dreamed of a summer retreat for faculty, students, and friends. This notion had the firm support of the Rand School's executive director, Bertha Mailly. Mailly was a New England Yankee, and she stood out in the New York socialist milieu, which was heavily Jewish. Mailly's mere presence suggested that the Rand School and its offspring, Tamiment, were at least notionally non-sectarian and multicultural.[17]

When Mailly learned that the Dress and Waistmakers' Union could not afford the entire Forest Park property, she saw her chance. On September 28, 1920, she dug into her pocket and paid one

FIG. 52
Folk dancing at Unity House. Resorts usually hosted far more women than men, and if this scene is typical, Unity House had more than its share. UNITE Archives, Kheel Center, Cornell University.

thousand dollars as an option on the remainder of Forest Park. On December 28, the People's Educational Camp Society, Inc. (or PECS, as it was commonly called) was established as the operating corporation. PECS sent letters to professionals of radical views, especially doctors, asking them to buy its bonds. PECS neither issued stock nor paid interest on its bonds. Controlling Camp Tamiment was its sole purpose. The "members" of PECS, as its directors were called, had to have publicly subscribed to socialism for at least two years. In truth, they were well-off members of the middle class. Their socialism was born of sentiment, not poverty.[18]

Once the property was bought, everything had to be built from scratch, since Lederer had sold Forest Park's buildings to Unity House. To be ready for the 1921 summer season, construction had to begin immediately—and in the dead of winter of late 1920, then, "[r]oads needed to be hacked through the wilderness, there were buildings and shelters to erect, furnishings and bedding to acquire, plumbing and kitchen equipment to install, food and water to provide." This was easier said than done. New Yorkers had street smarts. They could find their way through a city maze with all the confidence of a forest ranger in the wilderness; they could instantly size up a dark street, or even a corner, and know whether to avoid it. But they knew nothing about construction. In the words of Ben Josephson, who would eventually become the manager of Camp Tamiment, "[we] could not tell an oak tree from pickled herring." Bertha Mailly's solution was to call in Alexander (Sandy) Hayman, another New England Yankee, who was a carpenter and woodsman. She gave him the job of cutting timber, erecting buildings, laying out roads, and so on.[19]

Camp Tamiment opened on July 1, 1921. It had 30 guests the first week and 285 guests over Labor Day. The place reeked of socialist humility. In its first year, Tamiment used surplus army bedding, cots, and stoves. Guests sat on long benches and ate family style at tables without linen. Only the kitchen building had walls; the rest of the buildings had only ceilings, from which canvas flaps were dropped to keep out the rain. Although these modest facilities invited disaster, Camp Tamiment was a financial success, earning an operating profit the first year. After 1923 it was self-sustaining, and the PECS board stopped soliciting donations.[20]

Although the Rand School originally intended to have only an adult camp, it quickly established a bungalow colony named "Sandyville" on the same grounds. In 1922, Sandyville consisted of twenty bungalows and a children's playground. Although the Sandyville adults could use Camp Tamiment's facilities, children were not allowed in. It was said that Sandyville became a haven for socialists who had families, money, and a yen for intellectual stimulation.[21]

Tamiment received a mixed reception from its neighbors. In the first months, when Hayman and the New Yorkers were erecting the buildings, the owner of a nearby resort refused to house them and persisted in her haughtiness for years afterward, never referring to Tamiment by name, only to "the people who have this place up on the hill." However, money can break down all sorts of barriers. Ben Josephson recalled Tamiment's first account with a lumberyard: "We told the owner that there were three reasons why he would not do business with us: (1) we're New Yorkers; (2) radical New Yorkers; (3) and we're Jewish." The lumberyard man said, "No problem." On the other hand, buying dynamite was not so simple. When Sandy Hayman went to Stroudsburg to buy blasting material to pull up tree stumps, he was refused. The store owner "suspected we were reds and that we were using it for blowing up the town or something. It took some effort to change his mind."[22]

Despite the fears of Tamiment's neighbors, the camp was not a home for urban bomb throwers who were planning to destroy the Poconos. The Rand School people were very much opposed to communism and anarchism. Although the first summer of operation was marked by political lectures (often given outdoors, weather permitting), political subjects were progressively downplayed. Indeed, the reality of running a business faced the camp's managers during the first summer. The waiters demanded a day off each week, and the camp's business manager reported a "constant clash with the help." He suggested to PECS that Tamiment be run as an actual business instead of a socialist experiment.[23]

Both Mailly and Josephson agreed, realizing that a scruffy, proletarian camp would die. They wanted to turn Tamiment into a regular resort, but the PECS board preferred the original vision of a country summer school. The PECS board disapproved of dancing and similar frivolities, which they saw as distractions from the Rand School's mission. The PECS people lost out, however. In 1926, the former owner of a Catskill hotel was hired. He brightened Tamiment by bringing in linen tablecloths and napkins on tables, uniforms on waiters, and a new cook who specialized in Jewish foods. Camp Tamiment became middle-class, with students and alumni of New York University and City College of New York increasingly seen. By the end of the decade, nonpolitical topics such as art, music, and literature dominated the lectures. Swimming, tennis, and calisthenics attracted the largest audiences.[24]

Along the way, Mailly and Josephson injected Camp Tamiment with a new purpose. Aside from turning it into a resort, they also made it a source of money for the Rand School. In other words, Camp Tamiment would not serve the Rand School as a socialist Chautauqua, but as a cash cow. Camp Tamiment made a contribution to the Rand School every year during the 1920s—even in the three years when the profit margin was thin or nonexistent. By 1927, Tamiment had contributed $24,621.[25] Once Tamiment became a money-making resort, it also became a paradox. Ostensibly an institution devoted to the undermining of capitalism, it sought to make money in the best capitalist tradition. If John D. Rockefeller knew of Tamiment, he would have smiled with approval. But from his perch in the great beyond, Karl Marx would have frowned.

The Italians

Before 1918, the mountain village of Canadensis contained two small Italian boardinghouses, the Belvidere and the Villa Brentini. In 1918, the Italian-Swiss owner of the Villa Brentini tired of the resort business. He sold the Villa Brentini to Anthony Comazzi and his wife, Caterina, who wanted to leave New York City to escape the Spanish influenza. Like many owners of small resorts, the Comazzis had their version of the American dream. They ran the Villa Brentini as a family business. Mother and the three children did the chores, while dad cooked, having worked as a chef in New York City. His specialty was northern Italian dishes such as polenta, risotto, and gnocchi. During Prohibition, Comazzi

FIG. 53
Sandyville was the bungalow colony at Camp Tamiment. The bungalows without walls in this photograph were typical of Camp Tamiment's original buildings. Vacationers at Camp Tamiment had extra reason to hope that it would not rain. Tamiment Institute Library, New York University. Photograph by N. T. McClennon.

made his own wine and served it to guests. In the 1930s, the Italian consuls from Philadelphia and San Francisco stayed at the Villa, as did Vincente Minnelli, the Hollywood director and future husband of actress Judy Garland. Another prominent guest was boxer Primo Carnera, heavyweight champion in 1933–34; he is recalled as a big man who spoke little English, but loved to eat Italian.[26]

William and Bridget Giannini also stayed at the Villa Brentini. They liked the area so much that they opened their own resort, the William Inn. As always, an Italian place had to serve Italian food. William Giannini, who was of Italian-Swiss background, was an excellent cook. Unfortunately, he could not offer a real Italian meal, for he could not openly serve wine during Prohibition. The solution at the William Inn was stored in the third floor bedroom: the floorboards could be lifted, creating an ample hiding space.[27]

For some reason, this handful of Italian resorts was located in Barrett Township. There are no signs of a "plot" to have the Italians contained. The Comazzis' daughter, Clotilda, recalls that when her parents moved in, a local shopkeeper helped them by extending credit during the early lean years. The Italian resorts were near each other probably because people with similar backgrounds like to congregate.

Lutherans in the Poconos

Two Lutheran resorts, Lutherland and the Paradise Falls Lutheran Association, opened in the 1920s. Although most Lutherans in the Middle Atlantic states derived from German stock, Lutherland and

FIG. 54
An indoor race at Camp Tamiment. No "den mothers" at this camp for adults! The photograph is undated, but the clothes and the hairstyles are very 1920s modern. Tamiment Institute Library, New York University.

the Paradise Falls Lutheran Association were perceived as being religious instead of ethnic. German Americans may have endured suspicion during World War I, but they were far more assimilated than Italian Americans and Jews.

Paradise Falls Lutheran Association originated with Raymond Raff, a Philadelphia builder. Driven by poor health to the fresh air of the Poconos, he bought a farm in Henryville and called it the Abend Ruhe Farm. Once his health was restored, he became so enthusiastic about the Poconos that he offered his farm to the Lutheran Church as the nucleus of a resort. On October 17, 1922, a group of Lutherans from New York, Easton, and Philadelphia met with Raff and created the Paradise Falls Lutheran Association.

Rev. George Ammon recalls: "The publicity for the early operation of Paradise Falls was entirely within the confines of the Lutheran Church—through the national magazine, pamphlets, letters. There was a promotional 16-mm silent movie that was shown at the churches to drum up trade." Three cottages were erected in 1924, and others followed. By 1928, Lutherans had bought five hundred acres, including a half-mile of Paradise Creek. Unlike the Quaker Inn at Buck Hill Falls, the Paradise Falls Lutheran Association never sold cottage lots to outsiders, because it could rely on the rather large Lutheran community to buy them. Paradise Falls Lutherans also deviated from the Quaker model by not having a golf course.[28]

Lutherland, the other Lutheran resort, was created by a different branch of the Lutheran community. Whereas members of the United Lutheran Church built Paradise Falls, Lutherland was the work of Missouri Synod Lutherans—and it was a larger, more ambitious project. Lutherland started life as a children's camp, when a group of Lutheran ministers decided to provide young Lutherans with Christian vacations. A committee headed by Rev. Herbert H. Gallman and Henry Dahlen spent three years searching the eastern United States for a suitable site. They had good luck: the Pocono Pines Assembly declared bankruptcy after World War I, and its property included a casino, a hotel, and some thirty buildings in all. It had been vacant for two years before being purchased by the Missouri Synod Lutherans.[29]

Lutherland opened on July 5, 1926. Nearly two thousand Lutherans from New York City were present at the dedication ceremony. The fancy start set the tone for the rest of the 1920s. Everything at Lutherland seemed to be on a grand scale. To begin, there was Henry Dahlen himself, the president of Lutherland, or the Lutheran Conference and Camp Association, as it was officially called. Dahlen was no ordinary layman. He was a construction magnate who erected Woolworth stores as well as factories and commercial buildings. Originally from Minnesota, he was now based in New York City.[30]

The children's camp was only the beginning for Lutherland. Special trains from New York City brought in thousands of vacationers. Many were impressed—so much so that they bought fourteen hundred building lots, each 51 by 150 feet. In April 1929, Dahlen's annual report boasted that Lutherland was one of the largest camps of its kind, combining the original buildings with a large new hotel, a children's playground, and a playhouse. The damming of a creek had created the ninety-acre Lake Tamaque. In July of the same year, nearly twelve thousand guests visited Lutherland; in the following month, fourteen thousand visitors came, creating a success that could only lead to greater ambition. By the end of the year, plans were being laid for a dining room that would accommodate one thousand and for a dormitory that would house five hundred guests.[31]

Along with this physical expansion, attention was given to the spiritual life. Professor Walter Meier, a prominent educator and future host of radio's "Lutheran Hour," ran the religious program. An old drawing of a projected church for Lutherland suggests piety and imagination. The church, designed in the shape of a cross, had a glass roof so that airplanes flying overhead at night would see a crossed light that was a religious beacon. Whether this church was seriously planned or only a fantasy is not known.

In any case, the Great Depression was imminent. The enthusiasm so evident in the Lutherland of the 1920s would be severely tested.[32]

The Lutheran resorts, like the Italian and Jewish vacation spots, were business ventures. Other purposes are discernible as well, such as the reinforcing of ethnic, religious, or political ties. But upon careful examination, yet another agenda emerges, one that many of the promoters and guests may have followed unwittingly. The presence of ethnic resorts proclaimed the foreign-born and their children to be "American." Jews who went to Unity House and Camp Tamiment were doing the American thing—taking a vacation in the very American climate of the Poconos. Religious resorts had a somewhat similar function. They were a means by which various minorities would find approval or acceptance within the mainstream of American society. At Lutherland, this stealth operation was in full swing. During the xenophobia of the First World War, the Americanism of German American Lutherans had been called into question. At Lutherland, Lutherans affirmed their American identities by staging pageants with colonial themes. By wearing period dress and re-creating scenes from the American past, Lutherans not only had fun by dressing up, but they also assured the majority community (and themselves) that German Americans were safe. The colonial pageants made the Lutherland crowd as American as apple pie.

Methodists on a Roll

In the long run, what made ethnic groups "different" was not so much their names and foodways as their customs. During the process of Americanization, these customs would not necessarily be abandoned, though. Instead of completely disappearing, foreign traditions might enter the American mainstream, forever changing the flavor and appearance—if not the very substance—of "Americanism." Ethnics drank wine and beer, danced at weddings and parties, and saw no harm in card playing. With the exception of Lutheran Germans and Norwegians, they were not even Protestant. If ethnics ended up playing a stronger role in American life, their lifestyles might reinforce the tendency of many native-born Protestants to indulge in allegedly bad habits, thereby making booze, gambling, and dancing part of the mainstream.

The old-stock Americans in the Poconos who worried most about bad habits were Methodists. Publicly, Methodists never mentioned ethnics, reserving their ire for those "real" Americans—traitors, as it were—who had been seduced into dancing, gambling, and drinking. Yet the susceptibility of many Pocono Methodists to the 1920s version of the Ku Klux Klan suggests that their social activism contained a heavy dose of nativism. Methodists had an expansive view of sin. Methodist preachers regularly ranted against tobacco, gambling, and theater, and they had a special hatred for liquor. In the immediate postwar years, Methodists and their Presbyterian allies seemed like winners. After a long campaign for prohibition, they had the satisfaction of seeing the Eighteenth Amendment become part of the Constitution on January 16, 1919. The Volstead Act, passed later in the year, made illegal the sale of a beverage that contained more than one-half of 1 percent of alcohol.[33]

Having beaten the forces of demon rum, the Pocono Methodists were on the offensive in the immediate postwar years. All around, they saw sin waiting to be conquered. Stroudsburg's Methodist pastor preached a sermon in which he decried carnival gambling and billboards that lasciviously displayed the female form. He also denounced theater, a traditional Methodist target. But he paid special attention to dancing, which more than anything else made Methodist clergy see the hand of Satan.[34] Preachers could not help but know that dancing was a major attraction of the resorts. Although Pocono preachers directed their sermons at the local population and never mentioned vacationers, attacks on dancing were an indirect attack on resorts. Resorts and the churches occupied two separate worlds—but they still ran the risk of colliding.

The pointed attacks on dancing had started before the War. On April 23, 1914, the *Daily Record* reported that Rev. William Aiker of the Billy Sunday evangelist organization had spoken at the Stroudsburg Presbyterian Church and had condemned card playing, alcohol, dancing, and other evils. In the succeeding issues, the *Daily Record* reported on the latest dances, especially the tango, the sexy rage from Argentina. It gave instructions on movements and steps, even printing pictures of tango dancers. On May 4, the newspaper reported that Rev. Aiker was back, giving a "Solar Plexus to Modern Dance." Aiker should have punched harder. The same issue of the *Daily Record* reported that the owner of the Cataract House had hired a dancing master to teach the tango and other modern dances.[35]

In the summer of 1919, the borough of Stroudsburg organized a series of block dances. In the horse-and-buggy age, the block dances would have attracted only residents of the Stroudsburg area. But the automobile had ended the old isolation. At the first dance in July, thousands came from all over the county and from the resorts; the Gap hotels sent large delegations. Dozens of hay rides made the block dance their final destination. The streets had three hundred lights, and more than half of these were covered with Japanese lanterns.[36]

Public dancing was a gauntlet laid down to the Methodist clergy, and they accepted the challenge. In August 1919, before a congregation of 500, Rev. G. W. Sheetz flayed the block dances. The minister reminded his flock that the Hebrews had danced before the golden calf and that Salome had danced for the head of John the Baptist. Dancing, he insisted, led to sins of the flesh. The block dances continued for the rest of the summer, though. Thousands were present at the last dance of the season. According to the *Morning Press,* little tots danced and elderly people danced. At one point, 310 couples were dancing. The Rev. Sheetz was a major topic of discussion. Mayor Edinger remarked: "I can't seem to find any harm in this." Russell Hughes, editor of the *Morning Press,* wrote: "We went over and saw the Stroudsburgers go to hell last night. A nice time was had by all."[37] In the following summers, the borough of Stroudsburg again sponsored block dances and the Methodist clergy continued to fulminate. In August 1921, a block dance had a masquerade theme. Some 128 dancers in full costume participated in the grand march and competed for prizes.

In a letter to the *Morning Press,* the Rev. W. J. Crider added the evils of urban life to the usual sins of drunkenness, gambling, and dancing. As if to prove him right, a few weeks afterward, the newspaper confirmed the good reverend's assessment of city people. At a dancing pavilion, a brazen hussy from New York City was courting hellfire. She won first prize with a "daring costume," which was a "very Hawaiian, Hawaiian costume."[38]

The Methodist agitation in Stroudsburg may have been responsible for the raid on Katherine Rogers's whorehouse. Known as the "Island," it was located off lower Main Street in the marshes near Brodhead's Creek. In a small town like Stroudsburg, everyone must have known of its existence, especially since it had been in operation for some thirty years. But it was not closed until 1922, after repeated protests to the State Board of Health. There is the story about a band of young musicians who stopped at the "Island" after a gig. Not trusting their instruments in the car, they took them in. A band member saw a piano and started playing. That got the girls going. They started dancing with each other and with some of the men who were there. The entire band was soon playing. The madam came storming in and yelled: "This is a whore house, not a dance hall!"[39]

Rail as they might at dancing and sin, the Methodist clergy would lose these battles, just as they would lose with alcohol. Prohibition turned out to be a hollow victory. As early as July 1919, an illicit still was discovered a few miles from Stroudsburg. The *Morning Press* reported the rumor that a "foreigner" was selling illegal beer. The following month, the newspaper was surprised that intoxicated men were seen on Main Street. It wondered about the source of the liquor. In 1921, the *East Stroudsburg Press and the Jeffersonian* answered that question when it reported that alcohol was coming into Monroe County in high-priced automobiles, from Scranton in suitcases, and from Easton in trucks.[40]

Methodists had lost the 1920s version of the culture war. There was nothing left but to protest and scream. Some expressed their rage by joining the Ku Klux Klan, which had a significant following in the Poconos. This was the national Klan, founded in 1915, that hit its stride in the 1920s. Whereas the original Klan of the years following the Civil War was a southern phenomenon that directed its fury toward African Americans, the Klan of the 1920s was also popular in the northern states, especially in rural areas. The northern Klan, more often than not, aimed its venom at Catholics, Jews, immigrants, and big cities. It was said to be a protest against an America in which small-town Protestants were losing influence. The Klan was, so to speak, the last gasp of the rural WASP.[41]

The Ku Klux Klan was especially prominent in Pike County. In March 1924, forty-five Klansmen in full robes attended services at the Matamoras Methodist church. Their arrival was expected; pews were reserved. Only the leader took off his hood, and he was a stranger, allegedly from Philadelphia. The Klansmen came by auto and left by auto, disappearing into anonymity. A week later, Klansmen attended the Milford Methodist church. Said to be members of the local Milford chapter, they gave fifty dollars to the pastor, whose "sermon gave the Klan a good recommendation." The *Milford Dispatch* gave few other details, aside from noting that the sermon dealt with "Americanism"—a euphemism for wishing that big cities like New York and all its foreign-born inhabitants with strange names would disappear.[42]

The Klan's presence in Milford may have been partially motivated by the heavy summer presence of Syrians from New York City. The Syrian vacationers, though white, were as foreign as could be. They had strange names like Zaloom and Macksoud; they ate exotic foods such as stuffed grape leaves, creating a demand in Milford for lamb and Middle Eastern vegetables. Their children were pre-cocious city kids—at a time when "city" meant sophistication more than violence and drugs. Young Syrians often won community tennis and swimming matches in Milford. And most galling of all, their parents had money (made by importing rugs and other strange goods from distant lands). Klansmen would believe that America had failed when honest folk whose ancestors had fought with Washington and Grant were scrounging for a living while foreigners with swarthy skins who spoke accented English were buying nice houses and staying at fancy resorts.[43]

In a normal world, grown men who disguise themselves in sheets as if it were Halloween might be accused of drinking to excess. In the case of the Pocono Klan, however, drinking was unlikely: Klan members very much favored Prohibition. In April 1924, the Klan burned a cross on a high promontory overlooking Bushkill after hearing rumors of an illicit whiskey still. Placards with skulls and crossbones warned bootleggers. Although the press did not mention it, bootlegging may not have been the only reason for the Klan's eruption in Bushkill. Jewish resorts had opened in the area as well.[44]

Like Pike County, neighboring Monroe County was also a hotbed of nativism. The most famous politician in Monroe County's history was A. Mitchell Palmer. As President Wilson's Attorney General, Palmer was responsible for deporting countless aliens during the Red Scare of 1919. Compared with the Klan in Pike County, however, less is known of Monroe County's Klan. Newspapers in Monroe County paid less attention to their chapter of the Klan, regarding it as an embarrassment. Nonetheless, in 1922, an East Stroudsburg newspaper reported the visit of a Klan organizer, who took recruits to "a secluded spot" for ceremonies.[45]

Ida Jolley and her Jewish parents had recently moved to the Poconos. She recalls that the Klan burned crosses in East Stroudsburg on the hill near the site of today's Catholic church. The silk mill was nearby, and it had a Jewish manager. He left town. As a child, Ida had once sneaked into a theater that was having a private function. She had stumbled into a Klan meeting. Some of the Klansmen removed their hoods, and she was shocked to see "friends" of her Jewish parents. In 1920, Ida's father had opened a Jewish bakery in East Stroudsburg. Among his biggest customers were the newly opened Jewish resorts. The local American bakery did not use poppy seeds and caraway seeds on its rolls and bread. In fact, no one in the Poconos had even seen poppy seeds. Remembering the time that her father displayed rolls with seeds on the crust, Ida remarked, "the Gentiles thought it was dirt." They called the Health Department, and Ida's father had some explaining to do.[46]

The Ku Klux Klan soon disappeared. On the national level, it was beset with scandals. In the Poconos, it was ineffective. Unless the press was ignoring Klan violence, the Pocono Klan was essentially an exercise in posturing, grown men talking tough but unwilling to cross the line into violence. After all, Klansmen in the Poconos were Methodists, not hoodlums.

Klansmen were not the only vocal supporters of Prohibition. The Law Observance League sought to strengthen the enforcement of liquor laws in Monroe County. In 1924, it issued *The Monroe Citizen,* an angry periodical that accused the police of corruption and railed against moral decline. One issue claimed that white women in Stroudsburg were seen in the streets, looking for black men. Little is known of this risqué side of Pocono society, although a police raid on a speakeasy gives food for thought. The proprietress was black. According to the police report, she ran an operation that was "high, wide and handsome"—whatever that meant.[47]

The raid took place in 1932. In the following year, Prohibition would be repealed, and speakeasies would be history. Besides, the Great Depression had started. The main item of public debate in the Poconos and elsewhere had become the economy. "Americanism" was discussed less frequently, but the issue was not dead. In the early 1930s, when a newspaper editor from Stroudsburg returned from New York City, he complained of seeing many aliens who reeked of garlic.[48]

8

Laurel Blossom Time
Surviving the Great Depression

"May you live in interesting times" is a Chinese curse. The 1930s were indeed interesting times. The Great Depression ruined the lives of millions of Americans. Many lost their savings when the stock market collapsed and banks failed; many more lost their jobs. The more unfortunate had to swallow their pride and ask for charity. Americans of all classes hoped for good times to return, waiting for factories and offices to reopen and to rehire. Throughout the 1930s, they waited—and they waited in vain. Businessmen had no cure for the sick economy. Neither did President Herbert Hoover, nor did his successor, Franklin Delano Roosevelt, for all his good intentions and energy. Not until the Second World War did the economy revive and Americans again enjoy prosperity.

People economize when incomes fall. They make food their last sacrifice and luxuries their first. A vacation is a luxury. The Pocono vacation industry would have a rough time in the 1930s, but it survived. Forced to compete harder, some resorts did more than survive. They grew while weak resorts perished.

Slipping and Sliding into the Abyss of 1932–33

In the months after the stock market crash of October 1929, the looming retrenchment in the vacation business was not apparent. No one realized that the Great Depression was starting. The optimistic could believe that the stock market was experiencing rough corrections. Besides, by the summer of 1930, the Great Depression had not yet affected the upper class. Aside from few executives having lost their jobs, dividends remained intact, a sign of reassurance for the possessing classes. Economists continued to assure the public that the good times of the 1920s would continue.[1]

Vacationers still came to the Poconos. If the press can be believed, more came in 1930 than in 1929. During the Memorial Day weekend, local restaurants and hotels broke the records of the previous two years. The Lackawanna Railroad claimed that its Memorial Day traffic broke a three-year record. There was more good news during the Fourth of July holiday. Pocono Manor, Skytop, and Lutherland claimed increased business over the previous year. Buck Hill had a fabulous season, earning the highest profit of its nearly thirty-year existence.[2]

If anything pointed to optimism in the Pocono resort industry, it was an announcement made in June 1930. Wealthy investors from New York and Philadelphia were planning to erect a new hotel on the site of the old Montanesca Hotel in Mount Pocono. According to its promoters, the proposed Pocono Towers Hotel would have three hundred rooms and would cater to weekend motorists and to motorists who traveled short distances. The hotel would have an eighteen-hole golf course, twenty-five cottages, and a swimming pool, but it was never built. A motel before its time, it was, like television, a stillborn innovation—a casualty of the Great Depression.[3]

Despite the optimism of the well-to-do in mid-1930, the working class was already feeling the ravages of the Depression. Both in the nation and in the Poconos, factories had started closing in 1930. By June, the silk mill in East Stroudsburg and other businesses had closed. According to the 1930 census, Monroe County had 447 people who were jobless and looking for work.[4]

Although President Hoover insisted that prosperity was returning, the national economy continued to decline. From 1929 to 1932, the amount of money paid in salaries dropped by 40 percent, dividends by 56.6 percent, wages by 60 percent. Meanwhile, beginning in September 1931, banks started closing, and in March 1933 the banking system of the United States was near collapse. The day was long gone when the Depression affected only working people. The middle and upper classes lost their savings when banks failed, lost their jobs when the economy shriveled, and lost their discretionary income when stock dividends shrank. The vacation crowd had less money.[5]

For the Pocono resorts, the Memorial Day weekend of 1931 was a disappointment when the anticipated crowds did not come. Nonetheless, the rest of the 1931 season could have been worse. Both Tamiment and Buck Hill had less business than in 1930, but they still managed to turn a profit. By the end of August, the *Daily Record* was asserting a moral victory of sorts, insisting that Monroe County had escaped the worst of the Depression. As proof, it noted that Main Street in Stroudsburg had fewer than a half-dozen vacant stores. Where else, it asked, could this be seen? The *Daily Record* insisted that the resort season had been "fairly good." But its claim that "some" hotels had had a better season than in the previous year suggests that most had suffered. Pocono Manor was showing signs of desperation. In 1931, the Pocono Manor Association dropped the requirement that only Quakers could own shares of the stock and serve as managers and directors. During the winter of 1931–32, Pocono Manor closed its main building, which had stayed open in previous winters.[6]

Innkeepers and merchants were clearly worried. As if denying reality, they placed an ad in the *Daily Record* of October 13 that proclaimed: "Listen to the cheerful tones of Good Old Monroe County." Skytop, Lutherland, and Monomonoch all claimed that their 1931 season had surpassed that of 1930. No other resort made this boast, which belied the ad's bravado. That the ad appeared in October, after summer visitors had gone home, indicated that its purpose was to lift local morale.

The national economy continued to sink, reaching rock bottom in the summer of 1932. Signs of stress were likewise seen in the Poconos. In February 1932, Monroe County started a project to have resorts hire local labor. In the past, the resorts had been unable to find enough temporary help in the Poconos and had imported most of their summer workers. But with the closing of the silk mills and with the local economy shrinking, the local labor pool was now overflowing. It was expected that some two hundred of the unemployed would sign up for a new program of classes on hotel service taught in the local high schools by home economics teachers and hotel managers. Instead, nearly six hundred signed up, of which over half found jobs that summer. The opening of the resorts could not have come at a better time. According to the Pennsylvania Department of Labor and Industry, on the eve of the summer of 1932, 25 percent of Monroe County's working population was unemployed. In Pike County, 21 percent was unemployed.[7]

The 1932 season began well, with resorts doing good business on Memorial Day, the traditional start of the summer. The *Daily Record* reported a big gain compared with the previous Memorial Day. Tamiment had a great Memorial Day and had to turn away hundreds of visitors. The *Daily Record* continued its upbeat tone throughout the summer, at one point quoting a hotel manager who claimed that there was no such thing "as a Depression" in the Poconos. The Poconos did have a good Labor Day as well. The *Daily Record* noted that "scores of hotels" had turned away guests for the first time in the season. Here was an admission that resorts had not been full in July and August.[8]

The woes of three large resorts, though, tell the real story—the story ignored by the local press. According to Buck Hill's annual report, patronage fell by 20 percent in 1932. Rate reductions and an inability to lower expenses by the same proportion caused income to fall sharply. When the Inn suffered a deficit, Charles Thompson, the manager, was quick to react. In August, even before the season ended, he announced a 25 percent cut in salaries and wages. Edward Jenkins, who had recently been hired as advertising manager, later recalled being given the additional post of front office manager and having to skip a December paycheck.

Camp Tamiment and Unity House had rotten seasons in 1932 (despite Tamiment's remarkably successful Memorial Day that year). Camp Tamiment had steadily attracted fewer guests since 1929, and like Buck Hill, it reduced its rates, hoping to stop the decline. But nothing seemed to work in the summer of 1932, the low point of the Great Depression. The number of guest days fell by three thousand, forcing Tamiment to end the year in the red—the only time it did so in the 1930s. Unity House, Tamiment's neighbor, appeared desperate. Throwing caution and political solidarity to the winds, it made a clumsy attempt to steal Tamiment's bungalow renters.[9]

On July 8, 1932, J. Halperin, the Unity House manager, sent an alarming letter to David Dubinsky, the president of the I.L.G.W.U. Halperin revealed that Unity House was not only attracting fewer guests but also having to cope with the fear and paranoia in the Pocono business community. In what completely contradicted the public cheerfulness of the press, Halperin wrote that suppliers no longer waited for payment; they wanted to see their money up front. He begged for five thousand dollars "to eliminate any immediate attempts at collection." He added that he could not come to union headquarters in New York to plead his case because his "absence might cause suspicion" among local creditors. Unity House stayed afloat, but when the season ended, it owed ten thousand dollars in back wages to its employees.[10]

Although the press tried to be cheerful about Monroe County, it did not even try with Pike County, always the poorer of the two counties of Pocono vacationland. The 1932 summer season started badly, with boardinghouses, hotels, and bungalows unfilled. To add insult to injury, private homeowners in Pike County tried to make ends meet by taking in summer boarders. By July 1932, this competition caused hotels and boardinghouses to complain and led to a proposal to tax private residences that took in boarders. Although business picked up at the end of summer, Pike County had its worst season on record. The Chamber of Commerce lost 90 percent of its hotel and board-inghouse members, and it collapsed.[11]

The Monroe County Chamber of Commerce was also troubled. On September 8, 1932, W. L. Caley, its secretary, resigned. The Chamber of Commerce could not pay his salary because it was broke. At the beginning of 1933 it was still broke, having over two thousand dollars of unfilled pledges. The Chamber was not alone in having unpaid obligations. During the 1932–33 fiscal year, unpaid taxes in Monroe County increased by 50 percent. Times were tough, but the Chamber of Commerce in Monroe County managed to survive.[12]

Bad news seemed pandemic in 1932. Two banks merged to avoid embarrassment. They were the Security Trust Company and the Stroudsburg Trust Company, which combined to become the Stroudsburg Security Trust Company. Although the *Daily Record* claimed that they merged to give better service, the real reason was that the Stroudsburg Trust Company was in a precarious condition. Even the new bank was troubled. In October 1933, Harvey Huffman, who represented Monroe and Pike Counties in the Pennsylvania Senate, wrote to David Dubinsky of the I.L.G.W.U. Noting that the Stroudsburg Security Trust Company carried the mortgage on the Unity House property, he suggested a deposit of fifteen thousand dollars. "This would be very much appreciated." Senator Huffman did not explain why the bank needed the money. Everyone knew that cash-starved banks were collapsing throughout the nation. Within a week, Dubinsky replied that his union would deposit an initial ten thousand dollars in the Stroudsburg Security Trust Company. The bank survived.[13]

As 1932 wound down, jobs seemed to disappear in the Poconos. In Monroe County, the chairman of the Relief Board stated in December that unemployment was worse than in previous years. In January 1933, the Relief Board reported that twenty-eight hundred residents of Monroe County (about 10 percent of the population) were receiving public assistance. This dramatic increase in unemployment strained public resources, with the result that payments for relief, as public assistance was then called, were cut by 20 percent.[14]

During the winter of 1932–33, thirty resorts stayed open. Their owners were not necessarily committed to winter sports; they were only hoping that marginal business would pay for the overhead. In the case of Jeanac Farms near Cresco, Jean Haley recalls that her parents stayed open because they could no longer afford to live in Philadelphia during the winter. They moved to their resort and enrolled their children in the local schools.[15]

Around the nation, some believed that the American system was dead and that radical change was necessary. Most Americans disagreed, feeling that the best solution was something very traditional—

a change of presidents. Franklin Delano Roosevelt defeated Herbert Hoover by a landslide in the 1932 election, a victory for the former that meant more than a change of political parties and a new face. Unlike the dour Hoover, who seemed perplexed and pained by the Depression, Roosevelt projected a strong image. His voice and smile radiated the confidence that Americans wanted to see in a leader. Roosevelt set the right tone in his inaugural address, when he assured Americans that their only fear was "fear itself." At first, Roosevelt seemed to have a magic touch, for the economy rebounded. The Federal Reserve Board's Adjusted Index of Industrial Production had been 59 in March 1933, when Hoover left office. In April, the Index jumped to 66; in May, to 78; in June, to 91; and in July, to 100. The 1929 high of 125 seemed within reach.[16]

On May 15, 1933, the *Daily Record* reported good news. People were smiling again in the Poconos. The general feeling of hopelessness was gone, with merchants, manufacturers, innkeepers, and workers climbing out of the doldrums. In July, the newspaper reported that Independence Day business had increased, compared with the previous year's commerce. In August, it reported fewer persons on relief. The big resorts shared in this good news. At the end of the season, Tamiment boasted a 43 percent increase in guest days and showed a profit. Buck Hill was also in the black. Its profit was the smallest in six years, but no one complained.[17]

Unfortunately, the Great Depression was not over. In August 1933, the Federal Reserve Index of Industrial Production sank to 91, and it continued to sink, falling to 84 in September, to 76 in October, and to 72 in November. Two-thirds of the growth achieved in the spring had been lost. The sad truth emerged. The first months of the Roosevelt administration had been a honeymoon, an unreal time of exhilaration. The reality of the 1930s would be an economy that would never reach the golden levels of 1929.[18]

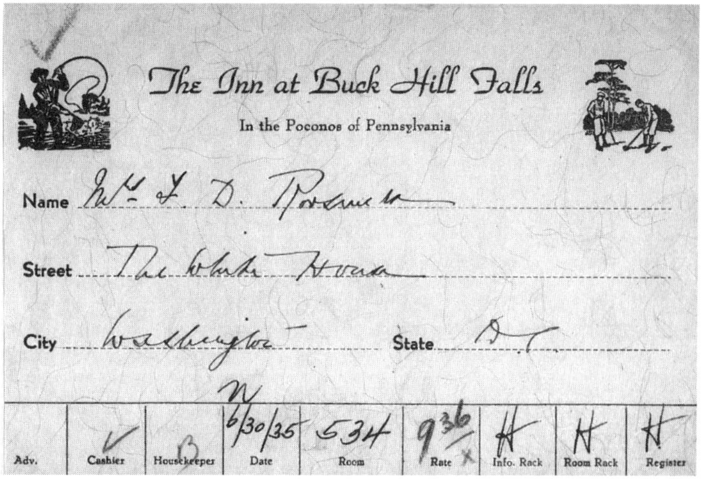
The Inn at Buck Hill Falls
In the Poconos of Pennsylvania
Name
Street
City
State
6/30/35
534
Adv.
Cashier
Housekeeper
Date
Room
Rate
Info. Rack
Room Rack
Register

FIG. 55
On June 30, 1935, First Lady Eleanor Roosevelt signed in at Buck Hill. She had come to address a conference that was explaining a New Deal program to resettle the homeless. That evening, she sat in the lounge, knitting and signing autographs. It was understood that no one would discuss politics. Buck Hill Collection, Barrett Friendly Library.

FIG. 56

This Maryland family visited Skytop Lodge in the summer of 1934. The automobile is a Pierce Arrow Silver Arrow. Skytop Collection.

The Blue Laws: Going but Not Gone

With the federal government unable to end the Great Depression, each community tried to help. In the Poconos, most people believed that they could weaken the Great Depression by abolishing Pennsylvania's blue laws, which were over a century old. The blue laws were seen as hostile to the Pocono economy because they criminalized recreation and behavior that was permissible in neighboring New York and New Jersey.

That blue laws were bad for business became very clear in 1930, when the East Stroudsburg chief of police arrested four young ladies from nearby camps. Their crime was violating a borough ordinance against wearing "indecent" clothes. The press did not explain the nature of the "indecency," only that camp shorts and blouses had been worn. Presumably, the clothes were too tight or too revealing. The publicity frightened city vacationers at nearby resorts and camps, who then stayed out of town. Complaining of lost business, local merchants met with the mayor of East Stroudsburg and the president of the borough council. Very quickly, ads appeared in a local newspaper, assuring summer visitors that camp clothes were permissible, provided that they were worn as "intended by their makers."[19]

In the summer of 1930, when this incident took place, the Great Depression was only beginning. As the economy deteriorated, people became more than willing to sacrifice traditional standards. In the nation at large and in the Poconos, Prohibition, already under severe attack in the 1920s, became a Depression casualty. The legalization of alcohol was seen as a way to provide jobs and to increase tax revenues. In 1931, at the American Hotel Association's national convention, the Pennsylvania delegation forced a vote on Prohibition. The vice president of the Pennsylvania State Hotel Association was W. Von Broock, the owner of the Penn Stroud Hotel in Stroudsburg. According to innkeepers in the Poconos, hotels were losing thousands of dollars to bootleggers and to foreign steamship lines that sold liquor on their cruises. In February 1933, Congress voted to repeal the Eighteenth Amendment. Three-fourths of the states also voted for repeal, and by the end of the year, America was again wet. In both Monroe and Pike Counties, most voters favored repeal.[20]

Regardless of what Pocono voters felt, they had to obey Pennsylvania state law. Governor Gifford Pinchot was a straight arrow, whose lips, it was said, would touch neither tobacco nor alcohol. Faced with repeal, Pinchot fought a rearguard action, simultaneously allowing liquor and creating obstacles to its purchase. His liquor code, for instance, closed bars on Sunday—an act that had a severe impact on the Pocono resorts, which were heavily dependent on the weekend trade. Pocono resorts lost business to competitors in New York and New Jersey.[21]

Other blue laws dealt with the observance of the Sabbath. Throughout Pennsylvania, Sunday was a special day: movie theaters had to close, and sports could not be played for money. Sunday vacationers in the Poconos could neither go to the cinema nor watch a semi-professional baseball game. The Pennsylvania State Hotel Association wanted these blue laws abolished. Their opponents were the churchgoers, especially the Methodists. As with liquor, the churches lost the vote. In a statewide referendum in November 1933, Monroe and Pike Counties (along with the rest of the state) voted for Sunday sports. The Monroe County Chamber of Commerce lost no time printing a schedule of

Sunday games for 1934. But the Sunday lobby did win a partial victory. Movie theaters remained closed on Sundays until long after World War II. And professional baseball and football could be played only between the hours of 2 P.M. and 6 P.M.[22]

Their Finest Hour

In fighting the Depression, Monroe County was far more energetic than its northern neighbor, Pike County. Perhaps as a result of its frontier past, when rafters and lumberjacks had swilled and caroused in Milford, public life in Pike County had always had an anarchic streak. In contrast, the New York-based Lackawanna Railroad had shown Monroe County the advantages of organization. Whereas Monroe County had an active Chamber of Commerce, public-spirited citizens, and a press that sought to galvanize the community, little communal effort—aside from opposing the blue laws—existed in Pike County.

Monroe County showed its spunk in how it handled the decline of the Lackawanna Railroad. From 1932 to 1939, the Lackawanna lost money, forcing it to retrench and reduce both service and maintenance. Fred Shoemaker, a lifelong resident of Delaware Water Gap, recalls the neglect of the flower beds adjoining the train station. The resort directories were another casualty: the Lackawanna published none between 1933 and 1939. The Monroe County Chamber of Commerce took up the slack. The Chamber had been formed in 1930 with the merger of smaller organizations: the Stroudsburg Chamber of Commerce, the East Stroudsburg Board of Trade, and the Monroe County Publicity Bureau. By 1932, the Chamber had fourteen committees, all chaired by local business- and hotelmen who donated their services. One of the Chamber's goals was to beautify tearooms and gas stations.[23]

A key project of the Chamber of Commerce in 1932–33 was putting out a booklet that promoted Monroe County. Since the Chamber was broke, it needed contributions. Unfortunately, Monroe County had no sugar daddy to cover the booklet's costs with one big donation. The Chamber had to beg the public at the very time when the Great Depression was at its worst. It succeeded in persuading 223 businessmen, resort keepers, and public-spirited citizens to donate $5,465 for the printing of fifty thousand booklets. In June 1933, the Chamber reported that it had mailed fifteen thousand of these booklets. Among the recipients were golf clubs throughout the nation, physicians and florists on the East Coast, and automobile clubs and tourist bureaus in the tristate area. In 1938, history repeated itself. The Chamber again begged for donations, raised roughly the same amount of money, and published another booklet to advertise Monroe County. Both the 1933 and 1938 booklets had one drawback, though. Although competent and thorough in noting the county's assets, the booklets were dull, with all the charisma and excitement of the Yellow Pages.[24]

The annual Mount Pocono Horse Show had more flair and imagination. Dubbed the "Arena in the Clouds," it was sponsored by the Chamber of Commerce for the benefit of the Monroe County General Hospital. The Horse Show was a community effort, with programs sold by the Ladies Aid of the Mount Pocono Methodist Church and refreshments by the Ladies Auxiliary of the Fire Department.

The first Horse Show was held in 1930 and the last in 1941. In the buildup for the first show, it was said that Governor Pinchot and Grover Whalen, a New York City celebrity, would be present. Neither appeared, but the very mention of their names inflated the Horse Show. At the third Horse Show, actress Ginger Rogers was a guest. Although the stated reason for the Horse Show was publicity, the unstated reason was image. By the 1930s, automobiles had turned horses into conspicuous consumption for the rich. By suggesting high society, a horse show glamorized the Poconos and enhanced all the resorts, even the poorer ones whose patrons would rarely see horses, unless they went to the racetrack.[25]

The people of Monroe County also cooperated in sponsoring the Laurel Blossom Time festival, which served much the same purpose as the Horse Show: it publicized and enhanced the Poconos. Unlike the Horse Show, Laurel Blossom Time was not sponsored by the Chamber of Commerce, whose finances were limited. It did not matter. Public-spirited citizens not only volunteered to run the festival, but they also advanced the money to pay preliminary expenses, depending on ticket sales to the ball and the pageant for reimbursement. If it rained and attendance was sparse, they had to absorb the loss. After the third Laurel Blossom Time festival in 1933, the *Daily Record* reported that all three festivals had lost money.

Laurel Blossom Time made no claims to originality. The organizers openly admitted their debt to Apple Blossom Time in Virginia's Shenandoah Valley, to Cherry Blossom Time in Washington, and to Georgia's Peach Festival. Because Pennsylvania's laurel flower bloomed in pink and white in June, especially in the Poconos, the laurel was convenient. It became the pretext for a festival that was partly nature worship, partly a beauty contest, and partly a pageant that celebrated the community.

The organizers of Laurel Blossom Time aimed for elegance and class. The beauty contest segment of the festival was not a vulgar skin show with women wearing bathing suits to titillate the public. The young ladies wore dresses and were seen by photographers only at their demure best. Never was there a hint of scandal, as the girls had the best of chaperons: their fathers. The editor of the *Daily Record* candidly wrote that Monroe County did not want visitors with a "Coney Island taste." Monroe County sought "the better class," and Laurel Blossom Time was an effort to attract "that element." To reinforce the point that the Laurel Blossom Time festival was not aimed at the motorcycle crowd, none of the contestants were waitresses or clerks with working-class parents. They were college students at a time when the great majority of young women did not attend college. The Laurel Queen at the first festival in 1931 was Elsa Beamish, a Philadelphia suburbanite whose father was an associate of the governor. The 1933 Laurel Queen also came from the Philadelphia suburbs. She was Beryl Temperton, the daughter of a chemical company executive. Another element of class in the contest—at least by the standards of the 1930s—was the absence of ethnic names among the contestants. All had safe northern European names—no Goldbergs, Russos, or Kowalskis.

In the first Laurel Blossom Time festival of 1931, no local women were among the contestants. The citizens of Monroe County had to wait for the coronation procession to participate in the festival: representatives of the Boy Scouts, Girl Scouts, Lions, Auto Club, Rotary, Kiwanis, and the Chamber of Commerce would march in the parade. The procession itself had an Indian theme called "The Spirit of the Poconos." This depiction of Native Americans revealed more about period trendiness than about actual Indians, though here, the Indians were neither savages nor politically correct victims. In keeping with the laurel flower theme, Indians came across as part of the natural world. One marcher was dressed as the Great Spirit; another two as "the pipes of peace."

An American history pageant and "The Ballet of the Flowers" followed the crowning in the 1932 festival. The ballet illustrated "the vicissitudes in the life of natural things and how all depend on the Sun, the great master of life." The 1933 pageant had a lighter touch, featuring characters from Mother Goose and the story of Cinderella and her prince. The 1936 pageant marked the hundredth anniversary of the founding of Monroe County by presenting thirteen episodes in the county's history. As with all the pageants, townspeople participated in costume.

The Laurel Blossom Time Queen and her princesses, as the runners-up were called, received their proverbial fifteen minutes of fame. In return, they were expected to spend a week in the Poconos, tour the region, dine and dance at selected resorts, and, finally, attend the coronation ceremony, the pageant, and the grand ball. Like modern British royals, their function was simply to be seen—and in this case, to publicize the Poconos. Governor Pinchot crowned the Laurel Queen in 1933; his successor, George Earle, was scheduled to do so in 1936, but was unable to appear. There was a rumor (false, as it turned out) that Eleanor Roosevelt would attend the 1933 festival. The participants in the beauty contest also served the publicity cause by living within a hundred miles of the Poconos—as did most of the resort guests. It was hoped that the hometown press of the contestants would play up the good fortune of their native daughters.

There is no doubt that Laurel Blossom Time generated publicity. The publicity gimmick of 1933 was having an autogiro fly the Laurel Queen, Barbara Vincent, from Philadelphia's Fairmount Park to Stroudsburg. Besides, everyone likes a pretty face. Barbara Vincent's picture appeared in hundreds of newspapers. Major wire services, such as United Press and Associated Press, carried Laurel Blossom Time stories. A Fox Movietone man with "his talkie apparatus" covered the Vincent "coronation," having the ceremony repeated three times before he was pleased. Aside from the intangible benefits of this publicity, restaurant and service station business increased during Laurel Blossom Time. Local banks reported heavier deposits after it was all over.[26]

One effect of Laurel Blossom Time endures today. Pennsylvania did not have an official state flower in the early 1930s. Inspired by Laurel Blossom Time, a campaign was started to make the laurel the state flower. Again the community came together. The local Garden Club, Rotary, Kiwanis, and other groups spoke out in favor of the laurel. A bill to this effect passed the Pennsylvania legislature, and on May 5, 1933, Governor Pinchot signed it.[27]

Size Matters: The Big Resorts Conquer the Great Depression

Although the entire Pocono region gained from the annual Horse Show and Laurel Blossom Time festival, the Big Three resorts—Buck Hill, Pocono Manor, and Skytop—probably gained the most. They were the classy hotels, and their patrons would prize equestrian skills and applaud the high tone

FIG. 57

Contestants and officials of the first Laurel Blossom Time contest in 1931 dine at the Kittatinny Hotel. Several months later, the Kittatinny was destroyed by a fire. Monroe County Historical Association.

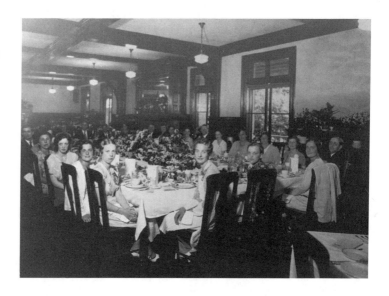

of Laurel Blossom Time. Nonetheless, these resorts were not content to bask in borrowed publicity. Each resort had to make itself attractive and let the public know its assets, or it would lose out to its competitors. The Big Three rose to the challenge. They maintained standards, generated publicity through innovation, and, most important of all, they made money.

Modernization of the facilities was important. A high-class resort can never afford to appear seedy. In the depths of the Depression, Buck Hill offered to assist cottage owners with renovations. Buck Hill also constructed a new swimming pool to replace the original pool of 1908 that no longer properly filtered and circulated water. The new Olympic-size pool was dedicated on July 4, 1936. Building a huge pool was a wise move, because it projected modernity. Nonetheless, a Quaker board member failed to understand, saying, "Thee has sold us a big white elephant—why, it is so big that you could just about float the Leviathan in it."[28]

Concern with standards made Buck Hill refuse to hire an advertising agency in the early 1930s. The directors believed that an insider could best publicize the resort and preserve its values. Their choice was Edward Jenkins, a proper Quaker graduate of Swarthmore College (itself a Quaker institution) and a nephew of a Buck Hill founder. Among other things, standards meant keeping out the "wrong" people. Buck Hill continued to expect new guests to produce a recommendation from former guests, and it kept an informal blacklist of former guests who were no longer welcome. Like Pocono Manor, Buck Hill refused to serve alcohol after Prohibition ended, thereby discouraging the tippling set. At Skytop, the private club arrangement was kept. No one could walk in off the street with a wad of money and expect service.[29]

There was always the danger that maintaining standards would lead to stagnation. The managers of the Big Three avoided this mistake. Their strategy was to innovate, but not seem faddish; to change, but

FIG. 58

Violet-Camille Foster, Laurel Blossom Time Queen in 1934, was truly regal with her long train. In real life, she was a student at Columbia University in New York City.

FIG. 59

Violet Clark and her masks. Clark
made masks like these for the Indian
ceremonial dance at the 1936 Laurel
Blossom Pageant. The masks were
made of papier-mâché and the hair of
unthreaded rope. To highlight the
masks in the evening, when the pageant was held, she used white paint
for the lips and around the eyes. Buck
Hill Collection, Barrett Friendly
Library.

not break with tradition—a strategy of "progressive conservatism." And if a particular novelty broke the
rules of decorum, it was no great crime. One advantage of being rich is being able to redefine decorum.

The Alaskan dog teams at Buck Hill, Pocono Manor, and Skytop showed how the Big Three could
change the rules. At lesser resorts, the dog teams might have seemed silly. At the Big Three resorts,
they were a public relations bonanza. Assembled in the late 1920s in order to publicize winter sports,
the dog teams remained intact in the dark days of the early Depression. The publicity more than paid
for the dog food. When Helen Keller stayed at Buck Hill, she was given a ride. From 1932 to 1942,
the Big Three raced their dogs in their annual sled derby and received national coverage from Fox
Movietone News. In December 1932, the Big Three took their dog show to Philadelphia and staged

a sled race in Fairmount Park. Perhaps the greatest public relations coup was using the dogsleds for rescue work. They carried supplies to the snowbound, once near Philadelphia and once across frozen Long Island Sound to Westport, Connecticut. This latter episode received heavy coverage from the *Daily News,* a New York City tabloid with mass circulation.[30]

Sam Packer, the manager of Skytop, had a knack for public relations. He sponsored an archery tourney, an exhibit of photo portraits, and a fashion show in which guests and cottagers did the modeling. In a totally different vein was the annual sports trophy exhibit, in which hunters displayed their catches. One entry, a 350-pound bear, had been kept in a freezer of the Stroudsburg Ice and Storage Company prior to the contest. Entries for the sports trophy came from Scranton, Wilkes-Barre, Philadelphia, and New Jersey. The annual Skytop Water Carnival was a spectacle befitting a Hollywood musical. A crowd of two thousand attended the 1931 carnival and saw floodlights illuminating twenty-five floats on Skytop lake. One float depicted the goddess of liberty; another consisted of an immense sea serpent; a float that portrayed Indian life won the grand prize. While an orchestra played, colored lights focused on the center of the lake, spotlighting a huge lily from which a young lady in a bathing suit stepped out and danced. As was the custom at fancy resorts, profits were donated to charity. The silliness was justified.[31]

By contrast, the Inn at Buck Hill Falls was subdued. The Inn made golf a family affair with parent-child tournaments, senior tournaments, and the like. But the Inn also realized that many vacationers had neither the energy nor the inclination to play tennis or golf. Hence, it launched the lawn bowling tournament, an ingenious attempt to reach older guests. Unlike resort games such as tennis, which caters to the fit, lawn bowling (like Italian bocce ball) does not require great flexibility and reserves of stamina— an ideal sport for those who want no reminders of the passing years. Lawn bowling became a Buck Hill specialty. In 1958, the Inn began sponsoring the United States Lawn Bowling Championships.[32]

The Buck Hill Follies also shifted its emphasis, becoming more mellow. An amateur talent show for guests, it originally had a satiric touch. The 1929 edition, for instance, featured male guests of varying ages and poundages, dressed in tutus, dancing "The Waltz of the Flowers." The Follies completely changed in 1930 when Earle Lewis, box office manager of the Metropolitan Opera Company, became a cottager. In the six years that he ran the Follies, stars of opera and radio performed. They attracted audiences from a fifty-mile radius.[33]

Another cultural triumph for Buck Hill was the Art Association. Founded in 1933, the Art Association held exhibitions and promoted local artists—among them Cullen Yates, the landscape impressionist. The Inn at Buck Hill Falls would match the dues of the Association's members and buy paintings from artists who wanted the prestige of a Buck Hill exhibition. Edward Jenkins recalled that "for six to eight hundred dollars, we got some great paintings."[34]

Along with innovations, though, there was retrenchment in the Buck Hill of the 1930s. The International House had invited foreign students to speak at Buck Hill, but during the Depression, the pool of international students shrank, causing the International House to be discontinued in 1935. Besides, the Buck Hill colony had lost interest.[35] It may be that during the throes of the Depression—

when dictators had seized control of most European countries, and when potential dictators were lurking in the extremes of American politics—Buck Hill's clientele wanted to forget current events. With its genteel, refined culture, the Inn provided a vacation not only from the stresses of the marketplace, but also from the anxieties of politics.

Ideals and Profits: The Dilemma of Tamiment and Unity House

By contrast, politics was the ostensible motive for Tamiment and Unity House. A promotional brochure for Unity House proclaimed that "Unity was divorced of the corroding crust of profit" and was "the creation of men and women who are of and for the working class." Not surprisingly, Unity House invited progressive speakers such as George Soule, editor of *New Republic* magazine. Its entertainment supplemented the familiar Jewish comedians and stars of Broadway and radio with

FIG. 60
Golf was not a male preserve at Buck Hill. Buck Hill Collection, Barrett Friendly Library.

social dramas. In 1935, Unity House staged "They Shall Not Die," a play about the Scottsboro Boys, the African Americans from Alabama who had been framed for murder. The main hall boasted paintings by Diego Rivera, the Mexican muralist who used his enormous artistic talent to depict the downtrodden and their exploiters.[36]

Camp Tamiment also had lofty ideals. Every year, except the two when it posted a loss, Tamiment gave part of its profits to the Rand School for the political training of young workers. It also demonstrated its commitment to the young by hosting the annual meetings of the League for Industrial Democracy, an intercollegiate organization for students interested in the social sciences and socialism. The League's conferences attracted leading socialists, one of whom was Norman Thomas, the Socialist candidate for president in 1932. After 1933, when the League stopped coming, Tamiment hosted its own Economic and Social Conferences. The topic of the three-day conference in 1938 was "Totalitarianism: Menace to Mankind." The 1939 topic was "The New Deal and the 1940 Election."[37]

Tamiment and Unity House fought the good fight, but they ended up compromising their original ideals. This was more true with Tamiment. Ben Josephson, who was assistant manager before Mrs.

FIG. 61
The annual sports trophy exhibit at Skytop Lodge. Hunters proudly display their catches. Note, too, the bear on the table. Skytop Collection.

FIG. 62
Girls want to have fun: frolicking in the snow at Skytop in the 1930s. Skytop Collection.

Mailly's retirement in 1947, clearly realized that Tamiment needed to be profitable, or it would close. The business-minded Josephson often fought with the directors. When they asked him to hire good socialist boys as waiters, Josephson replied that he wanted waiters who could wait. When the directors insisted on a proletarian camp, he forcefully demanded an attractive camp. After he retired, Josephson admitted that he had underestimated the costs of new buildings in order to gain the approval of the directors. He also installed showers in cabins without the directors' permission. He knew the importance of creature comforts.[38]

Tamiment's theater also contributed to subverting the political message. In the early days, the theater often consisted of serious drama, such as one-act plays by Eugene O'Neill, and socially conscious material such as "Spoon River Anthology." But serious theater was already in decline when Max Leibman took over the theater workshop in 1933. Leibman downplayed the serious stuff altogether and replaced it with satire and revues. He invented the Tamiment formula of a fresh show every week,

FIG. 63
Guests at Skytop working on their social skills. Skytop Collection.

writing satirical sketches for weekdays and a musical revue for Saturdays. Leibman wrote well, attracting talented unknowns who knew that a Tamiment gig would boost their careers. Among the Tamiment entertainers of the late 1930s were Jerome Robbins, Imogene Coca, and Danny Kaye. Among the writers was Sylvia Fine, who would later marry Kaye.

Leibman hit the big time in 1939 with *The Straw Hat Revue,* a collection of revues and sketches that ended up on Broadway and enjoyed a modest run of seventy-five performances. In *The Straw Hat Revue,* Imogene Coca did parodies of Carmen Miranda and Shirley Temple. Danny Kaye re-created his "Anatole of Paris" number from Tamiment. (Anatole hated women and designed outrageous hats to make them look ridiculous.) Danny Kaye was so good in his numbers that he was officially "discovered."[39]

The witty, sophisticated entertainment at Tamiment attracted the stylish and chic, or at least those with pretensions to style. Students and alumni from New York University and City College of New York were among the male guests, and they attracted single women who wanted to meet men with

FIG. 64
The happy fisherman was Richard Crooks, Metropolitan Opera tenor, who owned a cottage at Buck Hill. Crooks was also the featured singer of radio's "Voice of Firestone" show. Buck Hill Collection, Barrett Friendly Library.

these credentials.[40] The atmosphere was permissive. Patricia Shoemaker, then a student at the nearby state teachers' college, recalls working as a babysitter for a gorgeous young woman who lived at a Sandyville bungalow and gave no explanation when she was absent for most of the night. Her husband was in the city, and she paid Patricia to mind the baby.[41]

By the late 1930s, Camp Tamiment had become a middle-class resort, distinguished from its Pocono competitors only by its theater and Jewish flavor. Like the Quaker resorts, Tamiment faced the challenge of the Depression by expanding its facilities and its programs. As an incubator of show business talent and as a money-making venture, Tamiment was a success. As a socialist institution, it was a failure. Politics had become irrelevant to the guests, who were far more concerned with class

FIG. 65
These Russian dancers at Camp Tamiment were probably guests performing in a workshop. At the far right, second row, is Ben Josephson. To his left stands his wife, Irene. Tamiment Institute Library, New York University. Photograph by Kalart Commercial Photography.

distinctions than with social or ethnic solidarity. They shunned next door's Unity House, whose clientele was also Jewish, but sinned by being working-class. The Board of Directors candidly admitted that Tamiment's patrons "did not care for the social contacts which might be made at Unity House," preferring "to fraternize in their own circles."[42]

Unlike Tamiment, Unity House was not motivated by profit, since it was subsidized by the garment workers' union. Yet if loss of virtue is measurable, Unity House also lost some of its purity, although not to the extent that Tamiment did. Unity House suffered an enormous embarrassment when its college student waiters staged a work stoppage in 1937. When the waiters were not rehired for the 1938 season, they picketed the I.L.G.W.U.'s main office in Manhattan, thereby getting the attention of the New York press. An ex-waiter wrote to Dubinsky: "You are actually organizing Unity House as a capitalist venture. You intend to throw out all those agitators and those reds." In its defense, the union argued that working conditions were better at Unity House than at private resorts. "We cannot satisfy every disgruntled employee," Dubinsky wrote.[43]

More disconcerting than petty labor disputes was the failure of Unity House to achieve its original mission. In the early 1920s, the founders of Unity House wanted to elevate workers and create an institution superior to private resorts. When a fire devastated Unity House in August 1934, David Dubinsky was still a true believer. Instead of using the Great Depression as an excuse to close down Unity House, he rebuilt it. A publicity brochure boasted that the builders of Radio City in New York had provided the materials and skilled workers for the new fireproof building. Unity House had everything a New Yorker could want: handball, basketball, baseball, Ping-Pong, tennis, and swimming in a beautiful lake. The less active could take in movies, concerts, plays, and popular entertainment. The food was great.[44]

If only *people* could measure up to the ideal! Waiters were nasty if not tipped. Although union propaganda called Unity House the "workers' resort," some of the working-class guests had no proprietary feelings toward the place. They encouraged waiters to fight management. Some union members loaned their dues books to friends and relatives so that they could take advantage of the low union rates. The union was concerned enough to start checking credentials of incoming guests. Finally, the working-class patrons of Unity House did not care for the serious entertainment, nor did they want to be uplifted. A consultant reported that Unity House had too much culture, classical music, heavy drama, and surreal dancing. The consultant suggested that Unity House lighten up with lowbrow humor, dance contests, amateur nights, and costume balls. He was hired for the 1939 season.[45]

Survival Through Uniqueness

All resorts, large and small, had the same strategy to fight the Depression. They tried to convince the public of their unique excellence. In playing up their differences, the larger resorts had the additional advantage of a firm customer base. Buck Hill, Pocono Manor, and Skytop could count on the patronage of the rich. Unity House, with its subsidized vacations, could count on working-class Jews. Tamiment reached out to middle-class Jews who wanted a touch of style. But the other Pocono resorts, with the exception of the handful of small Italian and Jewish hotels, had no obvious constituency. They had to create their own cadre of clients. They needed a mystique, a distinct personality, to stand out.

To this end, many resorts reinvented themselves by offering a theme to go along with the room and board. Some Pocono resorts made courtship their theme by catering to young singles. Although young men and women went to these resorts allegedly to relax and play, they went in fact to find each other without having to see parents, married couples, and children. Another innovation for singles resorts was avoiding the sexual segregation of adult camps. In the 1920s, Kamp Karamac had assured parents that their daughters were safe. The owner of a popular singles resort of the 1930s instead told friends that he did not care what his guests did. (Don't ask, don't tell!)

Courting also took place at family resorts. The Unity House waiters complained of having to show up at the Recreation Hall and dance with female guests. After nine hours of waiting on tables, the men preferred to rest. By contrast, Tamiment's waiters did not object to fraternizing with women—it was a fringe benefit. At the opposite extreme stood Buck Hill. Edward Jenkins recalled with pride the absence of what he called "prowling" at the proper Quaker resort.[46]

A leading owner of singles resorts in the Poconos was Thomas Bridger. In the late 1920s, he bought Oak Grove, a venerable hotel in Marshalls Creek. There must have been money in romance, because in 1932, at the height of the Depression, Bridger leased the Glenwood in Delaware Water Gap. Bridger realized that he could not rely on advertising alone to attract business, since the Great Depression had reduced the discretionary income of young singles. His solution was visiting a firm's personnel department and getting permission to solicit employees. He offered a vacation plan that worked much like a bank's Christmas Club. Beginning in March, people would contribute every week, and by summer, they would have paid for their vacation.[47]

Like Bridger, Howard Knudson was not frightened by the Depression. In May 1933, he bought the Willow Dell Hotel at a sheriff's sale. He immediately announced that he would cater to young vacationers, promising to keep them occupied with a continuous program and to provide a collegiate orchestra the entire summer. Within a week, Knudson was in New York City to sign up guests.[48]

Activities at singles resorts may have been frivolous, but they gave men and women an excuse to meet. In the summer of 1938, the Oak Grove held an egg-throwing contest, a coed baseball game, and a "wild west corn roast" around a campfire. According to the *Daily Record*, there were "real cowboys and Indians mounted on horseback whooping it up." (Barnum in the Poconos?) The Willow Dell held a "kiddie kutup" in which five young men impersonated the Dionne quintuplets. The old clothes dance at the Willow Dell was somewhat more serious: a hobo party allowed guests to acknowledge, and then laugh away, the Depression.[49]

A resort's theme did not necessarily have to rely on hints of sex and romance. "Baron" Falkenhagen offered a Western theme in the dude ranch that he opened up at the old Brodhead Cottage near Delaware Water Gap. Dude ranches allowed city slickers to don Western clothes and ride horses like "real" cowboys. Actual dude ranches, of course, were located in distant places like Wyoming. A Pocono dude ranch seemed somewhat contrived, especially one run by a so-called baron who advertised German food instead of Western beans and beef. It did not matter. For the baron, the Western theme was the gimmick that made his place unique. And for his guests, the Pocono "Wild West" was a lot closer than the real thing.[50]

Alternative medicine had a market as well. The fire that had destroyed F. Wilson Hurd's sanitarium in 1911 had left a deficiency in the Poconos. That deficiency was rectified in 1932, when Dr. William Howard Hay and a group of investors bought the bankrupt Mount Pleasant House in Mount

Pocono and created Pocono Hay-Ven. Although Hay had graduated from New York University Medical School, he was something of a medical maverick: he crusaded against sugars, refined grains, and an excess of protein because they allegedly left too much "acid ash" in the body. A typical lunch at Pocono Hay-Ven consisted of lettuce soup, cheese ball salad, steamed broccoli, fruit cup, and—for active patients—broiled lamb patties. Parsley soup, sauerkraut, and steamed lima beans were among the dinner delicacies. (This less-than-appetizing menu seems to have been simply a modern version of the very old notion that misery leads to redemption.) Hay rejected guests with incurable or communicable diseases, preferring to improve the healthy. According to his publicity, guests could have a normal resort life and play both tennis and golf. Famous guests at Pocono Hay-Ven included show business stars Marie Dressler, Lily Pons, and Clark Gable. Dr. Hay died in 1940.[51]

Not every resort keeper could create a theme resort. Capital was necessary. The dude ranch required, at the very least, horses, a stable, and Western paraphernalia. Pocono Hay-Ven needed medical facilities for nurses and physicians. It was possible, however, to create a theme resort on the cheap by excluding selected ethnic groups. Exclusion would define the culture of a resort. The absence of African Americans was taken for granted. The absence of white Christian ethnics at some resorts was also apparent. Whether this exclusion was policy or accident is unknown. Resort ads did not address the issue.

There is no doubt that a fair number of resorts excluded Jews. Their ads bluntly stated "Christian clientele," or "Gentiles," or some other euphemism. During the 1930s, according to ads in the Lackawanna directories, more Pocono resorts than ever openly refused Jewish guests. At first sight, the rejection of paying customers at a time of economic stress makes no sense. The argument that more resorts were restricted in 1935 than in 1905 because second- and third-generation Jews, unlike their parents and grandparents, could afford a vacation, misses an important point. Driven by the Great Depression, resorts would be expected to scramble for every possible guest. Jewish money is just as green as gentile money. Exclusion makes sense only as a marketing move: rejecting Jewish guests was a cheap way for a resort to create a theme that would set itself apart from its competitors. Owners of "restricted" resorts realized that a fair number of vacationers preferred their own kind. By tapping into this market, they were trying to increase their income.[52]

A resort without a theme had to give the public at least one reason for its patronage. Many resorts relied on the old standby of food—a mere biological necessity for some, but a joy for others. Several resorts advertised German cooking, which, in the 1930s, seemed to be the standard ethnic fare for "Americans." The Cataract House stood out by advertising Hungarian food. Kamp Karamac advertised that it gave "second portions." Monomonoch Inn pompously claimed that its kitchen was "supervised by a feminine person, giving it the excellence of food served in your own private home."[53]

Schemes to lure the public varied as much as imagination allowed. Starlit Lodge insisted that it did not serve alcoholic beverages and asked guests not to bring their own. The Bluff House in Milford advertised nightly cabaret entertainment from New York. Onawa Lodge announced "Cruise-Way" vacations, meaning that it offered "all the activity, congeniality, carefree atmosphere and activities associated with cruise vacations." Compared with their Victorian predecessors, resorts were less likely to stress scenery and health, but more likely to mention amusements and games.

The best lure of all was competitive pricing. Some of the smaller resorts survived because owners worked long hours, pinched pennies, and passed the savings on to their customers. Irene Cramer, whose parents owned Sunnybrook House, recalls that her father raised chickens for Sunday dinner. He would kill them on Saturdays, clean them, and put them in ice water. On a good weekend, he would kill as many as thirty chickens. Florence Mack's family took her to Green's, near Saylors Lake. Three generations of the family worked at the resort, saving on hired help. Florence's mother used to wonder how the Greens could charge so little.[54]

Summing Up: The Poconos During the Great Depression

Was the Pocono press exaggerating when it claimed that the Great Depression was worse elsewhere? To begin, no one denies the suffering in the Poconos of the 1930s. Resorts near the Delaware River were especially affected. Delaware Water Gap, once the heart of the Pocono vacation industry, declined to the point that it had only five resorts listed in the 1938 Chamber of Commerce publicity booklet. The Castle Inn was not mentioned. The Kittatinny Hotel was already gone, having burned down on October 30, 1931. The Lackawanna resort directory of 1939 admitted that the Gap was no longer a vacation center, calling it instead "the gateway to the playground of the East." The travails of the resorts affected the entire borough of Delaware Water Gap. It was said that the banks took a very indulgent attitude toward unpaid loans, since buyers could not be found for foreclosed properties. The borough could not collect all of its taxes and had to cut back on streetlights. When the federal government initiated WPA projects in the late 1930s, some of the tax arrears were finally settled.[55]

The Gap had no monopoly on sad stories, though. Throughout the Poconos, notices of sheriff's sales were frequent. Jean Haley recalls that her parents' Jeanac Farms closed down, and the family returned to Philadelphia. They would not share in the American dream. Lutherland was a near casualty, surviving only because of a Reconstruction Finance Corporation loan from the federal government. In later years, massive indebtedness would bedevil the resort. Harry Ahnert recollects that his parents could not pay the mortgage interest on Fernwood, the resort they had built after World War I. Luckily, the Ahnerts had a guardian angel in the form of the Pennsylvania Power and Light Company, which was erecting a power line to Bethlehem and offered to pay six thousand dollars for the right-of-way through the Ahnert property. The Ahnerts were saved.[56]

The Ahnert experience may have been more typical for the Poconos than the Jeanac Farms debacle. The Pocono press—despite its shameless civic boosterism—may have been correct in claiming that the Depression was worse elsewhere. The big resorts, with the exception of the Castle Inn and the Buckwood Inn, survived, as did many smaller ones. As for the population, the mixed Pocono economy of services, farming, and some manufacturing provided options unavailable elsewhere.

When Pocono Hay-Ven opened in 1932, it hired seventy-five residents of the community. Mary Smith Nelson recalls that many of her neighbors were part-time farmers. They canned vegetables to supplement meager incomes. She herself worked at Emil Gropper's resort in Pike County to put herself through East Stroudsburg State Teachers College.[57]

The great achievement of the 1930s was not so much having survived the Great Depression than the manner in which people survived it. Residents of Monroe County came together for the Horse Shows, Laurel Blossom Time, and the publicity booklet. Here was a small-town synergy straight from a Norman Rockwell scene. Also remarkable was the refusal to compromise standards. People believed in maintaining the quality of life in their community.

One result of the 1930s had no connection to the Great Depression. The region gained a new name, a recognition that the decline of the old resorts along the Delaware River had made the Pocono plateau the center of the resort economy. By the end of the Depression, "Poconos," a unique name of Indian origin, was coming into general use. This forced traditionalists in Monroe and Pike Counties, who insisted that the Blue or Kittatinny Mountains were distinct from the Poconos, to readjust their thinking. By 1939, several hotels in Marshalls Creek and Minisink Hills (the new name for North Water Gap) were advertising in the Lackawanna directory, proclaiming that they were located in the "Eastern Poconos" or "the foothills of the Poconos." The vacation region had gained its modern name.[58]

9

The Poconos at Midcentury
The Last of the Good Old Days

The Great Depression ended when World War II defense spending revived the economy. The number of jobless dropped from nine million in 1939 to one million at the war's end in 1945. Indeed, by 1944, the total of all goods and services available to civilians was larger than it had been in 1940. A war was on, but for those not fighting, these were good years. As always, what was good for the general welfare was good for the Poconos.[1]

Beginning with the war and continuing into the 1950s, many resorts that had survived the Great Depression had good seasons. Although these resorts had aging buildings and facilities, their guests did not seem to mind—nor did they mind having a vacation that referred to earlier decades. Even the new postwar resorts honored the old ways. Many people simply enjoyed the vacation that they, or their parents, could not afford in the 1930s. Nonetheless, an era was ending. Not only were the prewar resorts having a final fling before consumer tastes changed, but so were the old standards and norms they embodied.

The Poconos During World War II

Certain Pocono resorts had some of their best years during World War II.[2] Some of their guests were newcomers; they included vacationers who normally would have gone to the shore, but the government had closed Atlantic City for the duration of the conflict. Other newcomers were servicemen who were stationed within driving distance and who met their girlfriends in the Poconos. Among the signs of boom times were the extra cars that the Lackawanna Railroad added in the summer of 1944 and the need for rooming houses to take in the resort overflow.

Resorts tried to provide their guests a 1930s vacation, a goal that was not always possible. As in the First World War, the nation had to make sacrifices. Foreign foodstuffs, such as sugar and coffee, were scarce; domestic foods, such as meats, fats, oils, and canned goods, were not always available. To ensure equity—to see that all Americans, even those with less money, would eat—the federal government had imposed rationing, giving consumers a fixed number of coupons for scarce goods. The system required consumers to present the required number of coupons when purchasing a rationed item. When they had used up their coupons, they had to wait for the next distribution. Although resort guests were expected to bring coupons for their meals, most did not cooperate, having come to the resorts in order to save their coupons.[3]

Resorts had to improvise to meet their food needs. The easiest way to stock a pantry was to break the law, pay extra, and buy on the black market. Many resorts took this option. An exception was Tamiment: according to Ben Josephson, Tamiment had excellent relations with the community because it promptly paid its bills. Josephson presumably meant that Tamiment got extra coupons from the food rationing board in Milford and could bypass the black market. In one bizarre instance, a guest showed up with his own food instead of coupons. Marie Hoffman, whose parents owned the Delaware House in Dingmans Ferry, recalls that the man had a huge leg of lamb that he sold to Marie's father for the evening dinner.[4]

Many resorts had to cut back on the quality of their meals. The *New York Times* reported in 1943 that chefs no longer had large dripping roasts to carve, nor could resorts offer the picnic roasts and barbecues of the prewar years. One hotel nonetheless tried to maintain the picnic tradition with chicken, hot dogs, and corn. Buck Hill's menus became limited, giving the impression that the fancy hotel could only serve items that were available. The sugar shortage, for example, restricted desserts. Sugar, in fact, was in such short supply that some guests at the Sunnybrook Inn stole it. Irene Cramer recalls that her parents could not leave it on dinner tables overnight. Nor could they leave tableware, which was also known to disappear.[5]

Gasoline and tires were also rationed, causing American motorists to drive one-third fewer miles in 1943 than in 1941. Pocono attractions that depended on automobile traffic were severely hit. Bushkill Falls suffered more than it did during the Great Depression, reaching a low point on one Fourth of July, ordinarily a busy day, when its parking lot contained only two automobiles. John Shinn, who rented bungalows to vacationers, recalls that his bungalows were often empty during the War. Unity House advised union members to save travel and gas by taking an entire vacation at one time rather than breaking it into segments.[6]

If motorists had no gasoline, they had to take the railroad. During the war, the Cresco station of the Lackawanna Railroad more than doubled its ticket sales. Resorts conveniently near the railroad did well. In its 1942 Annual Report, the Inn at Buck Hill Falls noted that New Yorkers were coming via the Lackawanna Railroad but that Philadelphians had a problem. The Inn was sending private cars to Allentown to meet Philadelphia guests halfway. In the following year, cuts in gasoline supplies closed this route.[7]

Aside from shortages of food and gasoline, resorts also had to cope with labor shortages, as the booming economy and conscription reduced the summer pool of temporary workers. According to the press, hotels were understaffed in the summer of 1944. Forced to rely on students, some hotels had to close in September, when the school year began. On Memorial Day in 1945, several resorts

FIG. 66
Lifeguards at the Buck Hill pool during World War II. The gentleman in the middle was Howard DeNike, an instructor at East Stroudsburg State Teachers College. He was hired by the Inn at Buck Hill Falls during the war years, when the regular staff was in the armed forces. Buck Hill Collection, Barrett Friendly Library.

could not open because of labor shortages, forcing them to wait until the end of the school year so that they could hire students. The Camp Club at Buck Hill could not find experienced male counselors; it improvised, as it often did during the war, and hired three seniors from a suburban Philadelphia high school to supervise the youngsters in the play camp. What the Inn at Buck Hill Falls could not replace were its sled dogs, which were drafted in 1943 and sent to an army camp in Montana for use in Alaska and elsewhere to rescue crews of downed airplanes.[8]

In a peculiarly perverse way, the war's privations served to diversify the attractions of the Poconos, giving a new twist to traditional activities. Because gasoline was scarce, horses were pressed into service, pulling wagons and carts that transported guests to tennis courts and golf grounds. Here was an unplanned and unintended nostalgia. At Tamiment's bungalow colony, women knitted for their country—making garments and blankets for the Red Cross—and sold war bonds. In the summer of 1942, the women in Tamiment's bungalows sold almost forty thousand dollars' worth of bonds. For the fifth national bond drive, Monroe County combined entertainment with patriotism. On July 1, 1944, Richard Crooks, the Metropolitan Opera tenor who had a house at Buck Hill, teamed with the Fred Waring orchestra to give four concerts. Crooks and Waring gave the first concert at Lutherland, after which they went to Buck Hill, then to the state teachers' college in East Stroudsburg, and they concluded the evening at Shawnee Inn (formerly Buckwood Inn, which Waring had recently bought). Admission was by ticket with bond purchases.[9]

At least two resorts missed out on the wartime resort business. The Fernwood in Bushkill closed voluntarily. At that time, Fernwood was not the mega-resort of today, but a small roadside inn whose main attraction was its Sunday chicken dinners. Its German-born owner saw more money in using his technical background to open a machine shop and supply the United States Navy. Pocono Manor, on the other hand, stayed open, but had a new clientele: the Navy made it a rest home for its personnel.[10]

The manager of the Inn at Buck Hill Falls wondered if his resort would also be leased by the Navy. As events turned out, he made a different contribution to the war effort when the Inn at Buck Hill Falls became a potential bomb shelter. It promised seventy-five rooms to the Standard Oil Company, which, fearing the worst, had a contingency plan to vacate New York City. Buck Hill would have the rooms available within a week, if requested. The request was never made. The oil company also leased part of Buck Hill's basement, made of reinforced concrete, to store a portion of its files. Throughout the war, the main office in New York City called for documents or sent a courier.[11]

Leasing rooms to the oil company during the war was extra money for Buck Hill, since it had enough of its usual business. In 1942, Buck Hill was tripling the profit it had made in 1940. The rest of the war years were even better, and the resort had to reject thousands of requests for reservations. Buck Hill also found renters for all the listed cottages, allowing the owners who could not sell during the Depression to have their chance at last. In 1945, seventeen properties changed hands.[12]

Tamiment and Unity House both had record-breaking years. At Tamiment, beginning in 1940, each successive season actually set *new* records. In 1943, the resort had to return hundreds of dollars to applicants because it had run out of empty rooms. It made so much money, in fact, that it invested eighty thousand dollars in war bonds. The following two years registered further gains. By the end of 1946, Tamiment could boast that during the war years it tripled its reserves to nearly one million dollars. Unity House, Tamiment's neighbor, also had a great war. Business was so good in 1942 that for the first time in its history, the union resort had an operating profit and it did not need its usual subsidy from the I.L.G.W.U. to cover its low rates. Although Unity House raised prices for the 1943 season to cover increasing food costs, the public kept coming. The resort was so overcrowded that the union considered limiting vacations to three weeks.[13]

Expansion of the Poconos

Prosperity continued with the coming of peace. Good times allowed more Americans to buy cars, loaded with extras such as heaters and radios that made driving more pleasant. According to a national survey, automobiles were used for 83 percent of vacation trips in 1953—a fact that implied a need for new roads. Postwar prosperity, through the agency of federal highway spending, gave these roads to the American motorist.[14]

Large-scale federal involvement in road building was a novelty, for prior to World War II, the provision of roads had been the obligation of state and local government. Few limited-access highways had been built, and highway construction in general had consisted of paving existing roads, which dated from the horse-and-buggy era. Driving was tedious, involving many stops for red lights, and drivers crawled on narrow, antiquated roads, getting stuck in long traffic jams during peak season. Stalled cars whose radiators had overheated were familiar sights.[15]

In the 1940s, driving in the Poconos was little changed from the days of the Great Depression. The first signs of transformation were seen in 1953 with the completion of three bridges over the Delaware River. The Milford and Portland bridges replaced existing structures that had been neglected in the threadbare 1930s. The Delaware Water Gap bridge became a new port of entry into the Poconos.[16]

Subsequent years saw the completion of superhighways that New Yorkers and Philadelphians could use to bypass the traditional routes to the Poconos, almost transforming drivers from tortoises into hares. The northeast extension of the Pennsylvania Turnpike ended the stop-and-go tedium of Route 611, which Philadelphians had once endured to reach the Poconos. Likewise, Interstate 80 saved travel time for New Yorkers, allowing them to drive without stopping through New Jersey and reach the Poconos within two hours. The Monroe County segment of Interstate 80, which started at the Delaware Water Gap bridge, become the main east-west artery of the Poconos and the terminus for smaller highways, such as Route 33 and Route 209. By linking with the northeast extension of the Pennsylvania Turnpike at the western fringe of the Poconos, Interstate 80 created a continuous (if convoluted) connection between New York and Philadelphia. Another highway, Route 84, connected Pike and Wayne Counties with the southern portions of New York State and New England.

Even before better roads and bridges drew the Poconos closer together, a new four-county resort association was performing the same function. The Pocono Mountains Vacation Bureau had been launched in the 1930s to promote the inland resorts, especially the Quaker resorts. In 1948, it merged with the resort branch of the Monroe County Chamber of Commerce. Over 400 resorts and 125 camps joined the newly expanded Pocono Mountains Vacation Bureau, which encompassed four counties: Monroe, Pike, Wayne, and Carbon. Located on the western fringes of the Poconos, Carbon County was the new member of the Pocono club, and it was eventually served by the new highways: both Interstate 80 and the northeast extension of the Pennsylvania Turnpike fell within its borders. Interstate 80 allowed New Yorkers to drive deeper into the Poconos and reach Carbon County in even less time than it took in the old days to reach Delaware Water Gap and the Stroudsburgs.[17]

The inclusion of Carbon County was more evidence that God may have made the mountains and the scenery, but man made the Poconos. Big Boulder and Jack Frost mountains, destined to be major ski centers, suddenly became part of the Pocono region. Likewise, Hickory Run State Park—with its boulder field, a legacy of the Ice Age—became a Pocono site. The boulders jut upward crookedly, resembling eggs in an egg carton, and create a unique form of hiking that favors the long-legged and the sure-footed. If hikers fall between the boulders, the boulders will never break, but ankles are at risk.

Carbon County was noted for Mauch Chunk, a charming village along the Lehigh River that had been a coal shipping center in the mid-nineteenth century. Among the men of affairs who once lived in Mauch Chunk were thirteen millionaires. Tourists were also attracted to Mauch Chunk, as its high

FIG. 67
Author at boulder field, Hickory Run State Park. The field appears as dead as the stone, but it isn't. Snakes and mice may be seen in the crevices between the boulders.

mountains and narrow, crooked streets can conjure visions of Alpine villages; the area reminded the well-traveled of Switzerland. In counterpoint, Mauch Chunk had its dark side of poverty and coal-miner rebels. Three members of the Molly Maguires were hanged in its jail.

After the Second World War, tourism was declining. Joe Boyle, the editor of the *Times News*, feared for the future of Mauch Chunk and devised a bold, imaginative solution. He made a deal with the widow of Jim Thorpe, the Native American athlete who had won two gold medals at the 1912 Olympics but who had lost them when his brief career as a professional ballplayer had been revealed. Today, Jim Thorpe is a multicultural hero. But in 1954, Thorpe was a dead Indian with a tarnished reputation. His widow believed that he deserved better; she had come into town with her husband's corpse, and for twenty-five thousand dollars, she handed over her dead husband to Boyle. Mauch Chunk buried Thorpe with honors and renamed itself after him—a posthumous revision of the great athlete's life, since he had never set foot in the place that buried his corpse and bears his name.[18]

Aside from a famous name, the little village of Jim Thorpe gives the Poconos still another tourist attraction. The house of Asa Packer, railway pioneer and founder of Lehigh University, draws many visitors, curious about the rich and famous of yesteryear. "Stone Row," sixteen row houses on Race Street built by Asa Packer in 1849, has been restored and placed in the National Register of Historic Places. Among the other attractions of Race Street are an art gallery, an antique store, a pricey restaurant, and St. Mark's Episcopal Church—which definitely deserves a second look. Built in 1869 into the hillside, the church has a spectacular interior that features Tiffany windows. Over the door, a winged-lion gargoyle surveys the good life below. He holds stone tablets with Greek letters (yet another European touch in Jim Thorpe).

FIG. 68
This billboard greets visitors to Jim Thorpe. The Swiss comparison is a holdover from the nineteenth century, when Americans felt inferior toward Europe and needed to justify interest in American sites with references to the Old Country.

Last Fling of the Old Resorts

During World War II, many Americans feared that when defense spending ended, the economy would devolve to its prewar state, and the Great Depression would return, almost as a cruel joke after the teasing wartime prosperity. Instead, the best of all possible worlds was born. The wartime prosperity continued, but without the shortages. There was a lot to buy and money to buy it, creating the conditions for boom times in the vacation industry. Kamp Karamac seemed to sense this happy future when, prior to its 1947 season, it invited the public to share the fun, noting in a publicity brochure that the end of wartime rationing had allowed it to stock its freezers with turkeys and delicacies. In a way, Kamp Karamac was announcing that the good times would get even better.

What changed little, if at all, during the midcentury years was resort life: it relied on the games and pastimes of former generations and reflected the customary formalities that society still honored. The 1940s and 1950s were the last time Americans agreed on standards, or at least paid lip service to the notion that public behavior had to fit traditional norms. An obvious example was dressing up in public. Whether going to church, to the office, to the theater, and even to restaurants, men wore suits and women wore dresses. Some Pocono resort owners can recall the mountains of luggage that vacationers, especially single women, would bring. Vacationers were allegedly seeking to relax, but instead of being casual in their clothes, they dressed up, often taking the trouble to put on suits or dresses for dinner. They felt it very important to show off their clothes, as if an abundant wardrobe was a sign of public virtue. Many vacationers changed clothes several times a day, having the goal of never repeating an outfit, a feat that was possible during a short stay.[19]

The old prewar formulas suited Buck Hill, Pocono Manor, and Skytop just fine. Buck Hill consistently maintained standards so that it would continue to attract a wealthy clientele. The dining room had "French service," code words for elegance. The enduring popularity of its high teas, an

FIG. 69
Stone Row, Race Street. Stone Row, in Jim Thorpe, dates from the 1840s. Note the mountains in the background, giving Jim Thorpe its "Swiss" look.

excuse to dress up and to exhibit manners, was a throwback to an earlier time when the American upper classes modeled themselves on their British counterparts. By the 1950s, no one could deny that the American century had arrived, but Buck Hill's conservative guests preferred tradition. As would befit a clientele that celebrated the ways of their parents and grandparents, tours in horse-drawn carriages remained popular. Nonetheless, concessions were made to changing times. In 1958, the Inn at Buck Hill Falls permitted liquor in the dining room, although it waited another four years before opening a cocktail lounge. (The other Quaker resort, Pocono Manor, had already bowed to John Barleycorn in 1951 when it acquired a liquor license and opened a cocktail lounge.[20])

By remaining true to its traditions, the Inn at Buck Hill Falls satisfied the needs of many well-off vacationers. The Inn had its best year in 1946, having over 116,000 guest days. That year's heights could not be sustained; they were the pent-up release of wartime savings. Nonetheless, in terms of guest days, Buck Hill kept surpassing its wartime records until 1950. And even the 1950s were prosperous times. When Buck Hill added a west wing and a new dining room in 1964, it was expecting continued good times in the coming years. Pocono Manor also did well after the war, and it offered new creature comforts: a fully equipped movie theater, an indoor swimming pool, and an artificial ice skating rink. Most important of all, a new golf course was completed in 1966.[21]

At Unity House and Tamiment, dressing up was an expression of 1950s conformity as well as an occasion for the children and grandchildren of immigrants to show that they had arrived. Both resorts managed to continue their watered-down political agenda of the 1930s and to attract their traditional clientele. For example, Unity House maintained its wartime momentum until 1949, when business reverted to normal and the union resort suffered its usual operating losses. The I.L.G.W.U. was not alarmed. Unity House had always been a union showcase where workers could have a rich man's vacation (or at least the illusion of one) at little cost.

FIG. 70
Tobogganing at Skytop. Skytop Collection.

FIG. 71
Charlie Walker was the head groom at
the Inn at Buck Hill Falls. Buck Hill
Collection, Barrett Friendly Library.

Showing off Unity House was the best way to humble the bosses, too. In May 1956, David Dubinsky, the president of the I.L.G.W.U., invited two hundred clothing manufacturers and their wives to Unity House, feeding them lobster and prime rib. The bosses, in turn, got into the mood of things: they serenaded Dubinsky (who had his own cottage on the grounds) with parodies of old favorites. To the tune of "Dixie," they sang: "We wish we were in the land of cotton, where labor rates are next to nothing." "Home on the Range" became "The Bosses' Lament":

Oh give us a home,
Where the union don't roam,
In a search for less hours and more pay,
Where it don't make no fuss,
Never buffaloes us,
Never causes grief and dismay.[22]

As would befit a union showcase, Unity House had to live by the highest union ideals. The I.L.G.W.U. seemed to learn from its labor troubles of the 1930s. In 1950, it allowed the Hotel and Restaurant Workers Union to organize Unity House workers. The I.L.G.W.U. also made sure that only union labor worked on the construction of the Unity House theater. Having made a fetish of the union label, the I.L.G.W.U. had to practice what it preached. It banned foreign-made goods from the Unity House gift shop.[23]

Unity House also had to provide entertainment that was both first-rate and acceptable by the norms of the 1950s—or at least the norms of New York liberalism. Acts not only had to be clean in order to accommodate the family trade, but they also had to be racially sensitive so as to avoid offending the union's black members. In 1956, the opening of a new theater allowed the I.L.G.W.U. to express its liberal ideals by having Marian Anderson, the African American contralto, sing at the dedication. The theater was the focus of Unity House entertainment, booking the road companies of Broadway hit shows during the middle of the week. Unity House was so proud of itself that in a 1957 brochure, it billed itself as the "Times Square of the Poconos" and claimed to be "the last word in theater." This was not entirely accurate. Unity House did give the best in popular entertainment, but it was never a creative force.[24]

As before the war, the cutting edge in popular entertainment was next door at Tamiment. Whereas Unity House was prosaic, Tamiment entertainment was ironic with a touch of the avant-garde, too original to stay in the confines of a summer resort. In 1953, Max Leibman brought his Tamiment acts to television and called his production "Your Show of Shows," which starred Sid Caesar and Imogene Coca. The blend of satiric sketches and parody made "Your Show of Shows" the archetype for television variety comedy and the ancestor of the long-running "Saturday Night Live" show. "Your Show of Shows" alone could have secured Tamiment's place in entertainment history, but Tamiment had much more to offer the world. To its prewar alumni, such as Danny Kaye and Jerome Robbins, it added new alumni, including Arte Johnson, Neil Simon, and Woody Allen.[25]

Ben Josephson, who became the manager of Tamiment when Mrs. Mailly retired, also offered highbrow entertainment. It had been obvious in the 1920s that Tamiment's clientele did not want serious theater, and so Josephson tried serious music. In 1952, Tamiment initiated its annual Chamber Music Festival, which featured the Curtis String Quartet from Philadelphia. The Festival attracted much attention, receiving endorsements from the governor of Pennsylvania and the mayor of

Philadelphia. In addition to the Chamber Music Festivals, Tamiment offered classical concerts on a weekly basis. Tamiment was the land of Mozart and Dvořák as well as Woody Allen.[26]

Tamiment managed to preserve a political agenda in the postwar years, although it no longer had the Rand School of Social Science to subsidize. The Rand School had died, a victim of prosperity and of the failure of socialism to attract young workers in the postwar years. The demise of the Rand School also deprived Tamiment of its justification for a tax exemption, which had been the support of the workers' school. To preserve its tax-exempt status, Tamiment needed a new outlet for its profits. Tamiment could have sought to fund social work, minority education, or other programs aimed at the less fortunate. Such was not the case. Tamiment did donate some money to Social Democrats in eastern Europe who were trying to stop communism. But political donations were peripheral to Tamiment's new mission. In general, Tamiment's money sought to enhance the New York left-wing, anticommunist elite. For example, Tamiment subsidized the *New Leader* magazine by placing public service announcements that promoted Radio Free Europe, the National Safety Council, Better Schools, and so on.[27]

As before the war, Tamiment sponsored annual seminars on problems of current interest. Among the topics were "Democracy in the Trade Unions" and "The Crisis in American Foreign Policy," with speakers ranging from Norman Cousins and Sidney Hook to Henry Kissinger. The 1948 seminar, "An American Program for World Peace," became the theme for the second annual college essay contest, which drew 160 essays from 117 colleges. The judges were the president of Hunter College in New York City, the editor of the *American Bar Association Journal,* and the director of the American Association for the United Nations. Another Tamiment-sponsored event was its annual book award. Among the winners were Carl Sandburg for his autobiography, Whittaker Chambers for *Witness,* and James MacGregor Burns for *Roosevelt: The Lion and the Fox.*

Tamiment's political activism was often divorced from the life of the resort. In the 1950s, the seminars met in New York City; the 1958 seminar, for example, was held in the auditorium of the Museum of Modern Art. The book award luncheons were held in Manhattan hotels. Resort guests were probably unaware of Tamiment's off-site agenda. They went to Tamiment for the food, the entertainment, the golf, the art lessons, and the opportunity to make friends.[28]

The Sandyville bungalow colony had become upscale, a sort of liberal Jewish version of the Skytop and Buck Hill cottage colonies. Sandyville parents sent their children to private schools and hired nannies for the summer. They are recalled by one of the workers as "an incredible group of people, all intelligent women and men. They were all into their arts and crafts and their stocks."[29]

New Resorts

The end of a victorious war is like the uncorking of champagne. It unleashes energies waiting to be released. In the Poconos, which had always attracted aspiring entrepreneurs, the end of World War II brought many Americans who had made money to the area, all seeking their version of the American dream.

A good example was Minnie Edwards, who had two wartime jobs: factory worker by day and hairdresser by night. Her earnings were just a means for her to achieve her real dream, which was to be her own boss. Along with her husband, she bought a cottage in Cresco and opened the Brookview Manor, a boardinghouse that could feed forty at most. It was an old-fashioned place that specialized in home-cooked meals and expected guests to fend for themselves recreationally—hiking, fishing, driving, and doing whatever else suited their fancy.[30]

Unlike Minnie's Brookview Manor, which always remained small, Dave Artzt started modestly and later became a major player on the resort scene. Artzt was a Temple University graduate and the son of a businessman who made hair tonic (according to Artzt, the "greasy kid stuff" once lampooned in commercials). Artzt hinted at a mysterious background. Having been a nightclub singer in Atlantic City in the 1930s, he was in the beauty supply business before arriving in the Poconos in 1946 with one hundred thousand dollars. He bought the Friedman brothers' resort in Bushkill, renamed it Pocmont, and made it into a major resort.[31]

Many new resort owners were ethnics. Artzt was Jewish, as were the Barrows of Bacon and Bagel and Lew Miller of Log Tavern Camp. Charles Poalillo and his wife, who bought the Penn Hills tavern in 1944, were Italian Americans. Like Artzt, they started small, at first catering to friends and relatives who wanted a good Italian meal in the country. After Charles died in 1953, his wife and son continued the business and transformed Penn Hills into a resort for honeymooners and couples. Penn Hills eventually became a multi-million dollar enterprise that branched into skiing and real estate.[32]

What really raised eyebrows was the opening of African American resorts. The Poconos had been segregated before the war, as Hillary and Agnes Bute, immigrants from the West Indies, realized during a country trip in 1938. While driving through the Poconos, the Butes could not find a room. Every resort, boardinghouse, and common flea trap was allegedly bulging with guests on that particular day during the Great Depression. The Butes were not fools. Aside from being annoyed, they sensed an opportunity. In 1948, Hillary and Agnes Bute opened a summer resort in Mount Pocono and advertised for "colored guests." Agnes ran the resort and Hillary joined her on weekends, when his auto repair business in Brooklyn was closed. The Butes did not arouse any community opposition, since they bought out an establishment that catered to black workers at the Mount Pocono resorts. In fact, the Butes were welcomed, since they ran a very quiet place. Hillary describes his guests: "They were mostly teachers, doctors, business people, and retired people. We didn't go in for the young crowd. We didn't allow any drinking at all. We had mostly people who sat on the porch and took little walks. We had shuffleboard. We took guests on drives up through the mountains, showed them around." Bute's was an old-fashioned little resort, one of a handful of the African American places, memorable only for its clientele.[33]

Judge Albert Murray's Hillside Inn had a convoluted origin. Albert Murray was a black Brooklyn attorney with a Jewish partner, Abraham Kaufman, and they bought the Hillside House near Marshalls

Creek. In 1955, a year after the purchase, Kaufman died of a heart attack while mowing the lawn at the Hillside. His family was not interested in the property, and Murray was given full title to the Inn. Murray and his wife, Odetta, moved in and caused a few Pocono jaws to fall. The head of the Vacation Bureau offered to buy out the Murrays, but the Murrays refused. Odetta ran the resort in the summer while Albert tended to his Brooklyn law practice. By the time Murray retired from the law in 1986, he was a judge on the New York State Supreme Court.

The Murrays had had to build up the Hillside Inn, which under its former owner had only eight rooms and no liquor license. Instead of borrowing for expansion, Murray invested the profits of his law practice. Murray remembers how he built up the Hillside:

> We advertised in *Ebony*, in the *Amsterdam News*, the Philadelphia *Tribune*, and a Brooklyn newspaper. We were loaded with customers. They had nowhere else to go. If you came to Hillside Inn, you got a swimming pool and that was a big thing. We built a pool in 1957. My capacity was about eighty. We had people who knew me, people who had served with me. We had top entertainment and we served three meals—southern cooking: fried chicken, ribs, sweet potato pie, peach cobbler, and definitely grits, eggs and all of that stuff.

The Murrays tried to avoid hiring their staff in New York City. They believed that they could advance African Americans by hiring students from southern black colleges to give them the opportunity to see role models. Albert Murray recalls: "When I brought the kids from the South, I said, 'Look at these people you're serving. They are teachers, lawyers and all of that. They got some information to give you. You want to be a teacher: this lady is a teacher in New York.' The students had the opportunity to see people who had made it and that was the same thing that happened to me when I came to New York. I saw other Blacks who were making it." Like Tamiment and Unity House, Hillside Inn was no ordinary resort. It had a mission, although it was far less known to the world of the majority.[34]

The best known of the new resort owners was Fred Waring, the big band leader, who bought the Buckwood Inn in 1943 and renamed it Shawnee Inn. Born in 1900 in Tyrone, Pennsylvania, Waring had long been in the public eye. Before the age of thirty, Waring and his band had been on Broadway, toured Europe, and appeared in *Syncopation*, the first movie musical. In 1933, his band—now a large glee club of seventy singers and orchestra members called the "Pennsylvanians"—appeared on the weekly "Old Gold Radio Show." In 1949, Waring became the first big band leader to have his own television program. But he found television confining, and he left it in 1954 to do road shows. His formula was simple. Rather than experimenting with new songs, he stuck with old favorites that he believed would "live forever." For his fans, Fred Waring would "do it better than anyone else."

Once Waring bought the Shawnee Inn, he made the Poconos his base of operations, and he broadcasted his radio shows from the Inn. In 1947, he launched the Fred Waring Youth Choral Workshop, an annual program based at the Shawnee Inn that attracted choral teachers, directors, and students from around the country. In the same year, Waring also formed the Shawnee Press to publish music.

In 1952, he moved his music enterprises to the empty Castle Inn in Delaware Water Gap. Aside from making the Poconos a music center of sorts, Waring attracted celebrities to his Shawnee Inn. At the height of his television fame, the portly comedian, Jackie Gleason, often played golf at Shawnee. The Fred Waring Four Ball golf tournament was one of the top ten amateur golf events in the country, attracting Arnold Palmer when he was the amateur champion. In addition, Waring held an annual cartoonists' convention at his Inn.

Waring projected a traditional image. His singers sang clearly, in contrast to the mumbling rock singers who were beginning to appear in the 1950s. His singers were also clean-cut. Right to the end, when Waring retired in 1980, the Pennsylvanians avoided the casual look that had become the norm for musicians after the 1950s. Even the composition of the Pennsylvanians reflected a time when "real" Americans were WASPs. The Pennsylvanians had WASP names, and it was commonly believed in the Poconos that Waring did not practice multiculturalism. Waring probably had much to do with the Poconos keeping a nativist image, despite the presence of the new ethnic resorts.[35]

"Dirty Dancing" in the Poconos

The 1950s and 1960s were the last years of the American singles resort—the last time that young people would leave home to socialize and meet members of the opposite sex. Part of the reason that courting took place in the country was the morality of the day, a remnant of Victorian taboos. Young people, especially women, worried over one's "reputation." It was best to have a fling in the boondocks, away from the prying eyes of neighbors, relatives, and peers. On the other hand, many resort guests did not want a fling, but did want to meet new people. Singles resorts provided the opportunity to meet individuals who would not be seen at school, on the job, or in the neighborhood. In short, when singles resorts brought people together, they harked to the past—but when they expressed a freer sexuality, they pointed to the wild and rebellious 1960s.

Much of the transition can be seen in Vacation Valley, a large postwar resort that had the distinction of being the only one that specifically referred to singles in its ads. Vacation Valley was self-consciously acknowledging the new youth culture of the postwar era. A 1957 ad in the *New York Daily News* noted the presence of a rock-and-roll band. At a time when nearly all Americans past the age of twenty considered rock music both juvenile and barbaric, Vacation Valley had no shame. It openly admitted its target market with music that suggested abandon. A former employee recalls that "Every night was New Year's Eve at Vacation Valley."[36]

Although the rock band was a concession to the youth culture of the 1950s, the brothers who owned Vacation Valley, Francis and John Shinn, did much to honor traditional mores. They served no liquor, and they expected guests to be discreet in their courtship rituals. The Shinns had a dress code for the dance floor that required jackets and slacks, but forbade blue jeans. (In the 1950s, jeans were working clothes that were not fit for polite company.) John Shinn recalls:

FRED WARING and THE PENNSYLVANIANS
"HOW IT ALL BEGAN"
FRED WARING SHOW

WILLIAM MORRIS AGENCY, INC

FIG. 72
Fred Waring and his band in 1919. Fred is by the piano. Even at the age of nineteen, Fred Waring had a talent for publicity. Monroe County Historical Association.

We were pretty strict on the dress code. We found less trouble when you make people dress. Women had to be in dresses or dress slacks, not jeans. People really like discipline. Our guests had as good a time here as elsewhere. Every time we had a band they had to dress. If you insisted, you didn't have the problems, the behavioral problems. When people are dressed, they have the tendency to behave a little better. If you got sloppy old clothes on, you don't give a damn if someone knocks you on your tail in the mud, do you?[37]

If Vacation Valley guests needed more excitement, they walked down the road to the Jungle Bar, recalled as the wildest young people's bar of the eastern Poconos.[38]

Raunchy bars existed, in part, because the singles resorts had activity programs that were little changed from the 1930s. Vacation Valley guests played golf, softball, and archery, much as the older married couples did at other resorts. At night, Vacation Valley had bingo games, comedians, and even a trained horse performing tricks on the dance floor. The waiters staged skits from Broadway plays. Kamp Karamac, which adjoined the Delaware River, offered the additional attraction of canoeing. Its highlight of the summer season was the beauty contest in which guests competed in bathing suits and formal wear.[39]

Although singles resorts strove to keep their clients occupied with games and amusements, everybody knew that guests came to find romance. The activities were a device to bring people together and break the ice. Singles resorts forced intimacy at meals by seating guests, family style, at tables with six to eight chairs. Unfortunately for the young ladies, women always outnumbered the men at the resorts. Guests came on Sunday, and by evening, some of the girls would have already counted the boys. Joseph O'Connor, who worked at Kamp Karamac, recalls the night that the ratio was ten to one. The next morning, the girls demanded their money back. Frank Tancredi recalls the same man shortage at Vacation Valley, where he waited on tables. Vacation Valley's owner improvised a temporary solution: he sent his Volkswagen van to East Stroudsburg State Teachers College, returning with male students in order to balance the sexes on the dance floor.

At each resort, the permanent solution to the shortage of men involved forcing waiters to dance with the girls. The waiters did not necessarily object, but fun stops being fun once it becomes mandatory. At times, the waiters were tired; they had been on their feet all day, but they had to "enjoy" themselves regardless of how they felt. What some regarded as a burden, though, others saw as an opportunity. John Shinn recalls the waiter who asked the hostess for the tables with homely women, whom he would take for boat rides on the lake and dance with at night. At the end of the week, this waiter—who was a psychology major at Cornell University—was well rewarded with tips. There is also the tale of the woman at Log Tavern Camp who complained about the food. The owner told the best-looking waiter to give her special attention. A few days later, she said that the food had greatly improved.[40]

Former guests and workers recall that often the women themselves would chase staff members, especially if there were not enough male guests to go around. Lifeguards and golf pros were at the top of the pecking order; next came riding instructors, social directors, and waiters. Less desirable were blue-collar workers, as they were less likely to be students or college graduates. Dishwashers were unacceptable. They frequently came from New York City's skid row after drying out. Either an employment agency sent them, or resorts sent vans to skid row to pick them up.[41]

The 1950s were the "dirty dancing" years, when many singles took advantage of being among strangers to shed any inhibitions they might have. Depending on the resort, management either strove to maintain some semblance of respectability or else turned a blind eye while taking the money. The owner of a well-known singles resort once boasted of his indifference to what guests did and claimed that he helped matters along by removing locks from room doors. He was not lying. Joseph

FIG. 73
Swimsuit contest at Kamp Karamac. Each resort tried to be different from its competitors. Kamp Karamac's gimmick was a beauty contest for its guests. Delaware Water Gap National Recreation Area.

O'Connor recalls that three young ladies once appeared at Kamp Karamac after suffering a fright at this other resort. Men tried to come into their room all night. The frightened women pushed the dresser to the door, and one kept guard while the others slept. The next morning, they complained about the "missing" locks to the manager, who acted as if it were nothing. The three young women spent the rest of their vacation at Kamp Karamac.

Kamp Karamac was very much a proper place. On the other hand, Oak Grove and Glenwood, which—like Karamac—predated the war, had a wild reputation. The wildest of all, according to observers, was Tamiment, which in its own way reflected the newer mores that in the 1960s would become mainstream. Although the Tamiment of the 1950s still had its political agenda, that agenda never intruded on the socializing. One waiter recalls that guests often returned to their rooms after the nightly dancing and carried on without even bothering to lower the blinds. Another observer saw sadness at Tamiment, a place where many lonely women desperately sought companionship.[42]

The Pocono Honeymoon Resorts

First the courtship, then the wedding, and finally the honeymoon. There was a marriage boom after World War II and, because of postwar prosperity, newlyweds could afford a honeymoon. Honeymooners had always come to the Poconos, but they had never defined the region until after World War II, when the Poconos became a favorite destination for newlyweds. If nothing else, honeymoons gave the Poconos what they had always lacked: a distinguishing feature that would make the region stand out from its competitors. The Poconos had become the land of love and romance. In 1959, the *New York Times* reported that the Poconos were rivaling Niagara Falls, which once was America's favorite honeymoon destination. The Poconos averaged 1,500 to 2,000 honeymooners each week, and business kept improving. Ten years later, *Newsweek* reported that the region was attracting about 115,000 newlyweds per year, an average of over 2,000 each week. *Newsweek* added that the Poconos contained twenty-five "love nests," resorts that catered to honeymooners.[43]

The honeymoon business was competitive. To gain the advantage over its rivals, a resort needed satisfied customers who believed that their first days of marriage had been special and would tell their friends. Ed and Claudine Glauser, who ran Honeymoon Haven, gave newlyweds something special by installing "Roman" or sunken tubs, square tubs for two, which evolved into the famous heart-shaped tubs of today. Another gimmick to enrich the honeymoon experience was to limit the clientele to newlyweds. One resort made sure of this by demanding to see the wedding certificate. The Pocono Mountain Inn believed it had a winning formula by advertising that "honeymooners are treated with studied neglect."[44]

The rule at typical honeymoon resorts was forced conviviality. As in the singles resorts, guests ate family style in order to get acquainted. During the day, games and amusements were the same as at other resorts, with a social director leading the way. Group activities were so much the norm that when a couple was late arriving in the morning, other couples would cry: "We know what you were doing."

The paradox of fostering association at a time when privacy would be expected is easily explained. The resort keepers knew that honeymooners were young. As late as 1969, the average age of guests at Penn Hills—a leading honeymoon resort—was nineteen, which of course means that many newlyweds were teenagers. Many brides had attended all-girl schools and had never left home. The sudden intimacy of the honeymoon was a jolt that they could not handle. Claudine Glauser of Honeymoon Haven recalls crying, frightened brides who needed to talk to a mother figure. Dario Belardi, a partner at Cove Haven, remembers one bride who left the room the first night and hitchhiked back to northern New Jersey. Sometimes, a couple would cut short the honeymoon, using excuses such as the death of a family member. With so many couples having problems, it is easy to

FIG. 74
Where the girls are: guests pose at Kamp Karamac. Singles resorts always attracted more women than men. If the ratio was too unfavorable, women were known to ask for their money back. Delaware Water Gap National Recreation Area.

see why resorts did not leave honeymooners alone and why honeymooners were kept busy at play during the day. Couples needed other couples as a support group.[45]

Another problem was less serious, but nevertheless could contribute to a sudden decision to cut short the honeymoon. Many working-class couples had never left the city, and they were frightened of the country. Claudine Glauser describes the city newlyweds:

FIG. 75
These professional models were posing as honeymooners at Buck Hill. All the resorts, even the staid ones, tried to cash in on the honeymoon business. Buck Hill Collection, Barrett Friendly Library.

We had cases of people from New York who had never heard bugs at nights. You know how they chirp at this time of year. They couldn't stand it and they had to go home. Never been out of the city. Some of them didn't even know what a cow looked like. There was an occasion when a couple was staying at one side of a cottage and another couple on the other side. One couple had some nuts in a drawer and they wound up on the other side in the other couple's drawer. A mouse or chipmunk was taking them from one side to the other. One of the girls thought it was the cutest thing. She put cheese in the middle of the floor. They were watching for the mouse to come out and they were waiting with their camera to take pictures. If that would happen today, you would get a lawsuit. They would scream and carry on. People are different today.

Yet the innocence and lack of sophistication of some of the newlyweds could never hide the fact that a honeymoon resort was another indication of America's growing acceptance of hedonism. Although honeymoons had long been a staple of the affluent classes, newlyweds once went to resorts that catered to all comers. The explicit postwar honeymoon resort not only celebrated marriage, but it also discreetly celebrated what took place after marriage. The honeymoon resort, more than anything else in the Poconos, typified the 1950s: traditional, with its games and pastimes, yet containing hints of the looser sexuality of the decades to come.

10

Prelude to Reinvention

A former manager of Skytop Lodge once remarked that a successful resort anticipates the needs of customers by providing services, comforts, and, if need be, a different vacation culture—even *before* the public is aware of its new needs.[1] In the postwar years, this rule was ignored by many resorts, either because they were unwilling to spot new trends or unable to make the necessary changes, or because they were trapped in aging buildings and facilities and could not raise enough capital for renewal. More than one resort closed down. But even if resort managers were shrewd and canny, minding all the p's and q's of the business, they could still be the victims of extraneous forces that ranged from severe weather to government policy that had other uses for resort property. In one case, a major resort was sold because of an adverse ruling from the Internal Revenue Service.

Dying Slowly

Some resorts never fully recovered from the Great Depression. Fatally wounded, they had somehow managed to survive, sickly and weak. The most spectacular example may have been Lutherland, which in 1936 had borrowed massively from a government agency, the Reconstruction Finance Corporation, and was never able to pay its huge debt. Desperate for business, any business, Lutherland had to downplay its religious mission in order to find paying guests. Ads in the *New York Times* for Beaverbrook, its young adult camp, made no mention of Lutherland—implying to non-Lutherans, who would not know any better, that Beaverbrook was a secular camp. In fact, many of Lutherland's guests were Catholics. Furthermore, its debt did not allow Lutherland to modernize by building a swimming pool and by maintaining its facilities. Rudolph Ressmeyer, a camp director of the 1940s, recalls his disagreements with Robert Ergang, the general manager, who was a retired New York University history professor. Ressmeyer would press Ergang to spend profits on improvements, and Ergang adamantly refused, insisting that he had to service the debt.[2]

To complicate matters, some of the bondholders were saddled with bonds that were losing value. They had little confidence in Ergang, whom they regarded as an amateur, hired only because he was available and pliant. They directed most of their ire toward Robert Dahlen, who had dominated Lutherland until he resigned its presidency in 1943. In 1947, to avoid litigation, Dahlen had surrendered all interest in Lutherland in return for a cash settlement and two mortgages. Dahlen was accused of profiting from the dying enterprise, receiving interest on the mortgages while the holders of the bonds (who regarded themselves as the "little people") received nothing. It was a sad denouement to the original hopes of the 1920s.[3]

Lutherland, beyond hope, filed for bankruptcy in 1951. A court-appointed trustee continued to run the business. In the 1960s, Lutherland was sold to Valparaiso University, which in turn sold it to Susqui Industries. The Philadelphia National Bank eventually acquired the property and sold it to the ever-present developers. Today, little remains of Lutherland. The hotels, the camp, and the casino are gone. Only the cottages survive: their owners still have the ninety-nine-year lease on the lots that Lutherland had started selling in the 1920s.[4]

The same fate befell the Paradise Valley Lutheran Association, the other Lutheran enterprise. But in this case, there was far less sting, because the Paradise Valley project never overexpanded and never borrowed from the federal government. Its decline can be traced to the fact that its hotel was inferior when compared to the new postwar motels. The late Reverend George Ammon, who had been closely associated with Paradise Valley, commented in a 1989 interview: "I think the rise of motels was the death knell for a place like this. You did not have a room with your own facilities and the automobile made it possible for people to travel farther away. People now borrowed money for leisure time activities. People were no longer interested in coming to what was a second-rate hotel."

The hotel closed, leaving the cottage colony behind. Several owners winterized their cottages and moved in permanently. To this day, cottage owners must be Lutherans. Rev. Ammon again recalled: "We had guest pastors coming from New York, New Jersey, and Pennsylvania. We still have that. That is the only remnant of the religious tradition that we have now: a Sunday morning worship service. All of the rest of the religious activities have gone by the board—no Sunday school, no midweek service. As clergy we regret that the religious impetus that started the thing has eroded to a great extent—in many ways parallel to what has happened in our culture."[5]

Resorts in Delaware Water Gap and the Stroudsburgs had a different problem. They were stuck in a location that had not been fashionable since the center of the vacation industry shifted inland, away from the Delaware River. Owners of several boardinghouses gave up the business altogether and converted their Victorian-era buildings to apartments. Other resorts hung on.

Stroudsburg and Delaware Water Gap resorts often ended their life cycle by transforming themselves into dormitories for East Stroudsburg State Teachers College. Mirroring the state of all institutions of higher education after the Second World War, the teachers' college in East Stroudsburg was crowded, unable to house all the returning veterans who could afford college on the G.I. Bill. But East Stroudsburg State Teachers College was not a typical school, surrounded by aging resorts that opened in mid-June and closed after Labor Day. Hence began a marriage of convenience: resorts would house students during the school year, and once the spring semester ended, they would revert to their usual vacationers. Among the resorts that participated in this arrangement were the Fenner in East Strouds-burg and the Bellevue in Delaware Water Gap. These resorts were considered extensions of East Stroudsburg State Teachers College. Students had to behave as if they were living on campus.

The Indian Queen in Stroudsburg differed from other student resorts in that it housed first-year women. Although they were two miles from campus, the women also lived under strict supervision—in fact, far more than the men. They were so much part of campus life that they could not even escape the rigors of hazing. Sophomores made special trips from the main campus to make sure that women in the Indian Queen would have the joy of doing push-ups at two o'clock in the morning. For the owners of the Indian Queen, the extra cash was handy, yet the resort was doomed. Situated on bustling Main Street, it made no sense in the automobile age. It was demolished in 1963, and a bank stands on its location.[6]

Resorts that were empty or losing business were usually razed. A few examples will suffice. In Delaware Water Gap, the Brodhead Cottage of the nineteenth century was demolished in 1960. It had been a dude ranch in the 1930s, allowing city people to play at being cowboys. Among the Mount Pocono resorts demolished were the Clairmont, the Mount Pocono House, and the Skyline Inn (for-merly the Devonshire Pines, which Edward Jenkins operated after he left the Inn at Buck Hill Falls).

Acts of God and Acts of Man

More than one Pocono resort burned to the ground. Invariably, the pattern was the same. An aging wooden building was either empty or neglected. Sooner or later, acts of God—such as a storm, light-ning bolt, or fire of natural origin—or vandals would cause a blaze that would destroy the resort. Among the many examples are the Belmont in Mount Pocono, which burned in 1963, and the Mount Pleasant House, which met its fate in 1968.

Another act of God was the great flood of August 1955, the greatest natural disaster in the history of the Poconos. The overture to the flood was Hurricane Connie, which had soaked the ground thor-oughly. When Hurricane Diane arrived days later with trillions of gallons of additional rain, the mountains could no longer absorb the water. The result was a deadly run-off on the night of August 18–19 that uprooted trees and lifted boulders, sweeping them along with tons of soil, giving an added punch to the water. By the time the fortified water reached the low-lying areas of Monroe County, it had become an irresistible force. Houses, cars, bridges, and man-made objects of all kinds were thrown about and broken, and, in some cases, they were included as part of the flood's deadly bag-gage. The residents of Greentown, Canadensis, Analomink, and the Stroudsburgs were caught unawares. Most managed to escape, leaving behind flooded basements and first floors. Eighty-seven people died, and thousands were homeless.[7]

FIG. 76
Remains of the Interboro bridge. The flood of August 1955 destroyed the Interboro bridge between Strouds-burg and East Stroudsburg. Monroe County Historical Association.

Once the floodwater receded, impassable roads and fallen bridges stymied relief workers. Communities and resorts were isolated. Marie Hoffman, who owned the other Delaware House (the one in Dingmans Ferry), took in mothers with children from a nearby bungalow colony. She recalls: "We had no lights. No water. We did get milk from a local farmer but it was unpasteurized so we rationed the pasteurized milk for anyone under two. I learned that we can get along without electricity, although it would be a hardship. But you can't get along without water. That was awful. When the water did come back after two weeks, it was so full of chlorine that it killed my goldfish."

At the Riverview Tavern alongside the river, the water covered the bar. Marie Hoffman recalls the cleanup at the Riverview: "You think of water as being clean; you don't realize the mud it leaves behind. We needed hoses to clean the walls. Everything touched by floodwater had to be thrown out."[8]

August is the peak season for the Poconos, but the flood effectively ended the season for most resorts. Although only five members of the Pocono Mountains Vacation Bureau closed down, average occupancy dropped dramatically, with less than 20 percent of the beds occupied six days after the flood. False stories circulated in city newspapers about typhoid scares, causing numerous reservations to be canceled. Onawa Lodge in Barrett Township had 225 guests at the time of the flood, but even though power was restored in two days and drinking water brought in, most vacationers went home, and few took their places. In less than two weeks' time, Onawa Lodge was nearly abandoned, reduced to 30 guests.[9]

Tamiment, by contrast, weathered the crisis rather well. Gasoline-powered generators provided limited power for the main buildings, the refrigerators, and for well pumps, although the theater and the cabins stayed dark. After the electric company restored power, Ben Josephson hastened to reassure the public. On Monday, August 22, he sent out 750 telegrams, informing reservation holders that the Milford bridge was passable. Once the guests arrived at Milford, they would be met by automobiles from Tamiment. As a result, nine out of ten reservation holders showed up.[10]

Every natural disaster leads analysts to wonder if better planning would have reduced the destruction. The flood of August 1955 was no exception, and the federal government decided that a dam was needed to prevent a similar flood in the future. This led to support for the Tocks Island Project, an ambitious plan to dam the Delaware River six miles upstream from Delaware Water Gap. The underside of this plan was that it inevitably meant that resorts and residences standing in the way of the dam were as doomed as the buildings ravaged by the 1955 flood.

Although the Commonwealth of Pennsylvania had been buying land for the dam for years, the August 1955 tragedy gave a certain urgency to the cause of flood control. The Delaware River Basin Commission, in cooperation with the Army Corps of Engineers, proposed a 160-foot-high dam at Tocks Island in the Delaware River that would create a thirty-seven-mile-long lake extending north to Port Jervis. The largest dam east of the Mississippi, the Tocks Island Dam was seen as producing all sorts of benefits. It would store water for consumption, generate hydroelectric power, regulate river flow, and provide recreation. The National Recreation Area surrounding the lake was expected to attract over ten million visitors a year. These formidable plans were given life in October 1962, when Congress enacted the Flood Control Act that authorized the Tocks Island Dam. Three years later, President Lyndon Johnson signed the bill creating the National Recreation Area, thereby combining flood control with a national park. The project would be operational by 1975.

Acquiring the land was all that remained. Through the power of eminent domain, the federal government in 1967 began to appropriate thousands of acres of land on both sides of the Delaware River upstream from Delaware Water Gap, evicting the tenants. As thorough as a storm or an earthquake, the government demolished over three thousand buildings that it had seized. Compensation was supposedly keyed to the physical value of the buildings, but this meant nothing for resorts whose real value was the intangible skills of their managers. Contesting the government's low offer required trips to federal district court in Scranton, an intimidating experience for those who are not naturally litigious. "We got peanuts," recalls Barbara Barrow, whose parents owned Bacon and Bagel in Bushkill. Marie Hoffman also remembers disappointment with the government's frugal settlement. Aside from the Hoffman and Barrow resorts, Honeymoon Haven, the Peters House, and various other inns near Delaware Water Gap also fell victim to the proposed Tocks Island Dam.

In the early 1960s, the Tocks Island Dam seemed inevitable. Construction was to begin in 1967, but it was delayed by the Vietnam War, when President Johnson had to choose between guns and butter. He chose guns. The federal government repeatedly cut funding for the dam, and by 1971, the Army Corps of Engineers had yet to issue a construction contract. Meanwhile, community opposition to the dam was growing. The same war in Vietnam that cut the dam's funding had also shown ordinary citizens that they could oppose the government. In addition, the fight against the dam was

FIG. 77
Tocks Island, in the Delaware River, was the site of a proposed dam—a dam that was never built, due to community opposition. Monroe County Historical Association. Photograph by A. Koster.

gaining the support of outsiders. The Save the Delaware Coalition had a membership that ranged from the Sierra Club to the Daughters of the American Revolution. And the alleged benefit of flood control was increasingly questioned.

Aside from winning over the public, Tocks Island's opponents won over many politicians. On July 31, 1975, when the Delaware River Basin Commission met, the governors of New York, New Jersey, and Delaware voted against funding the Tocks Island project. Only Governor Milton Shapp of Pennsylvania continued to support it, perhaps recalling the night in 1972 when the flooding Susquehanna River chased him out of the governor's mansion in Harrisburg. The Commission's vote effectively killed the Tocks Island project. All that remained was the signing of its death certificate: its deauthorization took place in 1992.[11]

Not all acts of man in the Poconos were necessarily baneful. In the 1950s, needing land for the Delaware Water Gap bridge and its arteries, the Delaware River Bridge Commission used its power of eminent domain to acquire fourteen properties in Delaware Water Gap. Among them were five hotels: the Delaware House (or the Hof Brau, as it was then called), the Riverview, the Hillcrest, the Howard, and the Bellevue (which had housed college students). These hotels had been in decline for years, so the forced closure may have been a blessing to the owners.[12]

Changing Vacation Patterns

A vacation both fits the needs of an age and reflects that age. The singles resort was the expression of the courtship culture of earlier decades, in which sexuality was hidden. The open sexuality of the 1960s made the singles resort an anachronism. Despite what some baby boomers felt, they did not discover sex in the 1960s; they merely chose to publicize it. With the Tamiments and Vacation Valleys no longer needed for secretive lovemaking, fewer young people bothered to visit singles resorts in the Poconos. It did not help that many resort owners failed to notice the changing youth culture. The jazz acts that Ben Josephson was booking at Tamiment in the early 1960s may have been cool a decade earlier, but were passé for twenty-year-olds who regarded Elvis as a has-been. Josephson also drove away customers by banning blue jeans on the dance floor. A few years earlier, young people would have obeyed house rules and dressed up. In the defiant sixties, though, they stopped coming.[13]

For the black resorts, the decade of the 1960s had its own special impact. Civil rights legislation forbidding discrimination in public accommodations meant that black vacationers now had options once denied them. Hillary Bute recalls retaining his long-standing customers, but failing to attract younger black vacationers. He and his wife ended up taking in the overflow from Mount Airy Lodge. The Hillside Inn, by comparison, struggled on and finally closed in 1982. The other African American resorts also closed.

Another significant change for the Poconos took place much farther away. In 1958, Seattle's Boeing aircraft company introduced the first passenger jetliner to America—the 707. It was faster and safer than traditional piston-engine aircraft. The smoother ride of the 707 allowed passengers to reach their destinations without nervous glances at the airsickness bag. Florida, the Caribbean, and even Europe were closer than ever. Easier air travel meant competition, and Ben Josephson would complain of it, especially since the upscale clients Tamiment attracted would be very susceptible to exotic vacations in distant places.[14]

Another form of competition for the Poconos was the option, strange as it seems, of staying at home. Ben Josephson called it an "abrupt change in the way of life in metropolitan areas." In a public statement made in 1958, Josephson described this new competition as follows:

> The development of swimming pools at Country Clubs . . . allows the family to have the facilities of a continuous summer vacation . . . without the necessity of a family leaving home for an expensive vacation at a resort hotel; the development of the Cabana Beach Club . . . allows mother to pack the family into the car each morning and take them to a beautiful facility and

FIG. 78

Ben Josephson and Willi Brandt. Brandt, the Social Democratic Chancellor of West Germany, stopped at Tamiment during his American visit of 1963. Josephson and Brandt shared the same leftist, anticommunist politics. Distinguished visitors gave an air of class to Tamiment, but its young singles were more interested in the fun. When Tamiment could not adjust to the 1960s, the singles stopped coming. Tamiment Institute Library, New York University. Photograph by Lewis Goren.

thus avoid the necessity of a summer vacation, and the suburban way of life now includes the home or community swimming pool and day camp for the children.[15]

As staying at home became more enjoyable, summer vacationers demanded additional services from resorts. They wanted private bathrooms in their rooms, not a walk down the hall to the public bathtub and water closet. And they wanted air conditioning, not the old-fashioned cool breeze offered by opening a window. More than anything else, vacationers wanted a swimming pool. It had evolved from vacation luxury to vacation necessity. The old swimming hole had seemed natural to swimmers of the nineteenth century, but in the 1950s, weeds, green slimy stuff that floated, pebbles under the feet, and live critters were uncivilized. City people wanted the reassurance that only chlorinated water would give, even if chlorine stung their eyes. The fanciest resorts had installed swimming pools prior to World War II, and the rest had to follow suit in the postwar years. Although swimming pools were expensive to build and difficult to maintain because chlorinated water was corrosive, they were necessary in order for a resort to remain competitive.[16]

The worst problem for resorts was the tendency toward shorter vacations that had begun earlier in the century and that showed no signs of abating. Prior to World War I, a resort could expect a good number of vacationers to stay for the "season"; by the 1930s, a resort had to settle for vacationers who stayed for several weeks. A postwar resort had to settle for even less. Marie Hoffman of the Delaware House recalls that the backbone of her business in the 1940s had been the weekly trade of guests who arrived on Sunday night and left the following Sunday. By the 1960s, fewer guests were staying for the week. Her growing reliance on transients had, for all practical purposes, turned her Delaware House into a motel. The only real difference was that the Delaware House had a restaurant and bar.

Like the small resorts, large resorts also lost the weekly trade. But unlike small resorts, the large ones could survive, provided they made the necessary adjustments. They had to give up the notion of relying on a continuous stream of guests and instead accept a feast-and-famine routine of conventions and one-day group outings. Doing business this new way had the very important implication that resorts had to remain open throughout the year. In turn, this required huge capital investments, for at the very least, resorts built for the summer trade had to install heating in order to have guests in January. If guests were attending a convention, they would expect private phones in their bedrooms. A winter trade also implied an indoor life. An outdoor swimming pool (a cutting-edge resort amenity in the 1930s) was useless in the winter, making an indoor pool a necessity, despite the cost. Also necessary was a nightclub—both for winter guests and for casual visitors who would stay only for a few hours. Ben Josephson wrote in 1963 that the old ballroom and stage where Tamiment had practically invented television variety comedy had become dated. Tamiment had to invest in a nightclub.

Along with the cost of providing new amenities, a sudden increase in liability insurance was another unwelcome burden, especially for the smaller resorts. Retired resort owners all remember the shock of seeing the bills. Unwilling to believe that her premium had doubled, Marie Hoffman checked with her agent, who confirmed the bad news. Reeve and Marie Price, who ran the Spruce Mountain House, recall that the insurance firm demanded sprinklers in the kitchen and coverage for horseback riding. The Prices finally got rid of the horse to save money on insurance. Faced with the prospect of having to incur debt for modernization, they decided to retire in 1968.[17] Joyce Kristoff, who ran the Blue Ridge Inn with her husband, noted that insurance was "one of the things we couldn't finance any more." She added, "Heavens! It kept going up. We couldn't afford it. The electric we couldn't afford any more. And that's why a lot of the resorts went out of business. They just couldn't keep up with the expenses. Even the ones who owned them outright couldn't keep up with the expenses. Only the largest businesses stayed in business."[18]

At the same time, a national movement rose to bring vacation workers under federal minimum-wage legislation. Resort owners were opposed, arguing that free room and board represented a form of remuneration and that the real wages of vacation workers were above the minimum wage. On March 13, 1964, the manager of Skytop, William Malleson Jr., testified before a Congressional Committee and spoke against the five-day workweek and overtime pay. He obviously spoke for the industry, but the politicians were not listening. On September 23, 1966, President Lyndon Johnson signed a minimum-wage bill that covered resort workers. The new law gradually raised hourly pay until it reached $1.60 in 1971. Although equity could easily justify applying the minimum wage law to resorts, the higher payrolls did come at a bad time. In the context of increasing expenses throughout the industry, a jump in labor costs was the last nail in the coffin for many small resorts.[19]

To complicate matters, the 1960s also produced new labor problems. Resorts had always relied on poorly paid, obedient workers who labored seven days a week and who had enormous patience with the public. During the Great Depression and even into the 1950s, with memories of the 1930s still fresh, people could be found who would work long hours. In the rebellious and prosperous 1960s, job expectations expanded, especially among younger workers who had no memory of hard times.

The Inn at Buck Hill Falls suffered a culture clash with its college-aged, baby-boomer workers. Fingerprinted, told to stay out of sight, and fed leftovers, they were resentful. After living in a comfortable college dormitory, Buck Hill seemed like a prison: small, spartan sleeping quarters, uncomfortable mattresses, and naked bulbs hanging from the ceiling. The guests seemed ancient, and in the 1960s, no one over thirty was to be trusted. One waitress dismissed the diners as "cranky old ladies" who kept on complaining. Another waitress received no tips the first week because she was in training. On the eighth day, having seen no tips and having been paid less than a dollar a hour, she quit. She found a job at Unity House and liked it. The union resort took better care of its employees, allowing them to use the recreational facilities and to swim in the lake. The food was also a lot better.[20]

In the 1960s, the Inn at Buck Hill Falls still had an aristocratic clientele, or at least what passes for aristocracy in the American Republic. It was a private world, an anachronism not only to its work-force, but also to the universe outside. One time, a young Italian American couple from Philadelphia were in the area. It was winter; they had been hiking in the snow; their boots were wet. They just wanted a glimpse of the place that was allegedly so "hoity-toidy." They burst into the Buck Hill lobby during high tea. The lobby was full of old women who were skinny because they had the money to wear fine clothes, whose hair was properly trimmed and primmed, and who had one glove off as they picked up their cups of tea. The young couple and these women would never have seen each other in Philadelphia, although they probably lived no more than several miles apart. They looked at each other in mutual shock. The Main Line and ethnic Philadelphia had had a close encounter in the Poconos.[21]

Pocono Twilight

Tourists of the new millennium who drive around the Poconos will see the many billboards for the large couples resorts. As they drive by empty lots, housing developments, and shopping centers, they will not know that Victorian resorts once stood on some of these sites. The tourists might even see some of the old wooden resorts—structures that have had former lives of grandeur—in changed form, recycled into apartment houses, private residences, restaurants, and whatever else makes a profit. Without a second thought, the visitors might dismiss these old buildings with their porches and cupolas as a quaint part of the scenery, deserving a brief glance, as they continue their drive to a modern, spiffy resort.

Travelers who tour with longtime residents will hear of a different Poconos, the one that has vanished. They will hear of old resorts in Milford and of the few that survive, kept afloat by their bars and restaurants. Outside of Milford, along the Delaware River, in Greeley, Lackawaxen, and other rural townships, they will hear of long-gone resort owners, the stories of their lives, the famous guests, and the fate of the resorts. The same is true for Mount Pocono and for many other little towns of the Pocono region.

Delaware Water Gap has reverted to being a sleepy country village. The abandoned railroad station can barely be seen from Interstate 80, even if one knows that it is there. Only a single resort survives: the Glenwood. Layton and Agnes Hauser stopped serving meals at their Mountain House in 1969. They took in boarders, leased the building for a few years, and in 1982 sold the Mountain House to Frank Brown. Brown tried to keep going, but in 1988, an arsonist struck. When caught, the arsonist insisted that he was a Native American and demanded a trial by his peers. The judge looked at the Irish name of the arsonist and refused to empanel an Indian jury. As for Brown, he left the Gap for Stroudsburg, purchasing the Best Western—the latest name for the hotel that began life in 1833 as the Stroudsburg House.[22]

The two Quaker resorts also changed hands. In 1967, Pocono Manor was sold to Samuel W. Ireland, who had made his money by supplying coffee to commercial establishments. The Quaker connection, rather tenuous in recent years, was severed. Ireland poured money into his acquisition, renovating and modernizing, and his family still owns the Inn. Pocono Manor has survived by catering to conventions, weddings, and group outings.[23]

The Inn at Buck Hill Falls was less fortunate, having made a strategic blunder in the 1960s. It assumed that its world would last forever, and it erected a west wing, expanding when the smart move would have been to modernize existing facilities. The Inn at Buck Hill Falls was aging, a curse for a resort that needed a new client base and that had to attract conventions and bus outings aggressively. Luckily, in 1977, the Buck Hill Quakers found a buyer. But unable to make a profit, he ended up defaulting on the mortgage. The next owners also declared bankruptcy. In the 1990s, the once proud inn was empty, its roof leaking badly.[24]

Like Buck Hill, Fred Waring also came to be seen as an anachronism. In the era of long hair, joints, and acid rock, Waring was anything but hip. He kept on touring with his Pennsylvanians and continued

FIG. 79
Going to the ski trail was half the fun at Buck Hill. The horse-drawn carriage matched the conservative Buck Hill tradition. Buck Hill Collection, Barrett Friendly Library.

playing old favorites. Buying a ticket to one of his concerts was almost a political act, an affirmation of an older music and of its social context. By the time Waring retired in 1980, the size of his group and his audiences had shrunk.[25]

Some resort keepers tried to wrestle with shifting economic realities. Early on, Lew Miller of Log Tavern Camp recognized the changing trends: vacationers were flying elsewhere, and if they came to the Poconos, they wanted amenities that required serious money. He converted his adult camp into a children's camp, Camp Indian Trails. In 1961, he sold his interest to his staff, and a few years later, the camp closed. Having had the foresight to keep the property around the camp, Miller began a second career as a house developer. The owners of Vacation Valley also saw a changing business. Guests were getting fewer and older; they may have been literally the same people who came in the 1950s. In 1976, the Shinn brothers sold Vacation Valley to Caesars, the gaming corporation then noted for its casinos in Las Vegas and Atlantic City. Vacation Valley became Caesars Pocono Palace. As John Shinn noted, "Caesars had the capital we never had. They are on the New York Stock Exchange." A leading competitor for Vacation Valley was Oak Grove. In the 1970s, it too closed, converted to a wrestling camp run by a faculty member from the local teachers' college.[26]

Victimized by changing trends, Tamiment also had a unique problem of its own: the Internal Revenue Service. In 1956, the IRS revoked the tax-exempt status it had granted Tamiment in 1936 and renewed in 1939. The IRS ruled that the main business of the People's Educational Camp Society (PECS), the parent corporation for Tamiment, was running a summer resort for profit and that promotion of the social welfare was secondary. In effect, the IRS defined Tamiment as a commercial enterprise that chose to donate some of its profits to charity. PECS appealed to the Tax Court to have the tax exemption restored, but lost the appeal in 1963. In the following year, the United States Court of Appeals affirmed the decision of the Tax Court, and the Supreme Court refused to review the case. PECS had to pay. In 1963, the tax bill was nearly ninety thousand dollars, and the lawyer's fee was half that amount.[27]

The adverse ruling from the Tax Court was the last straw. Since the late 1950s, Ben Josephson had been pessimistic about Tamiment's future. Besides, Josephson and his chief assistant, Ben Blaker, were looking to retire. On September 18, 1963, Josephson recommended to the PECS board that Tamiment be sold. Selling the resort was also a means to avoid debt for modernization. After refusing several offers (including one from Jackie Gleason), on May 15, 1965, Tamiment was sold.[28]

After the sale, Tamiment and PECS went their separate ways. The Tamiment resort still exists, but it no longer has the New York liberal Jewish flavor that made it unique. Once PECS lost the encumbrance of a commercial enterprise, it quickly regained its tax-free status. It used the proceeds of the sale to support liberal causes, such as granting scholarships, distributing public service pamphlets, and publishing *Labor History,* which was a scholarly journal. Its most important activity may have been the support of the Tamiment Institute Library, which was housed at New York University and over which Josephson presided before his death in 1980.[29]

The decline of Unity House began in the 1960s. In 1961, the union resort attracted about 68,000 guests. In the following year, attendance fell to 60,000, and it kept on falling, sinking to 43,000 in 1968.

FIG. 80

Walt Disney (front row, fourth from left) was a member of the Beverly Hills Lawn Bowling Club that participated in the 1964 Buck Hill Falls Men's Open Doubles tournament. Lawn bowling tournaments have survived the demise of the Inn; they continue to be held on the Buck Hill grounds. The cottagers offer lodging to the participants. Buck Hill Collection, Barrett Friendly Library.

Four years later, the annual report noted a substantial drop compared to 1968. No figures were given. Unity House was tied to a declining union and could not be saved. Because of cheap textile imports, the garment industry had fewer jobs, which meant fewer union members. Membership in the I.L.G.W.U. shrank from 451,000 in 1967 to about 170,000 in 1990. In addition, new union members were not the first- and second-generation Jews and Italians of the old days. They were Chinese, Puerto Ricans, and African Americans who could not relate to Unity House. The clientele of the 1970s and 1980s were often the guests who had come in earlier times. They were an older crowd that had little use for the tennis courts and even less for the children's camp. But dancing to an eight-piece orchestra remained popular. The older guests, after all, were from the big band era.[30]

In February 1969, the I.L.G.W.U. was given a great excuse to sell Unity House: the administration building had burned to the ground, along with its thirteen Diego Rivera murals. The sale of Unity House was discussed and rejected. Louis Stulberg, the I.L.G.W.U. president, saw a future for Unity House, and he predicted that the planned Tocks Island project would raise property values in the area. The real reason for keeping Unity House was, of course, emotional. Unity House had become part of the union's ethos, as natural as dues and shop stewards. The union did scale down the size of Unity House; remodeling in the early 1970s reduced guest capacity by half, to 600. Nonetheless, Unity House was doomed, kept alive by union subsidies. Finally, in January 1990, the I.L.G.W.U. grew tired of infusing a million dollars annually into the resort, and Unity House was closed.[31]

FIG. 81

The magnificent Oak Grove Hotel was one of the swinging singles resorts. When the singles resorts became passé, the Oak Grove was sold and became a wrestling camp. Fire destroyed it in the 1970s. Monroe County Historical Association.

The I.L.G.W.U. could not find a buyer for its property. Unity House had no swimming pool, and it was not winterized. A typical old Pocono resort that opened on Memorial Day and closed after Labor Day, Unity House was a relic that remained empty. Near the end of the decade, a use was finally found for the property: plans were announced to convert the old resort into an arts center, which the Philadelphia and Pittsburgh orchestras agreed to make their summer home. (All this was contingent on local funding being found.) The proposed arts center was symptomatic of an emerging Pocono resort culture for which nature was a backdrop. Indoor attractions were a greater draw than the sunshine and the scenery. In the late twentieth century, the Pocono vacation economy had been reinvented.

Welcoming a New Millennium

America is the land of reinvention, and the Poconos are a good example of that reinvention. When the old hotels shut down, the Pocono vacation industry could have faded from public consciousness. This has been the fate of other resort regions, and it could still be the fate of the Poconos—but not in the foreseeable future. The Poconos have adjusted to the times and remade themselves.

The new Poconos satisfy nearly every taste. Winter sports are bigger than ever, because artificial snow has made skiing a reliable business. In addition, the super-resorts and their expensive indoor facilities allow the modern Poconos to attract winter vacationers. Couples resorts, with their famous heart-shaped bathtubs, meet different needs, but are likewise very much in the modern spirit. Less conspicuous, but also important, are the specialty resorts that take advantage of America's increasingly diverse preferences.

For other vacationers, summer homes or time-shares are attractive. If visitors come for the day, they can choose from hundreds of day-tripper attractions that range from jazz and Irish festivals to celebrations of wine and garlic. There are nature trails, petting zoos, water parks, a NASCAR racetrack, and much more. Variety marks today's Poconos.

Winter Sports

Serious skiing is a recent arrival to the Poconos, because in the old days, the region had only three of the four requirements for skiing. Although the Poconos had high elevations, cold weather, and a huge nearby market, the region lacked the most important element of all—and that was snow. The inverse of the area's summer sunshine is a typically dry winter. Snow does fall in the Poconos, but the snowfall is too irregular for a profitable ski resort.

Prior to World War II, Buck Hill, Skytop, and Pocono Manor tried to offer winter sports as an added attraction whenever the weather was willing. These hotels had lists of winter visitors to whom they mailed postcards with last-minute information on what the weather would allow. When skiing

FIG. 82
Before machine-made snow guaranteed a skiing season, winter sports in the Poconos usually consisted of ice skating. These young vacationers of the 1940s were having a great time on the Buck Hill golf course. Buck Hill Collection, Barrett Friendly Library.

was not possible, winter guests went skating and toboggan sledding. If snow fell, golf courses doubled as ski areas. The Lackawanna Railroad would quickly assemble a ski special and bring in skiers from New York City.[1]

After World War II, less snow fell in the Poconos, driving skiers to the New York and New England resorts and nearly stopping the winter trade. Buck Hill and Big Boulder, which opened in 1947, tried to reverse this trend by using machine-made snow. Unfortunately, the technology was primitive and made the Poconos seem inferior, since the region lacked a ski area with a complete network of trails. New England ski resorts mockingly referred to Middle Atlantic skiing as the "banana belt." But the Poconos were not daunted. In 1960, when Squaw Valley, California, hosted the Winter Olympics, millions of Americans sat before their television sets, watched downhill skiing events, and got the urge to ski. Vermont could sneer all it wanted, but the so-called banana belt was closer to Philadelphia and

FIG. 83
Up, up, and away at Camelback.

New York City. In the winter of 1961–62, more than fifty Pocono resorts stayed open during the winter and operated free auto shuttles to the ski trails.[2]

Meanwhile, work was under way on the new Camelback ski area, the first in the Poconos devoted entirely to skiing. The story begins with the Bensinger brothers, Chud and Alex, who were attorneys in Stroudsburg—and loved to ski. During the winter of 1950–51, they installed a ski run near Tannersville on Big Pocono Mountain, as Camelback was popularly called. The operation was a sideline that was open only on weekends and relied on natural snow. Business was understandably bad. When the flood of 1955 damaged the trails, the Bensingers put their operation on hold.

The next step in the saga was taken by a group of Philadelphians, avid skiers who had tired of driving to Vermont. In 1958, Jim Moore, an attorney, and his wife were vacationing at Pocono Manor when they noticed Big Pocono in the distance and wondered if it could be used for skiing. Moore returned with Terry Lloyd, an executive with Drexel & Co., and with Dan Horan, a Philadelphia insurance man. The Philadelphians heard of the Bensingers, and a partnership was born, in which the Bensingers were the local connection and the Philadelphians had access to credit. The partners had much to do; they had to buy out the owners of various parts of Big Pocono and arrange a lease with the Commonwealth of Pennsylvania, which owned the top of the mountain. The masterstroke of the Philadelphians was insisting that Big Pocono be called by its official name of Camelback. They felt that "Big Pocono" might be confused with the many events and places in the region that had Pocono in their name, whereas "Camelback" sounded unique and had charisma.

On November 8, 1962, the Bensingers, Moore, Lloyd, Horan, and others formed the Camelback Ski Corporation. They raised capital, laid out trails, and installed infrastructure with parking, chairlifts, and an Alpine-style lodge. On December 14, 1963, when the Camelback ski area opened, it was the largest in the Poconos. Its new, improved technology guaranteed a reliable supply of excellent machine-made snow. The first season was a big success: more than fifty thousand skiers visited Camelback that year.[3]

Skiing allowed summer resorts to remain open in the winter, and Camelback imitated their successes by installing summer attractions. In 1977, an Alpine Slide opened. The slide was a type of bobsled on a concrete track that twisted and turned down the mountain. Camelback made its money by selling tickets for the chairlift that carried Alpine riders up the mountain. In later years, Camelback added a water slide and a baseball batting cage. Summer vacationers can easily pass an entire day at Camelback.[4]

FIG. 84
Snow tubing aficionados wait their turn.

FIG. 85
A winter wonderland for skiers in the Poconos.

Pocono skiing was on its way. In 1972, the Jack Frost ski area opened, followed in 1975 by Shawnee. By 1984, according to the Pocono Mountains Vacation Bureau, skiing accounted for 25 percent of the region's tourist income. And *Skiing* magazine noted that the Poconos boasted twelve ski areas in 1992. Outsiders have always been amazed that the Poconos have so little snow and so much skiing. The artificial snow at Jack Frost Mountain has been rated one of the best three man-made surfaces in the country.[5]

In the 1990s, downhill skiing stopped growing in the Poconos, but snowboarding—essentially, surfing down a mountain—was gaining in popularity. This has largely been a sport for teenagers. The latest craze is snow tubing, though, which can appeal to all ages. A drag lift pulls the tube uphill, and it then slides down like a sled. *Ski* magazine believes that the Poconos, with their fifty-four sliding chutes, might be the American capital of snow tubing.[6]

Although successful, Pocono skiing suffers from a lack of respect—and from the weather. The temperature must fall below freezing to allow machines to make snow. Unfortunately, cold weather does not begin dependably until after Thanksgiving and it lasts only into March. An early spring or a warm spell in December or January can cause financial disaster. Lack of respect is a less serious problem. Ski snobs will always regard Vermont and Colorado as superior, but ski resorts will remain in the Poconos as long as they make money. Besides, skiing has the side benefit of diversifying the Pocono vacation economy. It allows resorts to remain open throughout the year and to afford facilities that would not be feasible for those relying on a three-month summer season.

Casino Gambling: A False Start

To an outsider analyzing the modern Pocono economy, casino gambling may seem to represent a lost opportunity. But citizen opposition stopped it, and there are few regrets. In waging their battle, citizens believed that they were protecting their social environment. They were also bucking the national trend of having legalized gambling almost everywhere—in riverboats, cruise ships, Indian reservations, and hotel casinos. Legalized gambling has become so pervasive that someone who came of age in the 2000s might easily be led to believe that it has always existed. That is not the case, of course. In the 1950s, only the state of Nevada permitted casino gambling. But in the 1970s, when residents of Atlantic City approved it in a referendum, old taboos about gambling started collapsing—but not in the Poconos.

There was talk that gambling would come to the Poconos. Its advocates proclaimed this coming to be inevitable. The large resorts favored gambling, as did the Pocono Mountains Vacation Bureau. Casino gambling evokes images of fancy hotels, fine restaurants, and fabulous Las Vegas shows. Without gambling, its supporters argued, the Poconos would decline. Only hicks with bad teeth would oppose it. Besides, went the argument, gambling had the side benefits of bringing in tax revenue and jobs.[7]

Gambling interests moved into the Poconos. By the late 1970s, Caesars International, known for its casinos in Las Vegas and Atlantic City, owned four resorts in the Poconos. It was widely believed in the Poconos that Caesar had not come to ski. In 1982, singer Wayne Newton (who had owned Aladdin's Castle in Las Vegas) bought Tamiment. In the following year, Jilly Rizzo, a longtime associate of Frank Sinatra, announced plans to finance a fifty-million-dollar resort and sports complex on the site of the former Echo Lake Resort in Bushkill. Rizzo denied an interest in gambling, insisting that the projected three-hundred-room hotel and the indoor sports arena (seating five thousand) would host sporting events. Still, gambling never came to the Poconos, and neither did Jilly Rizzo's resort.[8]

Outside of resort circles, few people in the Poconos wanted gambling. The Pocono Chamber of Commerce opposed it, as did the local clergy. Rumors flew that gambling would bring in mobsters—although if Joan Weiner, the temporary head of the Pennsylvania Crime Commission, was to be believed, mobsters had already arrived. In April 1978, Weiner told the *New York Times* that organized crime figures were found throughout the Pocono resort business. "You can't turn right or left in the Poconos without bumping into gangsters," she insisted. Although Weiner supplied no names, her words sparked some debate over whether she had hard facts or whether she had met too many people whose names ended in vowels.[9]

The enemies of gambling argued that casinos would not improve the Poconos. They painted a scenario in which millions of gamblers would overrun the region, forcing massive increases in fire protection, health services, police, and sanitation, creating an enormous bill that local taxpayers would have to pay. As Atlantic City had shown, only outsiders would benefit from gambling. Instead of good times, insisted these critics, gambling would bring in druggies, prostitutes, loan sharks, and other assorted low-lifes.[10]

Supporters of gambling tried the incremental approach. Instead of calling for casino gambling, they called for the legalization of slot machines. Opponents replied that slot machines would create a casino atmosphere that would pave the way for roulette and blackjack. The opposition did more than argue. The Monroe County Clergy Association put the issue on the ballot and won. In May 1983, Monroe County voters, by a ratio of four to one, defeated proposals to allow slot machines and other forms of casino gambling. In November, Wayne County voters rejected slots and casinos by a ratio of five to two. The votes were nonbinding referenda, but they did express the popular will. The state legislature in Harrisburg allowed gambling legislation to die. One resort had been so sure that gambling would be approved that it had jumped the gun and bought slot machines. Foes of gambling note with glee that the machines have been gathering dust in a cellar ever since.[11]

Resorts Without Gambling

The anti-gambling crusade did not come out of a vacuum. Pocono residents have always set parameters for the vacation industry. In the past, much was allowed, but there were always limits. In the years prior to World War I, hotels had bars; some hanky-panky took place, but a certain public decorum was expected. (The Swiftwater Monks, it should be recalled, drank in private.) Likewise, during Prohibition, booze was available, but the Poconos were not openly lawless. The story of the Milford resort that violated the blue laws of the 1950s by serving after-hours liquor in the basement is illustrative. The law was broken, but behind closed doors. In the 1980s, when the people of the Poconos rejected casino gambling, they were rejecting a cultural sea change that would link the Poconos with vice. In opposing the creation of an inland Atlantic City, an area whose main attraction would be casino gambling, they were showing a true continuity: Pocono residents in earlier decades had likewise regarded the brothels and bars of New Jersey's "sin city" with loathing.

Large resorts have had to survive in a gambling-free Poconos. As Atlantic City shows, gambling is the easy way to run a resort. Most casino hotels in Atlantic City offer games of chance, food, nightclub entertainment, and little else. If gambling and the steady stream of customers it guarantees are taken away, resorts must be creative. The super-resorts achieve this creativity through sheer variety. They offer numerous amusements, giving vacationers the same problem they have with food on a buffet table—deciding what to take and what to reject. A glance at some leading resorts shows that they compete by changing the amusement package.

Split Rock Resort at Lake Harmony was founded in 1941 as a private hunting and fishing retreat for executives of the Lehigh Coal and Navigation Company. With Big Boulder mountain nearby, Split Rock was a natural site for a ski resort. The great expansion took place after the Kalins family bought Split Rock Resort in 1981; they have since poured over thirty-five million dollars into the property. Split Rock Resort is the largest employer in Carbon County, and it has continued to grow. In June 1999, it announced the purchase of the bankrupt Mountain Laurel Resort, which had abruptly closed in December 1997, idling 250 employees. Split Rock said that it would sell timeshares on its new property.

The main building, the Galleria, makes Split Rock an all-weather resort. An entire vacation or convention can be spent in the Galleria, which contains meeting rooms, a gym, an indoor pool, a bowling alley, a first-run movie theater, tennis courts, and restaurants. The Galleria has facilities for children who can be dropped off by parents planning to ski, golf, or do whatever else kids call "boring." The only requirement for entering the children's program is that kids be at least three years old and "potty trained." Special events at the Galleria bring in hordes of weekend guests and day-trippers. On Mother's Day, 2000, fitness maven Richard Simmons showed off his exercise program. Murder Mystery Weekends allow audiences to participate. "The Death of the Boogie Woogie" in December 2000 was billed as the weekend that will "live in infamy."[12]

Woodloch Pines is a unique super-resort, and it remains the least known, tucked away in Lackawaxen Township in northern Pike County. Residents of other parts of the Poconos are barely aware of its existence, although Woodloch Pines is more than forty years old. Woodloch Pines thrives, but it neither hosts special events nor accommodates large conventions. It did not even install a golf course until 1991. Woodloch Pines also breaks the rules by hardly advertising, yet it boasts an 83 percent

FIG. 86

John Kiesendahl and Debbie Martin of Woodloch Pines. One of the founder's sons, Kiesendahl believes in hands-on management. Martin is marketing director.

occupancy rate. It relies on guest referrals and repeat business. Its secret is simple. Unlike other super-resorts that spread a wide net, Woodloch Pines concentrates on families. All super-resorts have tennis and basketball courts, an indoor gym, and a swimming pool. Woodloch Pines has something extra: go-karts and bumper cars.

Also singular is the nightclub. Instead of booking the slick acts favored by other Pocono resorts, Woodloch Pines offers ventriloquists and jugglers for the family trade. Comedians are warned to keep their material clean. The nightclub does not feature big names, although one sign of its quality is its famous alumni. Ray Romano, the star of the television sitcom "Everybody Loves Raymond," played here. Another regular was Darrell Hammond, who became famous by impersonating President Clinton on television's "Saturday Night Live." Every year, the Woodloch troupe puts on a new theme show. The 1999 theme was "Countdown to the Millennium," a musical based on the highlights of the century.

Much careful planning has gone into Woodloch Pines. At other resorts, the main lobby contains a mixture of conventioneers, families, couples, and bus tours. At Woodloch Pines, the main building houses family vacationers. Senior citizens on bus tours and conventioneers are shunted off to another building. The beauty of the structures also points to careful planning. The main building, with its knotty pine walls and rustic decor, calls to mind a tasteful country inn. Beyond the lobby lies the dining room, whose huge show window reveals a spectacular view of postcard-perfect Lake Teedyuscung, surrounded by trees.[13]

Another version of good taste is found at Skytop Lodge, still the classiest Pocono resort. After turning off Route 390, motorists make a gentle ascent to reach the main building, which sits on a hill like a castle of old. The five-story modified Dutch colonial structure is a reminder of the days when millionaires paid no income tax. The interior has its own quaint charm, sporting dark wooden walls, fine old furniture, and a dining room with fresh flowers on the tables. Skytop Lodge is the aging beauty queen who still turns heads. Gentlemen are asked to wear suit jackets at dinner. Finger bowls appear after meals. Skytop tries to maintain these throwbacks to an older gentility without appearing old-fashioned and out of touch. In 1987, Skytop had to accept the fact that people were reading fewer books, and it installed television sets in its rooms. The lodge has also dropped its dress code for golfers.[14]

The *Philadelphia Inquirer* once described Skytop as one of the last true family resorts of the East. At Skytop, family values are not the go-karts of Woodloch Pines. Grandparents read in the ample library while grandchildren sip Shirley Temples. Like all super-resorts, Skytop has a children's program. Along with the scavenger hunts and face painting that can be found at other resorts, Skytop has something called "tea etiquette." One cannot help feeling that kids would prefer to romp at Woodloch Pines.

Skytop offers fewer amusements than its rivals. But it makes good use of its huge fifty-five-hundred-acre estate. A full-time naturalist leads nature walks and lectures on flora and fauna. Guests are urged to report animal sightings, which are posted on a list in the lobby. Trees are tagged with passages from Tennyson and the Psalms. A sign in the lobby announces that "solitude" is a side benefit of a walk in the woods.[15]

Skytop is selling a mood, the feeling that every trend of the baby-boomer era is not necessarily for the best. The Saturday night Elimination Dance and Grand March are revealing. More than two hundred people hold hands and then weave inside and outside the hotel as they loudly sing songs like "Zip-a-Dee-Doo-Dah" and "Battle Hymn of the Republic." Aside from being wholesome fun, this is also indulgent nostalgia—with a hint of a political statement.[16]

Mount Airy Lodge in Mount Pocono has been the most well known of the Pocono super-resorts. It advertised heavily on radio and television, especially in the New York City area. It was the largest of the Pocono resorts, able to accommodate two thousand guests per night, but it was troubled. In November 1999, when its creditors lost faith in the management and moved to take over the resort, its despondent owner committed suicide. On May 11, 2000, the resort was sold at a sheriff's sale to the company that held the mortgage.[17]

Mount Airy's problem may have been that it cast too wide a net. It sought honeymooners, couples, families, conventions, bus tours, and skiers—anyone, it seems, who could pay. Unlike Skytop and Woodloch Pines, Mount Airy lacked a distinct personality, although it may have sought to create one with its entertainment. The walls of its lobby were adorned with over three hundred photographs of show business personalities who performed at Mount Airy. They ranged from comedians Joan Rivers, Flip Wilson, and Andy Kaufman to singers Julius LaRosa, Bobby Vinton, and Tony Bennett. Everyone seems to have been at Mount Airy (with the exception of Frank Sinatra). The 1999 summer entertainers included the Marvelettes, the Drifters, and the Platters, acts from the 1950s and early 1960s that target baby boomers.

Making Whoopee in the Poconos

If Americans today are asked to name the image that best represents the Poconos, chances are that many will cite couples resorts and heart-shaped bathtubs. Couples resorts are the direct descendants of the honeymoon hotels of the postwar era. In the 1960s, honeymoon resorts had to relax their rules when married couples asked to return for their second honeymoon. In the 1970s, unmarried couples were clamoring for admission. With cohabitation replacing marriage, honeymoon resorts became couples resorts.

And the one name continually linked to couples resorts is that of Morris Wilkins. Of all the Pocono personalities of the postwar era, Wilkins has the best chance of being remembered. He will merit at least a footnote in the history of popular culture for having created the heart-shaped bathtub and the seven-foot-tall "Champagne Glass Whirlpool Bath for Two." In 1963, Wilkins was co-owner of Cove Haven, a honeymoon resort. He figured that bedrooms would take care of themselves, but that bathrooms needed sizzle. The heart-shaped tub was the result of his inspiration—and the first magazine ads that featured it brought in hordes of reservations.

In 1969, Wilkins received national attention when *LIFE* magazine ran a story on Cove Haven. A two-page picture showed a couple necking in a heart-shaped bathtub. *LIFE* asked if the nation had entered an era of "affluent vulgarity." Cove Haven's competitors did not care about the alleged vulgarity; seeing profits, they installed their own tubs. Wilkins countered by installing heart-shaped pools in the rooms. In the 1980s, he capped his career by patenting and installing the champagne glass whirlpool bath. Wilkins created the ultimate illusion: his pools and tubs proclaim that sex is not the same as it was in the Garden of Eden, where Adam first lusted after Eve. It *is* better in the Poconos.[18]

By 1995, the nine Pocono resorts with romance themes were attracting over one hundred thousand couples each year. Penn Hills Resort, Summit Vacation Resort, and Birchwood were well known in the business. Mount Airy Lodge owned Strickland's and Pocono Gardens, classic honeymoon meccas of the postwar years. But the four Caesars Pocono resorts—Cove Haven, Paradise Stream, Pocono Palace, and Brookdale—use their collective clout to get much attention. They attract sixty-five thousand couples a year. Besides, they benefit from the services of Morris Wilkins himself. He sold Cove Haven to Caesars in 1969.[19]

Cove Haven is tucked away on the shores of Lake Wallenpaupack in Wayne County. Driving to Cove Haven is a less-than-exciting trek through the rural America of parked pickup trucks. This world is abruptly left behind at the Cove Haven grounds, where a red heart-shaped sign announces, "You are entering the Land of Love." Although Cove Haven tries to appeal to all ages—booking classic rock acts of the 1950s and 1960s, such as the Platters and Ben E. King, to entertain middle-aged couples on weekends—the resort is really a theme park for consenting adults. A statue of the Greek god Pan, known for his lack of inhibitions, faces guests as they walk into the lobby to register.[20] The men's room is labeled "Gladiator," and the ladies' room, "Goddess." The nearby gift shop is worth a look as well. Although nearly all the items for sale are clothes and memorabilia typical of gift shops,

FIG. 87
This champagne glass whirlpool bath in the Roman Towers suite is featured in a Caesars publicity brochure.

one table displays rubber pop-up penises and edible body lotions. Guests walk to their suites, or they can ride in a white van that in the 1990s was called "The Love Machine," but has since been renamed "Chariot." The nightclub comedians are modern and naughty. Anyone offended by off-color jokes and X-rated parlor games does not belong at Cove Haven.[21]

Suites vary in price. Penny-pinchers in the "Garden of Eden" suites forego the champagne glass and the heart-shaped pool, but they do get a heart-shaped bathtub. The top-of-the-line "Champagne Towers by Cleopatra" are cozy, four-level town houses that have no windows (presumably to encourage skinny-dipping). The absence of windows, though, raises the question of how to decorate the walls. A resort called "Caesars" might be expected to have symbols of ancient Rome. Instead, the "Cleopatra" suites contain stylized Egyptian faces in profile that are surrounded by hieroglyphs. A mural with pyramids and camels overlooks the heart-shaped pool. In these top-dollar suites, modern lovers with an interest in history may be reminded of—or even inspired by—the ancient love affair between the fiftysomething Julius Caesar and the twenty-two-year-old Cleopatra.

In December 1998, the *Pocono Record* reported that fetishists of all sorts had been quietly visiting the Poconos. During the slow season of early spring and late fall, they would book entire resorts for themselves. With prying eyes banished, the fetishists would do their thing. Cross-dressing men held conventions, impersonating famous women such as actress Ann-Margret. Spankers and masochists had also come to the Poconos. According to the *Pocono Record,* the Birchwood Resort in Tannersville had planned to host its fourth annual spanking party on April 20, 1999. Roughly 120 spankers from around the world had each paid five hundred dollars for erotic play at the Birchwood. The following weekend was devoted to bondage. Masochists with black leather, whips, chains, and cages had booked the hotel. The story was picked up on the national news; comedians on late-night television even took time out from their usual fare of jokes about then-President Clinton to make a few wise-cracks about the Poconos.

Events at the Birchwood had not exactly been a secret. The police knew, and the Birchwood staff, which had the unpleasant task of cleaning up, knew. Neighbors of the Birchwood Resort had also known of the spankers, had heard of the naked hide-and-seek events in the woods, and had gossiped about the "spank the naked bowler" game. The spankers had an Internet website, and the curious could download all sorts of naughty pictures, but for the most part, the world outside had remained unaware of the activities at the Birchwood.

After the *Pocono Record* exposed the Birchwood, the world knew—and the publicity was unwelcome. Robert Uguccioni, executive director of the Pocono Mountains Vacation Bureau, claimed that the Poconos sought families, couples, and groups. Spankers and masochists did not fit "into the mix," he added. The Birchwood caved to the pressure and canceled the bookings. The promoter of the parties angrily blamed the debacle on "local blue noses." He should have blamed the long-standing Pocono tradition of shaping its vacation environment. The same spirit that demanded decorum in the Laurel Blossom Time festivals of the 1930s, and that opposed casino gambling in the 1980s, had once again shown itself.[22]

FIG. 88
Entrance to Cove Haven, the "Land of Love."

Specialty Resorts

Specialty resorts are small resorts that buck the super-resort trend of being inclusive. They aim at narrowly defined groups in the population, much as ethnic resorts did in the old days. By meeting unique needs, specialty resorts mirror American society at large: they recognize that a single model does not fit America's very heterogeneous population, divided not only by race and class, but also by lifestyle. Specialty resorts attract the vacationers that super-resorts overlook or will not accommodate.

In the case of the New Hillside Inn, there is a lineal descent from an old ethnic resort. The original Hillside Inn was the African American resort that closed in 1982, leaving its owner, Judge Albert

Murray, too young to retire. Murray got a bank loan, upgraded his facilities, and reopened in 1989 with thirty-six rooms. Murray calls his new resort a social experiment, an example of what minorities can achieve. Pictures of George Washington Carver, Martin Luther King, Malcolm X, and Booker T. Washington grace the walls. Although dead for nearly a century, Booker T. Washington may best express the spirit of the New Hillside Inn, for Washington realized the importance of money in American life. Washington advised African Americans to enter business and achieve power through wealth.[23]

Like the New Hillside Inn, Deerfield Spa in Marshalls Creek dates from the 1980s, but it boasts a totally different motif. It is a health spa that some would call a fat farm. Its patrons lose weight on supervised, mostly vegetarian diets and through exercises that include dancing, aquatics, hiking, and martial arts. Deerfield Spa works on the mind as well: it offers "mind-body-spirit" lectures to create the "new you." The small number of guests allows each one to enjoy a very personal program.[24]

Health is also a goal at Sunny Rest Lodge, a nudist colony near Lehighton in the western Poconos, which is tucked away in thick woods to conceal its 190 acres from voyeurs. Signs by the swimming pool warn that swimsuits are not an option: they are banned. Veteran nudists have no tan lines, which are readily observed on newcomers. In a sense, Sunny Rest Lodge is very traditional in that it is open only during the summer. (Nudists do not walk in the snow.) The activities range from family barbecues to musical talent contests and volleyball, a favorite pastime. Sunny Rest would be a carbon copy of many other little resorts scattered throughout the Poconos, except for the obvious. Everyone is naked.[25]

The Rainbow Mountain Resort is another resort founded in the 1980s that reflects modern lifestyles. It is the only gay, lesbian, and bisexual resort in the Poconos. According to its guest book, the Rainbow is about "privacy, peace and quiet, complete freedom and total acceptance." The Rainbow boasts a disco and piano bar in its Lizard Lounge. Its website features a gay advice columnist as well.[26]

A very visible category of specialty resorts are bed-and-breakfast inns and country inns. In spirit, they are close to the small boardinghouses of the old days whose most important service was the personal attention of the owners. Bed-and-breakfast inns are small, but not necessarily cheap. Travelers who prefer budget accommodations should stay at a Motel 6. A bed-and-breakfast inn allows its patrons to eat breakfast with the owners and soak in the atmosphere. Unlike the standardized rooms of chain motels, every room in a real bed-and-breakfast inn should have its own unique wallpaper, bed, and bureaus. The furniture looks old, but as long as the overall effect is nostalgic rather than seedy, bed-and-breakfast inns work their magic and justify their premium prices. Throughout the United States, bed-and-breakfasts have become quite the rage, and over twenty of these inns have opened in the Poconos. They may not do for a traveling salesman, but they satisfy the vacationer who is in no particular hurry. Aside from fitting a public need, they have the further advantage of allowing an ambitious couple to open their own business.[27]

Country inns are larger, serve dinner, and offer more services, but they are not super-resorts. Country inns are a base from which vacationers explore the surrounding countryside and create their own fun—as in the old days. More than bed-and-breakfast inns, country inns are the true heirs of the Victorian hotels that once dotted the region. In some cases, they are literally Victorian hotels, expanded and modernized. Pine Knob Inn in Canadensis dates from the Civil War. The Stroudsmoor Country Inn in Stroudsburg has its roots in the Quaker Highland Dell of the Foulke family. Sitting on top of a mountain, it offers a magnificent view of Cherry Valley below.[28]

Specialty resorts for children are called camps. The Poconos have housed camps for over a century; as in the case of the resorts, camps varied in price and catered to different ethnic groups, reflecting the diverse American population. This diversity still marks Pocono camps. In the 1990s, for instance, a summer camp for Muslims opened in Dingmans Ferry. Campers study Islam and pray to Allah before beginning their recreation.[29]

Finally, a few words are necessary about the hunting and fishing clubs. At one time unwelcome, they have long since made peace with their neighbors. If these clubs did not exist, developers would take over, and there would be fewer green acres in the Poconos. The larger hunting and fishing clubs, such as the Blooming Grove and the Forest Lake clubs, have cottages on the grounds that serve as summer homes. Several cottage owners have settled in on a year-round basis. They have *become* neighbors.

The Blooming Grove Hunting and Fishing Club people no longer hunt deer. The animals have realized this, and they boldly walk across the front lawn of the clubhouse in broad daylight. Club members prefer to hunt pheasants and fish for trout. Pheasants are kept in cages and freed the night prior to the hunt. Trout are conceived and born on the grounds: a worker grabs male and female fish, squeezes out sperm and eggs, creates the soup of life by mixing the two, and lets nature do the rest. Fish grow up in tanks and are set free when they are adults. In playing God with the trout, the rather benign Blooming Grove club of today hints at that iron control it wished to exert in the nineteenth century.[30]

Pocono Attractions

A century ago, many city folk visited the Poconos for the day. They might have gone to Island Park in Delaware Water Gap for a picnic or for a swim in the Delaware River. They might have danced at Shohola Glen, canoed in Saylors Lake, or bicycled down the River Road, as Route 209 was then called. Day-trippers still come to the Poconos, although now they drive rather than take the old railways. After arriving, day-trippers have a wider range of activities. The choice is so vast, in fact, that many vacationers bypass the resorts altogether, stay at a motel, and choose their favorite pastimes from the vast Pocono menu.

As with the resorts, no brief survey can mention all the contemporary Pocono attractions. To begin, there is the world of nature. The twenty-four-hundred-square-mile, four-county region contains nine state parks and twenty-one state game lands, an outdoors that attracts hunters, hikers, birdwatchers—the whole tribe of people who love trees and fresh air. During the fall, guided foliage tours are available. In the winter, there are snow sports and skiing. The Delaware and Lehigh Rivers both offer the pleasures of canoeing, rafting, and tubing. Lake Wallenpaupack extends over fifty-six hundred acres, has fifty-two miles of shoreline, and is big enough for vacationers to take scenic tours.[31]

The largest park of all, which includes almost seventy thousand acres of land, is the Delaware Water Gap National Recreation Area (DWGNRA). Administered by the National Park Service, the DWGNRA includes forty miles of the Delaware River—from Port Jervis to Delaware Water Gap—as well as the adjacent land in Pike and Monroe Counties in Pennsylvania and Warren and Sussex Counties in New Jersey. The DWGNRA comprises the land that the federal government had acquired for the abortive Tocks Island Dam project, and it shows that in the long run, environmentalists won a double victory: they not only stopped the dam's construction, but also created a huge park on land that otherwise would have been developed. Because no dam was built, the Delaware River will continue to be free flowing, used for canoeing, as it was a century ago—and with cleaner water. The many hiking trails, including twenty-five miles of the Appalachian Trail, can meet nearly every hiking need. Fishing, hunting, picnicking, and rock climbing are other options. Park rangers lecture on the local ecology. History buffs can visit restored buildings.[32]

Indeed, history is big in the Poconos. Visitors can see many old houses. Among the more famous are Grey Towers, the large castle-like mansion of Gifford Pinchot in Milford, and the Asa Packer mansion in Jim Thorpe. Historical societies display old tools, clothes, and all sorts of odds and ends. The Poconos also boast several museums. At the Quiet Valley Living Historical Farm, one can relive the past by watching how Americans of former centuries lived and farmed. Another thrill is riding an old train in Jim Thorpe. For a few moments, riders can imagine themselves in the old days of steam locomotives and piercing, railway whistles.

Shopping buffs come from afar. Outlet malls, such as The Crossings in Tannersville (off Interstate 80), have crowded parking lots. Lovers of old furniture will enjoy the antique shops. A huge flea market is located off Route 209. Wine lovers can visit the three wineries in the Poconos and be treated to free samples of wine. A pretzel factory and a candy kitchen are also open to the public. Garlic lovers have their day in the September festival that honors Pocono garlic growers. Aficionados can buy garlic-laced foods and listen to "America's Smelliest Band," which consists of garlic-munching oompah players.[33]

The Poconos have long catered to sports lovers. Hunters and fishermen were among the first visitors to the Poconos, and they still come in the new millennium. Parked pickup trucks along the sides of roads are common sights during deer-hunting season. Golf in the Poconos is over a century old, and today's golfers can choose from more than thirty-five courses. Another activity that can raise heads is the Shawnee Hot Air Balloon Festival in October. The curious can watch balloons ascend, and the adventuresome can take a ride and look down at the Poconos. Playful balloonists have been known to "shoot" the Gap, that is, to fly low between Mount Minsi and Mount Tammany and see how close they can come to the Delaware River.[34]

In 1969, the Pocono Raceway opened in Long Pond, off Interstate 80. The founder was Joseph Mattioli, a Philadelphia dentist who had tired of pulling wisdom teeth and wanted to enjoy himself. Mattioli made the Pocono Raceway a family business and is still very much in charge. During the 1970s and 1980s, Pocono Raceway offered both stock car and Indy car races. But Indy car drivers complained that the track was unsafe, and in 1989 the Raceway dropped those races. Pocono Raceway has prospered in the 1990s by offering two NASCAR races, five weeks apart, each attracting sellout crowds of 130,000.[35]

Cultural events—ranging from mildly highbrow to fairly common—are always taking place in the Poconos. The Pocono Playhouse opened in 1946, the first of many theaters in the region. The September jazz festival in Delaware Water Gap originated with the jazz musicians who play at the Deer Head Inn (the former Central Inn) in Delaware Water Gap. The festival started in 1978 and features jazz artists from northeastern Pennsylvania and beyond.[36]

Super-resorts sponsor many special events. Fernwood Resort has held wrestling spectacles and stage shows that celebrate classic rock music of the 1950s. Split Rock Resort and the nearby Big Boulder and Jack Frost ski areas keep busy when the ski season ends. Among their festivals have been celebrations of beer, of blues music, and of the Irish. The Bikers Music Rally of 1999 featured rebel acts of the 1960s, such as Steppenwolf, Dr. Hook, and Big Brother and the Holding Company. The "Gathering on the Mountain" appeals to "Deadheads" who still mourn the death of the Grateful Dead's Jerry Garcia. The 1999 version of the "Gathering" featured old and new bands that have a special meaning to those who have not switched to wine and beer.

The annual "Great Tastes of Pennsylvania Wine & Food Festival" at Split Rock Resort celebrates Pennsylvania wine. Since the Keystone State is not a leading wine producer, ranking fourteenth among the fifty states, connoisseurs (who believe that only wines from France, and perhaps California, are real wines) do not come here. The festival targets the average wine lover who, for the price of admission, can attend seminars and sample free wine from Pennsylvania wineries. Performances by American and international musicians enhance the event as well.

At one such festival, ten thousand people showed up—as did half of Pennsylvania's fifty wineries. The crowd was well behaved and put litter into trash cans. Near the end of the day, the leader of one band (a band that, according to the program, can "coax music from such unlikely objects as garden hoses, washboards, tubs, whistles, kazoos, anything not nailed down") noted that wine led to burping, and so announced a burping contest. After band members gave a demonstration, he called for contestants. Six volunteered and croaked their best. The audience of several hundred applauded to select the winner—a young woman whose burps may not necessarily have been the loudest or the longest, but who won over the crowd by belching her heart out.

A Summer Home

No human activity elicits the same reaction from all people. A stay in the Poconos is no exception. Some vacationers come once to the Poconos and never return. Other vacationers return every year and would go nowhere else. For more than a century, some of these vacationers have consummated their love for the Poconos by buying a summerhouse. Among the early examples were the cottagers connected to the Quaker hotels, Skytop, Lutherland, the Paradise Valley Lutheran Association, and

FIG. 89
Garlic grower Frank Pollock selling
garlic vinegar and garlic at the Pocono
Garlic Festival.

the hunting and fishing clubs. After the Second World War, the trend of buying summer homes accel-erated. According to the 1990 census, one of every four houses in Monroe County was a part-time residence. More than half of the houses in Pike County were not used full-time. When summer homes are part of a development, they have the atmosphere of a resort cottage colony. Summer home developments may have social directors, for example, who plan activities for young and old, and the grounds may feature tennis and basketball courts as well as a swimming pool. In effect, much of the life of a resort is present in a summer home colony.[37]

In recent years, the selling of time-shares by resorts has received much attention. For a single charge, which averaged nine thousand dollars in 1996, buyers reserve a lodging unit for the same week each year. The idea is that time-share owners will save money in the long run. Of course, buyers tie themselves to the Poconos, just as if they had bought a house. In the 1980s, the Poconos contained over twenty time-share operations, some of which seemed to rely on the hard sell, with fast-talking salesmen wearing gold chains around their necks. There were instances of people being browbeaten for five to seven hours—people who signed a contract just to escape. By 1996, only four time-share sellers remained. According to the *Pocono Record,* the abuses were gone.[38]

The Poconos of the 1990s

The rules for success in the resort business are the same today as they were in the nineteenth century. Tough competition turns complacent resorts into losers. Resorts must be well-run, offer great service, and anticipate what the public wants even before the public knows what it wants. In the first half of the 1990s, resorts forgot these rules. According to the *Pocono Record,* the resort industry was largely tacky and run-down. In February 1996, a *New York Times* reporter and her husband visited a leading super-resort for her third wedding anniversary. She found the main building uninviting, with faded carpets in the lobby. The sauna did not work, the fireplace had no wood, and the old television set had poor reception. The food was just as bad and the waiter surly. To top off her vacation from hell, the comedians were not funny. A few months later, *Philadelphia Magazine* also had a very negative review of this resort. In another press story, a couple went to another super-resort, found cobwebs in their Jacuzzi, and promptly left for Amish country.[39]

The Poconos have the perennial problem of heavy competition. The Poconos of the 1990s were competing with cruise lines, Las Vegas, Amish country, and the Caribbean. These competitors were just as expensive, but more exotic than the Poconos. For two thousand dollars, a couple could spend a week at a top Pocono resort or spend five days at Disney World. As if tough competition were not enough, the Poconos had run out of new ideas. The cutting-edge, heart-shaped pools and seven-foot-high champagne glasses of the 1970s had lost their novelty. In addition, the resort industry lost the customers who bought time-shares and second homes in the 1980s. All these problems came to a head at the wrong time—during the recession of the early 1990s. As always, a vacation is the first casualty of a poor economy.[40]

Some of the toughest criticism of the Pocono resort industry has come from the *Pocono Record,* which has noted that the top five domestic destinations for vacationers do not include the Poconos, nor is Pennsylvania among the ten leading tourist states. But the Pocono vacation picture does not deserve such dark colors. The Poconos have never been a world-class vacation area. Their major asset has always been their proximity to the large cities of the Middle Atlantic states. It was no accident that during the 1970s and 1980s the Vacation Bureau called the Poconos "the near country." Besides, the *Pocono Record* was aiming its criticism at resorts—but day-trippers have been coming in record numbers.[41]

The Pocono Mountains Vacation Bureau has the task of selling the Poconos. Since 1961, it has received funding through a matching grant program from the state of Pennsylvania. The executive

FIG. 90
The Delmar and District Pipe Band performs at the Annual Scottish and Irish Games and Music Festival at the Shawnee Mountain Ski Area.

director, Robert Uguccioni, has been the top cheerleader for the resorts for over thirty years. He supervises an office of thirty workers and spends a budget of over three million dollars. The Vacation Bureau has recently given much publicity to the natural assets of the Poconos. It issues a Nature Guide, and it has a special hotline for fall foliage.[42]

Nature obviously has its charms. In driving along the back roads, motorists can expect to see deer. There is a chance that they will see bears and wild turkeys, or spot a hawk swooping down on its prey. At Cove Haven, a herd of deer wander around the grounds, as if the couples resort were the Garden of Eden. The deer and the mood they create are an asset that Las Vegas and cruise ships will never match. Only time will tell whether nature will be the elixir that keeps the Poconos going. Nature, after all, was the original Pocono attraction. However, a dark cloud looms on the horizon. As Uguccioni has warned, continued development of the region will ruin the vacation industry. The population of Monroe County has tripled since 1960, and Pike County's has quadrupled.[43]

In the mid-1990s, the super-resorts poured money into renovations. Caesars, Fernwood, Pocono Manor, Skytop, Pocmont, and Mountain Manor Inn spent over one hundred million dollars. Caesars alone invested fifty million dollars into its love nests. Camelback has put four million into its water park. The super-resorts had a great August in 1998. Whether the renovations or the booming economy of the late 1990s deserve most of the credit is uncertain. But this much is certain—Pocono vacationing still has life.[44]

EPILOGUE

The modern Poconos seem to be evolving into a distant suburb of New York City. What has kept more New York and New Jersey residents from moving in is the long drive to work. This problem will be solved in 2005, when a new commuter rail line is scheduled to use the old Lackawanna track to reach New York City. The implications are enormous. Travel time from Monroe County to Manhattan will equal travel time to Manhattan from the New York City suburbs of Westchester County and Long Island. The Poconos (and especially Monroe County) might gain so many new residents that sometime in the twenty-first century vacationers will notice the overcrowding. When they are fed up with the number of housing developments, roads, and shops, they will stop coming. The vacation era of Pocono history will come to an end.

Or perhaps the Pocono vacation industry will survive by doing what it has done in the past: move. In the twentieth century, Pocono vacationing moved inland from its original home along the Delaware River. It may move again, into northern Wayne County, western Carbon County, or even beyond the four-county Pocono region. Ever since the anthracite coal mines closed, Lackawanna and Luzerne Counties (which border the Poconos in the west and northwest) and their cities of Scranton and Wilkes-Barre have been looking for a mission. They already refer to themselves as the Poconos, and they are clamoring to join the Pocono club.

Whatever the fate of Pocono vacationing, the industry has had a proud history. Not only have the Poconos been a major player among the nation's vacation regions for over a century, but they have also pulled ahead of many traditional competitors. The rival Catskills once contained more resorts than the Poconos, and they received more attention during most of the twentieth century. Since the 1970s, though, the Catskills have seemed moribund, and few of their large hotels remain. The smaller hotels that survived the invariable fires have been sold to religious sects and other organizations. Likewise, Atlantic City was once a leading rival of the Poconos. Its decline began after the First World War, and by the 1970s, before casino gambling was introduced, Atlantic City had fallen so low that it ranked among the poorest towns in New Jersey.

Some of the old competition that the Poconos had to endure is altogether gone. The villages and towns that housed spas are nearly forgotten. Even the once-mighty Newport, Rhode Island, where

Gilded Age millionaires built summer mansions, has fallen. In today's world, it is a huge museum that satisfies tourists who are curious about the super-rich of the nineteenth century. By contrast, the Poconos keep thriving. If not in the same league as the vacation supercities of Las Vegas and Orlando, the Poconos have a long history of success. They challenge Las Vegas and Orlando to have the same staying power and to remain on top, or at least near the top, a century from now.

Shrewd resort owners deserve the credit. The Poconos do not have a dominant geographic feature, such as Niagara Falls, that automatically generates a stream of tourists, nor does the region have a man-made gimmick, such as gambling. The Poconos have always had to try harder. Their greatest hour may well have been after World War II. Instead of resting on their laurels, expecting old customers to keep returning, thirty resorts made a firm commitment to the future when they took a chance on skiing. They supported the founders of Camelback by promising to buy thirty-five thousand dollars' worth of lift tickets during the first two years of Camelback's operation.

In addition, many owners of aging Victorian resorts were unwilling to accept a gradual decline. They embraced the trend toward greater hedonism, opening resorts that catered to young singles and honeymooners. As Americans continued to lose their inhibitions, the Poconos obliged with the couples resort. The private, heart-shaped bathtubs and swimming pools that invited skinny-dipping dismissed health, self-improvement, or getting close to nature—the typical nineteenth-century justifications for a vacation—and focused on sensuality instead.

Reinvention has come at a price, however. Although most vacationers of the 1930s did not stay at the classy Quaker resorts, the tone for the Poconos was set by Buck Hill, Pocono Manor, and Skytop. Today, although two of these big three survive, they no longer define the Poconos. In the minds of many (if not most) Americans, the Poconos have become defined by the couples resort. The image is somewhat tacky. Even in the new millennium, sex draws snickers.

The Poconos have been a momentary experience for vacationers, but a living—sometimes remarkably profitable—for resort owners. For some of the more ambitious owners, the resort business has been the key to great success. What the Brodheads did in the nineteenth century has been replicated in the twentieth century. In the 1920s, for instance, the Ahnert family of Fernwood Resort came from New York City, started a chicken farm, and by the 1930s, served chicken dinners on Sundays. The machine shop of the war years was an interlude that provided capital for the postwar expansion of Fernwood Resort. In 1988, the Ahnerts sold Fernwood and its related enterprises to the Rank Organization of Great Britain, and they received over two hundred million dollars. Harry Kiesendahl of Woodloch Pines began as a Long Island milkman. He bought Woodloch Pines in 1958 when it was a small resort, and in the following year acquired a partner in his good friend, Don Kranich. The families' second and third generations run the business today, which includes a huge real estate development next to the resort and a restaurant near Lake Wallenpaupack. John and Suzanne Martens, who founded Mount Airy Lodge, were immigrants from Czechoslovakia.

Today, ambitious people without a huge source of capital cannot open a super-resort, but they can open a bed-and-breakfast inn. The entrepreneurial spirit that has been an hallmark of the resort business lives on. Bed-and-breakfasts may, perhaps, be franchised like today's motels. At this moment, a tycoon of the future may be quietly frying eggs for visitors to her bed-and-breakfast.

In contrast with the mutable resort economy, nature itself has appeared relatively stable: it has always been a key reason for a vacation. But our use and perception of the outdoors has, in fact, changed over the years. For much of the nineteenth century, a stay in the country was an opportunity to experience the sublime, to be amazed and astonished by nature. Later in the nineteenth century, a country sojourn was the result of the back-to-nature movement that made cyclers, campers, and hunters seek the mystique of the countryside. Americans are still in love with nature, although their perception of the outdoors may be driven by New Age mysticism or environmentalism. Even those who pay little overt attention to nature—who come to the Poconos and swim in an indoor pool that is available at any suburban country club—still come to encounter the natural environment. Although trees and mountains may be seen from a distance, from the windows of hotel rooms and cars, they constantly remind vacationers that Philadelphia and New York City are far away. Nature, no matter how faintly experienced, also refers to the environmental awareness that has become a feature of American culture.

One considerable change in vacationing has been the reversal of the essential definition of a vacation. A vacation once meant doing little. People sat on porches, conversed, took walks after dinner, and in general did not exert themselves. But modern vacationing involves being busy. A vast range of activities is a chief draw of the super-resort. (One reason that Skytop Lodge seems somewhat quaint by comparison is that it proudly announces the virtues of "loafing.")

Another obvious change in resort life is the end of segregation. No resort would dare advertise an all-Christian clientele, as many once did. All but one of the African American resorts are gone, no longer needed as alternatives to formerly all-white resorts. What the integrated vacationing of the Poconos suggests about modern America is a very interesting question. It may be a sign that America is not, in fact, developing into a multicultural separatism—or it could simply mean that formal integration counts for little. In a modern resort, guests do not have to mix. They no longer sit on the porch and talk. They can ignore the attractions of the resort, drive away in their automobiles, and only return to sleep. Even dining is no longer communal. The traditional family style arrangement, where guests sat at long tables and scooped food from common trays, has been replaced by the buffet, where guests eat separately. The intimacy that a resort once forced on vacationers is gone. Besides, modern vacationing no longer needs a resort. Many people prefer camping trips or living in summer homes. Other vacationers come to the Poconos for a day or two, see the sights, visit state parks, enjoy commercial amusements, and sleep at a motel. No one mixes with strangers. And when we do mix, it does not matter. We are insoluble elements for whom formal integration is meaningless.

Another sign of atomization is seen in the increasing number of amusements. At the beginning of the twentieth century, the resort industry used the term "playground" to describe the Poconos. The term was a better indication of a growing acceptance of pleasure than it was a description of fact. Other than the traditional natural attractions, the range of activities was narrow. But during the course of the twentieth century, the playground became a reality. Both on and off the resorts, the number of amusements has grown extensively. *Choice* is the salient feature of today's Poconos.

Choice makes vacationing less of a civic, unifying experience than it was in the past. Vacationers opt for particular delights of the playground, and they return home with their separate, unmatching memories. What remains is the vacation itself and the Pocono setting. We indulge ourselves in a way that our ancestors never did when they took a holiday. We are freer beings. We are also alone.

NOTES

Notes to Chapter 1

1. William Cullen Bryant, *Letters of a Traveller or Notes of Things Seen in Europe and America,* 2d ed. (New York: G. P. Putnam, 1850), 307–10.

2. Roderick Nash, *Wilderness and the American Mind* (New Haven: Yale University Press, 1967), 45–46, 54–65; Hans Huth, *Nature and the American: Three Centuries of Changing Attitudes* (Berkeley and Los Angeles: University of California Press, 1957), 11; Barbara Novak, *Nature and Culture: American Landscape and Painting, 1825–1875* (New York: Oxford University Press, 1980), 34–38; Donald Keyes, ed., *The White Mountains: Place and Perceptions* (Hanover: University Press of New England, 1980), 41–43.

3. Ernest Schwiebert, *Remembrances of Rivers Past* (New York: Macmillan, 1972), 229–31; United States Department of the Interior, National Park Service, *National Register of Historic Places—Nomination Form, Henryville House,* 1980; *Pocono Today,* July 28, 1985.

4. For Dutot, see L. W. Brodhead, *The Delaware Water Gap: Its Scenery, Its Legends, and Early History,* 2d ed. (Philadelphia: Sherman, 1870), 256–63; Alfred Mathews, *History of Wayne, Pike, and Monroe Counties, Pennsylvania* (Philadelphia: Peck, 1886), 1078–79. For Prince Alexander, see Elizabeth D. Walters, "History of the Water Gap House, 1872–1915" (unpublished manuscript, June 1969, Monroe County Historical Association, Stroudsburg, Pa.), 7–8. The Monroe County Historical Association will be cited hereafter as MCHA.

5. *Jeffersonian,* October 30, 1884; Elizabeth D. Walters, "The Kittatinny: Pioneer Summer Resort of Monroe County, Pennsylvania" (unpublished manuscript, December 1968, MCHA).

6. Brodhead, *Delaware Water Gap,* 262–63; *Mountain Echo,* July 9, 1881.

7. Ledger, Stroudsburg House, MCHA.

8. The Poconos received little national attention before the Civil War. Nathaniel Willis's *American Scenery* (1840) contained numerous engravings of the White Mountains, the Hudson River Valley, Niagara Falls, and other scenic places, but nothing on the Delaware River Gap. *The Home Book of the Picturesque* (1852), whose contributors included Bryant, Cooper, and Irving, had a chapter on "The Scenery of Pennsylvania" that entirely ignored the Poconos, with the exception of a single reference to Delaware Water Gap. Disturnell's guide to vacation spots (1855) flatly stated that Pennsylvania was no tourist mecca.

9. Bryan Wolfe, "Review Essay: The Fall of Niagara," *Winterthur Portfolio* 22, no. 1 (1987): 81–87; Dona Brown, *Inventing New England: Regional Tourism in the Nineteenth Century* (Washington, D.C.: Smithsonian Institution Press, 1995), 41–74; John F. Sears, *Sacred Places: American Tourist Attractions in the Nineteenth Century* (New York: Oxford University Press, 1989), 12–86. Philadelphia publisher George W. Childs had the reputation of giving

the best dinners in the country. He reputedly paid his chef eight thousand dollars. He could have vacationed anywhere, but preferred the Poconos, where he spent his money and time "improving" the local scenery. See Jefferson Williamson, *The American Hotel: An Anecdotal History* (New York: Alfred Knopf, 1930), 215.

10. E. Digby Baltzell, *Puritan Boston and Quaker Philadelphia* (New York: Free Press, 1979), 160.

11. Robert Lewis, "Seaside Resorts in the United States and Britain: A Review," *Urban History Yearbook* 7 (1980): 44–52; Richard A. Savage, "Bar Harbor: A Resort Is Born," *New England Galaxy* 18, no. 4 (1977): 11–22.

12. Kenneth Myers, *The Catskills: Painters, Writers, and Tourists in the Mountains, 1820–1895* (Yonkers, N.Y.: Hudson River Museum of Westchester, 1987), 31–32. For the Poconos, see *Jeffersonian*, September 17, 1874, and May 13, 1880; see also the Delaware Water Gap Folder, MCHA.

13. Novak, *Nature and Culture,* 38–42.

14. Vertie Knapp to Nancy Graham, March 29, 1980 (Art Folder, MCHA). [Ms. Knapp was the director of the MCHA in 1980.] The Corcoran Gallery in Washington, D.C., held an exhibit of Delaware Valley painters in 1975.

15. Architectural League of New York, *Resorts of the Catskills* (New York: St. Martin's Press, 1979), 2–4; Alf Evers, *The Catskills: From Wilderness to Woodstock* (Woodstock, N.Y.: The Overlook Press, 1982), 322; Myers, *The Catskills,* 33–36; Sears, *Sacred Places,* 60–62; *Appleton's General Guide to the United States and Canada, Part 1: New England and Middle States and Canada* (New York: D. Appleton, 1901), 75.

16. Schwiebert, *Remembrances of Rivers Past,* 229–44. Heavyweight boxing champion John L. Sullivan and Buffalo Bill also stayed at the Henryville House.

17. Mathews, *History,* 854–57; *Jeffersonian,* May 31, 1888.

18. Paul A. W. Wallace, *Indians in Pennsylvania,* rev. ed. (Harrisburg: Pennsylvania Historical and Museum Commission, 1981), 162–66; Henry S. Cattell, *The Pocono Plateau* (New York: McBride, Nast, 1912), 31–32; Mathews, *History,* 79–80.

19. Mathews, *History,* 834–35.

20. Leslie C. Wood, *Rafting on the Delaware River* (Livingston Manor, N.Y.: Livingston Manor Times, 1934), 6–7; J. Herbert Walker, ed., *Rafting Days in Pennsylvania* (Altoona, Pa.: Times-Tribune, 1922), 54–57; *Jeffersonian,* May 29, 1873.

21. Elizabeth D. Walters, "The Delaware: Walpack to Delaware Water Gap" (unpublished manuscript, October 1944, MCHA), 4–5.

22. Gary Letcher, *Canoeing the Delaware River: A Guide to the River and Shore* (New Brunswick: Rutgers University Press, 1981), 10; Wood, *Rafting on the Delaware River,* 6–7.

23. According to Baltzell, the individualistic, antinomian spirit of the Quakers became the dominant ethos in America during the 1960s. In a telephone conversation with the author, Baltzell lamented that "we were once Puritans but now we are Quakers."

24. Charles E. Funnell, *By the Beautiful Sea: The Rise and High Times of That Great American Resort, Atlantic City* (New York: Knopf, 1975), 3–6.

25. John Appel, coord., *History of Monroe County, Pennsylvania: 1725–1976* (East Stroudsburg, Pa.: Pocono Hospital Auxiliary, 1976), 51–53, 91–94. For train schedules, see *Jeffersonian,* September 5, 1858, and *Mountain Echo,* September 19, 1885.

26. Thomas H. Knepp, *The Poconos: A Handbook and Guide to Pennsylvania's Vacation Land,* 3d ed. (Stroudsburg, Pa.: Thomas H. Knepp, 1963), 36; Norman Lehde, *An Illustrated Historic Survey of Milford,* vol. 9 of *Pike County Historic Site and Scenic Area Survey* (n.p., n.d.), 5. For the lady lumberjack, see Pauline Learn, "Things to Remember" (unpublished memoir, 1977, MCHA).

27. Mathews, *History,* 868–75; Norman Lehde, *Milford Pennsylvania, 1733–1983, Heritage: 250* (Milford, Pa.: Borough of Milford, 1983), 37–38; I. Daniel Rupp, *History of Northampton, Lehigh, Monroe, Carbon, and*

Schuylkill Counties (Lancaster, Pa.: G. Hills, 1845), 152; LeRoy J. Koehler, *The History of Monroe County, Penn-sylvania, During the Civil War* (Stroudsburg, Pa.: n.p., 1950), 23–25.

28. Carroll Tyson, *The Poconos* (Philadelphia: Innes & Sons, 1929), 74–75; Carl S. Oplinger and Robert Halma, *The Poconos: An Illustrated Natural History Guide* (New Brunswick: Rutgers University Press, 1988), 203.

29. Tyson, *The Poconos,* 77–85; Dennis N. Bertland et al., *The Minisink: A Chronicle of One of America's First and Last Frontiers* (Milford, Pa.: Four-County Task Force on the Tocks Island Dam Project, 1975), 133–34; George J. Fluhr, *Shohola: History of a Township* (Lackawaxen, Pa.: Alpha Publishing, 1992), 57–61; Roger Dunning, "Monroe County Tanneries" (unpublished manuscript, 1968, MCHA).

30. Peggy Bancroft, *Ringing Axes and Rocking Chairs: The Story of Barrett Township* (Mountainhome, Pa.: Barrett Friendly Library, 1974), 82–83; *Jeffersonian,* May 27, 1875, and May 10, 1877. For the census, see *Stroudsburg Times,* July 31, August 14, and October 2, 1890; see also *Milford Dispatch,* September 10, 1891.

31. *Jeffersonian,* October 30, 1884; *Mountain Echo,* July 9, 1881, and August 1, 1885; Walters, "The Kittatinny," 6–7.

32. The summer 1859 issues of the *New York Times* paid some attention to New England and the Catskills, but ignored the Poconos.

Notes to Chapter 2

1. Foster Rhea Dulles, *A History of Recreation: America Learns to Play* (New York: Appleton-Century-Crofts, 1965), 201–3; Donna R. Braden and Judith E. Endelman, *Americans on Vacation* (Dearborn, Mich.: Henry Ford Museum and Greenfield Village, 1990), 8–9; Oramel S. Senter, *The Health and Pleasure-Seeker's Guide* (Philadelphia, 1874), 1–7; Cindy S. Aron, *Working at Play: A History of Vacations in the United States* (New York: Oxford University Press, 1999), 46–57.

2. The combined populations of Newark, Trenton, and Jersey City more than tripled between 1860 and 1890. Scranton's population jumped from nine thousand to over fifty thousand in the two decades after 1860. Allentown borough's residents—a population of more than thirteen thousand in 1870—reached thirty-five thousand by 1900. For New Jersey, see John E. Bebout and Ronald J. Grele, *Where Cities Meet: The Urbanization of New Jersey* (Princeton, N.J.: Van Nostrand, 1964), 31–33. The author acknowledges the assistance of Ramona Hylton, Government Documents Librarian at East Stroudsburg University, for collecting the Allentown statistics from the U.S. Bureau of the Census.

3. John B. Bachelder, *Popular Resorts, and How to Reach Them* (Boston: J. B. Bachelder, 1874), 64; Huth, *Nature and the American,* 105–28. For the spas, see Robert S. Conte, "The Celebrated White Sulphur Springs of Greenbrier: Nineteenth-Century Travel Accounts," *West Virginia History* 42, no. 3–4 (1981): 191–221; Henry W. Lawrence, "Southern Spas: Source of the American Resort Tradition," *Landscape* 27, no. 2 (1983): 1–12. Disturnell's vacation guide of 1855 not only listed the nation's spas but also gave a detailed mineral breakdown for their water.

4. Martin V. Melosi, *Garbage in the Cities: Refuse, Reform, and the Environment, 1880–1980* (College Station: Texas A&M University Press, 1981), 26–27, 60–61.

5. Delaware, Lackawanna and Western Railroad, *Outings on the Lackawanna, 1899* (New York: B. E. Chapin, 1899), 59; *Mountain Echo,* July 9, 1881. *Outings on the Lackawanna* will hereafter be cited as Lackawanna, *1899 Outings.*

6. *Jeffersonian,* July 23, 1868.

7. Bachelder, *Popular Resorts,* 156. The idea of the vacation as an emotional necessity was promoted by such notables as Henry Ward Beecher, the famed New York clergyman, who held that city people needed a vacation to restore their energy. See Daniel T. Rodgers, *The Work Ethic in Industrial America, 1850–1920* (Chicago: University of Chicago Press, 1978), 94–98.

8. *Jeffersonian,* July 27, 1871.

9. Philip G. Terrie, "Urban Man Confronts the Wilderness: The Nineteenth-Century Sportsman in the Adirondacks," *Journal of Sports History* 5, no. 3 (1978): 7–20. For a study of "muscular Christianity" and its advocacy of the outdoor life, see David Strauss, "Toward a Consumer Culture: 'Adirondack Murray' and the Wilderness Vacation," *American Quarterly* 39, no. 2 (1987): 270–83.

10. Walters, "The Kittatinny," 9–10; for extinction, see *Jeffersonian,* February 12, 1874; for snakes, *Jeffersonian,* August 8, 1872.

11. *Jeffersonian,* June 5, 1873.

12. Huth, *Nature and the American,* 11–13, 67, 84; Novak, *Nature and Culture,* 34–42. Some of the best examples of the picturesque appeared in William Cullen Bryant's *Picturesque America* (1874), a lithograph collection of American scenery. It included the Delaware Water Gap and thereby recognized the Poconos. The Gap did not have the breathtaking vistas of the sublime, but it was picturesque.

13. *New York Times,* May 21, 1877.

14. *Stroudsburg Daily Times,* May 26, 1894; Sentner, *Pleasure-Seeker's Guide,* 6. Every year, Louis Fauchere (who was French Swiss) visited the old country after his hotel closed at the end of the season. See *Pike County Dispatch,* March 3, 1977.

15. Bancroft, *Ringing Axes,* 66–72. At Shohola, in Pike County, nearly all the German families accepted summer boarders. Wives ran the boardinghouses while the menfolk worked on the railroad, at the quarries, or in the lumber camps. See Fluhr, *Shohola,* 111–12.

16. Fluhr, *Shohola,* 98, 117; William F. Henn, *The Story of the River Road: Life Along the Delaware from Bushkill to Milford, Pike County, Pennsylvania* (Dingmans Ferry, Pa.: William F. Henn, 1975), 6, 49–50, 105–8, 126.

17. See Crissman House Folder, Pike County Historical Society; Mathews, *History,* 866.

18. Mathews, *History,* 867, 963–65; *Milford Dispatch,* August 6, 1896. For Greeley's attempt to launch a socialist cooperative in Pike County, see Don C. Seitz, *Horace Greeley: Founder of the New York Tribune* (Indianapolis: Bobbs-Merrill, 1926), 126–33. Greeley's own version is in *Recollections of a Busy Life* (New York: J. B. Ford, 1868), 151–52.

19. *Milford Dispatch,* June 11, August 13, and September 10, 1891; June 8, 1893; June 6, 1910.

20. Fulmer House Folder, MCHA; *Jeffersonian,* October 29, 1874, and July 15, 1875.

21. *Jeffersonian,* January 9, 1868, and February 6, 1873; *Commemorative Biographical Record of Northeastern Pennsylvania* [hereafter *CBR*] (Chicago: J. H. Beers, 1900), 111–12.

22. *CBR,* 571–72, 610; Henn, *River Road,* 27.

23. Layton Hauser, interview by author, May 5, 1993; *Philadelphia Inquirer,* July 1, 1876; *Pocono Record,* June 12, 1988.

24. Bancroft, *Ringing Axes,* 78; *Stroudsburg Times,* June 28, 1889; Emma LaBarre Miller Waygood, *Changing Times in the Poconos, 1872–1972* (Bethlehem: A.B.C. Printing & Photo Offset, 1972), 68.

25. Bancroft, *Ringing Axes,* 118–19; *CBR,* 706.

26. *Mountain Echo,* September 3, 1881; *CBR,* 1404–5; Henn, *River Road,* 106, 165–66; Mathews, *History,* 910–16, 924–26.

27. See materials in the Glenwood Folder, MCHA; Mathews, *History,* 1098–99.

28. Mathews, *History,* 1100–1103; *Mountain Echo,* September 8, 1881; *Pocono Record,* March 27, 1976; *CBR,* 585–87; Susan E. Cayleff, *Wash and Be Healed: The Water-Cure Movement and Women's Health* (Philadelphia: Temple University Press, 1987), 94–95.

29. Learn, "Things to Remember," 83–85.

30. The refugee supporters of Napoleon were the Pinchots, whose descendant, Gifford Pinchot, was the famous conservationist and two-term governor of Pennsylvania in the 1920s and 1930s.

31. *Milford Dispatch,* May 5, 1910, for Schanno; for Fauchere, *Milford Dispatch,* September 14, 1893, and April 20, 1911; *CBR,* 277–78; M. Nelson McGeary, *Gifford Pinchot: Politician Forester* (Princeton: Princeton University Press, 1960), 3–4.

32. *New York Times,* May 21, 1877.

33. Hotels Miscellaneous Folder, Pike County Historical Society; Norman Lehde, *Historic Survey of Milford,* 9; *New York Times,* May 21, 1877.

34. *New York Times,* May 21, 1877, and June 3, 1880.

35. Elizabeth D. Walters, "Water Gap House," i–vii, xvii–xviii.

36. Anne Goodwill and Jean M. Smith, eds., *The Brodhead Family: The Story of Captain Daniel Brodhead, His Wife, Ann Tye, and Their Descendants,* vol. 4 (Port Ewen, N.Y.: Brodhead Family Association, 1986), 321–24.

37. *New York Times,* August 11, 1880; *Jeffersonian,* June 27, 1872.

38. Walters, "Water Gap House," 4. Resort guests could be practical toward liquor. A convention of New Jersey newspaper editors once stayed at the dry Water Gap House, thus giving up the right to drink at meals, but they held their grand ball at the Kittatinny, where "adult beverages" were available. See *Jeffersonian,* July 3, 1873.

39. Walters, "Water Gap House," xvii–xviii, 32.

40. Walters, "The Kittatinny," 23–24.

41. Delaware Water Gap Folder (in Resorts A–O Box), MCHA; Warren F. Lee, *Down Along the Old Bel-Del: The History of the Belvidere Delaware Railroad Company* (Albuquerque, N.M.: Bel-Del Enterprises, 1987), 270–71.

42. *Jeffersonian,* May 9, 1895; *Stroudsburg Daily Times,* May 4, 1895.

43. *Stroudsburg Daily Times,* May 28, 1894; Walters, "Water Gap House," 9–11, 21–22.

44. *Stroudsburg Daily Times,* October 11, 1889; *Jeffersonian,* April 1, 1875, and August 23, 1883.

45. Erie Railroad, *Summer Excursion Routes and Rates to Popular Resorts* (New York, 1883), 20–22. All over America, the quick touring vacation had become an alternative for those who had neither the money nor the time to stay at a resort. See Aron, *Working at Play,* 137–50.

46. Brown, *Inventing New England,* 41–74.

47. For Cuyler, see *Jeffersonian,* July 9, 1868, and Walters, "The Kittatinny," 9–11; *Milford Dispatch,* August 1, 1889; *Stroudsburg Daily Times,* August 30, 1895.

48. Henn, *River Road,* 106.

49. *Jeffersonian,* July 17, 1879.

50. Barton Hill, "Paradise Valley," 1906 (Paradise Valley Folder, MCHA).

51. Joseph Jefferson, *Rip Van Winkle: The Autobiography of Joseph Jefferson* (London: Reinhardt & Evans, 1949), 172–73.

52. *New York Times,* May 21, 1877.

53. George J. Fluhr, *Pike in Pennsylvania: History of a County* (Lackawaxen, Pa.: Alpha Publishing, 1993), 89; Joseph Brent, *Charles Sanders Peirce: A Life* (Bloomington: Indiana University Press, 1993), 185–92.

54. Fluhr, *Pike in Pennsylvania,* 83–84; Mary Smith Nelson, interview by author, June 15, 1993.

55. *Jeffersonian,* August 31, 1871; July 31, 1879; June 17, 1880.

56. Peggy Bancroft, *Journey by Lamplight: From Indian Trails to Skyways* (South Sterling, Pa.: Gun-ni-ati Publishing, 1979), 96–99.

57. Brodhead, *Delaware Water Gap,* 35.

58. Ibid., 41–44.

59. *Milford Dispatch,* February 10, 1898. See notes by Elizabeth D. Walters in Childs Arbor Folder (Resorts A–O Box), MCHA.

60. Dulles, *History of Recreation,* 150–52, 182, 242, 360–62. The late 1860s and 1870s witnessed the spread of croquet, the revival of archery, and the adoption of lawn tennis by polite society.

61. *Jeffersonian,* August 14, 1879; *Mountain Echo,* August 1, 1885.
62. *Jeffersonian,* August 29, 1878; *Mountain Echo,* August 2, 1884.
63. *Jeffersonian,* August 1, 1878; *New York Times,* August 11, 1880.
64. *Jeffersonian,* August 22, 1878.

Notes to Chapter 3

1. Lackawanna, *1899 Outings,* 55.
2. *Stroudsburg Times,* May 17, 1894, and May 9, 1895.
3. Ibid., August 19, 1895, and June 7, 1897.
4. *Milford Dispatch,* October 18, 1894.
5. Delaware, Lackawanna and Western Railroad, *Summer Excursion Routes and Rates* (New York: Livingston Middleditch, 1895), 57–59; Lackawanna, *1899 Outings,* 11. The *Summer Excursion Routes and Rates* publication will be cited hereafter as Lackawanna, *1895 Excursions.*
6. Lackawanna, *1899 Outings,* 133.
7. Erie Railroad, *Rural Summer Homes on the Picturesque Erie* (New York, 1898), 45–47. Cited hereafter as Erie, *Rural Summer Homes 1898.*
8. *Milford Dispatch,* September 11, 1890.
9. Lackawanna, *1899 Outings,* 133.
10. Lackawanna, *1895 Excursions,* 56.
11. Ibid., 61; Lackawanna, *1899 Outings,* 133. The sanitarium treatment consisted of rest, nutritious food, moderate exercise, and open air. Since fresh air could only be found in a rural setting, sanitaria had to locate in the country. See Michael E. Teller, *The Tuberculosis Movement: A Public Campaign in the Progressive Era* (Westport, Conn.: Greenwood Press, 1988), 24–27.
12. Morris Evans, ed., *Picturesque Monroe County Pennsylvania* (Stroudsburg, Pa.: Times Publishing, 1897), contains many ads from the local resorts.
13. For Peters House, see Telephone Folder, MCHA; for the Kittatinny, Lackawanna, *1899 Outings,* 4; *Conashaugh Spring House* [1898 brochure].
14. Erie, *Rural Summer Homes 1898,* 45–47; Lackawanna, *1899 Outings,* 4, 7, 33.
15. Lackawanna, *1899 Outings,* 133; for the Hotel Bellevue, see *Milford Dispatch,* April 20, 1893.
16. Erie Railroad, *Summer Homes on the Picturesque Erie* (New York: Erie Railroad, 1896), 51–52.
17. John Higham, "The Reorientation of American Culture in the 1890s," in *Writing American History: Essays on Modern Scholarship* (Bloomington: Indiana University Press, 1970), 79–86; also see Dulles, *History of Recreation,* 201–2.
18. *Stroudsburg Times,* July 15, 1899.
19. Ibid., August 10, 1899.
20. Betsy Blackmar and Elizabeth Cromley, "On the Verandah: Resorts of the Catskills," in *Victorian Resorts and Hotels,* ed. Richard Guy Wilson (Philadelphia: The Victorian Society in America, 1982), 51–57. The sheer number of women at resorts was common everywhere; it was not an exclusively Pocono phenomenon. See Aron, *Working at Play,* 85–86.
21. *Stroudsburg Times,* June 26, 1895; Lackawanna, *1899 Outings,* 11. Tobacco was, of course, beyond the pale for women.
22. *Stroudsburg Times,* August 28, 1890; *Milford Dispatch,* September 2, 1897.
23. *Stroudsburg Times,* August 14 and August 28, 1890.
24. *Milford Dispatch,* July 10, 1890.

25. *Stroudsburg Times,* August 10, 1897.

26. Ibid., June 21, 1897; Walters, "Water Gap House, 1872–1915," 23; *Milford Dispatch,* May 20 and September 2, 1897.

27. *Mount Pocono Gazette,* Bicentennial Summer [1976]; *Stroudsburg Daily Times,* August 29, 1895.

28. Dulles, *History of Recreation,* 220–21; Aron, *Working at Play,* 185–86.

29. Fluhr, *Shohola,* 45–52; for Shohola's low-lifes, see *Milford Dispatch,* July 12, 1894. As could be expected, the Erie Railroad's *Rural Summer Homes 1898* ignored Shohola's seamy side and instead emphasized its natural beauties.

30. *Stroudsburg Times,* July 17, 1890, and July 16, 1891.

31. Ibid., July 20, 1888; *Jeffersonian,* September 12, 1878; Janet Wetzel, *Monroe County—Historic Legacy* (Stroudsburg, Pa.: Monroe County Planning Commission, 1980), 23.

32. *Stroudsburg Times,* July 20, 1888; August 11, 1892; July 13, 1898.

33. *Mountain Echo,* September 8, 1888; *Monroe Democrat,* June 20, 1889.

34. Violet Clark Eddy, interview by author, March 10, 1993.

35. Thomas Dunlap, *Saving America's Wildlife* (Princeton: Princeton University Press, 1988), 5–13; Theodore Whaley Cart, "The Struggle for Wildlife Protection in the United States, 1870–1900: Attitudes and Events Leading to the Lacey Act" (Ph.D. diss., University of North Carolina, 1971), 90.

36. Cart, "Struggle for Wildlife Protection," 90; Charles Hallock, *The Fishing Tourist* (New York: Harper, 1873); *The American Field,* October 13, 1894, 844–46.

37. *Stroudsburg Times,* November 9, 1893.

38. *Jeffersonian,* November 14, 1872, and April 3, 1873; Blooming Grove Park Association, *Objects, Charters, and By-Laws of the Blooming Grove Park Association* (New York: Powers & Macgowan, 1871); *The American Field,* October 13, 1894, 844–46.

39. Blooming Grove Park Association, *Objects, Charters, and By-Laws.*

40. *Milford Dispatch,* August 25, 1898.

41. Cart, "Struggle for Wildlife Protection," 92.

42. Blooming Grove Park Association, *Objects, Charters, and By-Laws;* Hallock, *The Fishing Tourist,* 227–29; Theodore Cart and Frank Froment, interviews by author, October 27, 1993.

43. Jean T. MacGregor and James T. MacGregor, *A Legacy of Wilderness: The Centennial History of the Forest Lake Club* (Lackawaxen Township, Pike County, Pa.: Forest Lake Club, 1984), 45, 60–61, 80, 85.

44. *Stroudsburg Times,* November 8, 1895.

45. Ibid., March 16, 1893, and October 26, 1897.

46. Gary Allan Tobin, "The Bicycle Boom of the 1890s: The Development of Private Transportation and the Birth of the Modern Tourist," *Journal of Popular Culture* 7 (Spring 1974): 838–49; Fred C. Kelly, "The Great Bicycle Craze," *American Heritage* 8, no. 1 (December 1956): 68–73.

47. *Milford Dispatch,* September 19, 1895, and August 19, 1897; *New York Daily Tribune,* June 16, 1895.

Notes to Chapter 4

1. William Frederick Dix, "American Summer Resorts in the Seventies," *The Independent* 70 (June 1, 1911): 1211–15.

2. Dale A. Somers, "The Leisure Revolution: Recreation in the American City, 1820–1920," *Journal of Popular Culture* 5 (Summer 1971): 125–47.

3. Dulles, *History of Recreation,* 201–3; Rodgers, *Work Ethic,* 107.

4. Robert J. Casey and W. A. S. Douglas, *The Lackawanna Story: The First Hundred Years of the Delaware, Lackawanna and Western Railroad* (New York: McGraw-Hill, 1951), 173–80; Thomas Townsend Taber and

Thomas Townsend Taber III, *The Delaware, Lackawanna and Western Railroad in the Twentieth Century, 1899–1960,* Part 2 (Muncy, Pa., and Williamsport, Pa.: by the authors, 1980), 394–99; Rodney O. Davis, "Earnest Elmo Calkins and Phoebe Snow," *Railroad History* 163 (Autumn 1990): 89–92; Earnest Elmo Calkins, *And Hearing Not* (New York: Charles Scribner's Sons, 1946), 224–25.

5. Taber and Taber, *Delaware, Lackawanna and Western Railroad,* Part 1, 17–18; Casey and Douglas, *The Lackawanna Story,* 103–4.

6. H. Roger Grant, *Erie Lackawanna: Death of an American Railroad, 1938–1992* (Stanford: Stanford University Press, 1994), 79–80; Taber and Taber, *Delaware, Lackawanna and Western Railroad,* Part 1, 29–32, and Part 2, 733; Casey and Douglas, *The Lackawanna Story,* 104ff.; Delaware, Lackawanna and Western Railroad, Passenger Department, *Mountain and Lake Resorts* (New York: Passenger Department, 1913), 26–28.

7. Casey and Douglas, *The Lackawanna Story,* 104ff.

8. Delaware, Lackawanna and Western Railroad, Passenger Department, *Mountain and Lake Resorts* (New York: Passenger Department, 1906).

9. Brown, *Inventing New England,* 9–12.

10. *Stroudsburg Daily Times,* January 16 and May 1, 1902.

11. Ibid., May 1, May 22, June 5, and August 21, 1902.

12. Ibid., October 23, 1902; October 22, 1903; April 7, 1904.

13. Ibid., October 22, 1903; Lee, *Down Along the Old Bel-Del,* 269–73.

14. A comprehensive view of the tiny railroad is in James N. J. Henwood, "Country Carrier of the Poconos: The Delaware Valley Railroad," *Railroad History* 174 (Spring 1996): 27–50. A brief account is in Peter Rickershauser, "The Life and Times of the Delaware Valley Pocono Shortline," *Train Sheet,* Spring 1977, 2–7.

15. *Stroudsburg Daily Times,* March 3, March 12, and October 8, 1903; February 25, 1904.

16. Ibid., May 11 and July 27, 1905; *New York Times,* June 17, 1906.

17. *Monroe Democrat,* April 22 and June 6, 1908; *Daily Record,* June 22, 1911.

18. In June 1908, residents along the River Road between Milford and Bushkill complained about drivers who were speeding at fifty miles an hour and running over fowls, pigs, and lambs, sparing only people and cows. Speeding was a statewide problem, and in 1909 the governor of Pennsylvania signed a bill that limited road speed to 24 miles per hour. See *Monroe Democrat,* July 1, 1908; *Milford Dispatch,* May 6, 1909.

19. *Daily Record,* May 31 and August 8, 1910; *Monroe Democrat,* July 6, 1910; *Milford Dispatch,* May 18, 1911.

20. Francis R. Drake, *The Borough of Delaware Water Gap: A Centennial Study* (Tallahassee, Fla.: Elsa Drake, 1992), 50–52.

21. *Daily Record,* August 31, 1910; *Morning Press,* August 13, 1913.

22. Richard Guy Wilson, "From Informality to Pomposity: The Resort Casino in the Later Nineteenth Century," in *Victorian Resorts and Hotels,* ed. R. G. Wilson (Philadelphia: The Victorian Society in America, 1982), 111–16; The Architectural League of New York, *Resorts of the Catskills,* 20.

23. George C. Hughes, ed., *The Bells: Ringing the Message of Progress in Monroe County and Tributary Country* (East Stroudsburg, Pa.: Hughes Press, 1915), 5; *Daily Record,* January 22, 1910.

24. For the aviary, see *Daily Record,* June 22, 1911. For the deer park, *Stroudsburg Times,* March 31, 1892, and April 18, 1907. Worthington failed to foresee that the absence of predators in his Edenic deer park would cause a population explosion. In a Malthusian nightmare, the deer outstripped their food supply one winter, and they would have starved if they had not been fed. Eventually, the deer park became a state preserve. It was protected by twenty-five wardens during the 1919 hunting season. When today's motorists pass by on Interstate 80, they might note the "Worthington State Forest" sign.

25. *Stroudsburg Times,* July 31 and August 7, 1902; *Daily Record,* May 22, 1911.

26. *Stroudsburg Times,* March 13, 1902.

27. The observer was the writer Norman Harsell in the *Milford Dispatch,* June 16, 1904. See also the *Stroudsburg Times,* June 1, 1905, and Walters, "The Kittatinny," 24ff.

28. *Stroudsburg Times,* March 20, 1907; Walters, "Water Gap House," 42–47.

29. *Daily Record,* September 28 and October 4, 1911.

30. For Atlantic City, see Funnell, *By the Beautiful Sea.* See also Tim Cain, *Peck's Beach: A Pictorial History of Ocean City, New Jersey* (Harvey Cedars, N.J.: Down the Shore Publishing, 1988); Charles Parker, "Ocean Grove, New Jersey: Queen of the Victorian Methodist 'Camp Meeting' Resorts," *Nineteenth Century* 9, no. 1–2 (1984): 19–25; and Floyd and Marion Rinhart, *Summertime: Photographs of Americans at Play, 1850–1900* (New York: Crown Publishers, 1978), 48, 54–56.

31. *Morning Press,* June 2, 1913; Layton Hauser, interview by author, May 5, 1993.

32. Hughes, *The Bells,* 5; John Appel and Roger Dunning, *Monroe County Sesquicentennial, 1836–1986* (Cresco, Pa.: Pocono Press, 1986), 106.

33. *Morning Press,* June 30, 1909, and June 12, 1913; Mary Owens Ballard, interview by author, August 18, 1989.

34. *Stroudsburg Times,* April 10, 1902, and February 28, 1907; see also *Morning Press,* May 31, 1913; August 10 and August 11, 1917; August 13, 1919.

35. *Milford Dispatch,* July 9, 1903, and March 3, 1905.

36. *Monroe Democrat,* Christmas issue, 1913. To this day, Ocean City remains a uniquely dry seashore community in New Jersey.

37. The *Mountain Echo* noted on July 12, 1902, that the six millionaires arrived with two racing autos. For Cleveland, see the *Stroudsburg Times,* May 2, 1907. The August 2, 1910 issue of the *Daily Record* speculated whether Roosevelt would return by the same route. There is no record of the former president returning to the Gap.

38. Charles Jenkins recalls the early days in his "Address Delivered at the Dedication of the Jenkins Woods in Celebration of the Fiftieth Anniversary of the Buck Hill Falls Company," August 26, 1951; Bancroft, *Ringing Axes,* 211–18.

39. Buck Hill History Committee, *Buck Hill History* (unpublished manuscript, 1964, Barrett Friendly Library, Mountainhome, Pa. [cited hereafter as *Buck Hill History*]), 1–5; Buck Hill Falls Company, *Second Annual Report to the Stockholders,* 1902; Buck Hill Falls Company, *Third Annual Report to the Stockholders,* 1903.

40. *Annual Reports of the Board of Directors, Pocono Manor Association,* 1905, 1907, 1908; *Pocono Inn,* 1907 [publicity pamphlet]. Pocono Manor was originally called "Pocono Inn," but was renamed in 1909.

41. *Stroudsburg Times,* February 13, 1902; Robert B. Keller, *History of Monroe County, Pennsylvania* (Stroudsburg, Pa.: Monroe Publishing Company, 1927), 465; Baltzell, *Puritan Boston and Quaker Philadelphia,* 433–38.

42. "Thumbnail History of Buck Hill" (unpublished manuscript, MCHA); Baltzell, *Puritan Boston and Quaker Philadelphia,* 166–75.

43. Bancroft, *Ringing Axes,* 214–16, 232–33; Gladys Rensen, "Golf," and Charles Biggs and J. B. Carr, "Those Were the Tennis Years," *Buck Hill History.*

44. Baltzell, *Puritan Boston and Quaker Philadelphia,* 160.

45. Bancroft, *Ringing Axes,* 216; Buck Hill Falls Company, *Seventh Annual Report to the Stockholders,* 1907; *Buck Hill Falls Breeze,* August 4, 1913; *Buck Hill Falls* [publicity brochure], 1912. By contrast, Pocono Manor reserved its lots for Quakers.

46. Henry Pleasants, *A Historical Account of the Pocono Region of Pennsylvania* (Philadelphia: John C. Winston, 1913), 60–62; Waygood, *Changing Times,* 96; David Morrison, interview by author, August 17, 1988.

47. Bancroft, *Ringing Axes,* 231; *Annual Report of the Board of Directors, Pocono Manor Association, For 1906;* Walters, "Water Gap House"; Dom Cavallo, "Social Reform and the Movement to Organize Children's Play During the Progressive Era," *History of Childhood Quarterly* 3 (Spring 1976): 509–22.

48. Peter J. Schmitt, *Back to Nature: The Arcadian Myth in Urban America* (New York: Oxford University Press, 1969), xv–xxii; Nash, *Wilderness and the American Mind,* 141–60.

49. Henry W. Gibson, "The History of Organized Camping in the United States," *Camping Magazine* 8, nos. 1–6 and 8–9 (1936): 3–21; Fluhr, *Pike in Pennsylvania*, 85; Tyson, *The Poconos*, 109; *Morning Press*, August 12, 1919.

50. *Stroudsburg Times*, January 29 and July 12, 1900.

Notes to Chapter 5

1. *Jeffersonian*, March 14, 1878. The *Jeffersonian* once claimed that sixty-five thousand criminals roamed New York, committing more crimes in a month than the total number of "depredations" of the Apaches and other Indians in an entire year; see April 17, 1873.

2. Ibid., August 1, 1867.

3. Ibid., August 20 and August 27, 1874.

4. Ibid., September 5, 1872, and July 22, 1880. There is always the possibility that the *Jeffersonian* may have been indifferent rather than tolerant toward the summer crowd. The newspaper could be very parochial, referring to communities no more than ten miles distant as being "abroad" (see January 17 and August 8, 1867). If nothing else, though, this was progress. After all, in a previous generation, Judge Dingman had said that New Jersey was off "the face of the earth."

5. Ibid., August 29, 1875; R. M. Wallace, ed., "Ebenezer or Memorial Discourse Commemorative of the Founding and Progress of the First Presbyterian Church, of Stroudsburg, Pennsylvania," 1877 (Presbyterian Folder, MCHA).

6. Barton Hill manuscript, 1906 (Paradise Valley Folder, MCHA); *Milford Dispatch*, November 26, 1896, and August 18, 1898.

7. Fred Strebeigh, "Pleasure in Creation," *American Heritage* 38, no. 5 (1987): 82–88; *Daily Record*, May 14, 1914; "Lenape Baskets," 1970 (Shawnee Folder, MCHA).

8. *Buck Hill Breeze*, July 18, 1913; Isabel Jenkins Booth, "Celebrations," *Buck Hill History*.

9. *Buck Hill Breeze*, August 15, 1914; *Morning Press*, August 27 and November 9, 1917.

10. Edward Jenkins, interview by author, July 28, 1988.

11. U.S. Bureau of the Census, *Twelfth Census of Population*, 1900, Pennsylvania, Vol. 137, Monroe County (National Archives, Philadelphia); *Thirteenth Census of the Population*, 1910, Pennsylvania, Vol. 178, Monroe County (National Archives, Philadelphia).

12. *East Stroudsburg Press and the Jeffersonian*, June 3, 1920.

13. Frank B. Michaels, "History of Banking in Monroe County, Pennsylvania" (unpublished manuscript, 1949, MCHA); Keller, *History of Monroe County*, 367–68.

14. *Times-Democrat*, Christmas issue, 1914.

15. *Stroudsburg Times*, October 23 and November 27, 1902; Pocono Protective Fire Association, *Condensed History, 1901 to 1937* (unpublished manuscript, MCHA).

16. *Monroe Democrat*, September 23, 1908; Commonwealth of Pennsylvania, *Report of the Pennsylvania Department of Forestry for the Years 1908–09* (Harrisburg: State Printer, 1910), 368–69. For the Slavic pickers, see Learn, "Things to Remember." For the observations of a travel writer, see Clifton Johnson, *Highways and Byways from the St. Lawrence to Virginia* (New York: Macmillan, 1913), 187–88.

17. Commonwealth of Pennsylvania, *Report of the Pennsylvania Department of Forestry for the Years 1908–09*, 68–71.

18. Dan Cupper, *Our Priceless Heritage: Pennsylvania State Parks, 1893–1993* (Harrisburg: Pennsylvania Historical and Museum Commission, 1993), 1; *Stroudsburg Times*, October 30, 1902.

19. Cupper, *Our Priceless Heritage*, 2–6.

20. Commonwealth of Pennsylvania, Department of Environmental Resources, *Chronology of Events in Pennsylvania Forestry* (Harrisburg: Bureau of Forestry, 1975), 11.

21. Ibid., 12; letters from Joseph Rothrock to John E. Potter, April 4, 1900, and from Joseph Rothrock to H. T. Frankenfield, May 3, 1900, in the Forestry Commission Correspondence, 1899–1900, Vol. 1 (microfilm #4237, Bureau of Forestry, Pennsylvania Department of Environmental Resources). Pike County's poachers were watched and heavily fined. By the end of 1902, two of the eight watchmen and detectives in the state forests were stationed in Pike County alone; see entries for February 5, August 6, and December 30, 1902, Forestry Reservation Commission Minute Book, No. 1, 1899–1909 (microfilm #4242, Bureau of Forestry, Pennsylvania Department of Environmental Resources).

22. Commonwealth of Pennsylvania, Department of Environmental Resources, *Chronology of Events in Pennsylvania Forestry,* 11–17; Commonwealth of Pennsylvania, *Report of the Department of Forestry of the State of Pennsylvania for the Years 1916–17* (Harrisburg: State Printer, 1910), 52–54.

23. Cupper, *Our Priceless Heritage,* 27–29; "Annual Report of Promised Land State Forest for 1915," Office of the Commissioner, 1901–21, Department of Forestry, Box 1; "Delaware State Forest—Promised Land State Park," Bureau of Parks, Department of Forests and Waters, Minutes and Reports, 1924–41, Box 1; Pocono Protective Fire Association, *Condensed History; East Stroudsburg Press and the Jeffersonian,* February 12, 1920.

24. *Stroudsburg Times,* November 5, 1891, and June 30, 1897; *Milford Dispatch,* July 14, 1898.

25. *Stroudsburg Times,* June 1, 1899; *Milford Dispatch,* November 26, 1891.

26. *Milford Dispatch,* March 6 and April 24, 1902; *Stroudsburg Times,* November 13, 1902.

27. *Milford Dispatch,* October 22, 1903; January 28, 1904; March 14, 1912; *Stroudsburg Times,* November 3, 1904.

28. *Milford Dispatch,* December 3, 1904, and February 23, 1905.

29. *Milford Dispatch,* May 11, 1905, and July 15, 1909.

30. *Stroudsburg Times,* June 14, 1900; *Milford Dispatch,* August 28, 1902, and January 26, 1905.

31. *Manzanedo Rod and Gun Club* [pamphlet, circa 1911–20]; *Morning Press,* June 18, 1913; *Milford Dispatch,* April 13, 1905; *Stroudsburg Times,* January 3, 1901.

32. Hughes, *The Bells,* 36–42; David L. Miller, ed., *East Stroudsburg Centennial, 1870–1970* (East Stroudsburg, Pa. Sun Litho-Print, Inc., 1970), 26–31; Wetzel, *Monroe County,* 19–21, 26–27.

33. *Daily Record,* September 4 and September 7, 1909, and May 13, 1911; *Monroe Democrat,* September 8, 1909.

34. *Jeffersonian,* June 29, 1871, and August 29, 1872; *Stroudsburg Times,* June 12, 1890, and April 6, 1895; *Stroudsburg Daily Times,* February 3, 1896.

35. *Milford Dispatch,* August 13, 1903, and May 5, 1904.

36. Ibid., May 6, 1909; *Daily Record,* April 6, 1914.

37. *Stroudsburg Times,* April 18, 1907; *Daily Record,* April 8, 1914; Bancroft, *Ringing Axes,* 295–96.

38. *Stroudsburg Times,* October 4, 1906, and January 31, 1907; Drake, *Borough of Delaware Water Gap,* 41–43.

39. *Stroudsburg Times,* March 11 and March 22, 1894.

40. Johnson, *Highways and Byways,* 188; *Milford Dispatch,* October 5, 1893; September 11, 1902; February 26, 1903; and August 11, 1904; *Stroudsburg Times,* January 25, 1900.

41. *Stroudsburg Times,* October 26, December 7, and December 9, 1897; Fluhr, *Shohola,* 133–35. The Pike County sheriff received fifteen dollars for selling Schultz's body to the State Board of Anatomy in Philadelphia. Part of this money was used to pay for the noose and the three-hundred-pound deadweight.

42. Edward Harold Mott, *Pike County Folks* (New York: J. W. Lovell, 1883); Norman Lehde, *Milford Pennsylvania, 1733–1983,* 64–67; *Milford Dispatch,* May 14, 1891, and February 6, 1896.

43. *Stroudsburg Times,* November 9, 1893.

44. Ibid., November 4, 1895, October 7, 1898, and August 10, 1899; *Milford Dispatch,* April 23, 1891.

45. *Milford Dispatch,* October 14, 1897, and October 23 and July 24, 1902.

46. Ibid., September 10, 1896.

47. In his *The Tourist Gaze: Leisure and Travel in Contemporary Societies* (London: Sage, 1991), John Urry argues that tourists stare and say little, as if they are observing natural phenomena. The natives, for their part, know

that their function is to be silently observed. Tourists return home with memories, the result of a brief gaze at the unfamiliar and exotic; the natives pocket the money.

48. Aron, *Working at Play*, 105–9. See also the works cited in Chapter 4 of this volume, in footnote 30.

49. At its founding in 1874, the National W.C.T.U. both attacked the liquor traffic and advocated equal rights for the sexes. Frances Willard, who led the W.C.T.U. from 1879 until her death in 1898, associated liquor with male dominance. See John Kobler, *Ardent Spirits: The Rise and Fall of Prohibition* (New York: Da Capo Press, 1993), 134ff.

50. *Daily Record*, March 28 and December 24, 1910, and March 31, 1911; Earl C. Kaylor Jr., "The Prohibition Movement in Pennsylvania, 1865–1920" (Ph.D. diss., The Pennsylvania State University, 1963), 291–93 and 358–60. The Brooks Law of 1887 gave judges the authority to grant and revoke retail liquor licenses.

51. *Daily Record*, March 27 and March 28, 1911; Walters, "Water Gap House"; Kaylor, "Prohibition Movement in Pennsylvania," 358–60.

52. In 1889, a proposed Prohibition amendment to the Pennsylvania Constitution lost by over 180,000 votes. In Monroe County, the vote was 2,585 opposed and only 970 in favor, a result that ran against the rule of most rural counties having favored the amendment. Kaylor, "Prohibition Movement in Pennsylvania," 276–78 and 358–60; *Jeffersonian*, June 20, 1889.

Notes to Chapter 6

1. *New York Times*, August 31, 1909.
2. *Morning Press*, July 14, 1916.
3. *Mountain Echo*, July 29, 1917; *Morning Press*, October 16, 1917; Dulles, *History of Recreation*, 360.
4. The period of American neutrality was fortuitous for the Spruce Cabin Inn. The fancy hunting lodge in Canadensis hired professional waiters from German ocean liners that were stranded in New York City when the war broke out in August 1914. Fear of the British navy kept the German ships from leaving. Since the United States was neutral, the German crews were free to fend for themselves. Some of the waiters found jobs at the Spruce Cabin Inn. When America entered the war in 1917, the waiters were interned as enemy aliens, and the Spruce Cabin Inn went back to having teenagers and housewives wait on tables. Paul Schaarschmidt, interview by author, June 14, 1989.
5. William McFadden, "A History of the Resort Industry at Delaware Water Gap" (unpublished manuscript, National Park Service, Bushkill, Pa.), 69; *Morning Press*, July 18 and December 15, 1918; *Times-Democrat*, December 15, 1918.
6. *Morning Press*, October 26 and November 5, 1917; August 31, 1918.
7. Ibid., July 23, July 29, August 5, and August 10, 1918.
8. Ibid., July 16, 1918.
9. Ibid., October 11 and October 16, 1918; Helen Dietz, interview by author, June 21, 1990.
10. *Morning Press*, April 11, 1918.
11. Ibid., March 27 and May 4, 1918; *East Stroudsburg Press and the Jeffersonian*, April 1, 1920.
12. *Morning Press*, December 3, 1917.
13. Ibid., August 14, 1919; Wilbur C. Plummer, "The Road Policy of Pennsylvania" (Ph.D. diss., University of Pennsylvania, 1924), 90–94.
14. *Morning Press*, October 29, 1921; *East Stroudsburg Press and the Jeffersonian*, October 22 and October 27, 1921; Appel, *History of Monroe County*, 167. Keller, *History of Monroe County*, 283, 498–99, is a contemporary view.
15. Martin Wilson, *Delaware Water Gap, 1993 Bicentennial* (Delaware Water Gap, Pa.: Antoine Dutot School and Museum, 1993), 12, 15–16; Henwood, "Country Carrier," 38–46; *Pocono Record*, July 27, 1983.

16. John A. Jakle, *The Tourist: Travel in Twentieth-Century North America* (Lincoln: University of Nebraska Press, 1985), 146–70.

17. Sally Walther, *The Story of Bushkill Falls* (Stroudsburg, Pa.: D. Hannan Associates, 1992), 33–39; Linda Pipher (Charles Peters's daughter), interview by author, June 19, 1990.

18. *Morning Press,* June, July, August, and September 1919, passim.

19. Ibid., June 1 and July 6, 1920.

20. Ibid., July 29, 1920.

21. *East Stroudsburg Press and the Jeffersonian,* August 25, 1921; *Milford Dispatch,* August 26, 1926; Fred and Patricia Shoemaker, interview by author, May 13, 1993.

22. Paul S. George, "Passage to the New Eden: Tourism in Miami from Flagler Through Everest G. Sewell," *Florida Historical Quarterly* 59, no. 4 (1981): 440–63. Florida had begun to promote its assets in the 1880s. By the mid-1920s, the Miami Chamber of Commerce was receiving one hundred thousand dollars of public money.

23. *Morning Sun,* December 29, 1928, and December 9, 1929; Keller, *History of Monroe County,* 226–27; R. E. Kintner, "History of Monroe County and the Stroudsburgs as It Is Today," *Founding of the Stroudsburgs,* August 27–29, 1930, 61.

24. *Morning Press,* June 25, 1924.

25. *Milford Dispatch,* August 28, 1924.

26. Jack Heilig, interview by author, February 27, 1992; *The Record,* July 31, 1930.

27. Frederick Lewis Allen's *Only Yesterday: An Informal History of the Nineteen-Twenties* (New York: Harper, 1931) is the classic account of the "roaring twenties." Written as the Great Depression was beginning, it was both a memoir of a zany period and a valediction to its end.

28. *Morning Press,* June 26, 1924; *East Stroudsburg Press and the Jeffersonian,* August 18, 1921; Carlyle Huffman, interview by author, July 30, 1987.

29. *East Stroudsburg Press and the Jeffersonian,* July 28, 1921.

30. *Milford Dispatch,* July 8, 1926.

31. *East Stroudsburg Press and the Jeffersonian,* August 25, 1921.

32. *Milford Dispatch,* October 29, 1925, and January 14, 1926.

33. *Morning Press,* July 25, 1928.

34. Gertrude Burlingame Hershey, "Things I Remember: From 1912 to 1974" (unpublished memoir, MCHA).

35. Milford Chamber of Commerce, Resort Department, *Milford and Its Environment Including All of Pike County, Pennsylvania* (Milford, Pa.: Milford Chamber of Commerce, 1922).

36. Floyd R. Lear to William F. Mosser, April 11, 1963, Maskenozha Rod and Gun Club Archive. (This archive is in the personal possession of Robert Lear, a Stroudsburg attorney.)

37. Kenneth and Dorothy Bates, interview by author, April 28, 1993.

38. *Milford Dispatch,* July 22, 1926; Commonwealth of Pennsylvania, Department of Environmental Resources, Bureau of Forestry, *Forestry: Programs and Services* (Harrisburg: Department of Environmental Resources, 1976), 15.

39. *Milford Dispatch,* July 15, 1926; Louis Bignami, "Past and Present Tents," *Westways* 73, no. 8 (1981): 35.

40. "Once Upon a Time," Personal Recollections and Memoranda of Dr. Edward E. Wildman; "Thumbnail History of Buck Hill"; Buck Hill Falls Company, *Twenty-Fifth Annual Report to the Stockholders of the Buck Hill Falls Company* (1925) and *Thirtieth Annual Report to the Stockholders of the Buck Hill Falls Company* (1930).

41. Tyson, *The Poconos,* 90–92.

42. See *Buck Hill History,* passim. Information on Pocono Manor supplied by Jean K. Wolf.

43. *Morning Press,* August 22, 1921.

44. Bancroft, *Ringing Axes,* 233; Harry Drennan, "Winter Sports," *Buck Hill History.*

45. *Morning Sun,* January 11 and January 18, 1929.

46. "Harry J. Drennan, Buck Hill's Winter Sports Director" [1966 Buck Hill Inn publicity brochure].

47. Edward Jenkins, interview by author, July 28, 1988; Tyson, *The Poconos*, 90–92, 102–3.

48. Evelyn R. Wolfe, "Lot and Cottage Owners' Association," *Buck Hill History;* Edward Jenkins, interview by author, July 28, 1988; Tyson, *The Poconos*, 97; *Twenty-Third Annual Report to the Stockholders of the Buck Hill Falls Company* (1923).

49. William Malleson Jr. (manager of Skytop), interview by author, June 19, 1989.

50. Patrick Fassano, *The Nature of Skytop* (n.p.: Patrick Fassano/Skytop, 1987), 12–17. An account by one of Skytop's founders is in Frederic W. Smith, *Skytop: An Adventure* (Skytop, Pa.: The Skytop Club, 1963), 5–33.

51. Bancroft, *Ringing Axes*, 247–52; Tyson, *The Poconos*, 102–3.

Notes to Chapter 7

1. International Ladies' Garment Workers' Union Archive, Martin P. Catherwood Library, Kheel Center for Labor Management Documentation and Archives, Cornell University, Ithaca, N.Y. (hereafter cited as "I.L.G.W.U. Archive"), Minutes of General Executive Board [I.L.G.W.U.], November 15, 1938.

2. *Stroudsburg Times*, November 3, 1894.

3. Ibid., August 16, 1894; December 27, 1895; June 6, 1899.

4. *Daily Record*, July 1, September 26, and September 28, 1909; William H. Truesdale to Chief Engineer, Lackawanna Railroad, Hoboken, N.J., October 6, 1909 (Truesdale Letterbooks, Corporate Records of the Lackawanna Division of the Erie-Lackawanna Railroad, Syracuse University Library.)

5. *Stroudsburg Times*, April 24, 1902; *Milford Dispatch*, March 13, 1902; Forest Brown (Norwegian American Historical Association), letter to author, October 26, 1993. For the views of a current resident of the area, see Jodielynn Kuhn, interview by author, June 24, 1993.

6. *Milford Dispatch*, August 21, 1902.

7. *Jeffersonian*, August 17, 1882, and August 8, 1889; *Milford Dispatch*, August 8, 1895.

8. *New York Times*, June 18, 1906.

9. *Stroudsburg Times*, August 1, 1894, and October 29, 1895; *Milford Dispatch*, September 15, 1892.

10. *The Origin of the Tamiment Facilities*, located at the Tamiment Institute Library, Elmer Holmes Bobst Library, New York University, New York (hereafter, "Tamiment Library"); *Morning Press*, May 12, 1919. The March 2, 1969, issue of the *Sunday Call-Chronicle* of Allentown recalled that Forest Park during World War I was "supposedly a hideout for pro Germans and was padlocked by the government." The newspaper gave no other details. The mysterious ending of Forest Park is also discussed in Martha Schmoyer LoMonaco, *Every Week, A Broadway Review: The Tamiment Playhouse, 1921–1960* (New York: Greenwood Press, 1992), 4.

11. "Application for Loan on Second Mortgage upon Camp Tamiment," September 21, 1921, Camp Tamiment Collection #7: Box 1, Tamiment Library; "Treasurer's Report at the Annual Meeting of the People's Educational Camp Society, Inc.," January 1922, Camp Tamiment Collection #7: Box 1, Tamiment Library.

12. Louis Levine, *The Women's Garment Workers: A History of the International Ladies' Garment Workers Union* (New York: B. W. Huebsch, 1924), 338, 352–53, 487, 492–93.

13. "Financial Report of the Unity House for Season of 1923," Collection #56: Research Department, Collected Documents, 1907–48, I.L.G.W.U. Archive. According to Aron, Unity House "in some ways resembled Chautauqua" (see *Working at Play*, 221).

14. Minutes of General Executive Board [I.L.G.W.U.], 1924–29 passim, I.L.G.W.U. Archive.

15. Morris Sigman to George Oliver [Unity House's manager], June 24, 1927, Collection #6: Morris Sigman Correspondence; "Unity Reunion: List of Complementary Tickets," Collection #49: Fannia Cohn. The fun activities at

Unity House were advertised in a brochure called "Twelfth Season: 1930 Unity House," Collection #56: Research Department, Collected Documents, 1907–48, I.L.G.W.U. Archive.

16. LoMonaco, *Every Week,* 2–15.

17. Rachel Cutler Schwartz, "The Rand School of Social Science, 1906–1924: A Study of Worker Education in the Socialist Era" (Ed.D. diss., State University of New York, 1984), 114; LoMonaco, *Every Week,* 5.

18. "Minutes of the People's Educational Camp: Meeting of the Board of Directors," February 9, 1921, Camp Tamiment Collection #7: Box 1, Tamiment Library. An overview of the early days is in the Tax Court of the United States, People's Educational Camp Society, Inc. v. Commissioner of Internal Revenue, February 12, 1963 (hereafter cited as "Tax Court"), 2076–77. See also the brief history (probably written in the 1950s) in "How It Started," People's Educational Camp Society, Box 2, Tamiment Library.

19. "Ben Josephson Reminiscences," Ben Josephson Papers, Tamiment Library (hereafter, "Ben Josephson Reminiscences"); "Broader Horizons," People's Educational Camp Society, Box 2, Tamiment Library.

20. "Application for Loan on Second Mortgage upon Camp Tamiment." For Tamiment's financial success, see Tax Court, 2078, and "Ben Josephson Reminiscences."

21. "Report of the Board of Directors to PECS, Inc.," January 15, 1923, Camp Tamiment Collection #7: Box 1, Tamiment Library; Martha Blaker, interview by author, April 5, 1990.

22. "Ben Josephson Reminiscences."

23. Ibid. The business manager at Camp Tamiment accused Sandy Hayman, the Yankee radical, of undermining the help's morale. See "Minutes of the People's Educational Camp: Meeting of the Board of Directors," December 12, 1921, Tamiment: Box 1, Tamiment Library.

24. "Ben Josephson Reminiscences"; LoMonaco, *Every Week,* 21–27.

25. "Report of President to Annual Meeting of the People's Educational Camp Society, Inc.," February 17, 1928, Camp Tamiment Collection #7: Box 1, Tamiment Library; "Ben Josephson Reminiscences."

26. Clotilda Comazzi Wile, interview by author, February 22, 1989.

27. Barrett Township Historical Society Bulletin, June 1994.

28. George B. Ammon and Clifford E. Hays, *The Story of Paradise Falls Lutheran Association, 1922–1972* (privately printed, 1972); Rev. George B. Ammon, interview by author, July 13, 1989. A contemporary view is in Keller, *History of Monroe County,* 457–58.

29. Tyson, *The Poconos,* 108; Keller, *History of Monroe County,* 450–53.

30. Laura Niebacher (Dahlen's daughter), telephone conversation with author, July 28, 1989.

31. Waygood, *Changing Times,* 44–45; Keller, *History of Monroe County,* 450–53; *Morning Sun,* April 29, 1929.

32. Rev. Rudolph Ressmeyer, interview by author, July 19, 1989.

33. Frederick A. Norwood, *The Story of American Methodism* (Nashville: Abingdon Press, 1974), 348–50. The Methodist Episcopal Church, at its General Conference of 1872, adopted a rule on amusements that condemned the buying, selling, or drinking of liquor. Dancing, card playing, and attending theater, horse races, and circuses were also forbidden. See William Warren Sweet, *Methodism in American History* (Nashville: Abingdon Press, 1961), 325.

34. *East Stroudsburg Press and the Jeffersonian,* January 20, 1921.

35. The new dances of the years immediately prior to World War I signalled that Victorian morality was declining. Although moralists lamented the change, the "best" people were rejecting nineteenth-century dances that exhibited control and sexual restraint in favor of freer dances that often originated in red-light districts. Lewis A. Erenberg, "Everybody's Doin' It: The Pre–World War I Dance Craze, the Castles, and the Modern American Girl," *Feminist Studies* 3 (Fall 1975): 155–56.

36. *Morning Press,* July 31, 1919.

37. *East Stroudsburg Press and the Jeffersonian,* August 21, 1919; *Morning Press,* August 30, 1919.

38. *East Stroudsburg Press and the Jeffersonian,* June 23 and July 21, 1921.

39. Ibid., September 21, 1922; Jack Heilig, interview by author, February 27, 1992.

40. *Morning Press,* July 25 and August 19, 1919; *East Stroudsburg Press and the Jeffersonian,* August 11, 1921.

41. Philip Jenkins, *Hoods and Saints: The Extreme Right in Pennsylvania* (Chapel Hill: University of North Carolina Press, 1997), 62–88. Although condemned by Methodist leaders, the Klan found favor among church members. One Methodist historian writes: "It appealed to many ministers and church members, some of whom became members, and not infrequently Methodist ministers became organizers and its active promoters." See Sweet, *Methodism in American History,* 384.

42. *Milford Dispatch,* March 6 and March 13, 1924. Church visitations were a common religious practice among Pennsylvania Klansmen. See Emerson Hunsberger Loucks, *The Ku Klux Klan in Pennsylvania: A Study in Nativism* (New York-Harrisburg: Telegraph Press, 1936), 118–33.

43. Warner DePuy, interview by author, August 10, 1993; Joanne Ambler, "The Syrian Summer Colony of Milford" (lecture delivered at the Northeastern Conference of Junior Historians, State Teachers College, East Stroudsburg, Pa., May 2, 1952). The *Milford Dispatch* ran stories on the Syrian summer colonies on August 21 and September 4, 1924.

44. *Milford Dispatch,* April 23, 1924.

45. An account of Palmer's Pocono career is in Stanley Coben, *A. Mitchell Palmer: Politician* (New York: Columbia University Press, 1963), 1–15; *East Stroudsburg Press and the Jeffersonian,* October 19, 1922.

46. Ida Jolley, interview by author, January 30, 1991.

47. *The Record,* June 17, 1932; George Chauncey, *Gay New York: Gender, Urban Culture, and the Making of the Gay Male World 1890–1940* (New York: Basic Books, 1994), 327–29. The *Monroe Citizen*'s linking of alcohol to interracial sex was not unique. In some parts of the United States, citizens noted that breaking the liquor taboo led to the breaking of other taboos, including racial ones.

48. *The Record,* April 8, 1931.

Notes to Chapter 8

1. Frederick Lewis Allen, *Since Yesterday: The Nineteen-Thirties in America* (New York: Harper, 1940), 30–31.

2. *Morning Sun,* June 2 and July 5, 1930. According to Buck Hill's Twenty-Ninth and Thirtieth Annual Reports, the 1930 profit was 45 percent higher than that of 1929.

3. *Morning Sun,* July 2 and July 3, 1930.

4. Ibid., June 13 and June 28, 1930; Allen, *Since Yesterday,* 30–31.

5. John Kenneth Galbraith, *The Great Crash,* 3d ed. (Boston: Houghton Mifflin, 1972), 146; Allen, *Since Yesterday,* 51–61.

6. *Daily Record,* June 1 and August 31, 1931; September 1, 1932. See also "Annual Financial Report of Camp Tamiment for the Year Beginning October 1, 1929, and Ending September 15, 1930," Collection #7: PECS, Tamiment Library; information on Pocono Manor supplied by Jean K. Wolf.

7. *Daily Record,* February 1, May 18, and September 17, 1932.

8. Ibid., May 31, July 5, and September 6, 1932.

9. See the annual reports for the years 1929 to 1932 in Collection #7: PECS, Tamiment Library.

10. Halperin to David Dubinsky, July 8, 1932, Collection #2: David Dubinsky Correspondence, I.L.G.W.U. Archive.

11. *Daily Record,* July 16, July 29, September 2, October 3, and October 29, 1932.

12. Ibid., November 15, 1932; see also February 18 and May 3, 1933.

13. *Daily Record*, December 15, 1932; Jesse Flory, talk delivered at MCHA dinner, East Stroudsburg State College, February 4, 1978; correspondence between Huffman and Dubinsky, October 4 and October 11, 1932, Collection #2: David Dubinsky Correspondence, I.L.G.W.U. Archive.

14. *Daily Record*, December 24, 1932; see also January 30 and February 3, 1933.

15. Ibid., November 16, 1932; Jean Haley, interview by author, October 24, 1994.

16. Allen, *Since Yesterday*, 124.

17. See the annual reports for Camp Tamiment for the years 1929 to 1932 in Collection #7: PECS, Tamiment Library; see also Buck Hill's annual reports for 1928 to 1933.

18. Allen, *Since Yesterday*, 162; Galbraith, *The Great Crash*, 173.

19. *Morning Sun*, July 10 and July 31, 1930.

20. *Daily Record*, July 25, 1931; *Morning Sun*, November 8 and November 9, 1933.

21. Paul B. Beers, *Pennsylvania Politics, Today and Yesterday: The Tolerable Accommodation* (University Park: The Pennsylvania State University Press, 1980), 72–76.

22. *Daily Record*, January 24, June 5, and November 9, 1933; John T. Jable, "Sport, Amusements, and Pennsylvania Blue Laws, 1682–1973" (Ph.D. diss., The Pennsylvania State University, 1974), 167–70, 204.

23. Taber and Taber, *Delaware, Lackawanna and Western Railroad*, Part 1, 115; John and Patricia Shoemaker, interview by author, May 13, 1993; *Morning Sun*, April 16, 1930; *Daily Record*, November 15, 1932.

24. *Daily Record*, June 15, 1933; see also April 14 and May 4, 1938.

25. *Pocono Record*, July 12, 1977; *Morning Sun*, July 28, 1930; *Daily Record*, July 30, 1932.

26. The *Daily Record* gave extensive coverage to the Laurel Blossom Time festivals. Other sources of information are the official programs and photographs that are found in the MCHA. Leroy Koehler, a social science instructor at the teachers' college in East Stroudsburg, served as chairman of the Laurel Blossom Time Committee in 1936. His report of July 30, 1936, to the Chamber of Commerce makes very clear the lack of popular interest in the festival (see MCHA). The lives of the masses were on a different track. Mary Smith Nelson, who had been a student at the teachers' college in 1933, recalls the time that she was walking through Stroudsburg and heard sounds from a church. Curiosity made her enter, and she witnessed a religious revival. A woman jumped on a table and loudly proclaimed that a heavenly plane was coming to Stroudsburg and that it would take her away. All along, the woman had an eye on Mary, who realized that she was in another Stroudsburg, one quite different from the college and from the resort where she worked. She left the church building, but never forgot the experience. Mary Smith Nelson, interview by author, June 15, 1993.

27. *Daily Record*, January 31 and April 27, 1933.

28. Buck Hill's Annual Report for 1935; Herbert Lorenz, "Swimming at Buck Hill," *Buck Hill History*.

29. Edward Jenkins, interview by author, July 28, 1988; Mary Ann Miller, interview by author, June 14, 1989.

30. *Daily Record*, November 21 and December 21, 1932; Bancroft, *Ringing Axes*, 233–34.

31. William Malleson Jr., interview by author, June 19, 1989; *Daily Record*, May 22, 1931; August 12, 1931; and December 12, 1932.

32. "Golf at Buck Hill Falls in the Pocono Mountains, Pennsylvania" [promotional brochure, 1933]; Theodore H. Banks, "Lawn Bowling," *Buck Hill History*.

33. Cornelia Stabler Gillam, "The Buck Hill Players, 1929–1954," *Buck Hill History*.

34. Marianna G. Packer, "Buck Hill Art Association," *Buck Hill History;* Edward Jenkins, interview by author, July 28, 1988.

35. Anna Pettit Broomell, "The Foxhowe Association," *Buck Hill History*.

36. The following are found in the I.L.G.W.U. Archive: "The Unity House Summer Review" [a 1934 brochure], Tamiment Collection, Unity House Vertical File; "Persons Who Will Lecture in Unity House During the Summer,"

May 19, 1937, Collection #49: Education Department Records; "Unity News," August 25 and August 29, 1935, Collection #56: Research Department, Collected Documents, 1907–48. Diego Rivera had been commissioned in 1932 to paint murals for the new Rockefeller Center in midtown Manhattan. As Rivera painted the murals, their radical nature gradually became obvious. The last straw for John D. Rockefeller Jr. was the mural that highlighted Lenin. Rivera was paid for his services, dismissed, and his murals destroyed. To get revenge, Rivera painted new murals on movable panels for the New Workers' School on West Fourteenth Street. When the building was demolished, thirteen of these murals found their way to Unity House. Bertram D. Wolfe, *The Fabulous Life of Diego Rivera* (New York: Stein and Day, 1963), 317–37.

37. *Daily Record,* June 20, 1933; "Ben Josephson Reminiscences"; and the annual reports of Camp Tamiment to the directors for 1936, 1937, and 1939, Collection #7: PECS, Tamiment Library.

38. "Ben Josephson Reminiscences"; correspondence between Louis B. Goldberg and Ben Josephson, June 13 and June 14, 1938, Collection #3: Ben Josephson Papers, Tamiment Library.

39. LoMonaco, *Every Week,* 35–95; "Ben Josephson Reminiscences."

40. Martha Blaker, interview by author, April 5, 1990.

41. Pat Shoemaker, interview by author, May 13, 1993.

42. "Ben Josephson Reminiscences"; "Report of Board of Directors, Rand School of Social Science, September 22, 1936," Collection #3: Ben Josephson Papers, Tamiment Library.

43. The following are in the I.L.G.W.U. Archive: "An ex-union waiter" to David Dubinsky, April 27, 1937, and Ernest Meyer [*New York Post*] to David Dubinsky, May 29, 1938, Collection #5: Frederick F. Umhey Correspondence; see also correspondence between Louis Kammerman and David Dubinsky, August 1 and August 3, 1937, Collection #2: David Dubinsky Correspondence. On May 14, 1938, the *New York World Telegram* reported that forty-two "college boys" had picketed the I.L.G.W.U. office in Manhattan. It quoted Frederick Umhey, executive secretary of the I.L.G.W.U.: "Just because we happen to be a union, they think they can blackjack us. We . . . pay a union scale as high as any in the country."

44. See Unity House publicity brochures in Collection #5: Frederick F. Umhey Correspondence; Minutes of General Executive Board [I.L.G.W.U.], December 6, 1935, I.L.G.W.U. Archive.

45. Abraham Ellner to union locals, April 12, 1938, and Herman Liebman to Charles Zimmerman, April 7, 1939, Collection #14, Charles S. Zimmerman Records; Minutes of General Executive Board [I.L.G.W.U.], January 6, 1937; November 15, 1938; and May 25, 1939; I.L.G.W.U. Archive.

46. Martha Blaker, interview by author, April 5, 1990; Edward Jenkins, interview by author, July 28, 1988.

47. *Daily Record,* May 23, 1932; Fred and Patricia Shoemaker, interview by author, May 13, 1993; John Shinn, interview by author, May 20, 1993.

48. *Daily Record,* May 8 and May 15, 1933.

49. Ibid., July and August 1938, passim.

50. Delaware, Lackawanna and Western Railroad, Passenger Department, *Mountain and Lake Resorts, 1939,* 10.

51. *Daily Record,* August 27 and October 10, 1932; *Pocono Record,* July 12, 1977. See also a publicity brochure that *Pocono Hay-ven* published in 1933.

52. The 1933 edition of the Lackawanna passenger directory contained ten resorts ads that explicitly stated a "restricted" policy toward Jews. In the 1939 directory, twenty-three resorts were restricted. The exclusion of Jews obviously escalated during the 1930s.

53. Ethnic food was a code to alert readers to an ethnic hotel. In the *New York Times* of May 22, 1938, the Oliver House and the Friedman Brothers' Bushkill Falls Villa advertised that they served Jewish food.

54. Irene Cramer, interview by author, September 30, 1993; Florence Mack, telephone conversation with author, July 5, 1988.

55. Fred and Patricia Shoemaker, interview by author, May 13, 1993; Drake, *Borough of Delaware Water Gap,* 76–78.

56. Author interviews: Jean Haley, October 24, 1994; Harry Ahnert, June 8, 1993; and Rudolph Ressmeyer, July 19, 1989; District Court of the United States for the Middle District of Pennsylvania, *Lutherland, Inc. Debtor, Report of Reorganization,* Scranton, Pa., September 20, 1952.

57. Mary Smith Nelson, interview by author, June 15, 1993.

58. *Daily Record,* May 7, 1931; May 12, 1931; and November 5, 1938.

Notes to Chapter 9

1. Allan M. Winkler, *Home Front U.S.A.: America During World War II* (Wheeling, Ill.: Harlan Davidson, 1986), 14–15; John Morton Blum, *V Was for Victory: Politics and American Culture During World War II* (New York: Harcourt Brace Jovanovich, 1976), 91–92.

2. Kevin McManus, "Pocono Resort Owners Dip into Pool of Success," *Insight* (June 15, 1987): 54–55; *The Record,* July 31, 1944. The forty-second annual report to the stockholders of the Buck Hill Company (1942) noted that its record business was partially due to the closing of many sea resorts, especially those in Atlantic City.

3. Richard Polenberg, *War and Society: The United States, 1941–45* (Philadelphia: Lippincott, 1972), 32; Winkler, *Home Front U.S.A.,* 38–39. For the Poconos, see Appel, *History of Monroe County,* 154.

4. "Ben Josephson Reminiscences"; Marie Hoffman, interview by author, November 6, 1996.

5. *New York Times,* November 7, 1943; Irene Cramer, interview by author, September 30, 1993.

6. Polenberg, *War and Society,* 18; Walther, *Story of Bushkill Falls,* 42.

7. "Statement of Local Ticket Sales by Stations as Shown for Months of Years Indicated," Box 23, Corporate Records of the Lackawanna Division of the Erie-Lackawanna Railroad, Syracuse University Library.

8. *The Record,* June 30, 1944, and May 31, 1945; see also Edna Renouf, "The Twenty-Five Middle Years of Camp Club," and Harry J. Drennan, "Winter Sports," both in *Buck Hill History.*

9. *New York Times,* August 12, 1945; "Statement for Camp Tamiment . . . Presented at the Annual Meeting of the PECS," April 30, 1943, Collection #7: PECS, Tamiment Library; *The Record,* June 23, 1944.

10. Harry Ahnert, interview by author, June 8, 1993; *New York Times,* February 6, 1943.

11. Edward Jenkins, interview by author, August 11, 1988.

12. See the annual reports from Buck Hill during the war years.

13. See the annual reports from Josephson to the PECS Board of Directors from 1942 to 1945 in Collection #7: PECS, Tamiment Library; likewise, see the reports of the Unity House Committee from 1941 to 1945 in Collection #5, Frederick F. Umhey Correspondence, I.L.G.W.U. Archive. I don't mean to suggest that Tamiment and Unity House were doing better than other resorts. I have precise information for them, which I do not have for others (Skytop, for example).

14. Braden and Endelman, *Americans on Vacation,* 44.

15. Jakle, *The Tourist,* 189–91.

16. Knepp, *The Poconos,* 54–55.

17. *New York Times,* June 6, 1948; Edward Jenkins, interview by author, August 11, 1988.

18. Charlotte Forbes, "Jim Thorpe Lines Up for Visitors," *Saturday Evening Post* 263 (March 1990): 86–87; Laura Outerbridge, "Town Thrives on an Athlete's Aura," *Insight* (June 20, 1988): 24–25; and Sears, *Sacred Places,* 182–208, for a discussion of Mauch Chunk in its nineteenth-century glory days.

19. Carlyle Huffman, interview by author, July 30, 1987; Edward Jenkins, interview by author, August 11, 1988.

20. *Philadelphia Inquirer,* June 6, 1982; Edward Jenkins, interview by author, August 11, 1988.

21. Statistics on Buck Hill's profitability and guest days are in the annual reports; see also Mary Anne Miller, interview by author, June 14, 1989. Information on Pocono Manor supplied by Jean K. Wolf.

22. "Management Sings to Labor," May 26, 1956, Collection #2: David Dubinsky Correspondence, I.L.G.W.U. Archive; *Philadelphia Inquirer,* August 12, 1990.

23. Minutes of General Executive Board [I.L.G.W.U.], October 6, 1955; Saul Gold to Gus Tyler, September 26, 1972, Collection #52: Assistant President, Gus Tyler, I.L.G.W.U. Archive.

24. *Variety,* July 2, 1952 (clipping is found in Collection #5: Frederick Umhey Correspondence); "Times Square in the Poconos" [a 1957 publicity brochure], Collection #11: Local 10 Records, I.L.G.W.U. Archive; Arthur Bolger, interview by author, February 7, 1990. Bolger served as the last manager of Unity House.

25. *Pocono Record,* September 1, 1985; LoMonaco, *Every Week,* 115–17, 121–39.

26. "Music Over the Poconos" [brochure] and "Report on Operations and Cultural Activities: 1953 Season," Collection #84: Ben Josephson Papers, Tamiment Library.

27. Tax Court, 2077–80; Ben Josephson obituary from *New Leader,* July 14, 1980 (clipping in Collection #84: Ben Josephson Papers, Tamiment Library).

28. Information on Tamiment's cultural program is found in the annual reports and brochures in Collection #84: Ben Josephson Papers, Tamiment Library; a summary is in Tax Court, 2077–80.

29. Martha Blaker, interview by author, April 5, 1990; Barbara Barrow, interview by author, July 18, 1989.

30. Minnie Edwards, interview by author, June 12, 1991.

31. David Artzt, interview by author, February 28, 1990.

32. *Pocono Record,* December 1, 1991.

33. Hillary Bute, interview by author, June 10, 1993.

34. Albert Murray, interview by author, May 18, 1993.

35. See press clippings in the Fred Waring Folder, MCHA; see also the Waring obituary, *TIME,* August 13, 1984.

36. Frank Tancredi, interview by author, September 22, 1993.

37. John Shinn, interview by author, May 20, 1993.

38. Jim Tiernan, interview by author, November 12, 1991.

39. Joseph O'Connor, interview by author, October 15, 1993.

40. Frank Tancredi, interview by author, September 22, 1993; see the *Pike County Courier,* October 1995, for the Log Tavern Camp waiter.

41. Author interviews with Frank Tancredi, September 22, 1993; Barbara Barrow, July 18, 1989; Arthur Bolger, February 7, 1990.

42. Author interviews with Karl Dickl, February 5, 1991; David Artzt, February 28, 1990; Barbara Barrow, July 18, 1989; John Lambert, February 21, 1991; Arthur Bolger, February 7, 1990.

43. *New York Times,* September 20, 1959; *Newsweek,* June 23, 1969; Martha Saxton, "The Bliss Business: Institutionalizing the American Honeymoon," *American Heritage* 29, no. 4 (1978): 80–87.

44. Claudine Glauser, interview by author, September 5, 1989; "Poconos of Pennsylvania" [a brochure published by the Pocono Mountains Vacation Bureau in the 1950s].

45. *Newsweek,* June 23, 1969; *Philadelphia Inquirer,* June 8, 1986.

Notes to Chapter 10

1. William Malleson Jr., interview by author, June 19, 1989.

2. Rev. Rudolph Ressmeyer, interview by author, July 19, 1989.

3. Henry Schaumloffel Jr. to Paul Friedrich, August 17, 1960, Lutherland Bankruptcy, The United States District Court, Middle District of Pennsylvania, National Archives, Philadelphia.

4. Rev. Rudolph Ressmeyer, interview by author, July 19, 1989; Lutherland, Inc. Debtor, Trustee's Amended Plan of Reorganization, November 3, 1958, The United States District Court, Middle District of Pennsylvania, National Archives, Philadelphia.

5. Rev. George Ammon, interview by author, July 13, 1989.

6. Lawrence Squeri, Neil Hogan, and Peter Nevins, *Pride and Promise: A Centennial History of East Stroudsburg University* (Virginia Beach, Va.: Donning, 1993), 59, 74–75; *Sunday Call-Chronicle*, May 5, 1963.

7. Thomas H. Knepp, *The Poconos: A Handbook and Guide to Pennsylvania's Vacation Land*, 5th ed. (Stroudsburg, Pa.: Thomas H. Knepp, 1971), 44–46.

8. Marie Hoffman, interview by author, November 6, 1996.

9. *Wall Street Journal*, August 29, 1955; *New York Times*, August 2, 1955.

10. "Manager's Report, September 11, 1955," Collection #84: Ben Josephson Papers, Tamiment Library.

11. Richard C. Albert provides a thorough account of the Tocks Island project in *Damming the Delaware: The Rise and Fall of Tocks Island Dam* (University Park: The Pennsylvania State University Press, 1987).

12. *The Record*, June 28, 1952; Drake, *Borough of Delaware Water Gap*, 97.

13. Bernard Franz, interview by author, April 5, 1991.

14. Managing Director's Reports, January 22, 1956, and January 20, 1957, Collection #7: PECS, Tamiment Library.

15. "Statement by Ben Josephson Before the Minimum Wage Board on August 15, 1958, Stroudsburg, Pennsylvania," Collection #84: Ben Josephson Papers, Tamiment Library.

16. That the public had higher expectations, especially with regard to a swimming pool, was a common sentiment among those interviewed for this project.

17. Reeve and Marie Price, interview by author, January 31, 1989.

18. Joyce Kristoff, interview by author, September 5, 1989.

19. William Malleson Jr., "Statement on Behalf of Resort Members of American Hotel and Motel Association and the Interstate Resort Committee," March 13, 1964, Collection #84: Ben Josephson Papers, Tamiment Library.

20. Author interviews with Margaret Ma Levy, January 20, 1996, and Barbara Barrow, July 18, 1989; Donna Coleman Redisch, telephone conversation with author, June 10, 1989.

21. Henry and Carmela Lunardi, interview by author, August 26, 1993.

22. Layton Hauser, interview by author, May 5, 1993.

23. Information supplied by Jean K. Wolf.

24. Mary Ann Miller, interview by author, June 14, 1989; Edward Jenkins, interview by author, August 11, 1988; *Pocono Record*, February 21, 1992; July 29, 1992; and April 6, 1996; *Philadelphia Inquirer*, February 9, 1994.

25. *TIME*, August 13, 1984.

26. John Shinn, interview by author, May 20, 1993; *Pike County Courier*, October 1995.

27. Tax Court, 2076–84; "Minutes of the Board of Directors," October 8, 1964, Collection #7: PECS; Internal Revenue Service to People's Educational Camp Society, August 4, 1967, Collection #84: Ben Josephson Papers, Tamiment Library.

28. Josephson's annual reports to the PECS Board of Directors from 1960 onward were quite pessimistic. See Collection #84: Ben Josephson Papers, Tamiment Library.

29. Internal Revenue Service to People's Educational Camp Society, August 4, 1967; Ben Josephson obituary from *New Leader*, July 14, 1980 (clipping in Collection #84: Ben Josephson Papers, Tamiment Library). In the 1980s, singer Wayne Newton bought Tamiment. It was said that he sold it because Las Vegas-style gambling did not come to the Poconos.

30. Minutes of General Executive Board [I.L.G.W.U.], September 1963; January 6, 1969; and February 26, 1973 in I.L.G.W.U. Archive; *Pocono Record*, January 25, 1990; Arthur Bolger, interview by author, February 7, 1990.

31. Minutes of General Executive Board [I.L.G.W.U.], March 10, 1969, I.L.G.W.U. Archive; *Philadelphia Inquirer*, August 12, 1990; Kenneth C. Wolensky, "Unity House: A Workers' Shangri-la," *Pennsylvania Heritage* 24, no. 3 (1998): 28–29.

Notes to Chapter 11

1. *New York Times*, June 12, 1942.
2. Jill Wechsler, *Camelback: The Downs and Ups of a Banana Belt Ski Area* (Tannersville, Pa.: Coolmoor Publishing, 1989), 39; *New York Times*, January 21, 1962, and December 5, 1965.
3. Wechsler, *Camelback*, 11–71; *New York Times*, December 1, 1963.
4. Wechsler, *Camelback*, 149–51.
5. *Philadelphia Inquirer*, December 2, 1984, and December 5, 1993; Mike Finkel, "Only the Poconos," *Skiing* 44, no. 6 (1992): 78–82.
6. *Philadelphia Inquirer*, December 3, 1995, and December 1, 1996; "Tubing Takes the Poconos," *Ski* 62, no. 5 (1998): 14. More than 50 percent of America's snowboarders are under seventeen years of age; most skiers, by comparison, are between twenty-five and thirty-four.
7. *Philadelphia Inquirer*, November 10, 1983; Harry Ahnert, interview by author, June 8, 1993; Leon Arons and Annette Arons, *Casino Gambling and Monroe County, Pennsylvania. A Report to the Pocono Mountain Chamber of Commerce and the Citizens of Monroe County* (privately printed, 1983).
8. *Pocono Record*, August 1, 1983.
9. Jim Nechas, "Pocono Mountain High," *Philadelphia* (February 1979): 97–103.
10. Arons and Arons, *Casino Gambling*, 1–13; *Philadelphia Inquirer*, January 10 and January 12, 1984.
11. *Philadelphia Inquirer*, May 19, October 6, and November 10, 1983.
12. Much of this section on Split Rock Resort, along with the rest of this chapter, contains the author's firsthand observations.
13. *Washington Post*, June 24, 1998. The author thanks Debbie Martin, Director of Public Relations for Woodloch Pines, for her kind assistance and tour of the grounds.
14. *Philadelphia Inquirer*, September 2, 1994.
15. *Philadelphia Inquirer*, April 14, 1991; *New York Times*, August 18, 1995.
16. *New York Times*, August 18, 1995.
17. *Pocono Record*, November 4, 1999, and May 12, 2000.
18. *Philadelphia Inquirer*, February 8 and June 8, 1986.
19. *USA Today*, February 10, 1995.
20. The statue in the Cove Haven lobby is not really the Pan of Greek mythology, although he is labeled as such. The real Pan had the legs, ears, and horns of a goat. The so-called Pan at Cove Haven is a handsome young man—lusty, naked, and mood-setting, but an illusion.
21. *Philadelphia Inquirer*, February 8, 1986, and July 31, 1988; *USA Today*, February 10, 1995.
22. *Pocono Record*, December 23, 1998; see also February 22 and February 23, 1999.
23. Albert Murray, interview by author, May 18, 1993; *Pocono Record*, August 14, 1991; Wendy Beech, "Poconos Haven," *American Visions* 10, no. 6 (1995): 50.
24. "The Go, You Chickenfat, Go Weekend," *Philadelphia* (March 1985): 170; see also the Deerfield Spa website on the Internet <http://www.deerfieldspa.com/>.
25. *Washington Post*, August 12, 1990; see also the Sunny Rest Lodge website on the Internet <http://www.sunnyrest.com>.
26. See the Rainbow Mountain Resort website on the Internet <http://www.rainbowmountain.com>.

27. *Pocono Record,* July 18, 1996; see also Kenneth R. Clark and Janet Bregman-Taney, *The Insiders' Guide to the Pocono Mountains* (Stroudsburg, Pa.: Pocono Record, 1997), 75–97.

28. *Pocono Record,* December 1, 1991, and July 18, 1996; *Philadelphia Inquirer,* September 2, 1994.

29. *New York Times,* August 26, 1995.

30. Ted Cart and Frank Froment, interview by author, October 27, 1993. The author thanks Messrs. Cart and Froment for the tour of the grounds.

31. *Pocono Record,* July 17, 1996; *Philadelphia Inquirer,* September 27, 1996.

32. Albert, *Damming the Delaware,* 173–75; *Philadelphia Inquirer,* October 6, 1990; Oplinger and Halma, *The Poconos,* 217–21.

33. Sharon Harris, "Meetings in the Mountains," *Tri-State Events Magazine* 2, no. 6 (1987): 4–6.

34. *Philadelphia Inquirer,* September 16, 1989, and July 23, 1990.

35. *New York Times,* July 19, 2000; Brian Hineline, "A Ride in the Country," *Pocono World* 1, no. 2 (1991): 8–12.

36. William Coursen, "Jazz in the Gap," *Pocono World* 1, no. 2 (1991): 17–21; Robert Lehr, interview by author, September 22, 1991; Knepp, *The Poconos,* 92.

37. *Pocono Record,* July 19, 1996; Charles Testa, interview by author, August 19, 1993.

38. Karen Cord Taylor, "4 Bedrooms, 3 Baths, 52 Owners," *Investment Vision* (September–October 1990): 68–69; *Philadelphia Inquirer,* June 9, 1988; *Pocono Record,* April 26 and July 19, 1996.

39. *Pocono Record,* July 15 and July 17, 1996; *New York Times,* February 2, 1996.

40. *Pocono Record,* July 14, July 15, and July 17, 1996.

41. Ibid., July 14, 1996.

42. Ibid., July 17 and July 20, 1996.

43. Ibid., November 20, 1994; see also April 26 and July 14, 1996.

44. Ibid., August 21, 1998.

BIBLIOGRAPHY

Books, Articles, and Dissertations

Albert, Richard C. *Damming the Delaware: The Rise and Fall of Tocks Island Dam.* University Park: The Pennsylvania State University Press, 1987.

Allen, Frederick Lewis. *Only Yesterday: An Informal History of the Nineteen-Twenties.* New York: Harper, 1931.

———. *Since Yesterday: The Nineteen-Thirties in America.* New York: Harper, 1940.

Appel, John, coord. *History of Monroe County, Pennsylvania: 1725–1976.* East Stroudsburg, Pa.: Pocono Hospital Auxiliary, 1976.

Appel, John, and Roger Dunning. *Monroe County Sesquicentennial, 1836–1986.* Cresco, Pa.: Pocono Press, 1986.

Appleton's General Guide to the United States and Canada, Part I: New England and Middle States and Canada. New York: D. Appleton, 1901.

Archambault, A. Margaretta, ed. *A Guide Book of Art, Architecture, and Historic Interests in Pennsylvania.* Philadelphia: John C. Winston, 1924.

Architectural League of New York. *Resorts of the Catskills.* New York: St. Martin's Press, 1979.

Aron, Cindy S. *Working at Play: A History of Vacations in the United States.* New York: Oxford University Press, 1999.

Bachelder, John B. *Popular Resorts, and How to Reach Them.* Boston: J. B. Bachelder, 1874.

Baedeker, Karl, ed. *The United States. A Handbook for Travellers, 1893.* New York, 1893. Reprint, New York: Da Capo Press, 1971.

Baltzell, E. Digby. *Puritan Boston and Quaker Philadelphia.* New York: Free Press, 1979.

Bancroft, Peggy. *Falling Feathers: The Pocono Indian Presence.* Pocono Pines, Pa.: Printing Craftsmen, 1991.

———. *Journey by Lamplight: From Indian Trails to Skyways.* South Sterling, Pa.: Gun-ni-ati Publishing, 1979.

———. *Ringing Axes and Rocking Chairs: The Story of Barrett Township.* Mountainhome, Pa.: Barrett Friendly Library, 1974.

Bebout, John E., and Ronald J. Grele. *Where Cities Meet: The Urbanization of New Jersey.* Princeton, N.J.: Van Nostrand, 1964.

Beech, Wendy. "Poconos Haven." *American Visions* 10, no. 6 (1995): 50.

Beers, Paul B. *Pennsylvania Politics, Today and Yesterday: The Tolerable Accommodation.* University Park: The Pennsylvania State University Press, 1980.

Bender, Thomas. *Community and Social Change in America.* New Brunswick: Rutgers University Press, 1978.

Bertland, Dennis N., et al. *The Minisink: A Chronicle of One of America's First and Last Frontiers.* Milford, Pa.: Four-County Task Force on the Tocks Island Dam Project, 1975.

Bignami, Louis. "Past and Present Tents." *Westways* 73, no. 8 (1981): 34–37.

Blackmar, Betsy, and Elizabeth Cromley. "On the Verandah: Resorts of the Catskills." In *Victorian Resorts and Hotels,* edited by Richard Guy Wilson. Philadelphia: The Victorian Society in America, 1982.

Blum, John Morton. *V Was for Victory: Politics and American Culture During World War II.* New York: Harcourt Brace Jovanovich, 1976.

Bok, Edward. "The Summer of Our Discontent." *Ladies Home Journal* 18 (May 1901): 16.

Braden, Donna R., and Judith E. Endelman. *Americans on Vacation.* Dearborn, Mich.: Henry Ford Museum and Greenfield Village, 1990.

Brent, Joseph. *Charles Sanders Peirce: A Life.* Bloomington: Indiana University Press, 1993.

Brodhead, L. W. *The Delaware Water Gap: Its Scenery, Its Legends, and Early History.* 2d ed. Philadelphia: Sherman, 1870.

Brown, Dona. *Inventing New England: Regional Tourism in the Nineteenth Century.* Washington, D.C.: Smithsonian Institution Press, 1995.

Brown, Phil. *Catskill Culture.* Philadelphia: Temple University Press, 1998.

Bryant, William Cullen. *Letters of a Traveller or Notes of Things Seen in Europe and America.* 2d ed. New York: G. P. Putnam, 1850.

Burrowes, Thomas H. *State-Book of Pennsylvania.* Philadelphia: Uriah Hunt & Son, 1847.

Cain, Tim. *Peck's Beach: A Pictorial History of Ocean City, New Jersey.* Harvey Cedars, N.J.: Down the Shore Publishing, 1988.

Calhoun, William Caldwell. *History of the Forest Lake Club, 1882–1932.* N.p.: privately printed, 1932.

Calkins, Earnest Elmo. *And Hearing Not.* New York: Charles Scribner's Sons, 1946.

Cart, Theodore Whaley. "The Struggle for Wildlife Protection in the United States, 1870–1900: Attitudes and Events Leading to the Lacey Act." Ph.D. diss., University of North Carolina, 1971.

Cartmill, Matt. *A View to a Death in the Morning: Hunting and Nature Through History.* Cambridge: Harvard University Press, 1993.

Casey, Robert J., and W. A. S. Douglas. *The Lackawanna Story: The First Hundred Years of the Delaware, Lackawanna and Western Railroad.* New York: McGraw-Hill, 1951.

Cattell, Henry S. *The Pocono Plateau.* New York: McBride, Nast, 1912.

Cavallo, Dom. "Social Reform and the Movement to Organize Children's Play During the Progressive Era." *History of Childhood Quarterly* 3 (Spring 1976): 509–22.

Cayleff, Susan E. *Wash and Be Healed: The Water-Cure Movement and Women's Health.* Philadelphia: Temple University Press, 1987.

Chauncey, George. *Gay New York: Gender, Urban Culture, and the Making of the Gay Male World 1890–1940.* New York: Basic Books, 1994.

Clark, Kenneth R., and Janet Bregman-Taney. *The Insiders' Guide to the Pocono Mountains.* Stroudsburg, Pa.: Pocono Record, 1997.

Clark, Robert Judson. *The Arts and Crafts Movement in America, 1876–1916.* Princeton: Princeton University Press, 1972.

Clemensen, A. Berle. *Historic Resource Study: Delaware Water Gap National Recreation Area, Pennsylvania/New Jersey.* United States Department of the Interior, National Park Service, February 1995.

Coben, Stanley. *A. Mitchell Palmer: Politician.* New York: Columbia University Press, 1963.

Commemorative Biographical Record of Northeastern Pennsylvania. Chicago: J. H. Beers, 1900.

Commonwealth of Pennsylvania. *Report of the Department of Forestry of the State of Pennsylvania for the Years 1916–17.* Harrisburg: State Printer, 1918.

———. *Report of the Pennsylvania Department of Forestry for the Years 1908–09.* Harrisburg: State Printer, 1910.

Commonwealth of Pennsylvania, Department of Environmental Resources. *Chronology of Events in Pennsylvania Forestry.* Harrisburg: Bureau of Forestry, 1975.

———. Bureau of Forestry. *Forestry: Programs and Services.* Harrisburg: Department of Environmental Resources, 1976.

Conte, Robert S. "The Celebrated White Sulphur Springs of Greenbrier: Nineteenth-Century Travel Accounts." *West Virginia History* 42, no. 3–4 (1981): 191–221.

Cornell, Frederic. "A History of the Rand School of Social Science, 1906–1956." Ph.D. diss., Columbia University, 1976.

Coursen, William. "Jazz in the Gap." *Pocono World* 1, no. 2 (1991): 17–21.

Cupper, Dan. *Our Priceless Heritage: Pennsylvania State Parks, 1893–1993.* Harrisburg: Pennsylvania Historical and Museum Commission, 1993.

Davis, Rodney O. "Earnest Elmo Calkins and Phoebe Snow." *Railroad History* 163 (Autumn 1990): 89–92.

DeCoster, Lester A. *The Legacy of Penn's Woods: A History of the Pennsylvania Bureau of Forestry.* Harrisburg: Pennsylvania Historical and Museum Commission, 1995.

Delaware, Lackawanna and Western Railroad. *Outings on the Lackawanna, 1899.* New York: B. E. Chapin, 1899.

———. *Sculpture of the Elfs: A Story of Delaware Water Gap and Pocono Mountains.* Chicago: Henry O. Shepard, 1900.

———. *Summer Excursion Routes and Rates.* New York: Livingston Middleditch, 1895.

Delaware, Lackawanna and Western Railroad, Passenger Department. *Mountain and Lake Resorts.* New York: Passenger Department, 1902–1940. [Published sporadically.]

Dix, William Frederick. "American Summer Resorts in the Seventies." *The Independent* 70 (June 1, 1911): 1211–15.

Drake, Francis R. *The Borough of Delaware Water Gap: A Centennial Study.* Tallahassee, Fla.: Elsa Drake, 1992.

———. *Pohoqualin. Delaware Water Gap Reflections: A Personal History.* Panama City, Fla.: Boyd Brothers, 1999.

Dulles, Foster Rhea. *A History of Recreation: America Learns to Play.* New York: Appleton-Century-Crofts, 1965.

Dunlap, Thomas. *Saving America's Wildlife.* Princeton: Princeton University Press, 1988.

Eaton, Rebecca. *Geography of Pennsylvania.* Philadelphia: Edward Biddle, 1837.

Erenberg, Lewis A. "Everybody's Doin' It: The Pre–World War I Dance Craze, the Castles, and the Modern American Girl." *Feminist Studies* 3 (Fall 1975): 155–70.

Erie Railroad. *Rural Summer Homes on the Picturesque Erie.* New York, 1898.

———. *Summer Excursion Routes and Rates to Popular Resorts.* New York, 1883.

———. *Summer Homes on the Picturesque Erie.* New York: Erie Railroad, 1896.

Evans, Morris, ed. *Picturesque Monroe County Pennsylvania.* Stroudsburg, Pa.: Times Publishing, 1897.

Evers, Alf. *The Catskills: From Wilderness to Woodstock.* Woodstock, N.Y.: The Overlook Press, 1982.

Faris, John T. *Seeing Pennsylvania.* Philadelphia: Lippincott, 1919.

Fassano, Patrick. *The Nature of Skytop.* N.p.: Patrick Fassano/Skytop, 1987.

Finkel, Mike. "Only the Poconos." *Skiing* 44, no. 6 (1992): 78–82.

Fluhr, George J. *An Illustrated Historic Survey of Lehman Township.* Vol. 10 of *Pike County Historic Site and Scenic Area Survey.* N.p., n.d.

———. *Pike County: Highlights of History in Northeastern Pennsylvania.* Shohola, Pa.: privately printed, 1975.

———. *Pike in Pennsylvania: History of a County.* Lackawaxen, Pa.: Alpha Publishing, 1993.

———. *Shohola: History of a Township.* Lackawaxen, Pa.: Alpha Publishing, 1992.

Fluhr, George J., and John McKay. *An Illustrated Historic Survey of Dingman Township.* Vol. 7 of *Pike County Historic Site and Scenic Area Survey.* N.p., n.d.

Forbes, Charlotte. "Jim Thorpe Lines Up for Visitors." *Saturday Evening Post* 263 (March 1990): 86–87.

Funnell, Charles E. *By the Beautiful Sea: The Rise and High Times of That Great American Resort, Atlantic City.* New York: Knopf, 1975.

Galbraith, John Kenneth. *The Great Crash.* 3d ed. Boston: Houghton Mifflin, 1972.

Gelber, Ben. *Pocono Weather.* Stroudsburg, Pa.: Uriel Publishing, 1992.

George, Paul S. "Passage to the New Eden: Tourism in Miami from Flagler Through Everest G. Sewell." *Florida Historical Quarterly* 59, no. 4 (1981): 440–63.

Getz, Gail M. "The Great Escape: Camping in the Nineteenth Century." *Pennsylvania Heritage* 11, no. 3 (1985): 18–25.

Gibson, Henry W. "The History of Organized Camping in the United States." *Camping Magazine* 8, nos. 1–6, 8–9 (1936).

"The Go, You Chickenfat, Go Weekend." *Philadelphia* (March 1985): 170.

Goodwill, Anne, and Jean M. Smith, eds. *The Brodhead Family: The Story of Captain Daniel Brodhead, His Wife, Ann Tye, and Their Descendants.* 7 vols. Port Ewen, N.Y.: Brodhead Family Association, 1986–.

Gordon, John Steele. "The American Environment." *American Heritage* (October 1993): 30–51.

Grant, H. Roger. *Erie Lackawanna: Death of an American Railroad, 1938–1992.* Stanford: Stanford University Press, 1994.

Greeley, Horace. *Recollections of a Busy Life.* New York: J. B. Ford, 1868.

Hallock, Charles. *The Fishing Tourist.* New York: Harper, 1873.

Harris, Sharon. "Meetings in the Mountains." *Tri-State Events Magazine* 2, no. 6 (1987): 4–6.

Harshberger, John W. "Nature and Man in the Pocono Mountain Region, Pennsylvania." *Geographical Society of Philadelphia Bulletin* 13 (April 1915): 64–71.

Henn, William F. *The Story of the River Road: Life Along the Delaware from Bushkill to Milford, Pike County, Pennsylvania.* Dingmans Ferry, Pa.: William F. Henn, 1975.

Henwood, James N. J. "Country Carrier of the Poconos: The Delaware Valley Railroad." *Railroad History* 174 (Spring 1996): 27–50.

Higham, John. "The Reorientation of American Culture in the 1890s." In *Writing American History: Essays on Modern Scholarship.* Bloomington: Indiana University Press, 1970.

Hillman, Ralf Ridgway. *Old Dansbury and the Moravian Mission.* Buffalo, N.Y.: Kenworthy Printing, 1934.

Hineline, Brian. "A Ride in the Country." *Pocono World* 1, no. 2 (1991): 8–12.

Hoffman, Luther S. *The Unwritten History of Smithfield Township.* East Stroudsburg, Pa: Artcraft Press, 1938.

Howe, Daniel Walker. "Victorian Culture in America." In *Victorian America,* edited by D. W. Howe. Philadelphia: University of Pennsylvania Press, 1976.

Hughes, George C., ed. *The Bells: Ringing the Message of Progress in Monroe County and Tributary Country.* East Stroudsburg, Pa.: Hughes Press, 1915.

Huth, Hans. *Nature and the American: Three Centuries of Changing Attitudes.* Berkeley and Los Angeles: University of California Press, 1957.

Jable, John T. "Sport, Amusements, and Pennsylvania Blue Laws, 1682–1973." Ph.D. diss., The Pennsylvania State University, 1974.

Jakle, John A. *The Tourist: Travel in Twentieth-Century North America.* Lincoln: University of Nebraska Press, 1985.

Jefferson, Joseph. *Rip Van Winkle: The Autobiography of Joseph Jefferson.* London: Reinhardt & Evans, 1949.

Jenkins, Philip. *Hoods and Saints: The Extreme Right in Pennsylvania.* Chapel Hill: University of North Carolina Press, 1997.

Johnson, Clifton. *Highways and Byways from the St. Lawrence to Virginia.* New York: Macmillan, 1913.

Kaylor, Earl C. Jr. "The Prohibition Movement in Pennsylvania, 1865–1920." Ph.D. diss., The Pennsylvania State University, 1963.

Kaynor, Faye Campbell. "The Golden Era of Private Summer Camps." *Vermont History News* 41, no. 3 (1990): 46–50.

Keller, Robert B. *History of Monroe County, Pennsylvania.* Stroudsburg, Pa.: Monroe Publishing Company, 1927.

Kelly, Fred C. "The Great Bicycle Craze." *American Heritage* 8, no. 1 (December 1956): 68–73.

Keyes, Donald, ed. *The White Mountains: Place and Perceptions.* Hanover: University Press of New England, 1980.

King, Doris Elizabeth. "The First-Class Hotel and the Age of the Common Man." *Journal of Southern History* 23, no. 2 (1957): 173–88.

Kintner, R. E. "History of Monroe County and the Stroudsburgs as It Is Today." *Founding of the Stroudsburgs,* August 27–29, 1930.

Knepp, Thomas H. *The Poconos: A Handbook and Guide to Pennsylvania's Vacation Land.* 3d ed. Stroudsburg, Pa.: Thomas H. Knepp, 1963.

———. *The Poconos: A Handbook and Guide to Pennsylvania's Vacation Land.* 5th ed. Stroudsburg, Pa.: Thomas H. Knepp, 1971.

Kobler, John. *Ardent Spirits: The Rise and Fall of Prohibition.* New York: Da Capo Press, 1993.

Koehler, LeRoy J. *The History of Monroe County, Pennsylvania, During the Civil War.* Stroudsburg, Pa.: n.p., 1950.

A Landscape Book by American Artists and American Authors. New York: G. P. Putnam, 1868.

Lasch, Christopher. *The New Radicalism in America: The Intellectual as a Social Type.* New York: Alfred Knopf, 1965.

Lawrence, Henry W. "Southern Spas: Source of the American Resort Tradition." *Landscape* 27, no. 2 (1983): 1–12.

Lears, T. J. Jackson. *No Place of Grace: Anti-Modernism and the Transformation of American Culture, 1880–1920.* New York: Pantheon, 1981.

Lee, Warren F. *Down Along the Old Bel-Del: The History of the Belvidere Delaware Railroad Company.* Albuquerque, N.M.: Bel-Del Enterprises, 1987.

Lehde, Norman. *An Illustrated Historic Survey of Milford.* Vol. 9 of *Pike County Historic Site and Scenic Area Survey.* N.p., n.d.

———. *Milford Pennsylvania, 1733–1983, Heritage: 250.* Milford, Pa.: Borough of Milford, 1983.

Lesh, William S. *Landmarks of Monroe County.* Compiled and edited by Henry C. Hoffman. N.p., n.d.

Letcher, Gary. *Canoeing the Delaware River: A Guide to the River and Shore.* New Brunswick: Rutgers University Press, 1981.

Levine, Louis. *The Women's Garment Workers: A History of the International Ladies' Garment Workers Union.* New York: B. W. Huebsch, 1924.

Lewis, Robert. "Seaside Resorts in the United States and Britain: A Review." *Urban History Yearbook* 7 (1980): 44–52.

LoMonaco, Martha Schmoyer. *Every Week, A Broadway Review: The Tamiment Playhouse, 1921–1960.* New York: Greenwood Press, 1992.

Loucks, Emerson Hunsberger. *The Ku Klux Klan in Pennsylvania: A Study in Nativism.* New York-Harrisburg: Telegraph Press, 1936.

MacGregor, Jean T., and James T. MacGregor. *A Legacy of Wilderness: The Centennial History of the Forest Lake Club.* Lackawaxen Township, Pike County, Pa.: Forest Lake Club, 1984.

Mann, Maybelle. "American Landscape Prints." *Art & Antiques* (May–June, 1981): 90–98.

Mathews, Alfred. *History of Wayne, Pike, and Monroe Counties, Pennsylvania.* Philadelphia: Peck, 1886.

McClintock, Gilbert S. *Valley Views of Northeastern Pennsylvania.* Wilkes-Barre, Pa.: The Wyoming Historical and Geological Society, 1948.

McGeary, M. Nelson. *Gifford Pinchot: Politician Forester.* Princeton: Princeton University Press, 1960.

McManus, Kevin. "Pocono Resort Owners Dip into Pool of Success." *Insight* (June 15, 1987): 54–55.

Melosi, Martin V. *Garbage in the Cities: Refuse, Reform, and the Environment, 1880–1980.* College Station: Texas A&M University Press, 1981.

Menzies, Elizabeth G. C. *Before the Waters: The Upper Delaware Valley.* New Brunswick: Rutgers University Press, 1966.

Miller, David L., ed. *East Stroudsburg Centennial, 1870–1970.* East Stroudsburg, Pa.: Sun Litho-Print, Inc., 1970.

Mordden, Ethan. *That Jazz! An Idiosyncratic Social History of the American Twenties.* New York: G. P. Putnam's Sons, 1978.

Mott, Edward Harold. *Pike County Folks.* New York: J. W. Lovell, 1883.

Murphy, Raymond E. *Pennsylvania: A Regional Geography.* Harrisburg: Pennsylvania Book Service, 1937.

Myers, Kenneth. *The Catskills: Painters, Writers, and Tourists in the Mountains, 1820–1895.* Yonkers, N.Y.: Hudson River Museum of Westchester, 1987.

Nash, Roderick. *Wilderness and the American Mind.* New Haven: Yale University Press, 1967.

Nechas, Jim. "Pocono Mountain High." *Philadelphia* (February 1979): 97–103.

Newsom, Jon. "The American Brass Band Movement." *Quarterly Journal of the Library of Congress* 36 (Spring 1979): 114–39.

Noel, Thomas. "Paving the Way to Colorado: The Evolution of Auto Tourism in Denver." *Journal of the West* 26, no. 3 (1987): 42–49.

Norwood, Frederick A. *The Story of American Methodism.* Nashville: Abingdon Press, 1974.

Novak, Barbara. *Nature and Culture: American Landscape and Painting, 1825–1875.* New York: Oxford University Press, 1980.

Oakley, Amy. *Our Pennsylvania: Keys to the Keystone State.* New York: Bobbs-Merrill, 1950.

Oplinger, Carl S., and Robert Halma. *The Poconos: An Illustrated Natural History Guide.* New Brunswick: Rutgers University Press, 1988.

Outerbridge, Laura. "Town Thrives on an Athlete's Aura." *Insight* (June 20, 1988): 24–25.

Parker, Charles. "Ocean Grove, New Jersey: Queen of the Victorian Methodist 'Camp Meeting' Resorts." *Nineteenth Century* 9, no. 1–2 (1984): 19–25.

Pennsylvania Game Commission. *Pennsylvania's Wildlife Conservation History.* 3d ed. Harrisburg: Pennsylvania Game Commission, 1970.

Picturesque America. Illustrations from the Original 1874 Edition. New York: American Heritage Publishing, 1974.

Pleasants, Henry. *A Historical Account of the Pocono Region of Pennsylvania.* Philadelphia: John C. Winston, 1913.

Plummer, Wilbur C. "The Road Policy of Pennsylvania." Ph.D. diss., University of Pennsylvania, 1924.

Polenberg, Richard. *War and Society: The United States, 1941–45.* Philadelphia: Lippincott, 1972.

Pratt, Mary Louise. *Imperial Eyes: Travel Writing and Transculturation.* London: Routledge, 1992.

Rickershauser, Peter. "The Life and Times of the Delaware Valley Pocono Shortline." *Train Sheet,* Spring 1977, 2–7.

Rinhart, Floyd and Marion. *Summertime: Photographs of Americans at Play, 1850–1900.* New York: Crown Publishers, 1978.

Rodgers, Daniel T. *The Work Ethic in Industrial America, 1850–1920.* Chicago: University of Chicago Press, 1978.

Rosenwaike, Ira. *Population History of New York City.* Syracuse: Syracuse University Press, 1972.

Rupp, I. Daniel. *History of Northampton, Lehigh, Monroe, Carbon, and Schuylkill Counties.* Lancaster, Pa.: G. Hills, 1845.

Savage, Richard A. "Bar Harbor: A Resort Is Born." *New England Galaxy* 18, no. 4 (1977): 11–22.

Saxton, Martha. "The Bliss Business: Institutionalizing the American Honeymoon." *American Heritage* 29, no. 4 (1978): 80–87.

Schmitt, Peter J. *Back to Nature: The Arcadian Myth in Urban America.* New York: Oxford University Press, 1969.

Schwartz, Rachel Cutler. "The Rand School of Social Science, 1904–1924: A Study of Worker Education in the Socialist Era." Ed.D. diss., State University of New York, 1984.

Schwiebert, Ernest. *Remembrances of Rivers Past.* New York: Macmillan, 1972.

Sears, John F. *Sacred Places: American Tourist Attractions in the Nineteenth Century.* New York: Oxford University Press, 1989.

Seid, Bradford S. "The Perceptions of Residents of Monroe County on the Impact of Tourism in Monroe County, Pennsylvania." Ph.D. diss., Temple University, 1994.

Seitz, Don C. *Horace Greeley: Founder of the New York Tribune.* Indianapolis: Bobbs-Merrill, 1926.

Senter, Oramel S. *The Health and Pleasure-Seeker's Guide.* Philadelphia, 1874.

Singal, Daniel Joseph. "Toward a Definition of American Modernism." *American Quarterly* 39 (Spring 1987): 7–26.

———. *The War Within: From Victorian to Modernist Thought in the South.* Chapel Hill: University of North Carolina Press, 1982.

Smith, Frederic W. *Skytop: An Adventure.* Skytop, Pa.: The Skytop Club, 1963.

Somers, Dale A. "The Leisure Revolution: Recreation in the American City, 1820–1920." *Journal of Popular Culture* 5 (Summer 1971): 125–47.

Squeri, Lawrence. "The Pocono Resort Economy: Economic Growth and Social Conservatism, 1865–1940." *The Pennsylvania Magazine of History and Biography* 115 (October 1991): 475–501.

Squeri, Lawrence, Neil Hogan, and Peter Nevins. *Pride and Promise: A Centennial History of East Stroudsburg University.* Virginia Beach, Va.: Donning, 1993.

Statement of Work Done by the Pennsylvania Department of Forestry During 1901 & 1902. Harrisburg: State Printer, 1902.

Stielow, Frederick. "Grand Isle, Louisiana, and the 'New' Leisure, 1866–1893." *Louisiana History* 23, no. 3 (1982): 239–57.

Strauss, David. "Toward a Consumer Culture: 'Adirondack Murray' and the Wilderness Vacation." *American Quarterly* 39, no. 2 (1987): 270–83.

Strebeigh, Fred. "Pleasure in Creation." *American Heritage* 38, no. 5 (1987): 82–88.

Sweet, William Warren. *Methodism in American History.* Nashville: Abingdon Press, 1961.

Taber, Thomas Townsend, and Thomas Townsend Taber III. *The Delaware, Lackawanna and Western Railroad in the Twentieth Century, 1899–1960.* Parts 1–2. Muncy, Pa. and Williamsport, Pa.: by the authors, 1980–81.

Taylor, Karen Cord. "4 Bedrooms, 3 Baths, 52 Owners." *Investment Vision* (September–October 1990): 68–69.

Teller, Michael E. *The Tuberculosis Movement: A Public Campaign in the Progressive Era.* Westport, Conn.: Greenwood Press, 1988.

Terrie, Philip G. "Urban Man Confronts the Wilderness: The Nineteenth-Century Sportsman in the Adirondacks." *Journal of Sports History* 5, no. 3 (1978): 7–20.

Tobin, Gary Allan. "The Bicycle Boom of the 1890s: The Development of Private Transportation and the Birth of the Modern Tourist." *Journal of Popular Culture* 7 (Spring 1974): 838–49.

Trego, Charles B. *A Geography of Pennsylvania.* Philadelphia: Edward Biddle, 1843.

"Tubing Takes the Poconos." *Ski* 62, no. 5 (1998): 14.

Tyson, Carroll. *The Poconos.* Philadelphia: Innes & Sons, 1929.

Urry, John. *The Tourist Gaze: Leisure and Travel in Contemporary Societies.* London: Sage, 1991.

U.S. Department of Commerce. *Historical Statistics of the United States. Colonial Times to 1970.* Bicentennial Edition, Part 1. Washington: U.S. Bureau of the Census, 1976.

Walker, J. Herbert, ed. *Rafting Days in Pennsylvania.* Altoona, Pa.: Times-Tribune, 1922.

Wallace, Paul A. W. *Indians in Pennsylvania.* Rev. ed. Harrisburg: Pennsylvania Historical and Museum Commission, 1981.

Walther, Sally. *The Story of Bushkill Falls.* Stroudsburg, Pa.: D. Hannan Associates, 1992.

Warner, Sam Bass Jr. *The Private City: Philadelphia in Three Periods of Its Growth.* Philadelphia: University of Pennsylvania Press, 1968.

Watts, Ralph L. *Rural Pennsylvania.* New York: Macmillan, 1925.

Waygood, Emma LaBarre Miller. *Changing Times in the Poconos, 1872–1972.* Bethlehem: A.B.C. Printing & Photo Offset, 1972.

Wechsler, Jill. *Camelback: The Downs and Ups of a Banana Belt Ski Area.* Tannersville, Pa.: Coolmoor Publishing, 1989.

Weslager, C. A. *The Delaware Indians: A History.* New Brunswick: Rutgers University Press, 1972.

Wetzel, Janet. *Monroe County—Historic Legacy.* Stroudsburg, Pa.: Monroe County Planning Commission, 1980.

Wildes, Harry Emerson. *The Delaware.* New York: Farrar & Rinehart, 1940.

Williamson, Jefferson. *The American Hotel: An Anecdotal History.* New York: Alfred Knopf, 1930.

Willis, Nathaniel P. *American Scenery.* New York: R. P. Martin, 1840. Reprint, Barre, Mass.: Imprint Society, 1971.

Wilson, Martin. *Delaware Water Gap, 1993 Bicentennial.* Delaware Water Gap, Pa.: Antoine Dutot School and Museum, 1993.

———. "Delaware Water Gap: Birth and Death of a Resort Town." *Pennsylvania Folklife* 35, no. 2 (1985–86): 80–92.

Wilson, Richard Guy. "From Informality to Pomposity: The Resort Casino in the Later Nineteenth Century." In *Victorian Resorts and Hotels,* edited by R. G. Wilson. Philadelphia: The Victorian Society in America, 1982.

———, ed. *Victorian Resorts and Hotels.* Philadelphia: The Victorian Society in America, 1982.

Winkler, Allan M. *Home Front U.S.A.: America During World War II.* Wheeling, Ill.: Harlan Davidson, 1986.

Wolensky, Kenneth C. "Unity House: A Workers' Shangri-la." *Pennsylvania Heritage* 24, no. 3 (1998): 20–29.

Wolfe, Bertram D. *The Fabulous Life of Diego Rivera.* New York: Stein and Day, 1963.

Wolfe, Bryan. "Review Essay: The Fall of Niagara." *Winterthur Portfolio* 22, no. 1 (1987): 81–87.

Wood, Leslie C. *Rafting on the Delaware River.* Livingston Manor, N.Y.: Livingston Manor Times, 1934.

Other Printed Sources

Archival Materials

Commonwealth of Pennsylvania, Department of Environmental Resources. Bureau of Forestry. Forestry Commission Correspondence. 1899–1900, Volume 1. Record Group 43. Microfilm #4237. Pennsylvania State Archives, Harrisburg.

———. Forestry Reservation Commission Minute Book, No. 1, 1899–1909. Record Group 43. Microfilm #4242. Pennsylvania State Archives, Harrisburg.

———. Report of J. G. Rothrock, March 15, 1895. Record Group 43. Microfilm #4236. Pennsylvania State Archives, Harrisburg.

Commonwealth of Pennsylvania, Department of Forestry. Biennial Reports. Record Group 6. Box 1, Slot 1673. Pennsylvania State Archives, Harrisburg.

———. Office of the Commissioner, 1901–21. Record Group 6. Box 1, Slot 0186. Pennsylvania State Archives, Harrisburg.

Commonwealth of Pennsylvania, Department of Forests and Waters. Bureau of Parks. Record Group 6. Box 1, Minutes and Reports, 1924–41, "Delaware State Forest" Folder. Pennsylvania State Archives, Harrisburg.

———. Office of the Commissioner. Correspondence of Foresters and Rangers, 1901–23. Record Group 6. Box 7, "Pocono State Forest, Analomink. John L. Strobeck, 1918" Folder. Pennsylvania State Archives, Harrisburg.

Delaware, Lackawanna and Western Railroad Records. Department of Special Collections, Syracuse University Library.

International Ladies' Garment Workers' Union Archive. Martin P. Catherwood Library, Kheel Center for Labor Management Documentation and Archives. Cornell University, Ithaca, N.Y.

Lutherland Bankruptcy. The United States District Court. Middle District of Pennsylvania. National Archives, Philadelphia.

Tamiment Institute Library. Elmer Holmes Bobst Library. New York University, New York.

United States Bureau of the Census. *Thirteenth Census of the Population.* 1910. Pennsylvania, Vol. 178, Monroe County. National Archives, Philadelphia.

———. *Twelfth Census of Population.* 1900. Pennsylvania, Vol. 137, Monroe County. National Archives, Philadelphia.

Newspapers

Allentown Sunday Call-Chronicle
East Stroudsburg Morning Press
East Stroudsburg Morning Sun
East Stroudsburg Press and the Jeffersonian
Milford Dispatch
Monroe Democrat
New York Daily Tribune
New York Times
Philadelphia Inquirer
Pike County Courier
Pocono Record
Stroudsburg Daily Record
Stroudsburg Daily Times
Stroudsburg Jeffersonian
Stroudsburg Times
Stroudsburg Times-Democrat
USA Today
Wall Street Journal

Miscellaneous

Ambler, Joanne. "The Syrian Summer Colony of Milford." Lecture delivered at the Northeastern Conference of Junior Historians, State Teachers College, East Stroudsburg, Pa., May 2, 1952.

American Field, The. October 13, 1894.

Ammon, George B., and Clifford E. Hays. *The Story of Paradise Falls Lutheran Association, 1922–1972.* Privately printed, 1972.

Annual Reports of the Board of Directors, Pocono Manor Association. 1905, 1907, and 1908. Monroe County Historical Association, Stroudsburg, Pa.

Arons, Leon, and Annette Arons. *Casino Gambling and Monroe County, Pennsylvania. A Report to the Pocono Mountain Chamber of Commerce and the Citizens of Monroe County.* Privately printed, 1983.

Blooming Grove Park Association. *Objects, Charters, and By-Laws of the Blooming Grove Park Association.* New York: Powers & Macgowan, 1871.

Brown, Forest (Norwegian American Historical Association). Letter to author. October 26, 1993.

Buck Hill Falls. [Publicity brochure.] 1912.

Buck Hill Falls Breeze. [Resort newsletter.] Barrett Friendly Library, Mountainhome, Pa.

Buck Hill Falls Company. *Annual Reports to the Stockholders.* Barrett Friendly Library, Mountainhome, Pa.

Buck Hill History Committee. *Buck Hill History.* 1964. Unpublished manuscript. Barrett Friendly Library, Mountainhome, Pa.

Dunning, Roger. "The Growth and Variety of Monroe County Resorts." Unpublished manuscript. Monroe County Historical Association, Stroudsburg, Pa.

———. "Monroe County Tanneries." 1968. Unpublished manuscript. Monroe County Historical Association, Stroudsburg, Pa.

"Harry J. Drennan, Buck Hill's Winter Sports Director." [Buck Hill Inn publicity brochure.] 1966. Barrett Friendly Library, Mountainhome, Pa.

Hauserville Folder. Monroe County Historical Association, Stroudsburg, Pa.

Hershey, Gertrude Burlingame. "Things I Remember: From 1912 to 1974." Unpublished memoir. Monroe County Historical Association, Stroudsburg, Pa.

Jenkins, Charles. "Address Delivered at the Dedication of the Jenkins Woods in Celebration of the Fiftieth Anniversary of the Buck Hill Falls Company." August 26, 1951. Monroe County Historical Association, Stroudsburg, Pa.

Knapp, Vertie. "The Natural Ice Harvesters of Monroe County." 1972. Unpublished manuscript. Monroe County Historical Association, Stroudsburg, Pa.

Learn, Pauline. "Things to Remember." 1977. Unpublished memoir. Monroe County Historical Association, Stroudsburg, Pa.

"Lenape Baskets." Shawnee Folder. Monroe County Historical Association, Stroudsburg, Pa., 1970.

Manzanedo Rod and Gun Club. [Pamphlet, circa 1911–20.]

McFadden, William. "A History of the Resort Industry at Delaware Water Gap." Unpublished manuscript. National Park Service, Bushkill, Pa.

Michaels, Frank B. "History of Banking in Monroe County, Pennsylvania." 1949. Unpublished manuscript. Monroe County Historical Association, Stroudsburg, Pa.

Milford Chamber of Commerce. Resort Department. *Milford and Its Environment Including All of Pike County, Pennsylvania.* [Publicity brochure.] Milford, Pa.: Milford Chamber of Commerce, 1922. Pike County Historical Society.

Monroe County Chamber of Commerce. *Pennsylvania's Picturesque Playground, Monroe County.* Stroudsburg, Pa.: Monroe County Chamber of Commerce, 1942.

———. *Pocono Mountains, Delaware Water Gap, Delaware Valley, The Stroudsburgs.* Stroudsburg, Pa.: Monroe County Chamber of Commerce, 1933.

———. *Pocono Mountains, Delaware Water Gap, Delaware Valley, The Stroudsburgs.* Stroudsburg, Pa.: Monroe County Chamber of Commerce, 1938.

Mountain Echo. [Resort newsletter, irregularly published from 1879 to 1922.] Monroe County Historical Association, Stroudsburg, Pa.

A Mountain Paradise: The Water Gap House. [Publicity brochure.] 1911. Monroe County Historical Association, Stroudsburg, Pa.

National Park Service, Delaware Water Gap National Recreation Area. *Twenty-fifth Anniversary Symposium.* East Stroudsburg University, East Stroudsburg, Pa., April 6–7, 1991.

"New York Commercial Advertiser." September 17, 1839. Delaware Water Gap Folder. Monroe County Historical Association, Stroudsburg, Pa.

"Obituary Book." October 10, 1941–January 7, 1950. Monroe County Historical Association, Stroudsburg, Pa.

"Once Upon a Time." Personal Recollections and Memoranda of Dr. Edward E. Wildman.

Pocono Inn, 1907. [Publicity pamphlet.]

Pocono Pines Assembly Hotels, 1920, Nineteenth Season. Pocono Pines, Pa. Monroe County Historical Association, Stroudsburg, Pa.

Pocono Protective Fire Association. *Annual Report of the Board of Directors.* November 19, 1914. Monroe County Historical Association, Stroudsburg, Pa.

———. *Condensed History, 1901 to 1937.* Unpublished manuscript. Monroe County Historical Association, Stroudsburg, Pa.

Stroudsburg House Ledger Book, 1859–67. Monroe County Historical Association, Stroudsburg, Pa.

Thompson, Charles. "History of Creeks Adjacent to Bright Creek." 1944. Unpublished memoir. Monroe County Historical Association, Stroudsburg, Pa.

"Thumbnail History of Buck Hill." Unpublished manuscript. Monroe County Historical Association, Stroudsburg, Pa.

United States Department of the Interior, National Park Service. *National Register of Historic Places—Nomination Form, Henryville House.* 1980.

Wallace, R. M., ed. "Ebenezer or Memorial Discourse Commemorative of the Founding and Progress of the First Presbyterian Church, of Stroudsburg, Pennsylvania." Presbyterian Folder. Monroe County Historical Association, Stroudsburg, Pa., 1877.

Walters, Elizabeth D. "The Delaware: Walpack to Delaware Water Gap." October 1944. Unpublished manuscript. Monroe County Historical Association, Stroudsburg, Pa.

———. "History of the Water Gap House, 1872–1915." June 1969. Unpublished manuscript. Monroe County Historical Association, Stroudsburg, Pa.

———. "The Kittatinny: Pioneer Summer Resort of Monroe County, Pennsylvania." December 1968. Unpublished manuscript. Monroe County Historical Association, Stroudsburg, Pa.

Interviews

Ahnert, Harry. Interview by author. Fernwood, Pa., June 8, 1993.

Ammon, Rev. George B. Interview by author. Paradise Valley, Pa., July 13, 1989.

Artzt, David. Interview by author. Bushkill, Pa., February 28, 1990.

Ballard, Mary Owens. Interview by author. Buzzards Bay, Ma., August 18, 1989.

Barrow, Barbara. Interview by author. East Stroudsburg, Pa., July 18, 1989.

Bates, Kenneth and Dorothy. Interview by author. Paradise Township, Pa., April 28, 1993.

Battisto, Angelo. Interview by author. Mount Pocono, Pa., March 3, 1993.

Beville, Cecil. Interview by author. Delaware Water Gap, Pa., May 6, 1990.

Blaker, Martha. Interview by author. East Stroudsburg, Pa., April 5, 1990.

Bolger, Arthur. Interview by author. Unity House, Pa., February 7, 1990.

Bute, Hillary. Interview by author. Mount Pocono, Pa., June 10, 1993.

Cart, Ted. Interview by author. Blooming Grove, Pa., October 27, 1993.

Cramer, Irene. Interview by author. Marshalls Creek, Pa., September 30, 1993.

DePuy, Warner. Interview by author. Milford, Pa., August 10, 1993.

Dickl, Karl. Interview by author. Stroudsburg, Pa., February 5, 1991.

Dietrich, Harry and Verna. Interview by author. Wynnewood, Pa., August 20, 1993.

Dietz, William and Helen. Interview by author. Paradise Valley, Pa., June 21, 1990.

Eddy, Violet Clark. Interview by author. Stroudsburg, Pa., March 10, 1993.

Edwards, Minnie. Interview by author. Cresco, Pa., June 12, 1991.

Frankenbach, Charles. Interview by author. Forest Lake, Pa., December 22, 1991.

Franz, Bernard. Interview by author. Stroudsburg, Pa., April 5, 1991.

Froment, Frank. Interview by author. Blooming Grove, Pa., October 27, 1993.

Glauser, Claudine. Interview by author. Stroudsburg, Pa., September 5, 1989.

Haley, Jean. Interview by author. Gladwynne, Pa., October 24, 1994.

Hauser, Layton. Interview by author. Delaware Water Gap, Pa., May 5, 1993.

Heilig, Jack. Interview by author. Stroudsburg, Pa., February 27, 1992.

Hoffman, Marie. Interview by author. Milford, Pa., November 6, 1996.

Huffman, Carlyle. Interview by author. Marshalls Creek, Pa., July 30, 1987.

Hutton, William. Interview by author. Wayne, Pa., September 1, 1993.

Jacobson, Morris. Interview by author. East Stroudsburg, Pa., December 12, 1989.

Jenkins, Edward (Ted). Interviews by author. Buck Hill, Pa., July 28 and August 11, 1988.

Jolley, Ida. Interview by author. Stroudsburg, Pa., January 30, 1991.

Kaiser, Robert. Interview by author. Delaware Water Gap, Pa., June 17, 1993.

Kristoff, Joyce. Interview by author. Stroudsburg, Pa., September 5, 1989.

Kuhn, Jodielynn. Interview by author. Lackawaxen, Pa., June 24, 1993.

Lambert, John. Interview by author. East Stroudsburg, Pa., February 21, 1991.

Lear, Robert. Interview by author. Stroudsburg, Pa., November 3, 1993.

Lehr, Robert. Interview by author. Delaware Water Gap, Pa., September 22, 1991.

Levy, Margaret Ma. Interview by author. Philadelphia, Pa., January 20, 1996.

Lunardi, Henry and Carmela. Interview by author. Broomall, Pa., August 26, 1993.

Mack, Florence. Telephone interview by author. July 5, 1988.

Malleson, William Jr. Interview by author. Skytop, Pa., June 19, 1989.

Messerle, Louis. Interview by author. Bushkill, Pa., July 24, 1991.

Mikels, Mary. Interview by author. Stroudsburg, Pa., June 11, 1990.

Miller, Mary Ann. Interview by author. Mountainhome, Pa., June 14, 1989.

Morrison, David. Interview by author. Harrisburg, Pa., August 17, 1988.

Murray, Albert. Interview by author. Marshalls Creek, Pa., May 18, 1993.

Murray, Joan and Jerome. Interview by author. Havertown, Pa., August 14, 1993.

Nelson, Mary Smith. Interview by author. Lackawaxen, Pa., June 15, 1993.

Niebacher, Laura. Telephone interview by author. July 28, 1989.

O'Connor, Joseph. Interview by author. Broomall, Pa., October 15, 1993.

Pipher, Linda. Interview by author. Stroudsburg, Pa., June 19, 1990.

Place, Margaret. Interview by author. Marshalls Creek, Pa., September 30, 1993.

Price, Reeve and Marie. Interview by author. Monroe County, Pa., January 31, 1989.

Redisch, Donna Coleman. Telephone interview by author. June 10, 1989.

Ressmeyer, Rev. Rudolph. Interview by author. Pinecrest Lake, Pa., July 19, 1989.

Schaarschmidt, Paul. Interview by author. Mountainhome, Pa., June 14, 1989.

Schall, Jim and Doris. Interview by author. Philadelphia, Pa., August 19, 1993.

Schaumloffel, Henry. Interview by author. East Stroudsburg, Pa., March 4, 1992.

Shinn, John. Interview by author. Marshalls Creek, Pa., May 20, 1993.

Shoemaker, Fred and Patricia. Interview by author. Delaware Water Gap, Pa., May 13, 1993.

Sitkoff, Irma Pines. Interview by author. Swarthmore, Pa., September 27, 1993.

Tancredi, Frank. Interview by author. East Stroudsburg, Pa., September 22, 1993.

Testa, Charles. Interview by author. Wayne, Pa., August 19, 1993.

Thomas, Warren. Interview by author. Saylors Lake, Pa., October 13, 1993.

Tiernan, Jim. Interview by author. Pen Argyl, Pa., November 12, 1991.

Viola, Carl. Interview by author. Narberth, Pa., August 30, 1993.

Vliet, Jack Van. Interview by author. Stroudsburg, Pa., February 12, 1992.

Walter, William and Marjorie. Interview by author. Wynnecote, Pa., August 14, 1993.

Why, Larry Van. Interview by author. Bushkill, Pa., June 18, 1991.

Wile, Clotilda Comazzi. Interview by author. Cresco, Pa., February 22, 1989.

Williams, Robert. Interview by author. Shawnee on Delaware, March 13, 1991.

INDEX

African Americans, 125–26, 181, 182, 197, 220–21, 231.
    See also Hillary Bute; Albert Murray
Ahnert, Harry, 166
Atlantic City
    alternative to the Poconos, 32
    contrasted with the Poconos, 48, 68–69
    and gambling, 203, 213, 204
    model for the Poconos, 69, 71
    origins, 10
automobile
    auto carnivals, 63
    auto runs, 63
    changes American vacation, 99
    changes Pocono vacation habits, 100, 105
    impacts Pocono trolleys and railroads, 105
    leads to new roads, 105, 173
    negative effects on Delaware Water Gap and Milford, 108
    replaces carriage rides with touring cars, 63

Baltzell, E. Digby, 9–10, 62. *See also* Quakers
Bacon and Bagel resort, 181, 195
Barrett Township, 71, 81, 84, 91, 134
Barrett Township Fair, 91, 84, 101, 117
bed-and-breakfast inns, 221, 231
Bellevue Hotel (Delaware Water Gap), 69, 193, 197
Bensinger brothers, 209–10, 212
Best Western (Stroudsburg), 20, 102, 221. *See also* Burnett House; Fulmer House; Penn Stroud Hotel; Stroudsburg House
Bickley, Isaac, 3, 14
Big Boulder ski area, 173, 208, 224. *See also* skiing; winter sports
Blooming Grove Park Association, 51–52, 88, 89, 222.
    See also hunting; fishing

Bluff House, 23, 109, 165
Brentini. *See* Villa Brentini
Brodhead, Benjamin Franklin, 23, 26
Brodhead, Daniel, 23
Brodhead, Edward Livingston, 25, 26
Brodhead, John Davis, 25, 26
Brodhead, Luke, 15, 23–26, 25, 93, 96. *See also* Water Gap House
Brodhead, Thomas, 23, 25
Brodhead, William, 15, 25, 26
Brodhead Cottage, 26, 193
Bryant, William Cullen, 1, 2, 4, 236 n. 12
Buck Hill. *See* Inn at Buck Hill Falls
Buckwood Inn. *See also* Charles Worthington; Shawnee Inn
    bankruptcy during Great Depression, 166
    bought by Fred Waring, 171, 182
    during World War I, 100
    swimming pool, 111
    World War II concert, 171
    Worthington aviary, 63
Burnett House, 20, 31, 34, 41, 47. *See also* Best Western; Fulmer House; Penn Stroud Hotel; Stroudsburg House
Bute, Hillary, 181, 197. *See also* African Americans

Caesars International, 213, 219, 227. *See also* honeymoon resorts
Caesars Pocono Palace, 203, 217. *See also* Caesars International; honeymoon resorts
Caley, W. L., 108–9, 146. *See also* Monroe County Publicity Bureau
Camelback ski area, 209–12, 230. *See also* skiing; winter sports
Camp Tamiment. *See* Tamiment

camping, 87, 114
camps (children's), 77, 222
casino gambling, 212–13
Castle Inn, 66, 104, 168, 183
Catskill Mountains, xvii, 4, 5, 15, 17, 127
Champagne Glass Whirlpool Bath, 219. *See also* honeymoon resorts; Morris Wilkins
Childs, George W., 33
Churleigh Inn, 67
Cleveland, Grover, 7, 71
Cole, Thomas, 5
Colton, Wendell, 62
Conashaugh Spring House, 43, 44, 99
Cooper, James Fenimore, 5
Cope, G. Frank, 67, 69
Cope, John Purdy, 67, 96, 100
country inns, 221
couples resorts, xvi, xvii, 216–19, 230
Cove Haven, 190, 217, 219, 254 n. 20. *See also* Caesars International; honeymoon resorts; Morris Wilkins
Cramer, Irene, 168, 170
Crissman House, 20, 47
Crooks, Richard, 156, 171
Cullen, George A., 99–100
cycling, 52–54

Dahlen, Henry, 136, 192. *See also* Lutherland
day tripping, 31–32, 48–50, 54, 222–24
Deerfield Spa, 221
Delaware House (Delaware Water Gap), 41, 43, 48, 67, 104, 180
Delaware House (Dingmans Ferry), 54, 170, 193–94, 199
Delaware, Lackawanna and Western Railroad. *See also* Erie Railroad
    comes to Monroe County, 11
    cuts ties with Resort Association during World War I, 103–4
    future plans to resume service, 229
    improved by Truesdale, 58–61
    increases business during World War II, 169–70
    original eight stations in Monroe County, 11
    passenger directories publicize Monroe County, 38, 61
    Phoebe Snow promotion campaign, 55–58
    reduces service during Great Depression, 150
    shortens travel time, 11, 58, 62
    sponsors Resort Association, 62
    stone crusher, 91
    transforms Mount Pocono, 29

Delaware Valley Railroad, 62, 63, 105, 127
Delaware Water Gap
    description of, xviii
    example of the "picturesque," 236 n. 12
    ignored by antebellum writers, 233 n. 8
    visited by William Cullen Bryant, 1–2
Delaware Water Gap (village). *See also* Brodheads; Kittatinny Hotel; Water Gap House
    automobiles, 63–64
    bears, 89
    Brodhead family, 23
    Church of the Mountain, 80
    cyclists, 54
    decline, 108, 182, 192, 201
    Delaware House guests, 48
    first visitors, 3
    formerly "Dutotsburg," 2
    founded by Antoine Dutot, 2
    Lackawanna Trail, 105
    natural appeal of, 1–2, 17–18
    Phoebe Snow visits, 56–58
    postbellum guests, 31–32
    promoted by Jesse Graves, 26–28
    railway station, 58, 201
    stone crusher opposed, 91
    travel time from New York City, 12, 58
    vacation pastimes, 32–36, 69, 127
    during World War I, 101, 105
Delaware Water Gap National Recreation Area, 223–24
Diana's Bath, 24
Dimmick, Frances, 20
Dimmick, Samuel, 20
Dimmick House, 20, 31
Dingman, Daniel, 7, 242 n. 4
dogsleds, 118, 155–56
Dubinsky, David, 146, 168–69, 177. *See also* I.L.G.W.U.; Unity House
dude ranch, 180, 181, 193. *See also* Brodhead Cottage
Dutot, Antoine, 2, 3, 33

Erie Railroad. *See also* Delaware, Lackawanna and Western Railroad
    burns hard coal for clean smoke, 41
    cancels passenger directories, 61
    connects with the Poconos, 10, 11
    offers waterfalls tour, 29
    publicizes Pike County in passenger directories, 38
    used by 1890s cyclists, 54

Fernwood Hotel, 167, 171, 227, 230
fishing, 2, 7, 38–39, 88–89, 223. *See also* Blooming Grove
    Park Association; hunting; nature; Spruce Cabin Inn
Flood of 1955, 193–94
Forest Lake Club, 52, 89
Forest Park Hotel, 127–28, 130, 132, 246 n. 10. *See also*
    Arthur Lederer; Jacob Ottenheimer
Fulmer, Philip, 21, 30, 31
Fulmer House, 20, 102. *See also* Best Western; Burnett
    House; Penn Stroud Hotel; Stroudsburg House

Glauser, Claudine, 187. *See also* honeymoon resorts
Glenwood Hotel, 22, 101, 180, 187, 221
golf, 33, 48, 66, 69, 73, 223
Gonzales House, 21
Graves, Albert, 27–28
Graves, Jesse, 26–28, 30
Greeley, Horace, 20, 124
Grey, Zane, 31–32

health, 15–16, 22, 41–42, 49, 181, 221
heart-shaped bathtubs and pools, 217–19. *See also* hon-
    eymoon resorts; Morris Wilkins
Henryville House, 2, 7
High Falls Hotel, 21, 31
Highland Dell, 30, 126, 222
Hillside Inn, 182, 217, 221. *See also* African Americans
Hoffman, Marie, 170, 193–94, 195, 199. *See also*
    Delaware House (Dingmans Ferry)
Honeymoon Haven, 187. *See also* Claudine Glauser
honeymoon resorts, xvi, 186
Horse Show, 108, 150–51
Hotel Fauchere, 22, 93
Hudson River School, 5
hunting, 2–3, 38–39, 88–89, 156, 223. *See also* Blooming
    Grove Park Association; fishing; nature; Spruce
    Cabin Inn
Hurd, F. Wilson, 22, 42, 181
Hygiene Park, 49

I.L.G.W.U. *See also* David Dubinsky; Unity House
    closes Unity House, 204
    helps Pocono bank during Great Depression, 146
    invites garment manufacturers to Unity House, 177
    membership mostly Jewish, 123
    shrinking membership, 203
International Ladies' Garment Workers' Union. *See*
    I.L.G.W.U

Indian Queen Hotel, 20, 193
Inn at Buck Hill Falls. *See also* Pocono Manor; Quakers
    boom years during World War II, 171–72
    coping with World War II shortages, 170, 171
    cultural program, 116
    decline and bankruptcy, 201
    deficit of 1932 and salary cuts, 145
    discontented 1960s workers, 200
    expansion after World War II, 177
    guest activities, 117–18, 156–59, 203
    liquor policy, 118
    maintaining standards, 153, 170, 175
    origins of, 71
    pre-1914 growth, 73
    Quaker ethos, 73, 74, 116, 118
    relations with neighbors, 81
    tree planting, 86
    winter sports, 100, 118, 188
    World War I patriotism, 100
Irving, Washington, 5
Island Park, 49, 109, 222
Italians, 123, 137

Jack Frost Mountain, 173, 212, 224. *See also* skiing; win-
    ter sports
Jazz Festival, 224
Jeanac Farms, 146, 166
Jefferson, Joseph, 31, 81
Jenkins, Edward, 145, 153, 156, 180, 193. *See also* Inn at
    Buck Hill Falls
Jim Thorpe, 174
Josephson, Ben. *See also* Bertha Mailly; Tamiment
    copes with 1955 Flood, 194–95
    describes changes in resort business, 217
    hosts Willi Brandt, 197
    ignores 1960s youth rebellion, 197
    introduces highbrow entertainment, 169
    recalls Tamiment's neighbors, 132–33, 170
    recommends sale of Tamiment, 203
    wants Tamiment to be profitable, 133, 159

Kamp Karamac, 158, 165, 175, 194, 195
Kittatinny Hotel. *See also* John Purdy Cope; Minsi
    Pioneers
    advertises in *New York Times*, 30
    amenities, 42–43, 67
    bought and expanded by William Brodhead, 14
    bought by Isaac Bickley, 3

destroyed by fire, 182
1890s renovation, 43
entertainment, 69
founded by Antoine Dutot, 2–3
guests, 80, 127
hosts Laurel Blossom Time Festival dinner, 152
Lackawanna Trail completion celebration, 105
located by the Delaware River, 25
owned by John Purdy Cope, 67, 101–7
Ku Klux Klan, 139–40, 248 nn. 41, 42

Lackawanna Railroad. *See* Delaware, Lackawanna and
    Western Railroad
Lake Poponoming. *See* Saylors Lake
Laurel Blossom Time Festival, 151–52, 249 n. 26
Lederer, Arthur, 127, 128, 132
Leibman, Max, 167, 168, 169. *See also* Tamiment
Lutherland. *See also* Paradise Falls Lutheran Association
    decline and bankruptcy, 191
    early success, 137
    founding, 136
    Henry Dahlen, 136, 192
    suffers from Great Depression, 144, 145, 167
    World War II concert, 171

Mailly, Bertha, 130, 132, 133, 156, 179. *See also*
    Tamiment
Manunka Chunk, 13, 62
Mathews, Alfred, 8, 13
Mauch Chunk, 173–74. *See also* Jim Thorpe
Methodists, 13, 69, 96, 137–41, 247 n. 33. *See also*
    Prohibition
Minsi Pioneers, 33
Monroe County Chamber of Commerce, 146, 150, 152,
    166
Monroe County Mountain Resort Association, 62, 63,
    100, 103, 108
Monroe County Publicity Bureau, 108, 112
Monomonoch Inn, 144, 165
Montanesca, 66, 99, 144
Mott, Edward, 92
Mount Airy Lodge, 216, 217, 231
Mount Minsi
    burro rides, 69
    defaced by stone crusher, 91
    improved by Minsi Pioneers, 33
    painted by artists, 7

view from summit, 2
Mount Pleasant House, 43, 181, 193
Mount Pocono House, 29, 41–42, 43, 193
Mount Tammany, 1, 7, 224
Mountain Echo, 27, 34, 71, 111, 112
Mountain House (Delaware Water Gap), 21, 183
Murray, Albert, 182, 242. *See also* African Americans;
    Hillside Inn

nature. *See also* Blooming Grove Park Association; fish-
    ing; hunting
    bears, 89
    better in the Poconos, 38–41
    changing views of, 231
    forest protection, 84–86
    hunting and fishing clubs, 88, 89
    makes vacationers healthier, 15–17
    modern attraction, 227
    picturesque, 16–17
    primeval Pike County, 93
    rattlesnakes, 2, 16, 88, 93
    sublime, 1–2
    as wilderness, 2, 16, 30–31
Niagara Falls, 16, 17, 27, 187. *See also* waterfalls
Norwegians, 124, 137

Oak Grove Hotel, 180, 187, 222, 223. *See also* singles
    resorts
Ottenheimer, Jacob, 88, 127
Onawa Lodge, 182, 194–95

Packer, Samuel, 120, 121, 156
Palmer, A. Mitchell, 63, 84, 124, 140
Paradise Falls Lutheran Association, 135, 192. *See also*
    Lutherland
Peirce, Charles Sanders, 31
Penn Hills Resort, 181, 188, 217. *See also* honeymoon
    resorts
Penn Stroud Hotel, 20, 102, 149. *See also* Best Western;
    Burnett House; Fulmer House; Stroudsburg House
Pennsylvania Railroad, 11, 29, 62
Peters House, 21, 42
Phoebe Snow, 56–58, 61
Pinchot, Gifford
    creates tough liquor code, 149
    crowns Laurel Queen, 152
    donates to Milford advertising fund, 112

French refugee ancestors, 236 n. 30
Grey Towers home tourist site, 85, 222–23
makes laurel the state flower, 152
Pocmont, 181, 227
Pocono Hay-Ven, 43, 181, 183
Pocono Lake Preserve, 74
Pocono Manor. *See also* Inn at Buck Hill Falls; Quakers
coping with Great Depression, 144
expansion after World War I, 115–16
expansion after World War II, 177
founding of, 72
Labor Day athletic rivalry with Buck Hill Quakers, 116–17
Liquor policy, 153, 177
sold to Samuel Ireland, 201
standards of decorum, 152–56
tree planting, 86
winter sports, 100, 118, 188
Pocono Mountains Vacation Bureau, xvii, xix, 173, 212–13, 227
Pocono Raceway, 224
Pocono Record, 219, 225–26
Price, Milton, 21, 40. *See also* Spruce Cabin Inn
Price, Wesley, 21, 40, 52. *See also* Spruce Cabin Inn
Prohibition, 70
and the Ku Klux Klan, 139
Law Observance League, 140
Methodist support, 137, 138
popular opposition to, 97, 244 n. 52
and the resorts, 109, 134, 149, 237 n. 38
Women's Christian Temperance Union, 96–97

Quakers. *See also* E. Digby Baltzell; Inn at Buck Hill Falls; Pocono Manor
concern for nature, 84–85
first vacationers to Delaware Water Gap, 3
in Philadelphia, 4
religious services, 118
schism between Hicksites and Orthodox branches, 73, 117
Quick, Tom, 7, 8

rafters, 3, 7–8
Rainbow Mountain Resort, 221
Rand School of Social Science, 130, 132, 133, 156, 179
residents of the Poconos. *See also* horse show; Ku Klux Klan; Laurel Blossom Time Festival; Methodists
affected by city vacationers, 79–81
backward by city standards, 92–94
complain about highway speeding, 240 n. 18
challenge city views of nature, 88–89
early nineteenth-century boorishness, 11–13
embrace the vacation industry, 13–14
fight the Blue Laws, 149
ignore resort needs, 90–91, 249 n. 26
indifferent to conservation, 84–85, 243 n. 21
oppose casino gambling, 212–13
suffer during Great Depression, 145–47
work in the vacation industry, 83
resort business. *See also* couples resorts; honeymoon resorts; singles resorts; skiing; winter sports
anticipating the public's needs, 191
boom times in 1919–20, 107
changing vacation patterns after World War II, 196–97
closing of resorts, 191–92, 196–98, 201–4
expansion after Civil War, 17–23
expansion before World War I, 65–68
future of the resort industry, 229
during Great Depression, 143–47
in 1990s, 225–26
reinvented in late twentieth century, 207
uniqueness as goal, 37–38
resort life. *See also* couples resorts; honeymoon resorts; singles resorts
atomization, 231
automobile's effect, 63–64
block dances in Stroudsburg, 137–38
conservative lifestyle of mid century, 175
fetishists, 219
growing acceptance of leisure, 55–56
guest expectations raise costs, 197–99
at Inn at Buck Hill Falls, 117, 156–58, 184
interaction with local residents, 80
redefinition in late nineteenth century, 45–48
in Roaring Twenties, 109–14
at Skytop Lodge, 156, 215–16
at Tamiment, 170, 175, 187
theme resorts, 179–82
Roosevelt, Theodore, 7, 55, 71, 76, 241 n. 37
Rothrock, Joseph, 85

Sandyville, 132, 133, 166, 180. *See also* Tamiment
Saylors Lake, 49, 111, 166
Schwiebert, Ernest, 5

Shawnee Inn, 171, 182, 182, 183. *See also* Buckwood Inn; Fred Waring

Shinn, John, 170, 183, 222. *See also* Vacation Valley resort

Shohola Glen, 48, 222

singles resorts, 69, 179, 180, 183–85, 196–97

skiing, xvii, 207–12, 229–30

Skinner, Daniel, 8

Skytop Lodge
    built in 1920s, 119–20
    maintains standards, 120, 153, 215
    mountain location, 120
    profitable during Great Depression, 144, 153
    program for guests, 156, 215–16
    winter sports, 175, 207–8

Snyder, Samuel, 3

Split Rock Resort, 213–14, 224

Spruce Cabin Inn, 21, 40, 52, 83, 244 n. 4

Stroudsburg House, 3, 20, 102, 183. *See also* Best Western; Burnett House; Fulmer House; Penn Stroud Hotel

sublime, 1, 2, 5, 7, 17

Sunny Rest Lodge, 221

swimming pools, xvi, 112, 111, 197–99

Tamiment. *See also* Forest Park; I.L.G.W.U.; Arthur Lederer; Unity House
    decline, 196–97
    founded as adult camp, 132–33
    during Great Depression, 144–46, 147
    highbrow entertainment, 177
    IRS problems and sale, 203
    Jewish clientele, 132–33, 168
    neighbors, 132–33, 170
    during 1955 Flood, 194–95
    political mission, 132, 133, 159, 179
    singles scene, 180, 185
    during World War II, 170, 171–72

tanneries, 13–14

Thompson, Charles, 100, 117, 120, 145. *See also* Inn at Buck Hill Falls

Tilennius, Carl, 48, 84

time shares, 225–26

Tocks Island Dam, 194–96, 222–23

tuberculosis, 42, 61, 62

Truesdale, William, 58–59, 124. *See also* Delaware, Lackawanna and Western Railroad

Uguccioni, Robert, 219, 227. *See also* Pocono Mountains Vacation Bureau

Unity House. *See also* Forest Park; I.L.G.W.U.; Arthur Lederer; Tamiment
    decline and closing, 203
    entertainment, 176,
    failure of its mission, 169
    founding, 128–29
    Great Depression, 145
    high-brow flavor, 129, 130
    labor troubles, 178, 180
    murals by Diego Rivera, 176, 204, 249 n. 36
    union showcase, 129, 168, 175
    during World War II, 170, 171–72

vacation homes, 224–25

Vacation Valley resort, 183–84, 222. *See also* singles resorts

Van Allen, Charles, 85

Villa Brentini, 125, 133–34

Waring, Fred, 171, 182–83, 222. *See also* Shawnee Inn

waterfalls, 17, 29, 33
    Bushkill Falls, 17, 106, 170
    Caldeno Falls, 17, 27, 33
    Dingmans Falls, 17
    Raymondskill Falls, 17, 29

Water Gap House. *See also* Luke Brodhead; John Purdy Cope
    children's facilities, 75–77
    destroyed by fire, 67, 99
    exterior appearance, 25
    founded by Luke Brodhead, 25
    liquor policy, 25, 96
    outdoor recreation, 63, 80
    owned by John Purdy Cope, 67
    Theodore Roosevelt's visit, 71

Wilkins, Morris, 216, 218. *See also* couples resorts

Wine and Food Festival, 2224

winter sports, 100, 112, 118, 187–90. *See also* dogsleds

Woodloch Pines, 214–15, 231

Worthington, Charles C., 66, 69, 81, 96, 240 n. 24